Women Playing Men

WOMEN PLAYING MEN

Yue Opera and Social Change in Twentieth-Century Shanghai

女子越劇

JIN JIANG

University of Washington Press
Seattle and London

The publication of *Women Playing Men: Yue Opera and Social Change in Twentieth-Century Shanghai* was generously supported by the Chiang Ching-Kuo Foundation for International Scholarly Exchange and by the Donald R. Ellegood International Publications Endowment.

Printed in United States of America
Designed by Veronica Seyd
14 13 12 11 10 09 5 4 3 2 1

University of Washington Press
PO Box 50096, Seattle, WA 98145
www.washington.edu/uwpress

Library of Congress Cataloging-in-Publication Data

Jiang, Jin.
Women playing men : Yue opera and social change in twentieth-century Shanghai / Jin Jiang.
p. cm.
Includes bibliographical references and index.
ISBN 978-0-295-98843-6 (hbk. : alk. paper) — ISBN 978-0-295-98844-3 (pbk. : alk. paper)
1. Theater—China—Shaoxing—History and criticism. 2. Folk drama, Chinese—China—Shaoxing—History and criticism. 3. Women in opera. 4. Popular culture—China—Shanghai. I. Title. II. Title: Yue opera and social change in twentieth-century Shanghai.
PN2876.S53J53 2008
792.0951'132—dc22 2008024174

The paper used in this publication meets the minimum requirements of American National Standard for Information Sciences—Permanence of Paper for Printed Library Materials, ANSI Z39.48–1984.

Dedicated to the memory of my dear mother

PANG WENRUI (1920–2002)

and to my father

JIANG PEINAN

Contents

Preface

This book attempts to seize a moment in the history of Chinese women, of Shanghai, and of China's nascent modernity before it is lost. It presents a social and cultural history of the unique phenomenon of an all-female theater, "women's Yue opera" (*nüzi Yueju* [lit., "women's Zhejiang opera"]), or simply "Yue opera" (Yueju), in the context of the rise of an urban popular culture in modern Shanghai. Women's Yue opera, which originated in the Zhejiang countryside, became a popular form of theater, specializing in love dramas, between the 1930s and 1960s in the metropolis of Shanghai. Banned during the Cultural Revolution (1966–76), it was revived immediately after, only to become a theater enjoyed by a small number of fans and art professionals in more recent decades. If each era has its own popular culture, and if China's reform era has adopted a globalized popular culture of rock and roll and *gongfu* movies, then women's opera represents a popular-culture phenomenon of a past era. Although the opera has retained its artistic identity and will continue to be performed into the conceivable future, the social, political, and cultural significance it bore in previous periods is rapidly being replaced by a new set of contemporary meanings. The actresses and audiences who made Yue opera a popular phenomenon were aging as I began my research in the mid-1990s, and many have since passed away. It is urgent to preserve the voices of the women of Yue opera, speaking directly about their relationship with the opera and what the opera has meant to them. Moreover, while some earlier performances have been preserved on audio- and videotapes, the historical context and human relationships that shaped these productions must be rescued, or they will be lost.

I arrived on the scene in time to carry out some of the rescue work, conducting the first round of interviews in 1995–96 and following up with more interviews and conversations. The most important of these were interviews with actresses in the first and second generations of Yue opera, who personified the opera's success. Born during the 1920s into rural and peasant families in the poor countryside of Zhejiang, these women, who were mostly illiterate, joined opera schools in their early teens in order to make a living; they drifted to Shanghai with the flow of Zhejiang immigrants in the 1930s and 1940s and, with their performances both in the theater and in society, established Yue opera as the most popular theater in the city during the ensuing decades. The stories they told about their lives and careers not only testify to the genre's history but also reveal the ways in which these women allowed various rhetorics to mediate their narratives of this history and their own experiences.

The audience members I interviewed were mostly from middle- or upper-class families with education levels ranging from primary school to college. They are representative of the most important part of the audience, those who helped shape the opera with their financial, social, and emotional support. Their stories, combined with the actresses' recollections of female patrons and fans, provide access to the social and imaginary worlds of middle-class housewives and daughters. These women, the Yue opera actresses and audience members, represented a large segment of the female population in Shanghai in the middle decades of the twentieth century.

This segment of the city's population and Yue opera as a major popular-culture production of this group have so far been overlooked in studies of modern Chinese history. The negligence has much to do with the modern Chinese political and intellectual leadership, which, for most of the twentieth century, was not interested in popular culture but focused on rescuing China from imperialism and building it into a modern nation and state. The Nationalist government (1928–49) and the People's Republic of China (PRC [1949–present]) each made efforts to mobilize the population for its version of nation building, and both attempted to use popular arts as means of mass education and mobilization. In the eyes of this leadership, market-oriented popular arts that focused on the private, mundane concerns of individual citizens were unnecessary, selfish, and trivial, to say the least, and harmful and dangerous, at worst, as they encouraged people to indulge their personal feelings and kept them from devoting themselves to the nation. Thus, both left-wing and Nationalist intellectuals criticized popular literature of the Republican period (1912–49), lumping different strains together under the pejorative term "mandarin ducks and butterflies school of fiction," and studies of popular literature did not begin to emerge until the 1980s. Similarly, while the Nationalist government despised popular theaters and entertainments, the PRC government tried to transform them into state propaganda tools with which to glorify the communist revolution.

Besides suffering the elite bias against popular genres in general, women's opera was stigmatized further because of lingering prejudices against women and women's culture. Modern China's intellectual and political leadership promoted and popularized the concept of liberating women from the "feudal" tradition marked by bound feet, arranged marriage, and lack of access to education and work outside the home. The problem is that the elite assumed the role of liberator, and the concept of women's liberation was shaped largely within the framework of nation building: women had to be liberated in order to better serve the nation as good mothers, good wives, good teachers, good workers, and even good soldiers. Both the Nationalist Party (Guomindang) and the Chinese Communist Party (CCP) demanded that women revolutionaries act within the frameworks of their respective Party ideologies, considering a separate women's movement narrow-minded, unnecessary, and unacceptable. While giving women intellectuals little room to establish their subject position as women,[1] both parties also shared a contemptuous attitude toward women who had little interest in or appeared unsusceptible to political and intellectual nation-building discourses—the Nationalists largely counted these women out, and the Communists tried to reform them. For both Nationalist and Chinese Communist parties, the illiterate actresses and bourgeois housewives and daughters associated with Yue opera appeared to be a backward mass indulging in its own small, mundane concerns of sex, love, and the family, ignorant of national politics. The opera also became notorious for elaborating the purportedly excessive, trivial emotions of love and desire while having little concern for the nation's struggle. Thus, in the name of the nation, the old misogynist bias sneaked back in under the new rhetoric of women's liberation, denying historical significance to a large number of women and their culture.

These elite biases against popular and women's cultures were compounded with a methodological pitfall in the study of modern China's history, namely heavy reliance on written texts and printed discourses. Reliance on written materials inevitably gives privilege to elite activities, since intellectual and political elites, mostly men, produced much of the written texts of the period. While such research is not necessarily thereby rendered invalid and may be valuable when taken on its own terms, collectively it nonetheless may have produced an understanding of history that overemphasizes elite influences while viewing popular activities only as "resistance" to elite intentions. The paucity of voices coming directly from the nonwriting public could have the effect of reducing the majority of Chinese people to objects of elite intentions. Similarly, the lack of women's voices could render Chinese women subalterns in history, with the result that feminist and women's histories of China are framed as critiques of male elite use of women's issues for men's political purposes rather than focusing on issues and significations that concerned women. It is thus crucial to find the voices of these subalterns through oral and performance-related materials outside the print media, and Yue opera provides precisely such a source.

My discovery of Yue opera was actually a rediscovery of an experience from my Shanghai childhood. When I entered primary school in 1962, the government assigned my mother to work as an administrator for the Shanghai Yue Opera House. I often went to the theater with my mother for evening performances because there was no one at home to take care of me. My mother would put me on one of the front seats reserved for her while she worked backstage. My classmates and friends considered me extremely fortunate because the opera was very popular and tickets were hard to obtain. But college-educated Chinese revolutionaries, including my mother, who was not happy with her job assignment, generally looked down on local operas as old-fashioned and backward, and Yue opera, with its love stories, was considered particularly vulgar and trivial. Sure enough, this childhood experience was buried in my memory after I entered college in the late 1970s. Absorbed in the grand narratives of the nation's modern destiny, I stopped going to the opera. It was during my years at Stanford University in the 1990s, informed by the emerging trend of cultural studies in the most general sense, that I reconnected with this childhood experience and became determined to register the voices and experiences of these women in historical writings.

When I went back to Shanghai in 1995–96 to research the topic, I found that my mother loved Yue opera. In her retirement, she enjoyed listening to Yue opera and Beijing opera tapes and watched the opera channel almost every day. My father, also a college-educated New Culturist and a fan of spoken drama, had considered local opera backward and feudal when he was younger; now local operas on television were his favorite entertainment. Among a variety of local opera genres, Yue opera and Beijing opera were my parents' favorites: my mother favored Yue opera over Beijing opera, while my father preferred Beijing opera to Yue opera (a typical gender division in China's opera culture). Though it was now too late, my mother even regretted that she had not learned to write scripts for Yue opera. My parents never explained their newfound appreciation of native operas to me, as if it had all happened naturally and there was nothing to explain. They were retired from their job assignments and perhaps also from the revolution and revolutionary rhetoric, at least to some degree. They could now just enjoy themselves or be entertained by anything that appealed to their senses, without feeling the need to judge their tastes according to external standards. Their appreciation of native operas, in other words, was not the result of a sudden realization of the social and political significance of these forms. They were indeed puzzled by my interest in Yue opera, thinking that important historical events and figures would have been more appropriate subjects, not an insignificant type of theater that only entertained. Mother had great respect for her actress colleagues at the Shanghai Yue Opera House, whom she regarded as independent, resourceful, and hardworking women, and introduced many of them to me for interviews, but she still thought I should have picked a more important topic than Yue opera.

Interestingly, the majority of Yue opera actresses and audience members were not concerned about the stigma placed on them by people who were better educated in elite ideologies. The women of Yue opera functioned within a world of value of their own making and made judgments based on their own perspectives. Yue opera plays were considered shameless in depicting excessive romantic emotions, while Yue opera fans were thought to be notorious for their unrestrained public displays of passion for their favorite actresses and for the genre. Political and intellectual elites dismissed the theatrical and social world of Yue opera as trivial and meaningless, as they were unable to understand it within their own ideological frameworks. In order to understand the world of Yue opera, the historian must enter it by exploring the mundane experiences of the women of Yue opera and leave ideology at the door. "Courageous, empirical fidelity to experience can, under certain circumstances at least," as Peter Fuller points out, "cut through ideology. Experience is not *wholly* determined by ideology: it is very often at odds with it, causing constant ruptures and fissures within the ideological ice-floes."[2] An empirical study of Yue opera is likely to produce different pictures and refresh our understanding of the history of modern China.

Grounded in testimonies of Yue opera's women and theatrical productions, and aided by archival, newspaper and tabloid, and other historical records, this work attempts to reconstruct a meaningful world of Yue opera as it existed for the opera's actresses and fans. A variety of oral and performance-oriented sources provides access to the experiential and imaginary world of Yue opera women. Onstage performances (recorded or live), their reception in the larger public arena, performers' narratives of their lives and art, and audience members' accounts of the impact this art had on their lives are fascinating materials for historical analysis of what I call the "Yue opera phenomenon," a highly visible public display of women's emotions in a growing urban society.

Such an approach yields a history that shows, in contrast to the elite bias, that Yue opera was an important cultural production answering the needs of a newly forming urban society. The Yue opera love drama represented an effort to explore dramatic changes in sex, gender, and family relations in a rapidly modernizing city, and it helped the new urban dweller connect with these changes. Supported not only by women but also by the general public, the Yue opera love drama developed an artistic sophistication that brought the genre national and international recognition. Yue opera masterpieces, including *Liang Shanbo and Zhu Yingtai* (Liang Shanbo yu Zhu Yingtai), known since the 1950s as *The Butterfly Lovers*, and *Dream of the Red Chamber* (Honglou meng), had a far-reaching influence on the popular understanding of love and desire, gender and family relations, and the ethics and aesthetics of a modern urban life.

Viewed within the vast world of popular culture, it becomes clear that popular genres such as Yue opera mattered; elite ideologies appeared to be remote and often irrelevant, while the radical leftist invasion during the Cultural Revolution was destructive. Also, contrary to elite bias, popular-culture genres in general were not at all opposed to building a modern, strong Chinese nation, and many major productions placed their stories against the backdrop of landmark national events. The difference lies in the focus: while elite ideologies made the nation-state their top concern, requesting people to serve the state, popular productions focused on people and their mundane lives, oftentimes influenced by the status of the nation-state. In short, the popular-culture regime had its own value and was full of meanings that were important to the population. These values and meanings may not have entirely agreed with elite ideologies but were equally influential in shaping the nation's modern citizenry.

While the agenda of popular history is to give voice to the subalterns in historical studies, such projects are undertaken not by the silenced people themselves but by historians on their behalf, and most historians write for their academic colleagues. Yet, as Stuart Hall points out in his discussion of Gramsci, there would be no "organic intellectual formation . . . without 'an analogous movement on the part of the mass'" who "rise themselves to higher levels of culture and . . . extend their circle of influence towards the stratum of specialized intellectuals, producing . . . groups of more or less importance."[3] That is, the alleged subalterns, in fact, have raised their voices in the popular realm and asserted their influence in society; in that regard, they needed no help from professional historians. These people and the popular phenomena they created, however, are underrepresented in written history, and it is up to the historian to incorporate their stories into broader historical narratives. This book thus does not intend, and cannot claim, to speak for the people who created the Yue opera phenomenon; it is rather an effort to register the experiences and imaginations of these people and to understand the significance of their stories in the history of modern China.

Acknowledgments

I am eternally grateful to two great mentors, Harold L. Kahn and Lyman P. Van Slyke, who not only taught me high standards of scholarship but moreover continuously exemplified for me ways to live a moral and fulfilling life. Their wisdom, humor, and guidance have supported me through the past years. Van shared with me the story of his beloved aunt, who became an actress and, although disowned by her father for her choice of profession, provided for Van's father's education—a story that resonates with the experiences of the Chinese actresses featured in this book. Hal's comment that "drama imitates life imitating drama" helped me to see the Yue opera history as a process by which the actresses, the audience, and the opera mutually constructed one another in creating a public-culture phenomenon. It was during numerous such interactions with my teachers that this project was incubated and began to take shape.

I am also grateful to Gail Hershatter, Hanchao Lu, Edward Gunn, and Timothy Brook, who carefully read through an early version of the entire manuscript and offered constructive and detailed suggestions for revision. Their insights helped me to make the book conceptually clearer, more focused, and better structured. Bryna Goodman, Thomas Metzger, Elizabeth Perry, Charlotte Furth, Susan Mann, Wen-hsin Yeh, Dorothy Ko, P. J. Ivanhoe, Chen Jian, Mary Lou Roberts, Paul Robinson, Ann Waltner, Tobie Meyer-Fong, and Shannon Sweeney read and commented on parts of the work at various stages, and their questions and critiques were very useful as I struggled to make sense of the manifold materials. I especially want to thank Reiko Shinno and Mark Swislocki for their friendship and generous assistance. Reiko's enthusiasm about the project and our numerous conversations were both fun and inspiring, while Mark faithfully proofread every chapter for ideas as well as for errors.

I want to thank my former colleagues Martha Kaplan, John Kelley, Shao Jing, Yu Zhou, Peipei Qiu, Aili Mu, Maria Hoehn, and Ismail Rashid for reading and commenting on various parts of the work. Questions and criticisms from Max K'o-wu Huang, Chien-ming Yu, Ping-chen Hsiung, Chen Yung-fa, I-chun Fan, Hsiao-T'i Li, and other colleagues at Academia Sinica and from Kohama Masako, Suetsugu Reiko, Nishimura Shigeo, Shao Yingjian, Egami Sachiko, Maeyama Kanako, Ishikawa Teruko, and Sato Masayuki over my various talks on the subject in Taipei and Tokyo were challenging and stimulating. I especially want to thank local Yue opera researchers Ding Yi and Qian Yonglin at the Yue Opera Museum in Shengzhou (formerly Shengxian), Zhejiang; Gao Yilong, Lu Shijun, and Huang Dejun in the research branch at the Shanghai Yue Opera House; and Qiu Yawei and Qiu Wenguang with the Shengxian Native Place Organization in Taipei, who generously shared their ideas with me and allowed me to have access to their collections, interview records, stage photos, and precious old Yue opera recordings. In addition, Chang P'eng-yuan at Academia Sinica kindly gave me his personal copies of the precious eight volumes *The Complete Works of Qi Rushan*. Credit is also due to Zhang Jishun, Xu Jilin, Yu Weimin, and Li Beibei for their support and wonderful collegiality.

Special appreciation goes to the librarians who assisted me in the East Asian Collections at Stanford University, the Harvard-Yenching Library at Harvard University, the Shanghai Municipal Library, the Shanghai Municipal Archives, the District Archives of Hongkou and Huangpu in Shanghai, the Yue Opera Museum in Shengzhou, the Library of the Tōyō bunka kenkyūjo at Tokyo University, the National Library of Japan, the Foreign Affairs Archives in Tokyo, the Fu Ssu-Nien Library of the Institute of History and Philology, and the libraries in the Institute of Literature and Philosophy and the Institute of Modern History at the Academia Sinica in Taipei. Without their efforts, patience, and willingness to help, this project would not have been possible.

I would like to express my gratitude to Lorri Hagman at the University of Washington Press for her faith in this project as well as for her patience and guidance. The comments from an anonymous reviewer for the Press pushed me to further revise and improve the chapter on the audience for opera. Laura Iwasaki proved to be an excellent copyeditor who meticulously corrected typos and inconsistencies in the rendering of translated terms and smoothed the flow of the text. Correspondence with Mary Ribesky has been a pleasant experience as she is always warm, professional, and responsive. Because of them, the production process was an enjoyable experience.

Risako Ide kindly checked romanization for Japanese sources. My students also helped prepare the manuscript: Mauricio Castro checked the references and notes, Jin Tao helped with stylistic details, and Li Bin aided in the preparation of the Index. I am deeply grateful to the many friends, students, and colleagues who helped to make the book better, although I have no way to list everyone who has helped. All remaining mistakes are, of course, mine.

A Fellowship for the Study of Women in Asia from the Center for East Asian Studies at Stanford University funded a four-month research trip to mainland China, and a grant from the American Council of Learned Societies/Chiang Ching-Kuo Foundation enabled me to spend six months at the Tōyō bunka kenkyūjo in Tokyo, Japan, and three months at the Academia Sinica in Taipei. Summer grants from Vassar College supported multiple research trips to mainland China, and a grant from the Pujiang Talents Program sponsored by the Shanghai Municipal Government supported the final stage of this work.

This book is dedicated to my late mother, whose aspiration to live a meaningful life by expressing her literary talent beyond political and domestic boundaries has inspired and shaped my academic career, and to my father, who provided an open, liberal, and intellectually stimulating family environment for me and my brothers and sister to grow up in freely.

Women Playing Men

Geographical expansion of Shengxian opera

言情

Introduction

Opera, Gender, and the City

One of the most important cultural changes in modern China was the feminine opera culture that grew out of its Qing period (1644–1911) masculine predecessor. This modern feminine opera culture achieved its most mature form in several popular opera genres, including "*ping* opera" (*pingju*), which flourished in Tianjin; Yue opera, which became popular in Shanghai; and the "boy-singers' opera" (*gezaixi*), which thrived in Xiamen (later Taipei). The rise of a feminine opera culture in coastal cities reveals much about the gendered nature of social and cultural changes in the twentieth century.

Women's Yue opera, a popular social and cultural phenomenon created by the actresses and audiences of Yue opera in Shanghai, was a concentrated expression of the historical rise of women in public culture in modern Chinese society. It was also the most popular theater in Shanghai for half a century, from the late 1930s through the 1980s. Although women's Yue opera originated in the countryside of Sheng county (Shengxian, present-day Shengzhou City), Zhejiang, it took shape in Shanghai in the 1930s, where it underwent two major transformations—from a rural to an urban entertainment and from all-male to all-female performers. The opera thrived in Shanghai in the 1940s to such an extent that it overtook Beijing opera and the native "Shanghai opera" (Shenqu or Huju) to become the most popular theater in the city. In the 1950s and 1960s, the opera gained national and international influence through frequent performance tours as well as films of Yue opera master plays such as *The Butterfly Lovers*, of 1953, and *Dream of the Red Chamber*, of 1962, and became, arguably, second only to Beijing opera on a nationwide scale in terms of the size of its personnel and audience. Why and how did a female opera capture such a large audience, and what does Yue opera's success tell us about the gendered nature of China's cultural modernity? More specifically, perhaps, as Shanghai nurtured women's Yue opera, in what sense did the opera embody some of the city's peculiar gender and popular characteristics?

One answer to these questions lies in the love drama that tied the opera, the audiences, and the city together in forging a peculiar urban popular culture. Romantic love became one of the most important themes in popular culture as new patterns of family, gender, and sexual relationships began to emerge in twentieth-century Chinese society, which was undergoing tremendous modernization. While this transformation was occurring nationwide, changing family, gender, and sexual relationships had their most concentrated manifestations in treaty-port cities and generated an overflow of cultural products that reflected these changes in the form of the love drama. The love drama became an essential element in various genres, encompassing elite melodramatic productions of leftist films in the 1930s and 1940s as well as popular literature and entertainment such as "mandarin ducks and butterflies" fiction,[1] "Shanghai-style" (Haipai) literature, Shanghai opera, and women's Yue opera. As a response to the popular need to address these deeply felt changes, this culture of love in turn discursively shaped popular perceptions and understandings of changing sex and gender relationships.

Ever since the May Fourth New Culture Movement (roughly 1915–23), popular fiction and entertainment focusing on the emotion of love, or *yanqing* (lit., "elaborating on feelings") culture, was a target of criticism from China's intellectual and political elites, and international scholars overlooked it as they privileged studies in elite culture. This situation began to change dramatically in the 1980s, and a great number of monographs on Republican Shanghai's popular culture have since appeared. Perry Link led the way with his pioneering study of the "mandarin ducks and butterflies" school of fiction, while in the 1990s, Wei Shaochang, Wang Dewei (David Wang), Zhang Gansheng, Yang Yi, and Wu Fuhui followed up with more detailed and expanded studies of popular fiction in Republican era Shanghai. In the meantime, Paul Pickowicz, Yingjin Zhang, and Poshek Fu examined popular film of the period, and Leo Ou-Fan Lee's 1999 study surveyed the fields of fiction, film, and café as representatives of a modern urban culture in Republican Shanghai. Together, these works created a rich literature of popular fiction and film in Republican Shanghai and explored the question of the city's cultural modernity.[2]

Building on the existing literature, this investigation of women and gender in Shanghai's popular-culture scenes intervenes with its chosen temporal and spatial strategies. Temporally speaking, the existing scholarship focused on Republican Shanghai, with an underlying assumption that the communist takeover in 1949 caused a rupture in the city's cultural development. However, as an increasing number of China historians question whether the change of regimes in 1949 should be taken as the line dividing modern Chinese history, the cultural historian needs to follow cultural changes into the People's Republic of China in order to examine continuities and ruptures after 1949 and to develop a fuller picture of cultural changes in modern China. As the footsteps of Yue opera actresses crossed the 1949 divide, and Yue opera continued to develop under communism, this investigation follows its subjects into the popular-culture scenes of CCP-run Shanghai.

Spatially, this volume is designed as a social history of popular culture in modern Shanghai and, as such, is located at the intersection of social history and cultural studies. Cultural studies treats cultural phenomena as meaning systems that individuals and social groups create for themselves under certain circumstances. The strategy of the social history of culture is to focus on the producers and recipients of culture and thereby to observe changing social structures and power relations. Viewed from this angle, women's Yue opera was a social phenomenon closely related to the emergence of women into urban public space and changing gender relations in urban society during the period. The story of Yue opera thus takes us to areas that have not yet been adequately explored in studies of the city's public culture, namely, women's cultural activities and "traditional" native operas as important components of an overall picture of Shanghai's cultural modernity.

Women's Culture

Feminist and gender analysis provides the most important framework for this study, one that enables the historian to "discover" a women's culture centered on Yue opera in modern Shanghai's public space. The rich text of this women's culture reveals three historical processes: the rise of the opera, the rise of its actresses, and the rise of a large female audience in Republican Shanghai. Furthermore, an investigation centered on Yue opera reveals a more general trend of feminization of popular entertainment. Researchers of Shanghai culture, such as Leo Lee and Yingjin Zhang, have noticed the prominence of women and female images in Shanghai's popular-culture industry. They, however, have concerned themselves mainly with questions such as how men produced and consumed female images in the public domain, or what kind of meanings women and female images provoked in the minds of urban men. Few saw women as active producers of culture, and the important phenomenon of feminization of popular entertainment went unnoticed.

This volume focuses on women as historical agents and cultural builders who created the Yue opera phenomenon. The core narrative of this work concerns the trio of the opera, its actresses, and its female audience in modern Shanghai, exploring how the female producers and consumers of Yue opera made the opera such a success, and how the rise of the opera in turn helped these women redefine their social status and identity. It follows the lead of a cluster of inspiring feminist studies in the history of women and gender in China offered by such historians as Charlotte Furth, Gail Hershatter, Dorothy Ko, and Susan Mann that find women actively contributing to and at the center of historical changes.[3]

In his study of the means by which jazz was transmitted from black American ghettos to British suburbs, Simon Frith notes: "To understand why (and how) the worlds of jazz (and rock) are young men's worlds we have, for example, to understand what it means to grow up male and middle-class; to understand the urge to 'authenticity' we have to understand the strange fear of being 'inauthentic.'"[4] Similarly, to understand Yue opera is to understand what it meant to be female and immigrant in a modern metropolis during an era of profound social change, and in order to understand the urge to display emotions publicly through staging or attending Yue opera performances, we have to understand the pain of being silenced or not taken seriously, for such existential conditions sparked the particular experiences and emotions that underlay the ethics and aesthetics of the opera. As the actresses and audience of Yue opera struggled for respect and status, and for the right to express themselves publicly, they created a distinct women's culture—a defining monument in Shanghai's cultural landscape.

The rise of women in society represents arguably the most fundamental change in China in the twentieth century, a change that affected every aspect of Chinese life. Women's entrance into the cultural market, both as consumers and producers, represented perhaps the most important force in shaping a modern culture of love in twentieth-century Shanghai, while women's Yue opera was the most concentrated manifestation of this feminine power. Through the success of women's opera, the actresses and audience of Yue opera helped establish private feelings and mundane experiences as a major theme of modern life, making the "feminine" concerns of the everyday equally as important as the "masculine" public discourse of nationalism and modernity.

Popular Opera

Studying Shanghai culture at the level of popular opera opens a way toward probing a world outside the print universe. Chinese opera is an important subject for historical research because it was, until the mid-1980s, a prominent part of Chinese life and culture. Contrary to the idea, common among non-Chinese, that Chinese opera is defined by Beijing opera, numerous opera genres have existed in China over the past millennium; Beijing opera and Yue opera are relatively new genres, having originated only in the late eighteenth and late nineteenth centuries, respectively. Opera traditions in China have been traced back to at least the "southern opera" (*nanxi*) that matured during the Southern Song dynasty (1127–1279) and the "miscellany opera" (*zaju*) of the Yuan dynasty (1271–1368), and, in the five centuries between the mid-Ming (1500s) and the last decade of the twentieth century, local operas made up the most important form of popular entertainment for the vast majority of Chinese people.[5] While all Chinese operas shared a basic artistic format combining music, singing, speech, dance, and postures in order to narrate a story, each genre distinguished itself mainly by the local tunes and dialect it used in singing and speech. Theoretically, there were as many genres as there were dialects; in fact, various official statistics indicate that there were more than three hundred genres during the nineteenth and the twentieth century up to the 1980s.[6]

Although Chinese operas shared a basic format and a rich repertoire of plays, which developed and accumulated over centuries, each genre had its own ways of rendering these plays in order to cater to local taste. For a modern scholar trying to grasp the idea of "Chinese opera," it is imperative to note that what was most important for the artists of each genre and their audiences was the local identity of the opera, an identity manifested in the operatic rendering of the tunes, dialects, and vocabularies that reflected a local population's particular sentiments and tastes. Sung in local dialects and tunes for the local population, local-opera and storytelling genres were the most direct and authentic expressions of the life experiences and imaginations of the Chinese people in their various local environments. As such, these local operas contain a great deal of information about local populations—their living environment, their daily struggles, and their identities. As these genres also shared a common repertoire of plays across geographic and dialect areas and across time, they provide firsthand materials with which to study Chinese life and culture, both as locally and temporally specific and as a dynamic system that connects the historical with the contemporary and local or regional experiences with national imaginations.

Most important, the oral and performance-oriented materials of local operas provide access to the real "popular" world outside the discursive spaces produced by the writings of elite men and women. Most local operas had humble origins in rural populations. While some were transformed into more elaborate forms, such as Beijing opera and Yue opera, most remained local, small-scale phenomena. Most local operas in the latter half of the Qing dynasty were initially oral and performance oriented. As access to written opera scripts was limited, and owing to the generally low rates of literacy among peasants who became actors, performances of local operas were based mostly on actors' improvisations, albeit with the help of some sketchy plot outlines and a few lines of lyrics established by famous actors. Improvisation was such an important element of Chinese opera that, until the 1950s, few actors followed script lyrics closely, even though by then the literacy rate among actors had gradually risen, and scripts had been widely available, at least in cities, for almost the entire Republican period. Most so-called playwrights were in fact story writers whose main job was to create the plot and main characters and who only sometimes included a few lines of lyrics in their scripts. Actors would take these bare-bones scripts and flesh out the story onstage by adding lyrics and speeches of their own, inspired by interactions with their stage partners and in reaction to audience responses. Most scripts of popular plays published during this period were not created by playwrights for opera troupes but were written records of well-established performances.

Modern China's political and intellectual leadership tended to view oral and local traditions as barriers to the creation of a national identity. During the May Fourth New Culture Movement, they set off to overcome these barriers by promoting and popularizing standard Chinese (Mandarin) as the national spoken language and developing a new standard vernacular literary system based on it. A new standard, Chinese-based national language began to be established in the ensuing decades as it was used in education, official communication, and the mass media. Despite these efforts, local dialects and sentiments continued to be a major feature in Chinese lives in urban centers as well as in villages and small towns, and local operas continued to express these local sentiments.

Most Western-language monographs on Shanghai's popular culture, however, have focused on the petty intellectuals closely involved in the production and consumption of popular fiction and film based on standard Chinese, while overlooking local-opera and storytelling genres and their native-place supporters, who formed a large urban population characterized by low literacy and/or low status along with a lack of interest or ability in reading and writing. This has been the case in part because of the difficulties the foreign researcher faces in accessing local dialects. Chinese scholars, in contrast, worked to produce histories and gazetteers of various local operas during the 1980s and 1990s as part of state-sponsored local gazetteer projects. Each established genre in modern Shanghai—including Yue opera, Shanghai opera, Huai opera (Huaiju [lit., "the opera from the Huai River," i.e., northern Jiangsu, also known as Jiangbeixi, Subeixi]), and Beijing opera in Shanghai—was honored with a gazetteer.[7] As the most popular opera genre in the city and the Jiangnan region, Yue opera also became the subject of a few popular histories, including Gao Yilong's *The Story of Yue Opera* (Yueju shihua) and Ying Zhiliang's *History of Yue Opera in China* (Zhongguo Yueju fazhan shi).[8] Yet these publications have not received adequate attention from historians, partially because these works focus on operatic developments instead of considering the social and political significance of the genres in the history of modern Shanghai.[9]

Focusing on Yue opera and drawing on other local-opera forms, the following chapters show that, in twentieth-century Shanghai, dynamic native-place and linguistic politics were basic elements in the daily lives of millions of new residents, and the status of various local operas was closely related to the status of their native-place patrons. Even with the current dominance of standard Chinese in the mass media and the educational system, most people still speak local dialects within their family and native-place groups, and native-place politics continues to play an important role in people's lives. In fact, most Shanghai women interviewed for this project could not speak standard Chinese (though they could understand it) let alone use it to communicate subtle and complex feelings.[10]

Urban Space

The story of Yue opera and its women must also be a story about the modern city of Shanghai. Two factors formed the backdrop for the dramatic rise of Yue opera. First, women's Yue opera was part of the city's dynamic popular culture, shaped during the formation of Shanghai's capitalist economy and bourgeois population, a modern transformation that occurred first and foremost in Shanghai. Second, one salient feature of the city's popular culture was its obsession with women and love, a response to fundamental changes in gender ideologies and gender relations that, while taking place nationwide, were felt most intensely in the modern metropolis.

Shanghai, the largest semicolonial treaty-port city in China, was not only a physical place defined by its ports of call and complicated political jurisdictions; it also fueled China's modern transformation under Western influence. Shanghai is located at the mouth of the Yangzi River delta, backed by one of traditional China's richest areas, which is also noted for its cultural vitality, and facing the East China Sea, beachhead of the West's impact on China. Owing largely to its location, Shanghai developed rapidly into a regional and national center of the nation's modern economy and gained renown for its hybrid cosmopolitan atmosphere.

Colonial Shanghai provided a safe haven for economic development, as foreign powers sheltered China's most modern sectors and wealthiest industrialists from political disturbances and civil wars, and the city quickly grew into the largest industrial and commercial center in China.[11] In more concrete terms, modern Shanghai was built by large numbers of domestic migrants, who formed the largest share of the city's population. Shanghai in the late nineteenth and early twentieth centuries had already become the largest city in China, and the foreign settlements comprised its most economically and culturally vibrant sectors. By 1935, Shanghai's population reached 3.6 million, of which approximately 1.6 million lived in foreign settlements, alongside about 60,000 foreigners.[12] The population in foreign settlements continued to grow, to 1.67 million by 1936, and then exploded, to 4.5 million in 1938, with the influx of refugees fleeing invading Japanese troops.[13]

The combination of the foregoing factors—ambiguous political sovereignty, a lack of ideological control, a high concentration in resources, and the rapid growth of a diverse population—produced a dynamic market for all kinds of cultural products, native and foreign, traditional and modern. Skyscrapers were erected along the Bund and Nanjing Road to house banks, customs offices, and department stores where imported luxury goods were displayed, showcasing the city's modernity. A few streets away in the narrow lanes along Fuzhou Road, brothels and opium dens prospered alongside publishing houses, bookstores, printing services, and newspaper headquarters. Because it combined modern and traditional as well as native and foreign cultural forms, Shanghai captured the imaginations of both Chinese and foreigners. Their image of Shanghai was captured in turn by a distinctive urban popular culture manufactured by artists who availed themselves of the city's flourishing print industry and numerous entertainment venues.

Republican-era Shanghai manufactured modern romances in print. Ever since the Ming dynasty (1368–1644), the Jiangnan area had been home to China's most advanced printing industry, with the cities of Nanjing, Suzhou, and Hangzhou leading the way. Shanghai's printers built on this Jiangnan tradition by incorporating Western machinery and paper, and they soon became the nation's leading force in modernizing China's print culture. Shanghai's printing industry was the backbone of the city's commercial culture and helped shape cultural trends ranging from clothing fashions like the "cheongsam" (*qipao*), a modern urban dress for women, to the popular "mandarin ducks and butterflies" fiction.[14] Shanghai's printing industry was as capable of producing large numbers of inexpensive books in a short period of time as it was of producing refined prints. This capacity proved indispensable for the manufacturing of popular literature and gave Shanghai's popular literature its physical form. As the literary scholar Zhang Gansheng has pointed out, the great expansion of popular literature began with the appearance of daily newspapers with literary supplements in the early Republican period.[15] These literary supplements, with daily installments of serialized fiction, were soon rivaled by literary magazines, which published weekly, three times a month, semimonthly, and monthly and featured as many as a dozen fictional works in a given issue, often including three or four installments of longer works. If a series proved popular, an offprint would soon be produced. While the format of serialized fiction built on traditional links between storytelling and storytelling-style literature, it also made the mass consumption of fiction possible.[16] Popular fiction soon became an important part of everyday life for many Shanghai residents. As Zhou Shoujuan, the famous "mandarin ducks and butterflies" fiction author and editor of many popular literary supplements and magazines, including *Saturday* (Libai liu), recalled in his later years:

> There were not that many magazines in the early Republican period, so *Saturday* was very popular at that time. Every Saturday morning, readers waited at the door of the Zhonghua Library, where *Saturday* was distributed. As soon as the door opened, people rushed in to be the first to buy the maga-

zine. The situation somewhat resembled the morning rush for pancakes and deep-fried dough sticks at the neighborhood restaurants.[17]

People from all over the country flowed into the metropolis, attracted by its promise of opportunity, dazzled by its prosperity, amazed by its openness and sophistication, and frustrated by its coldheartedness and deception. Perhaps because they lived in such a legendary place, Shanghai people liked legendary stories. The best-selling writer Zhang Ailing, who began her career as a Shanghai writer in the early 1940s, titled her first collection of short stories *Legendary Stories* (Chuanqi). Commenting on the characteristics of Shanghai people, she wrote: "Shanghainese are abnormal products made of traditional Chinese people tempered by the high pressure of modern life and experienced in complex interactions among all kinds of old and new cultures. The result may not be so healthy, but there is a marvelous wisdom in it."[18]

These immigrants also carried with them their native-place identities, habits, and cultures. The largest immigrant groups, including those from Jiangsu, Zhejiang, and Guangdong, deployed their native cultures as they competed for recognition in Shanghai's public spaces; native opera houses as well as regional restaurants, grocery stores, and native-place halls became marks of their claims to cultural significance. Major native theaters in Shanghai included Yue opera from Guangdong (which used the same pronunciation as Yue opera from Zhejiang but was written with a different character), "Suzhou story-singing" (*pingtan*), Huai opera from northern Jiangsu, Yue opera from Zhejiang, Shanghai opera from the nearby countryside, and "Shanghai-style Beijing opera" (Haipai Jingju). While first-rate Beijing opera troupes performed in high-class teahouses and theaters in the foreign settlements during the early twentieth century, and major Yue (Zhejiang) opera companies relocated to upper-tier theaters when Yue opera became popular in the 1940s, other minor operas continued to be performed mostly on the peripheries of the downtown areas, where their constituencies were concentrated. Jiangbei opera, for example, was performed mainly in small, shoddy theaters in working-class neighborhoods in Yangshupu or in the shantytowns of Zhabei for lower-class northern Jiangsu immigrants, while Shanghai opera was performed mainly in Nanshi, Huxi (western Shanghai), and Pudong (across the Huangpu River) for a mixed lower- to lower-middle-class local audience.[19]

Although the historical kinship between popular theatrical entertainment and popular literature is well known to modern scholars, it is worth noting that a dynamic intertextuality between the two media created a symbiosis of popular culture in Republican era Shanghai. Virtually every popular novel published in Shanghai was adapted for popular theaters and storytelling genres as well as for the cinema.[20] Moreover, intertextuality went in both directions, for not only did local operas and storytelling venues compete to stage popular fiction works but writers also rewrote popular opera plays and Suzhou story-singing pieces as fiction.[21] Zhang Henshui's *Fate in Tears and Laughter* (Tixiao yinyuan) is one of the most remarkable examples of this intertextuality. Zhang's novel first appeared in daily installments, from November 1929 to 1931, in *Joyful Forest* (Kuaihuolin), a literary supplement to the major newspaper *Daily News* (Xinwen bao). A complete offprint first appeared in 1932. The novel was extremely popular in Shanghai and was quickly adapted to many forms of entertainment. An article published in *Coral* (Shanhu) magazine in May 1933 documented this phenomenon:

> Since Zhang Henshui published his novel *Fate in Tears and Laughter*, the novel has been used as a blueprint for various forms of entertainment, such as film, storytelling, Beijing opera, Guangdong opera, new drama [*xinju*],[22] Western opera, comic shows, puppet shows, Shaoxing opera [Yue opera], open ground operas, comic books, and folk songs. At the same time, several "sequels" and "alternative endings" have appeared on the market. . . . There are three versions of *Fate in Tears and Laughter in Suzhou Story-Singing* (Tixiao yinyuan tanci) being broadcast on Shanghai's radio stations, scripted by Yao Min'ai, Qi Fanniu, and Lu Dan'an, respectively.[23]

This intertextuality among various forms of popular literature and entertainment contributed to a diverse yet interconnected popular culture, organized by the marketplace and reflective of a distinctly Shanghainese sensibility.

One salient characteristic of this Shanghainese sensibility was its obsession with women and love stories. As the literary historian Yang Yi remarked about Shanghai-style, or Haipai, literature, referring to several generations of Shanghai writers from Bao Tianxiao to Zhang Ailing:

> *Yanqing* [elaborating on feelings] was the largest genre of Haipai literature. It seems no work could claim to be Haipai if it did not elaborate on the question of love. They [Haipai writers] especially appreciated the tears of Venus, and so their love stories were always sentimental. . . . The narrowness of the theme made it easy for Haipai writers to fall into the trap of

scholar-beauty boilerplate, but once they rose above such hackneyed formulations, they could gain some insight into the mystery of sex and love between men and women.[24]

Regardless of its bias against "scholar-beauty boilerplate," Yang Yi's comment nonetheless aptly describes the orientation of Shanghai's popular entertainment and, indeed, Shanghai-style popular culture as a whole. The genre of love melodrama dominated literature, film, drama, opera, storytelling, and radio broadcasting. The prevalence of love dramas may be understood as a cultural convergence in modern Shanghai between the *yanqing* genre of the East and the melodrama of the West.

The cultural historian Paul Pickowicz explained the origins of the genre of melodrama as it first emerged in industrial Europe:

> Melodrama, as Peter Brooks and others have suggested, is characterized by rhetorical excess, extravagant representation, and intensity of moral claim. It is an aesthetic mode of "heightened dramatization" that refers to pure and polar concepts of darkness and light, salvation and damnation. The melodramatic genre was developed first in French theater in the immediate aftermath of the revolution, at a time when a significant post-revolutionary democratization of culture was taking place. Although melodrama is a distinctively modern form, its initial political thrust was conservative. The audience for melodrama included people from all social classes who were frightened and confused by the modern transformation of society. This new and powerful mode of representation had a major impact on European fiction in the mid- and late nineteenth century and has been kept alive by filmmakers and television producers in the twentieth century.[25]

The melodramatic genre, as Pickowicz has also pointed out, dominated the Shanghai-based Republican era film industry. Despite their efforts to infuse Chinese films with May Fourth thought in the 1930s, leftist filmmakers such as Sun Yu, Cai Chusheng, Wu Yonggang, Shen Xiling, and Xia Yan all became captives of the powerful melodrama format. Although Xia Yan and PRC film scholars claimed that 1930s films embodied the tenets of social realism, leftist filmmakers in the 1930s, as Pickowicz argued, "accepted without question the dominance of the melodramatic genre and thereby doomed to failure any chance they had to introduce complex May Fourth ideas."[26]

Perry Link, in his pioneering study of early Republican era popular literature, put forth a similar interpretation of the "mandarin ducks and butterflies" school of fiction, albeit without using the word "melodrama." He pointed out that various aspects of the historical setting and literary characteristics of "mandarin ducks and butterflies" fiction resemble those of popular literature in other industrializing and industrialized societies:

> The extent to which modern life patterns are inherent consequences of industrialism may not be entirely clear; but modern-style entertainment fiction (or television, in recent decades) has, for one example, consistently appeared in tandem with industrialism around the world. From its beginnings in eighteenth-century England this kind of fiction spread to Western Europe and America, in many cases through direct borrowing as stories were reprinted or translated across international boundaries.[27]

The genre of melodrama as summarized by Pickowicz, or that of popular fiction as defined by Link, was introduced to Shanghai in the early twentieth century via Japanese translations of Western fiction being mass-produced in Osaka.[28] It is of course no coincidence that Osaka and Shanghai, the foremost industrial cities of Japan and China, respectively, were the national centers of melodramatic productions.

Despite the fact that the development of the melodrama in China, Japan, and the West were all related to the process of industrialization and urbanization, the Chinese perception of this process, which shaped a Chinese version of the melodrama, was in many ways not the same. While the English word "melodrama" has no easy counterpart in Chinese, the two popularly used native terms, *chuanqi* and *yanqing*, capture much of the peculiarity of popular culture in Republican Shanghai.

First, the Chinese were not just "frightened and confused" by modern changes, as Pickowicz suggested of their Western counterparts, with regard to their uncertain future. For Chinese of the time, "modern," a term applied mostly to things Western, was a known quantity, and for many, modern things were both necessary and fascinating: necessary because China had to become modernized in order to save itself from foreign dominance, and fascinating because of the novelty and exotic origins of these things. Indeed, many welcomed the coming of the modern age with feelings of wonder and excitement, favorably impressed by the steamboats, trains and railways, telegrams, and skyscrapers as well as by the foreign gunboats and powerful rifles that threatened China's sovereignty. This sense of excitement and wonder toward modernity is captured in the native phrase *chuanqi*, which means "romance," "legend," or "strange story."[29] Although the term originated to refer to a genre of fiction that was popular during the Tang dynasty (618–907), and later also was associated with a genre of Ming drama, it had also been used liberally to refer to fiction that recounted legendary or bizarre happenings. It thus struck Chinese of this period as appropriate for describing the wonder of Shanghai in the first half of the twentieth century.

Second, the most common form of melodrama in Republican Shanghai was the love story. The Chinese term *yanqing* probably comes closest to describing the content and style of the city's popular culture. *Yanqing*, as a genre of literature and entertainment, is characterized largely by a thematic focus on love relationships and a mode of aesthetics involving complicated plots and exceedingly sentimental expressions of emotions. *Yanqing* authors rarely exhibited much interest in politics in their work, and any political topic on which they touched for narrative purposes never interfered with their principal concern, the poetics of *qing*, or feelings. While some *yanqing* stories, like those related to mundane relationships among friends and siblings or between parents and children, do deal with the full range of human emotions, the majority focuses on love.

Yanqing literature and entertainment of this period also had deep historical and regional roots. Love stories in China can be traced back to at least the Tang dynasty, when they were a subgenre of *chuanqi* and therefore consisted of tales of unusual events. *Yanqing* arts emerged as an independent genre only in the seventeenth century, a period during which the Taizhou School, which argued for gender equality and intellectual-spiritual companionship, became influential in literary circles.[30] In the wake of the bloody Manchu conquest in the mid-seventeenth century, *yanqing* themes dominated literary and theatrical production in the highly commercialized urban areas of Jiangnan. Seventeenth-century scholar-beauty fiction and such famous *chuanqi* plays as Hong Shen's *The Hall of Eternity* (Changsheng dian) all focus on love.[31]

The Republican era fixation on *yanqing* signals one of the most far-reaching and deeply felt changes in twentieth-century China: the social and ideological remaking of the family and the redefining of gender relations. Concomitant with the May Fourth rhetoric of free love and marriage and gender equality were changes in family structure, most notably among immigrant families in large urban centers. The new urban settlers largely abandoned the traditional model of the multigenerational household and established nuclear families centered on an adult couple with children.[32]

Polygamy, another feature of traditional family structure for elite families, was discouraged by emerging Republican social norms and, albeit with exceptions, middle- and upper-middle-class men kept their second (and sometimes third) wives in locations separate from the main household. The relationship between husband and wife therefore became increasingly important within the family. As young people began to explore new ways of finding a dream husband or wife, courtship between young men and women became a common, although still shocking, feature of Shanghai's public life. The spectacular nature of Haipai courtship was captured in an article published in the October 1939 issue of the popular magazine *Shanghai Life* (Shanghai shenghuo), which quoted a war refugee who had only recently come to Shanghai after fleeing invading Japanese troops:

> Somebody who had not been to Shanghai would have no way of knowing that relationships between men and women could be so close. Every time I go to the park, I see that most people there are couples. One man and one woman closely accompany each other, and they interact only with each other: one is a gorgeously dressed new woman with hanging long hair, a powdered face, red lips, [clad] in stockings and high-heeled leather shoes, and the other is a smartly coiffed and creamy-faced young man wearing a Western suit. As they stroll along, they laugh freely, holding arms or leaning close to each other, as if they are the only ones there. In the hinterland, such behavior would surely cause gossip and be considered shameless.[33]

This degree of public intimacy between a young man and a woman may not have been typical of ordinary Shanghai residents, but its shocking effect on people is no exaggeration.

The need to reflect on changing family and gender relations was also manifested in elite arts, as seen, for example, in Lu Xun's short story "Remembrances of the Past" (Shangshi) and numerous spoken drama renditions of Henrik Ibsen's play *A Doll's House*. However, the most popular pieces of elite spoken drama in the 1930s—including Cao Yu's *Thunderstorm* (Leiyu), set in a modern coal mine, and *Sunrise* (Richu), which took place in a menacing metropolis (Shanghai)—were quintessential love melodramas, structured by the trials and tribulations of romantic relationships and intensely focused on the conflict between good and evil.[34] Indeed, the struggle between good and evil became even more intense in the leftist films and spoken dramas that aimed for an ideological or moral transformation of the audience, compared to the more market-oriented popular-culture productions. Ironically, intellectuals also participated in creating the phenomenon of the love drama, by using the genre to showcase core leftist values and criticisms, framed in a set of dichotomies such as good versus evil, modern versus feudal, national pride versus foreign invasion, the working people versus the ruling class, women versus the feudal, patriarchal system, and the unspoiled native countryside versus the decadent, foreign urban center.

As Shanghai's economic, social, and demographic development in the mid-twentieth century created a fertile breeding ground for modern love dramas, women's Yue opera emerged as a master theater of this genre. Western observers tend to view Yue opera, or any Chinese native opera, as traditional theater and see film as the modern form. For many Chinese familiar with native operas, however, women's Yue opera was young compared to operas such as "Kun opera" (Kunqu)—opera from Kunshan, Jiangsu—and Beijing opera, which were hundreds of years old. Its aesthetics were modern, as it was influenced by film and spoken drama and acquired a modern cosmopolitan quality. As the love drama refined its modern aesthetics, women's Yue opera became the leading type of theater in Shanghai. In fact, several theatrical genres active in Shanghai—such as Yue opera, Shanghai opera, and Huai opera—were new forms of Chinese opera, while imported spoken drama and film were not necessarily newer. Film, for example, became established in Shanghai during roughly the same period, and its popular success, beginning in the mid-1930s, owed much to the development of the cinematic love drama. Women's opera in Shanghai achieved popular success beginning in the late 1930s, after the film boom. Note that while most theatrical performances were carried out in various local dialects and tended to have separate audiences among dialect-based groups, film dialogue used mostly standard Chinese and drew a large crowd of the young and educated that cut across native and dialect origins. The growing popularity of film, however, did not deplete the audience for dialect-based theaters in any significant way, and many people enjoyed both the cinema and their favorite opera, just as they were capable of comprehending both standard Chinese and their local languages.

Wartime Shanghai

The years 1937–45, during the War of Resistance against Japan, represent a crucial period in women's Yue opera history. During these years, the genre took root in Shanghai and became a dominant presence in the city's popular entertainment. The opera matured rapidly, and the foundations laid during this period ensured its further development in the postwar and Civil War (1945–49) periods. These twelve years before the end of the Republican era, in 1949, witnessed the establishment of women's Yue opera as a major modern art form in Shanghai. The following statistics illustrate the dramatic rise of women's Yue opera in wartime Shanghai and afterward. Among Shanghai's theaters in 1938, two were devoted to spoken drama, three to Shanghai opera, and one to Kun opera; only Beijing opera's twelve stages competed with the twelve dedicated to women's Yue opera.[35] The popularity of women's Yue opera continued to increase throughout the 1940s and eventually overtook that of Beijing opera to become the most popular theater in Shanghai. A 1947 tourist guidebook lists thirty-two theaters for women's Yue opera, compared to only six Beijing opera houses, six theaters for Shanghai opera, five for spoken drama, and four for comic shows plus thirty-four movie theaters.[36]

What was the relationship between the Yue opera boom and the conditions of wartime Shanghai? Was the success of Yue opera somehow a consequence of war and occupation? Or was the rise of Yue opera only a coincidence?

The Japanese occupation of Shanghai began in November 1937, in the wake of the three-month-long Battle of Shanghai. As Chinese troops retreated, Japanese forces took control of most of the city, leaving only the French concession and the largely Anglo-American International Settlement intact, making this area a "solitary island" (*gudao*), until the outbreak of the Pacific War on December 8, 1941. As the Japanese advanced into the hinterland, refugees flooded into this "island" from neighboring areas, contributing to the considerable wartime prosperity of "island" Shanghai. Various local operas—such as Jiangbei opera, Yangzhou opera, and Yue opera—thrived as performers from the surrounding area arrived in the city and continued to entertain their fellow provincials, who were swelling the city's population.[37] Many female Yue opera troupes, entering the city with large number of Zhejiang refugees, flourished in Shanghai during this unusual period. Yue opera continued to develop even when the population began to decrease after 1942, when the Japanese completed their occupation of the city and began to deport refugees back to the countryside in an effort to strengthen their control over the local population and reduce pressure from the worsening food shortage.[38]

Wartime politics were also favorable for Yue opera and popular-entertainment genres in general. Previously, in the face of the escalating Japanese invasion of China during the 1930s, an intellectual-led "resistance culture" (*kangzhan wenhua*) mounted in the public sphere and reached its height after the outbreak of the War of Resistance in July 1937.[39] In Shanghai, however, resistance culture began to wane toward the end of the decade. As Chinese troops and the national government withdrew deeper into the hinterland, and as European authorities in charge of "island" Shanghai were under increasing Japanese pressure to crack down on resistance culture, intellectuals and young patriots gradually left Shanghai for Wuhan, Chongqing, Guilin, Kunming, and Yan'an. The elite resistance culture disappeared from the scene entirely after Japanese forces completed their occupation of Shanghai at the end of 1941.[40] In the meantime, much to the disgust of intellectuals and political leaders, popular culture remained active.

The occupation authority favored popular culture over the more nationalistic, elite culture. It carefully censored intellectual institutions, including major newspapers, the publishing industry, spoken drama venues, and the film industry, to suppress the circulation of resistance propaganda.[41] Among their first acts upon entering "island" Shanghai, Japanese forces took over major newspapers and publishing houses.[42] They then proceeded to arrest, interrogate, and torture nationalistic and left-wing intellectuals.[43] While the occupation authority placed intellectual activities under tight surveillance and ruthlessly suppressed any hint of resistance, it deliberately left all forms of popular entertainment alone, as these were deemed apolitical and therefore not a threat. Indeed, the occupation authority made a systematic effort to boost popular entertainment in order to create a false appearance of peace and prosperity in occupied Shanghai. It tried, for example, though without success, to persuade Mei Lanfang, who had lived quietly in Shanghai since the fall of Hong Kong, to return to the stage.[44] The occupation authority also banned Hollywood movies while encouraging Wang Jingwei's collaboration government to take over the city's film industry and produce films centered on love stories.[45]

The occupation authority's cultural policy also had a profound impact on literary productions in wartime Shanghai. Writers could no longer frame their stories as nationalistic, anti-Japanese narratives, which many had considered their patriotic duty in the 1930s, but they were unwilling to endorse the Japanese rhetoric of the so-called Greater East Asian Co-Prosperity Sphere, which subordinated China to Japan's imperial ambitions. Consequently, the ostensibly innocuous and personal topics of love, marriage, and family, or of modern metropolitan life in general, became favorite themes. Some seasoned romantic-fiction writers, now long-term Shanghai residents, who had been dormant during the height of resistance culture, became active again on the literary scene. Zhou Shoujuan, for example, resumed the famous romantic-fiction magazine *The Violet* (Ziluolan) in 1943, and Chen Dieyi published *Phenomena* (Wanxiang) and, later, *Chatting in Wind and Rain* (Fengyu tan).

The censorship of patriotic themes pushed wartime writers to concentrate on aspects of China's experience with modernity on a more personal, and hence more universal, level, even as their environment was being shaped by an oppressive foreign occupation. A saddened sensibility that spoke of Shanghai residents' ambivalent experience with urban modernity and foreign occupation thus prevailed in wartime literature. Like the city itself, the residents of wartime Shanghai were captives who had no choice but to live their everyday lives in an occupied city. Consequently, they were tied to the city more than ever before, and their identity as Shanghainese, as opposed to that of accidental sojourners, became ever stronger. This new awareness of and identification with the city are evident in the dozens of literary magazines that published explorations of the experience of modern life between 1942 and 1945.[46] In the absence of a cultural elite, popular-fiction writers enjoyed the status of cultural celebrities, and wartime popular culture became centered on personal narratives and sentimental love stories, the very specialty of popular opera genres such as Yue opera.[47]

The rise of women's voices in wartime Shanghai was particularly beneficial to the development of women's Yue opera. The occupation authority's suppression of elite resistance rhetoric also set the stage for women's voices to be heard clearly and distinctly. Moreover, Japanese authorities willingly supported the rhetoric of women's liberation as a way of promoting Japan's modernist outlook and finding common ground with Chinese intellectuals, and "women's questions" (*funü wenti*) became one of the very few politically meaningful topics that could be freely discussed in the print media in wartime Shanghai. Unlike the periods before and after the occupation, this period witnessed women themselves, not a patriarchal government or a male intellectual elite, initiating and setting topics for public discussion and assuming authority in leading the discourse. A new generation of "young lady writers" (*xiaojie zuojia*) emerged, and it is important to note that the period's most popular writers include two young women, Su Qing and Zhang Ailing.[48] These women were less concerned with the abstract principles of women's rights than with the mundane concerns of a wide range of women—professionals, working women in general, housewives, and students.

In "About My Writing" (Ziji de wenzhang), Su Qing observed, "I write mostly about relations between men and women. That's my life. I cannot help it."[49] Zhang Ailing also remarked, at a well-publicized women authors' roundtable: "Women act in a limited social sphere, and we cannot do much about this. . . . Women writers write mostly about family and love; their style is softer, naive, exotic, sentimental, and sensible, which has to do with each writer's environment, education, and personality."[50] During the roundtable discussion, most young lady writers admitted that their works were based on personal experiences. While Zhang Ailing claimed that her stories were derived not necessarily from her personal life but more from observation and imagination, these stories nonetheless focus on personal odysseys, the family, and love relationships. It is not surprising that these women artists would consider their focus on love, marriage, and the family to be "natural," given the long-standing gender system that defined women as subordinate to men and having no role to play beyond the domestic sphere, a system still very much a reality despite the efforts of its challengers during the Republican period.[51]

Women writers' prominent position in wartime Shanghai and their public discussion of women's issues provided an important context for the growth of women's Yue opera and its exploration of love, the family, and gender relations from a woman's perspective; however, there are also some specific historical connections between women writers and women's Yue opera. Zhang Ailing was so amazed by a Yue opera show she attended in rural Zhejiang that she wrote an essay recounting the experience.[52] Based on various remarks about Yue opera in her writing, it is apparent that Su Qing, a native of Ningbo, attended Yue opera shows from time to time with her mother and relatives. She obviously enjoyed the opera and, in the early 1950s, became a professional Yue opera playwright.[53]

Thus, while the influx of large numbers of war refugees, many of whom were wealthy and had both the time and the money to go to the theater and buy popular fiction, stimulated an initial popular-culture boom in "island" Shanghai, wartime politics and the emergence of women's culture in general helped sustain women's Yue opera and other popular-culture forms in occupied Shanghai. But, for several reasons, wartime Shanghai was ultimately a rupture only in political and military terms, not in terms of fundamental cultural and social development in urban life.

First, contrary to what scholars have generally assumed, the wartime popular-culture boom in Shanghai was not an "abnormal" (*jixing*) phenomenon but a normal phenomenon reasserting itself during an unusual period.

Popular culture was in fact the mainstay of Shanghai's cultural market throughout the Republican period, while elite arts, though a powerful cultural presence, were popular only for a short period in the late 1930s, an "abnormal" period when the resistance culture ran high.

Second, the rise of women's voices in wartime Shanghai was a result of continuous efforts to integrate women into society since the 1911 Republican Revolution. Like the young actresses in women's Yue opera, Zhang Ailing and her cohorts were born during the May Fourth era, roughly 1915–23, and were in their early twenties; Su Qing, born in 1914, was only slightly older than the rest. If wartime circumstances made these women the center of attention in public culture in occupied Shanghai, the preceding three decades of work on women's education, women's right to work, and equal rights for women laid the groundwork for this development. Professional women, including salesgirls in department stores, nurses, and schoolteachers, became a significant part of the city's workforce, and their experiences and problems were shared and articulated by women writers.[54] Su Qing had been an English major at the Central University in Nanjing, while Zhang Ailing attended St. Mary's, a Catholic women's school in Shanghai, and St. John's College. These young authors belonged to a generation that grew up under the mixed influence of the New Culture, popular romantic fiction, and Western literature. Of writing, Zhang said: "I have experimented with different styles of fiction writing, including storytelling literature [*huaben*] of the late Ming, as collected in *Legends of the Past and the Present* [Jingu qiguan],[55] historical romance, miscellaneous notes, 'mandarin ducks and butterflies' fiction, and orthodox New Literature [Xin Wenxue]."[56] Stylistic experimentation aside, Zhang Ailing and her generation of women writers had grown up with the rhetoric of women's liberation and witnessed the difficulties of, and progress toward, achieving that goal, and they now began to explore women's issues and experiences in the modern metropolis from perspectives that were both personal and representative of those held by the city's new professional women.[57]

Third, the influx of war refugees may be viewed as one of the many waves of migration to the great treaty-port city since the mid-nineteenth century. Yue opera's establishment in Shanghai was indeed a cultural ramification of Zhejiang natives' massive migration to Shanghai, a long-term process that encompassed the wartime period. Thus, while war and occupation were not crucial in the development of women's Yue opera, it was crucial that they did not alter the dynamics of these developments in urban migration, urban popular culture, and women's integration into society, which underlay the formation of such a women's culture. The rapid transformation of women's Yue opera into the most popular theater in wartime Shanghai was, therefore, a ripening of these longer-term historical processes that ran through the entire Republican period. The politics of occupation, however, helped push a popular phenomenon, which might otherwise have been overlooked, to the forefront of the cultural scene.

The Story Unfolds

A group of recent works map out the social and cultural contexts within which women's Yue opera evolved. The people featured in this volume generally lived in crowded townhouses along Shanghai's narrow lanes; their living environment has been discussed in Hanchao Lu's *Beyond the Neon Lights*. The actresses were, generally speaking, a lucky group of women who managed to obtain full citizenship in the nation's modern transformation while their traditional "sisters," the prostitutes, were denigrated as a social ill to be eliminated by the same process, as described by Gail Hershatter in *Dangerous Pleasures* and Christian Henriot in *Prostitution and Sexuality in Shanghai*. Susan Mann's article, "The Cult of Domesticity in Republican Shanghai's Middle Class," which examines Shanghai housewives from Ningbo, and Emily Honig's *Sisters and Strangers*, a study of Shanghai's female cotton-mill workers, are helpful for understanding the Yue opera audience, while Bryna Goodman's *Native Place, City, and Nation* and Emily Honig's *Creating Chinese Ethnicity* help us to place the city's popular entertainment in the background of native-place politics. Frederic Wakeman Jr.'s excursion into the world of police operations, *Policing Shanghai*, provides a social and judicial background for understanding actresses' relationships with various social elements, including local strongmen and gangsters. In *Shanghai Modern*, Leo Lee details Shanghai's popular culture, and Andrew Jones, in *Yellow Music*, describes a jazz scene. Both were dominated by male artists and consumers, providing a contrast to the social and poetic world of women's opera. Elizabeth Perry's study of Shanghai's working class provides another useful contrast to the lives of the women of Yue opera.[58]

Chapters 1 through 5 of this volume are arranged chronologically. Chapter 1 traces the development of the opera from its origins in Shengxian's countryside in the late nineteenth century to its establishment in Shanghai in the 1930s and discusses the opera's twofold transformation, from rural to urban and from male to female. Chapters 2 through 4 examine the rise of a women's culture in Shanghai's public space in the middle decades of the twentieth century, focusing on the challenges Yue opera actresses faced and their efforts to overcome them, female patrons and patronage, and the re-making of lowly female entertainers into art workers and public icons in the city's mass media. Chapter 5 traces the vicissitudes of the opera and actresses into the PRC period, analyzing their complex relationship with the communist revolution and the PRC state. Chapter 6, the final, thematic chapter, explores the distinctly feminine aesthetics and narrative schemes embedded in Yue opera masterpieces, which influenced popular senses of and sensibilities toward love and gender relations in modern China.

女班

Chapter 1

The Origins of Yue Opera

Yue opera originated with a peasant form of story-singing in the Zhejiang countryside in the mid-nineteenth century. In the late nineteenth and early twentieth centuries, this form underwent great transformations and was a popular urban spectacle in Shanghai by the end of the 1930s. Significantly, the latter phase of the opera's early development overlapped with the rise of women's Yue opera, as "all-female troupes" (*nü ban*) gradually replaced traditional "all-male troupes" (*nan ban*). While all-male troupes largely disappeared by the end of the 1930s, a gender-straight troupe (in which men play men's roles and women play women's roles) appeared in the Communist guerrilla area of Siming Mountain (Siming Shan) in eastern Zhejiang during the War of Resistance against Japan (1937–45), representing an insignificant variation of Yue opera. Women's Yue opera has since become the mainstay and the most distinctive feature of the genre.

The double transformation in the early development of Yue opera—from rural to urban and from all male to all female—took place amid dynamic tensions between Zhejiang's countryside and the emerging treaty-port city of Shanghai. These changes also occurred in the context of social, political, and economic upheavals brought about by the 1911 Republican Revolution, which terminated China's long imperial history, and the May Fourth New Culture Movement, which advocated adoption of a wide range of Western ideas, such as science, democracy, and women's liberation. These economic, political, social, and cultural upheavals generated a popular-culture phenomenon—the rise of folk operas throughout the country in the early twentieth century and the consequent feminization of opera culture, of which Yue opera is only one, but distinct, example.

Beijing Opera and the Male-Centered Opera Culture of the Qing Dynasty

In order to understand the historical significance of the rise of this modern feminine opera, it is necessary first to historicize its predecessor, Beijing opera, and the male-centered opera culture it represented. Beijing opera has been commonly understood as the standard Chinese opera, and its all-male cast is considered typical of this peculiarly traditional cultural form. Studies of Chinese opera in general and Beijing opera in particular have often overlooked the fact that Beijing opera developed into an all-male theater in order to serve a predominantly male audience only during the second half of the Qing dynasty, and that its homo-social character represented a rupture from the hetero-social opera culture of the seventeenth century.

The most popular opera form during the late Ming (1368–1644) and early Qing (1644–1911) dynasties was a genre known as *chuanqi*, which literally means "romance," "legend," or "bizarre story." Like some other literary forms of the time, *chuanqi* celebrated the cult of *qing*, meaning "feelings" or "passion," and featured romantic stories about talented scholars and faithful beauties.[1] The conquering Qing state, however, deemed the late Ming indulgence in sentimental love stories decadent and a cause of the fall of the Ming house; it therefore imposed strict moral codes on public culture by cracking down on what it considered "obscene theater" (*yinxi*).[2] The Qing state's effort to purge the public morality of sexually provocative elements won the support of the scholar-official elite and local Confucian gentry, who shared the Manchu criticism of the late Ming cult of *qing*. Emerging amid these circumstances, Qing opera culture assumed distinctive masculine characteristics that set it apart from the heterosexual Ming theaters that preceded it and the more feminized Republican opera culture that followed it.

The Qing state adopted a strict Confucian ideology that defined women's proper place as within the home, while social customs discouraged women from entering public arenas.[3] Women were, by law and custom, largely excluded from public entertainment venues, such as theaters, teahouses, and gambling halls, where opera was staged. Upper-class women could view performances only inside their homes or in the homes of relatives and friends, while lower-class women had access to shows only during local festivals, lineage or religious ceremonies, and community celebrations, when operas were performed in public, free of charge. Even during these public events, women's attendance was minimal. While household responsibilities and custom required wealthier women to stay at home (especially after dark), poorer women had to work long hours to earn a living and hardly had time to remain for long at the few shows they could attend; additionally, they were also bound by the social customs that discouraged all women from appearing in public.[4] Women in general, therefore, rich and poor alike, had limited access to public opera shows and were entirely excluded from performances in commercial venues.[5] Since they were not significant patrons or paying customers, they had little influence in shaping this major form of entertainment.

Moreover, as the Qing state considered women performers to be a kind of prostitute and the source of sexually provocative performances, its suppression of so-called obscene theaters went hand in hand with repeated prohibition of women performers. The earliest such prohibition was issued in 1671, the tenth year of the reign of the Kangxi emperor. Similar bans appeared many more times during the Kangxi reign, as well as during the Yongzheng and Qianlong reigns, and the last ban was issued in 1774, the thirty-ninth year of the Qianlong reign.[6] In the countryside, female performers were prohibited from participating in religious and lineage ceremonies, the most popular occasions for staging opera. Owing to relentless central and local government crackdowns, women performers generally disappeared from public view after 1774, except for a small number who appeared in the foreign settlements in Shanghai and Tianjin in the late nineteenth century.[7]

In the absence of female performers, boy actors and female impersonators came to occupy prominent roles in popular theater. The most famous female impersonator was Wei Changsheng, a Sichuan native who played young female roles in "Shaanxi clapper opera" (*Shaanxi bangzi*). Wei made his first appearance in Beijing in 1779, and his beauty, skill, and unrestrained eroticism immediately created a sensation. Wei and his cohorts made Shaanxi clapper opera the most popular theater in the capital, until the court expelled him from Beijing and disbanded his troupe in 1785.[8] Wei then joined a Kun opera troupe and soon left Beijing for Yangzhou and the Jiangnan area (the Yangzi River delta surrounding Suzhou, Hangzhou, and Shanghai), while Shaanxi clapper opera eventually retreated to its home in the northwest. In the 1790s, four *pihuang* opera troupes from Anhui,[9] who had entered the capital for the celebration of the Qianlong emperor's eightieth birthday, created a similar sensation with their leading female impersonators, resulting in another crackdown on "obscene" opera in the capital by the new Jiaqing emperor in 1798.[10] The opera troupes from Anhui eventually won official approval by shifting the focus of their performances from women's to men's roles and thereby managed to take root in Beijing. Over the ensuing decades, as the Anhui troupes absorbed the influence of official ideology and catered to the tastes of a capital-based political and intellectual elite, they developed a new opera form known as Jingju, or opera of the capital city of Beijing.

Thus, by the nineteenth century, through state and elite intervention, a new opera culture took shape. Not only did operatic representations of women become the exclusive purview of men, as female roles were performed by and for men, but female roles were further reduced to supporting positions, as love stories gave way to plays that accorded with Qing ideology. In contrast to the Ming *chuanqi* genre, Qing opera typically told grand narratives about the empire and the dynasty and featured emperors, ministers, and generals as protagonists. The form of the performance grew rigid and formulaic, as a strict system of role designs and highly formalized postures developed for portraying stereotypical characters. In general, male roles included *laosheng* (bearded males), for moralistic civil officials; *wusheng* (military males), for spirited generals; *jing* (known as *hualian* [lit., "painted faces"]), for simple-minded or mean officials; and *chou* (clowns). Typical female characters were serious young women known as *qingyi* (lit., "blue-clothed ladies"); outgoing young women, or *huadan* (lit., "colorful women"), who were in most cases servants of the main female characters; and old women, or *laodan*.

The artistic transformation of Anhui opera into a capital-city form was complete when it made imperial narratives the main theme of its performances while establishing male roles as the leading roles. Soon thereafter, a cluster of leading actors rose from the status of lowly entertainers to cultural celebrities who enjoyed imperial patronage and the support of a sophisticated male audience composed of officials, generals, imperial students, courtiers, clerks, government runners, examination candidates, and Manchu aristocrats.[11] A dozen or so famous actors—the most famous of whom were Cheng Changgeng, Tan Xinpei, Yang Yuelou, Yang Xiaolou, and Li Chunlai—personified ministers and generals and played out stories drawn from official as well as popular histories. Even a cursory examination of the plays developed during this period leaves no doubt that they dealt mostly with historical battles and major events, as the following titles indicate: *The Battle of Chengdu* (Zhan Chengdu), *Borrowing Arrows from the Enemy* (Caochuan jie jian), *Dingjun Mountain* (Dingjun shan), and *Capturing and Releasing Cao Cao* (Zhuofang Cao).[12] One of the most frequently performed plays, *Generals of the Yang Family* (Yangjia jiang), tells the story of a family that sacrificed almost all its men to the Song dynasty's war against invading barbarians. In the latter half of the nineteenth century, Beijing opera spread throughout the country with the support of a national political and intellectual elite, from provincial capitals to local market towns and villages, setting new standards of content and style for local operas to follow.

Major regional opera genres of the time, including clapper operas in the north and *luantan* (southern variations of clapper operas) and *pihuang* operas in the southern and central provinces, underwent similar transitions during the nineteenth century. Although regional major operas maintained their local color by singing tunes in local dialects, they shared a repertoire of plays and acting styles with Beijing opera. Together, these major operas and their patrons fashioned the male-dominant opera culture of the Qing dynasty.

Parallel to these major operas were folk operas active at the lower level of society.[13] The term "minor operas" (*xiaoxi*) has been used loosely in opera circles in China in order to distinguish the numerous folk operas from "major operas" (*daxi*), which encompassed more sophisticated and influential national and regional genres such as Beijing opera and various clapper operas.[14] Minor operas emerged in rural areas throughout China during the nineteenth century; they were part of the local peasant economy and offshoots of local peasant culture. The best-known genres include *yangge* in Shaanxi and other parts in the north, "flower-drum" (*huagu*) in Hunan, "flower-lantern" (*huadeng*) in Yunnan, various "storytelling" (*tanhuang*) genres in Zhejiang and Jiangsu, and "tea-picking" (*caicha*) among the Hakkas, as well as boy-singers' opera in Fujian, "lotus tone" (*lianhua luozi*) in Hebei (predecessor of *ping* opera), and "little opera" (*xiaogeban*) in Shengxian, Zhejiang (a forerunner of Yue opera).[15] Often started by poor peasants trying to scrape together extra income during the agricultural off-season, minor operas held low social status and were usually not allowed to be performed at religious ceremonies or in ancestral halls. The peasant artists staged their performances mainly in local gambling houses, low-end teahouses, and sometimes in the homes of rich local families on celebratory occasions, charging low fees so that they could stay in business in the poorer rural areas. Indeed, many minor operas were known locally as "the beggar's opera" (*taofan xi*), as the peasant performers sang while begging for food and money in the streets and in front of wealthy households. The performances were rough around the edges: costumes, if they were worn at all, were shabby;

lyrics were composed in local colloquial dialects; melodies were simple and repetitive; acting was unpolished and bawdy.[16]

Minor operas also differed from major operas with respect to their repertoires, narrative focus, and style. The repertoires of minor operas were drawn from a variety of sources, including popular religious scripts, folk songs and tales, popular ballads and storytelling traditions, and accounts of the daily lives of the peasantry. The main roles in minor operas were a young man and a young woman who played out scholar-beauty love stories such as *Pearl Pagoda* (Zhenzhu ta), or moments of local, real-life drama, as suggested by such titles as *Selling Charcoal* (Mai qingtan) and *Child Bride Returns Home* (Yangxifu hui niangjia).[17] Minor-opera plays were concerned with individual fortunes, not the fate or vicissitudes of the empire, and told stories about love and desire, loyalty and betrayal, and fortune and misery. Drawing on folk religious motifs and local superstitions, such as retribution and ghost stories, as well as such officially endorsed moral themes as filial piety, these stories delivered mixed messages and ambiguous moral lessons. Good performances were both entertaining and full of folk wisdom. Although not always clear-cut in practice, a general difference between minor and major operas existed beyond doubt.

Minor operas were part of the male-dominant opera culture of the time, with all the ambiguities and contradictions that attended the local practice of gender. In minor operas, as in major operas, all the performers were men. Even within all-male companies, gender hierarchies were prevalent, as male roles were higher in status than female roles. The bias against female roles was closely related to local superstitions but had little to do with actual professional ranks. A popular actor specializing in female roles, for example, was often the leading actor in the company and earned the highest salary, but he was still not allowed to sit on the dressing boxes backstage or walk in front of actors playing male roles when the troupe hiked to the next site.[18]

On the whole, the gender hierarchy was less rigid in minor-opera culture, which absorbed less official ideology and existed more as part of the daily life of the countryside. As seen in Shengxian little opera, the content of minor opera, which focused on everyday peasant life and scholar-beauty love stories, was more appealing to rural women, while the performances were more accessible. Because of their small size and light instruments, minor-opera troupes could perform inside homes or in the open space in front of a sponsor's house, and neighbors and villagers could attend performances for a token contribution. Such performances, unlike the much more elaborate events of "major-opera performance" (*chang daxi*), were informal and required much less consideration of the status and propriety of village women than did elaborate public performance of major operas.

Both historical records and oral histories point to periodic official prohibitions of minor operas for their heterodox content and vulgar style, while local elites vilified them either out of ideological conviction or for personal gain.[19] Authorities failed to eliminate minor opera, however, for it was part of the social and economic structure of late Qing rural life. The performers often desperately needed whatever income they could scratch together from their seasonal performances, and the local population needed entertainment at the lowest possible cost. For the same reasons, however, minor operas remained minor and relatively undeveloped during the nineteenth century. Their audiences had little purchasing power, their performances drew the wrath of officials, and their styles were too local to attract an audience beyond regional colloquial boundaries.

The Feminine Transformation of Opera Culture during the Republican Era

Opera culture underwent a major transformation during the twentieth century, as industrialization, urbanization, and revolution changed Chinese society. The decline of major operas, the rise of minor operas, and a general trend of feminization marked the century's new opera culture. This new opera culture came about first and foremost by feminizing the operatic body, which occurred when a critical mass of actresses and female audience members entered the opera world. When the 1911 Republican Revolution overthrew the imperial system and opened up Chinese society to wide-ranging social and political changes, women's liberation became one of the most championed issues within a broader national discourse about making China a strong and wealthy nation. The May Fourth New Culture Movement that followed made women's liberation a benchmark of China's social reform and cultural modernity and sought to popularize its rhetoric among a nationwide reading population. Related issues, such as free love and marriage, women's education, women's work and economic independence, and women's position in the family and society all became heated topics in popular and intellectual publications. Women were eager to take advantage of the opportunities these changing circumstances offered them. Upper-class women began assuming new roles and responsibilities outside the home. Some joined revolutionary organizations, others devoted themselves to education, and young women from wealthy families enrolled in new schools. Still others enjoyed newfound freedoms by going to theaters. At the same time, working-class women found in acting a means of earning a living. Gradually, a great number of women became participants in the entertainment industry, as audience members and performers. The presence of women eventually made operatic explorations of women and women's issues no longer the exclusive purview of men.

The increasing numbers of women operagoers brought about a shift in emphasis from male to female roles in Beijing opera in the early Republican period, as is evident in the emergence of the "four great female impersonators" (*sida mingdan*): Mei Lanfang, Shang Xiaoyun, Cheng Yanqiu, and Xun Huisheng. Qi Rushan, an intellectual and expert in European and Chinese operas who was much involved in Mei Lanfang's Beijing opera reforms, reasoned that the success of any actor depended on his ability to attract women spectators. Qi considered that an actor could become popular and successful only if he appealed to women, and that his success would be compromised if he appealed only to male patrons. Qi paraphrased popular sayings of the time to explain:

> Take a couple: if the husband wants to see a show but his wife is not interested, the wife will prevent the husband from going. If, however, the wife wants to go but her husband does not, the wife will make her husband go with her. In a family situation, a husband could go to the theater by himself without bringing the children along. But if the wife wants to go, then she would most likely bring her children with her. Among circles of friends, men often go to the theater by themselves or with one other friend, but they rarely treat their friends to opera shows. Women, on the other hand, like to gather in groups and go together. Thus, if an actor can make one woman come, she will bring many more with her to the theater. If an actor can make one man interested, the man may not come at all if his wife is not interested. As the saying goes: "A popular, good actor is one who can appeal to women."[20]

Lending support to Qi's views, Mei Lanfang attributed his own popularity to the growth of female audiences and testified to the profound impact of female operagoers on Beijing opera:

> In the past, neither night opera performances nor female audience members were allowed in Beijing's theaters. Social custom deemed the mixing of men

> and women in public injurious to public morality, as if opera were specifically sung for men, and women did not have the right to enjoy this kind of legitimate entertainment. This was indeed a stubbornness of the feudal age. Since the Republican era, great numbers of female patrons have poured into theaters and thus brought about sudden changes to the performing arts as a whole. In the past, bearded characters [*laosheng*] and male military characters [*wusheng*] reigned in Beijing opera, because members of a generally male audience had become connoisseurs of the art of performers of bearded men and military figures, due to their long-standing patronage of Beijing opera. Female audience members were new to the theater and thus naturally lacked expertise. Since they came only to view the lively atmosphere [*kan re'nao*], they would certainly pick out the pretty ones first. Therefore, female characters [*dan*] became their favorites. In a few years, *qingyi* [or serious young female characters] were attracting large crowds and in one jump became the leading roles in theatrical art.[21]

Aside from their lack of expertise, which prevented them from appreciating male roles, as Mei explained, women's interests in female roles may also have had to do with their greater facility in relating to female characters than to emperors, generals, and court officials. In any case, the correlation between the rise of women audiences and the new emphasis on female roles is unmistakable.

The rise of the four great female impersonators was accompanied by new plays centered on female protagonists, which created a twentieth-century dimension in Beijing opera and changed both its repertoire and its acting style. During the first two decades of the Republican period, Mei Lanfang, a pioneer of Beijing opera's modern reforms, created a dozen or so new works in an effort to explore various historical and literary female figures, including the mythological figure Chang'e, the Tang dynasty beauty Yang Guifei, the legendary female soldier Hua Mulan, and Lin Daiyu, the sickly beauty in the Qing dynasty novel *Dream of the Red Chamber*. In an attempt to present his characters as real and complex human beings, rather than as stereotypes, Mei was forced to break the strict codes of stylized performances pertaining to *qingyi*, or serious young women, and *huadan*, or lively young women, characters. Mei's reforms made his characters capable of expressing both sorrow and happiness and being both reserved and outgoing; the personalities of his characters thus blurred the traditional line between *qingyi* and *huadan*.[22]

When the female impersonator Shang Xiaoyun staged the new plays *A*

Modern Nun (Modeng jia'nü) and *Zhuo Wenjun* (Zhuo Wenjun), he was hailed by a commentator, in typical May Fourth hyperbole, as follows: "I think that Zhuo Wenjun was the first woman in several thousand years of Chinese history who believed in free love. The fact that she worked as a cook in her own restaurant proves that she was the first woman who embraced the idea of [economic] independence. Now Shang Xiaoyun has put this history onstage, in an effort very much in accordance with the trend toward women's liberation."[23] Cheng Yanqiu was known for his impersonation of unfortunate but virtuous women in traditional society, such as Su San in *Spring of the Jade Hall* (Yutang Chun). One commentator wrote about the significance of Cheng's characters by combining May Fourth rhetoric with an old ethic, as if no effort were required to reconcile the May Fourth condemnation of the old society that had made women suffer and the traditional female virtue of self-denial: "Chinese women have been suppressed by men for the past several thousand years under the feudal system. All of the commemorative arches erected in the past in honor of chaste women actually represent countless sorrowful life histories. Cheng Yanqiu's characters indeed represent the most precious female role models in Chinese history."[24]

As female audiences grew in size and female roles and protagonists became increasingly popular, female performers also began to prosper in Beijing opera circles. The first generation of female performers was born around the time of the 1911 Republican Revolution and began to study the art during the May Fourth period. Meng Xiaodong was perhaps the first accomplished female Beijing opera performer who specialized in *laosheng*, the leading male role. Other well-known women performers of the period—Xue Yanqin, Xin Yanqiu, and Wang Yurong—specialized in leading female roles and began to make a name for themselves around the mid-1920s. The next generation, including some of the best Beijing opera performers, such as Yan Huizhu, Tong Zhiling, and Li Yuru, studied with the four great female impersonators and became established in the 1940s.[25] From that time onward, female performers generally replaced the much celebrated male masters in the performance of female roles.[26]

Other major local operas from the Qing period also opened up to accommodate female performers and women's taste. These pro-women reforms, however, could not reverse a general decline of major operas in the early Republican period.[27] The dilemma for major operas was as follows: on the one hand, with the dismantling of the emperor system and the replacement of ministers and generals with new kinds of political representatives, imperial narratives became increasingly irrelevant and unappealing to the new Republican audience, half of which now consisted of women; on the other hand, however, the masculine style of major operas, which developed with their male-centered content, was too integral a part of these operas' artistic identity to be cast away or sufficiently reformed to accommodate more feminine narratives. In short, the male-centered Qing major operas could not adapt to the new era without losing their identity, and thus their decline was inevitable. By 1949, at the founding of the People's Republic of China, many major operas were on the verge of extinction and were rescued only because of the new government's efforts to preserve the national cultural heritage.[28]

Beijing opera retained its popularity a little longer owing to its high political and social status, its historical and ongoing association with officials, military figures, and men of letters, and its evolving artistic sophistication as perhaps best exemplified by the modern reforms of the four great female impersonators. During the Republican period, patronage of Beijing opera became a marker of taste and status for rich and powerful men, and male elites in political, intellectual, and business circles supported Beijing opera for various reasons. While old-fashioned wealthy men found nostalgic pleasure in the opera, reform-minded intellectuals and Nationalist government officials found in it authentic Chinese aesthetics useful for the construction of a national identity that could balance the rapid trend toward Western-style modernization. Yet, despite such political and intellectual support, Beijing opera's popularity was ultimately challenged and surpassed by emerging folk forms of minor operas, most dramatically by *ping* opera in the Tianjin-Beijing area and Yue opera in Shanghai and the Jiangnan region, but also by numerous other local minor operas, such as Lü opera in Shandong, Yu opera in Henan, and Chu opera in Hubei.[29]

With the decline of masculine major operas, minor operas rose to answer the call of the new era. Although minor operas shared the male-centered characteristics of Qing opera, they proved capable of accommodating the trend of feminization, as their content was more "feminine" to begin with and their styles less formulaic. Given the importance of Western influences on China's modern changes, much early modernization was concentrated in treaty-port cities where new ideas and cultural forms were first tried out. Shanghai, Tianjin, and Xiamen, therefore, became exciting places for minor operas where a rising urban mass audience, of which women made up a large part, helped shape their transformation into popular urban forms.

Broadly viewed, the rise of minor operas in urban centers was a direct response to mass urban migrations, the rhetoric of women's liberation, and women's entrance into the popular-culture market. The early twentieth century witnessed the growth of lower-income urban populations, owing to large-scale migration to, and industrialization in, coastal cities. Peasants moved to cities to become factory workers, clerks, barbers, and laborers such as rickshaw pullers and porters. There were also large numbers of female migrants, whose occupations ranged from housewives, to domestic helpers, to factory workers. Minor operas moved into the city along with their native-place and lower-class constituencies and developed rapidly in urban centers. The connection between minor operas and their constituencies within this modern urban transition was partially captured in a contemporaneous commentary on the "*didu* opera" (*diduban* or *diduxi*, nicknames for Shengxian little opera among Shanghai residents of the time) troupe.[30] The author, Xiao Wo, proposed taking a modern view:

> The twentieth century is an age of the people. For this reason, everything reflected in the arts is simple, easy to understand, and hence of the people. One example in our country is that our written language has changed from classic to vernacular, and then to the language of commoners. In painting, the popular cartoon has appeared, while in theater, there is a call for popular drama. In short, all these changes represent the spirit of the age, which is to make the masses understand the arts. Then, how can you say *diduxi* [*didu* opera] is not a product of the age? If someone thinks this statement is a slight exaggeration, then let's ask why *didu* opera is so popular with the masses nowadays. Why do we see the growing number of troupes and audiences only of *didu* opera and not of any other opera? The fact is undeniable. *Didu* opera's singing is simple, easygoing, and straightforward, which is not only in accordance with the spirit of the age but moreover fits the taste of the masses, as it is easy to follow.[31]

Presenting *didu* opera as in tune with the Republican ideology of popular rights, Xiao defended and promoted the opera of his native place in the face of the traditional class bias against minor operas. Moreover, he sought further to enhance minor operas' political legitimacy by arguing, in the new rhetoric of theatrical reform, that they were valuable tools for mass education. Xiao continued by comparing Shengxian opera and Beijing opera, pointing out that the long, complicated tunes of Beijing opera made it difficult for the audience to understand the lyrics and follow the plots. As a tabloid author, who hailed Shengxian little opera as a purveyor of mass education for poorer urban constituencies, put it:

> *Didu* opera is the most valuable and most educational drama. *Didu* opera's simple lyrics are like words as elementary as "people, hand, foot, knife, ruler" in the first lesson of a textbook, enlightening young students and educating the masses. *Didu* opera is particularly useful in our country where education has not yet become popularized. Kun opera, in contrast, declines rapidly because it is too abstruse [for the populace] to understand.[32]

At the same time, the new Republican ideology of women's liberation lifted traditional imperial sanctions against minor opera and its love stories. Supported by the May Fourth New Culture idea of free love and marriage, as opposed to Confucian puritanism and the traditional institution of arranged marriage, the love theme became prominent in theatrical representations. Minor-opera artists needed only to recast traditional scholar-beauty stories in the new rhetoric of free love and marriage and women's rights to adapt to the new fashion.

The entrance of women into the entertainment market as both performers and paying consumers greatly affected the modern transformation of minor operas. Women's impact is clearest in the cases of women's Yue opera in Shanghai and *ping* opera in Tianjin. More than other minor operas, Yue opera and *ping* opera were centered on love stories, women performers, and female or feminized male roles and were aimed at women audiences. *Ping* opera was originally an all-male theater, and women appeared on its stages only in the foreign settlement of Tianjin around the turn of the twentieth century. However, women performers and female characters soon thereafter took center stage, with the opera becoming increasingly popular in the Beijing-Tianjin area and spreading to the northeastern provinces and Shanghai in the 1930s and 1940s. During roughly the same period, all-female Shengxian opera troupes created a sensation in Shanghai, quickly displacing the all-male Shengxian troupes and making Yue opera exclusively an actresses' domain. In the process, *ping* opera overtook both Beijing opera and Hebei clapper opera in popularity in the north, and women's Yue opera overtook Beijing opera and the local Shanghai opera to become the most popular genre in Shanghai and Zhejiang.[33] That these two forms of theater should have become the most popular operas in their respective areas strongly suggests a close connection between women's entrance into the cultural market as consumers and the rise of minor operas.

The Story of Shengxian Little Opera

It was within this context that the early history of Yue opera unfolded.

"In the thirty-second year of the reign of the Guangxu emperor, 1906, Yue opera was born," or so Ma Chaoshui (1895–1975) declared in his *On the Early Development of Yue Opera* (Yueju fazhan shu).[34] This proclamation is part of an oral history transmitted through three generations of story-singers and performers and collected in the late 1950s, when a group of twenty-five retired Yue opera actors gathered together for a government-sponsored oral-history workshop in Shengxian. Ma Chaoshui, one of the twenty-five retirees, put this oral history on paper in 1960. This and a cluster of individual oral histories, studies of family and lineage books published in *Tracing the Origins of Yue Opera* (Yueju suyuan), a collection of original lyrics from the story-singing tradition,[35] and supplementary historical documents provide a glimpse of the opera's origins and early development.

Yue opera went through several stages in its early development. Not unlike the hip-hop originating among entertainment-hungry black youth in the inner city ghettos of the late twentieth-century United States, Yue opera began as a local tune of peasant self-entertainment in the countryside of Shengxian, Shaoxing prefecture, Zhejiang. Talented young peasants would sing about everything in a simple tune based on the *sigong* scale system, or *sigong diao*.[36] Jin Qibing, an admirable talent from a certain Horse Pond Village (Matang Cun) who was later remembered as the founding father of Yue opera, was said to be skilled at not only filling in original lyrics but also telling stories drawn from historical novels and Buddhist literature that he heard from storytellers. Jin apparently inspired and taught many young peasants, and when harvests were poor, he and his disciples made some extra income with their singing. At first, Jin and his followers sang at the doors of better-off households in villages and towns not too far from home during the lunar New Year. In return for the auspicious words they sang, they hoped to be rewarded with a couple of New Year cakes or dumplings. If all went well, they would return home with enough food to sustain their families over the holiday season. The singers thus earned the nickname "beggar's stories" (*taofan shu*). Before long, story-singers started to take advantage of the agricultural off-seasons and went out regularly on singing tours; it is said that some masters of the younger generation spent more time singing than plowing and became semiprofessional singers.[37]

The younger generation, according to oral histories, managed to increase the professional level of their art significantly, with singers from artisan backgrounds, such as Jin Zhitang and Xiang Jintang, playing important roles in this process. Jin Zhitang, it is said, used to station his shoe-repair stand outside major teahouses so that he could listen to the master singers inside. Apparently, Jin learned a great number of long stories and became familiar with storytelling skills while repairing shoes for his customers. Meanwhile, increasing numbers of Shengxian natives were turning to story-singing as a form of livelihood, making it into a countywide industry in the late nineteenth century when the rural economy deteriorated.

As their numbers increased, Shengxian story-singers began to expand into market towns in the rich area centered on Hangzhou, Jiaxing, and Huzhou in the Yangzi River delta, the Hang-Jia-Hu area. Shengxian masters competed with storytellers of the Hangzhou and Suzhou styles, two major storytelling genres long established in this area, and, when necessary, used their fists to fight for their share of the market.[38] A serious altercation apparently broke out in 1869 between Hangzhou-style masters and newly arrived Shengxian masters over the right to perform in a major teahouse in Yuhang, a market town near Hangzhou. Local officials, interestingly, ruled that both parties had the right to perform under the condition that they pay a tax to local government. An official stone tablet was thereupon erected and inscribed with four large characters that read "Sing stories and pay taxes" (Chang shu wan liang).[39] The Shengxian story-singers, as oral histories have it, then started a golden age of performing at market towns in the Hang-Jia-Hu area.[40]

By the early years of the 1900s, however, Shengxian story-singing was losing ground in market towns, and Ma Chaoshui and his colleagues had to move back to the countryside. While oral histories do not provide any specific reason for this development, it is likely that the illiterate story-singers from Shengxian were at the end of their wits in attempting to compete with the more learned and sophisticated Suzhou and Hangzhou masters. It was at this moment, however, that Shengxian story-singing masters began to turn to operatic performance.

Shengxian storytelling had its own style, and performers were aware of the difference between their style and that of major forms such as Suzhou and Hangzhou storytelling. As Ma Chaoshui noted:

> In major storytelling, one master told the whole story by himself, while in our minor storytelling, there was the master and one or two companions who sang fixed repetitive melodies on the side. Major-storytelling forms featured tales like *Romance of Yue Fei* [Shuo Yue quanzhuan] and *Romance of the Three Kingdoms* [Sanguo yanyi]. Minor storytelling told mostly tales like *Story of the White Snake* [Baishe zhuan], *The Golden Dragon Whip* (Jinlong bian), *Seven Beauties* (Qimei tu), and *Pearl Pagoda*.[41]

The division between major- and minor-storytelling traditions was as clear as the division in opera traditions. While major-storytelling forms focused on historical, military, and political narratives, minor-storytelling forms elaborated on love, betrayal, and personal fortunes. Other differences were that the Shengxian style combined speaking with singing and chanting on the side and required two or three performers who had to remain standing onstage to carry out the story. Compared with the conventional storytelling method featuring one master who relied primarily on his oral skills to tell the story, the Shengxian style involved more physical movements, which made its transition to opera quite easy.

Early in 1906, two or three groups of Shengxian story-singers began, separately but simultaneously, to perform the stories they had thus far only been narrating and thus gave birth to Shengxian little opera. Ma Chaoshui recounted how this occurred on a cold winter night in the countryside of Yuhang, when Ma and his master ran into two pairs of touring singers. They all stayed at the patron Chen Wanyuan's home, which was, as they knew, always open to singers. Excited by the presence of three pairs of singers, villagers gathered at Chen's home and asked to be entertained. In order to include all the singers in the performance, Chen suggested they act out a story together, instead of each pair singing its own story. Apparently, the suggestion was well taken. Using Mr. and Mrs. Chen's clothes as costumes, the singers staged a four-hour performance of *Pearl Pagoda*, punctuated by occasional outbursts of friendly laughter from the audience, in Chen's living room.

News of the innovation spread fast, and other story-singers also turned to acting. Some singers, upon returning home in the spring to work in the fields, met with requests from fellow villagers that they put on plays, and the villagers promised to take care of the singers' lands in exchange. Quickly, all storytellers turned to acting, and a new minor opera began to take shape. Because of its unpretentious style and small scale, the villagers gave it the endearing nickname "little opera," in contrast to "Shaoxing major opera" (*Shaoxing daban*).

Over the next few years, little-opera troupes multiplied in Shengxian, but the opera remained part of the local peasant culture. Actors were mostly peasants who worked in the fields during busy agricultural seasons and performed only during off-seasons or on special occasions. Troupes usually had seven or eight members; troupe formation and performances were rather casual. An actor might join an ongoing performance, and another actor might leave one performance to join another. The only musical instruments used in these days were a pair of small drums and a wooden clapper, played by any performer who was not onstage, to keep the rhythm. Costumes were mostly everyday clothing, and audiences did not mind when the plaster casts that some performers used to heal muscle and tendon injuries were exposed. There were few props to speak of, and troupe members carried the few they owned from village to village on their shoulders. Later, some troupes accumulated small funds and rented costumes and instruments from Shaoxing major-opera troupes, but there was never anything elaborate about little-opera performances. The troupes also charged very low fees for a full program, which lasted from afternoon to dawn. Their fees were so low that even small villages could afford them. Performances at gambling gatherings, commonly known as *xing pengzi* (lit., "to raise an awning [for a gambling gathering]"), were another source of income for little-opera troupes.[42]

Because of its high mobility and low overhead, little opera flourished at the lowest level of rural society, and the nature of the rural market in turn informed the opera's style. Villagers appreciated major-opera performances for their bustling atmosphere and the variety of snacks sold by food peddlers; they did not mind if they could not actually hear the lyrics, because everyone was already familiar with the stories. Their reasons for appreciating little opera were very different. Little-opera performances created a much more intimate relationship with audiences, as performances were casual and small in scale. Moreover, little opera used plain vernacular language, simple local tones for speech and singing, and hardly any musical instruments. All these features made it easy for local audiences to hear the lyrics and speeches clearly and to follow the plot more closely.

The content of little opera, which inherited a generous repertoire of established stories from its story-singing predecessor as well as drew on local peasant culture and Buddhist texts, was also of great interest to rural residents. From story-singing, little opera inherited a set of stories known as "news" stories, which vividly described local peasant life, as seen in such titles as *Ten Rare Things* (Shi xiqi) and *Ten Weird Things* (Shi guguai).[43] "Sing the news" (*chang xinwen*) segments often served as a popular prelude to a program. In a well-known piece, *Selling the Mother-in-Law* (Mai po ji), a wicked daughter-in-law plots to get rid of her aged mother-in-law. She bribes a matchmaker to marry off the old lady, and the greedy matchmaker cheats a poor young peasant by making him spend his life savings for the bride. The young man happily takes the bride home, only to discover that she is a teary-eyed old woman. After hearing the woman's sad story, the young man's anger turns to sympathy, and he decides to adopt her as his mother. Deeply moved, the old woman tells him about a fortune her late husband secretly handed to her just before his death, and she advises the young man to find a nice wife and start a small business with the money. The bad daughter-in-law regrets that she has thrown away her good fortune, the matchmaker repents and finds the young peasant a nice bride, and the old woman and young couple live a happy life thereafter.[44]

Little opera also inherited the romance from its story-singing predecessor. When Shengxian story-singers entered market towns, they learned longer pieces from the rich repertoires of storytelling traditions, and one of these, among the most performed tales in both Shengxian story-singing and little opera, is *Pearl Pagoda*. It tells a long, complex story about a young scholar named Fang Qing. Fang hails from a scholar-official family in Henan. The family becomes impoverished after Fang's father dies, and Fang visits his aunt to ask for a loan so that he can go to the capital and take the civil-service examination. His snobbish aunt humiliates him and gives him nothing. The aunt's daughter overhears their conversation and, sympathetic to her cousin, secretly gives the young scholar her pearl pagoda to pawn for the money he needs. His uncle also sees a promising scholar in Fang and grants the young man his daughter's hand in marriage. On his way home, Fang is robbed and almost freezes to death in the snow. The person who stole from Fang is exposed when he takes the pearl pagoda to the local pawnshop, and Fang is presumed dead. But Fang had in fact been rescued, passes the exam, taking first place, and is appointed to an official position. One day, Fang disguises himself as a Daoist priest and is invited into his aunt's house. In the process of telling her fortune, he purposefully criticizes his aunt while hinting at his true identity. In the end, Fang's identity is revealed, the aunt repents, and Fang happily marries his loving cousin.[45]

Little opera also drew on Buddhist traditions for its materials. *Buddhist Daughter of the Liu Family* (Liu Xiangnü), a story adopted from the popular Buddhist text *Precious Volume about Liu Xiangnü* (Liu Xiangnü baojuan), tells the story of the enlightened daughter of the Liu family, who practices filial piety, saves her parents from misfortune, and, at long last, enlightens them. Historians of popular religion in late imperial China have shown that Buddhism had considerable influence on the lives of rural women, and the Liu Xiangnü story is but one example of the spread of Buddhist messages through forms of peasant entertainment.[46]

Oral accounts of the early history of little opera describe the opera's difficult relationship with authorities and some members of the local elite. While local moralists may have disapproved of the opera's heterodox message and bawdy style, local bullies considered the actors easy prey in their power games, and government agencies flexed their muscles by going after the actors. According to Ding Yi, a local Yue opera researcher in Shengxian, a little opera show at its home village in the summer of 1906 was almost ruined by a bully, Fan Jinhuan, who controlled an eighteen-man militia. It was an unspoken rule that anyone planning a show in this area had to send gifts to Fan in advance. The show, Ding Yi said, was put together at the last minute by local actors, who had just returned from a performance tour, to entertain their fellow villagers. No gift was sent to Fan, and Fan dispatched his men to arrest the singers. Outraged, the villagers selected eighteen young men from the peasant association to protect the singers and also plead their case with a member of the local gentry, Li Haifa, who was well connected to officials in both Shengxian and Dongyang Counties. Li, who had been disgusted by Fan's behavior for some time, took the opportunity to lead a rebellion against Fan. On the day of the show, a big audience, including many supporters from nearby villages, gathered around the stage. Li sat right in the front row, and the eighteen young men were positioned on both sides of the stage. When Fan's men heard about this, they fled before they reached the spot.[47]

In 1908, *Regulations of Self-Government of Shengxian* (Shengxian zizhi zhangcheng), an official edict issued by the local government as part of the national Constitutional Reform Movement, prohibited minor-opera performances of any kind, and the newly formed police force welcomed this opportunity to show its power.[48] Ma Chaoshui recounted another dramatic incident in which he and his troupe were arrested in a small village and taken to the police station in Sanjie. An elderly gentry man bailed them out, and then the man's wife wanted to see them perform. A simple stage of planks placed on top of haystacks was erected outside the man's yard, facing the police station, and the actors performed two plays for the villagers, *Double Golden Flowers* (Shuang jin hua) and *Pearl Pagoda*. The show was well received, and the audience was moved to tears by the scene in which the daughter gives her pearl pagoda to her beloved cousin. The show went on for several days, until the head of the police force became so embarrassed that he begged the old man to end it. "We felt victorious," Ma commented, and he even dared to lecture the head of the police force, or so he claimed in his account, arguing: "Opera is one of the three persuasions. The first is the emperor's law, a tough measure that promises capital punishment for those who dare to violate it. This is not the best way. The second is the Buddhist way that makes people study sutras and learn about retribution. The third is playful persuasion through opera. We show the people the crystal-clear [difference between] good and evil by means of our vivid performance."[49] Although Ma's depiction of the event need not be taken on faith, his speech is a clear example of peasant appropriation of the elite idea of "persuasion of the people" (*jiaohua*) with which to argue his case.[50]

The troupes were not so lucky when performing outside of Shengxian. Once, in Paito, Zhuji County, Ma Chaoshui and seven fellow actors were charged with obscene performance and arrested in the middle of a show by the local police chief, Zhou Zhongzen. Zhou, a Shengxian native himself, seems to have been ashamed of his native-place fellows' lowly trade and shows. He ridiculed the actor who played young female roles by parading him through the streets in his womanly makeup and stage costumes. Then he had all the costumes burned. According to Ma, those who had attended the show were not convinced that Zhou was in the right, as they had witnessed nothing obscene, and so they stormed the police station. "I took my men and fled to Sandu," Ma wrote. "We did not have any money but still had seven or eight mouths to feed, so we had to perform some story-singing in teahouses." Later, they borrowed some costumes and props and staged an opera; again, "the police objected and imposed a four-yuan tax for each night of performance, while all we could earn from one night's show was about three or four yuan. We had no choice but to leave."[51]

Ma's account is rife with similar incidents of persecution but also reveals a sense of pride at little opera's rise from such adversity. Despite repeated persecution, Shengxian little-opera troupes mushroomed all over the countryside, attesting to, among other things, the deep rural market for minor operas.

The rapid increase in the number of little-opera troupes in Shengxian was also closely related to a downturn in the local economy. From 1907 to 1911, a drought in Shengxian destroyed all the crops. Many young men joined little-opera troupes and left the county in search of a new livelihood. Opera singing became a countywide industry, and little opera was the main Shengxian export to adjacent areas.[52] The troupes traveled along three traditional trade routes: through Xinchang and Yuyao to Ningbo in eastern Zhejiang; through Dongyang and Zhuji to Jinhua in central Zhejiang; and through Shangyu, Shaoxing, and Xiaoshan to the Hang-Jia-Hu area in western Zhejiang.[53] The Hang-Jia-Hu area, highly developed and a long-term base for Shengxian story-singers, was the most popular destination for little-opera troupes. Such a troupe performed in Hangzhou for the first time in 1910, and in Ningbo and Jinhua in 1915. Two years later, in 1917, little opera staged the first show in Shanghai.[54]

Shengxian Opera in Shanghai

Shengxian little opera entered Shanghai along with a large flow of immigrants from Zhejiang, especially the Ningbo-Shaoxing area. Yang Shaochun, a Shengxian native and a Beijing opera agent in Shanghai, brought the first little-opera troupe to Shanghai in 1917. The twenty-odd members of the troupe boarded a Ningbo-Shanghai steamboat and arrived at the Shiliupu dock along the Huangpu River, where Zhejiang immigrants dominated. As news of their arrival spread, Zhejiang natives crowded the New Theater (Xin Wutai) to watch the city's first show of Shengxian little opera. When the actors appeared onstage in their funny-looking costumes and began their clumsy singing and acting routines, the audience burst into laughter. Many left before the end of the program, and few came back for a second viewing. Yang Shaochun held out for a few weeks but eventually gave up and disbanded the troupe; most of the actors sold their bedding to buy tickets home.[55] A few months later, a Shaoxing major-opera agent in Shanghai sponsored a second little-opera troupe. Despite an initial success that lasted a few months, the troupe disbanded within half a year. A few further attempts were made in 1918 and 1919 without much success.[56]

The turning point came in the winter of 1919, as little opera's effort to enhance its production values converged with a new wave of social awareness related to such issues as women's liberation and free love and marriage after the May Fourth Movement. Shengxian opera returned to Shanghai with new plays boasting better-developed plots and characters as well as more-refined music, costumes, makeup, and acting.[57] Most plays during the foundational phase of Shengxian opera in Shanghai were centered on love stories, and the most successful plays included *Liang Shanbo and Zhu Yingtai* (or *The Butterfly Lovers*),[58] *Emerald Hairpin* (Biyu zan), *Tale of the Lute* (Pipa ji), and *Meng Lijun* (Meng Lijun), all with positive portrayal of the heroines.

The development of *Emerald Hairpin* and *Liang Shanbo and Zhu Yingtai* best illustrates the success of Shengxian opera in Shanghai. Set in the Ming dynasty, *Emerald Hairpin* tells the tragic story of a young couple. Minister Li Tingfu marries his only daughter, Li Xiuying, to Wang Yulin, son of a member of the imperial academy. Li Xiuying's cousin, Gu Wenyou, who is secretly in love with her, conspires to separate the new couple. Gu arranges to have a forged love letter supposedly written by Li and a stolen emerald hairpin of hers placed in the new couple's bedroom on their wedding night. When Wang sees the items, he falls for Gu's trick and concludes that Li is having an affair with Gu. Furious, Wang rejects Li and berates her repeatedly or ignores her. Unaware of the source of Wang's anger, Li submits to his abuse with the hope that her loyalty and love will eventually win his heart.

In the original Wu opera (from adjacent Dongyang County) version of this story, Li's father kicks his daughter to death upon hearing about her alleged violation of chastity. Then, after the truth comes to light, Wang commits suicide in remorse and Gu is arrested and executed. In a previous Shengxian version of this play, Li Xiuying eventually dies of melancholy, while Gu Wenyou succumbs to lovesickness.[59] The play had never been popular because the tragic ending involved the deaths of all the main characters and the loss of heirs for all three families. But in Shanghai in the winter of 1919, it was presented with an innovative and completely different ending. As Ma Chaoshui, who participated in the Shanghai adventure and was in fact responsible for the revised ending, recalled:

> The fourth time we went to Shanghai to perform in the Star Theater [Minxing] in Tianbao Lane, off Haining Road, I thought to myself: "Even though

Shanghai's market is really good, we still have to find our way into it." I thought that the Dongyang Wu opera *Emerald Hairpin* was a moving story and maybe a good choice. We had more than forty actors at the time. I went out to the street to look for scripts and found a storybook in which Wang Yulin abuses Li Xiuying until she dies. I thought that the ending was too negative. Later I found a Buddhist edition that has Wang Yulin become a *zhuangyuan* [first place in the metropolitan civil-service examination] and present the phoenix cap to Li Xiuying [seeking reconciliation]. I then wrote the act "Presenting the Phoenix Cap" and had Zhang Yunbiao play Wang Yulin. During the show, the audience was moved to tears as the story unfolded.[60]

Ma Chaoshui and his actors changed the story line and gave the play a happy ending. Instead of simply accepting Wang's allegation regarding his daughter's chastity, Li Xiuying's father investigates and discovers that the handwriting in the love letter, the evidence on which Wang based his accusation, does not match his daughter's. The story that follows was then completely altered: Gu's conspiracy is exposed, while Li Xiuying returns to her natal home to recuperate, and Wang is left alone to rue his bad behavior. In an effort to redeem himself, he studies hard and wins the title of *zhuangyuan*. Upon his return from the capital after the examination, Wang presents Li Xiuying with a phoenix cap, a gift he solicited specially from the emperor in order to honor his wife. Li, however, refuses to accept it, nor is she willing to go home with Wang, declaring instead that she wants to live in a monastery for the rest of her life. In the closing act, everyone, including all the characters in the play as well as members of the audience, must listen to Li Xiuying complain at length about her sufferings, while Wang, the honorable *zhuangyuan*, is made to kneel at Li's feet and apologize. At the end of the play, the two are gloriously and happily reunited.[61]

This positive ending to an otherwise tragic story, with its vindication of the heroine and criticism of the male protagonist, was most sympathetic to women and accorded with the new concept of women's liberation, representing a clear departure from the misogynist operatic tradition of the Qing period. The play was Shengxian opera's first big hit in Shanghai and subsequently became a classic of the Yue opera repertoire.

Liang Shanbo and Zhu Yingtai was a celebration of love that originated from a folktale set in neighboring Shangyu County.[62] Some scholars believe that the first written record of the story appeared during the Tang dynasty (618–907) and told the following tale:

> Yingtai, daughter of the Zhu family in Shangyu, disguised herself in men's clothing and traveled in search of a school education. At school, she met Liang Shanbo, a classmate from Guiji [present-day Shaoxing], whose style name was Churen [lit., "with benevolence"]. Yingtai returned home first; one year later, Shanbo visited her at her home, only to discover that Yingtai was a woman. He was deeply affected. Upon his return home, Shanbo asked his parents to arrange for his marriage with the Zhu family, but Yingtai had already been betrothed to the son of the Ma family. Shanbo later served as the magistrate of Yin county [present-day Ningbo], where he passed away from sickness. He was buried in the western side of Maocheng [east of Yin County]. On her way to Ma's house as a bride, Yingtai's boat was held up by storms and big waves when it passed the site of Shanbo's tomb. Having learned that Shanbo was buried nearby, Yingtai landed and cried passionately before his grave. Suddenly, the ground below her split open and collapsed, and Yingtai was thus buried with Shanbo. Prime Minister Xie An [320–385] of the [Eastern] Jin dynasty [317–420] issued a memorial to the throne on the matter and accordingly honored the grave as "the grave of a righteous woman."[63]

A Southern Song (1127–1279) version of the story transforms the two lovers into a pair of butterflies fluttering over the gravesite.[64] The story later spread widely, taking different forms in various entertainment media; modern examples include the Sichuan opera play *Liang Shanbo and Zhu Yingtai* (Liuyin ji) and the Huangmei opera play by the same title.

In the Shengxian opera version premiered in Shanghai in the winter of 1919, Zhu Yingtai, disguised as a man, meets Liang Shanbo at Straw Bridge, outside of Hangzhou, on her way to school in the city. The two young students are so taken with each other at their first meeting that they immediately become sworn brothers. They then study and live in the same room for three years without Shanbo ever suspecting Yingtai's true sex. Upon leaving for home, Yingtai secretly asks the teacher's wife to arrange a marriage between her and Shanbo. Soon after Yingtai returns home, however, her father accepts a request from a certain wealthy Ma family and betroths her to Ma Wencai. When Shanbo finally arrives with his request for marriage, Yingtai can only promise to be with him in their next life. Returning home, Shanbo soon dies of lovesickness. On her way to Ma's house on the wedding day, Yingtai stops to pray in front of Shanbo's tombstone, and when it opens up in response to her prayers, she jumps in to join him. Ma Wencai tries to hold her back, only to be dragged into the tomb along with her, and the two go thereafter to the court of the underworld. Checking the book of life and death, the King of the Underworld finds that Shanbo and Yingtai are actually the Golden Boy and the Jade Girl who serve the Jade Emperor in heaven. The Jade Emperor had sent them down to earth to experience a few cycles of incarnation, and they have just completed the last reincarnation. The king accordingly sends the two back to the Jade Emperor and returns Ma Wencai to earth, where he marries his own predestined bride.[65]

The play's highlights came in four separate acts: "Eighteen-*Li* Farewell" (Shibali xiangsong), "Remembering the Eighteen-*Li* Farewell" (Hui shiba), "Meeting at Yingtai's Chamber" (Loutai hui), and "Yingtai Crying at Shanbo's Bier" (Yingtai kuling). In "Eighteen-*Li* Farewell," Liang Shanbo sees Zhu Yingtai off as she heads home, accompanying her for eighteen *li* (roughly six miles). Along the way, she tries to reveal her true sex and her love for him by invoking eighteen metaphors of love, including flowers, butterflies, mandarin ducks, the story of the Cowherd and the Girl Weaver, monks and nuns, and the hall of the bodhisattva Guanyin where young couples pray for sons. Yingtai cannot keep herself from expressing her feelings for Shanbo before they depart. But, as a well-educated woman, she knows how a proper lady must carry herself, and as a young girl, she is also too shy to express her love and desire in a straightforward manner. "Eighteen-*Li* Farewell" captures Yingtai's dilemma and beautifully illustrates the young girl's grace and complex psychology, a mixture of desire, passion, shyness, determination, and intelligence. "Remembering the Eighteen-*Li* Farewell" is a solo act in which Liang, having learned from the teacher's wife about Yingtai's true identity and her wish to marry him, leaves school for the Zhu Family Village (Zhujia Zhuang) to ask for Yingtai's hand in marriage. As he encounters familiar scenes along the way, a happy Liang Shanbo recalls the eighteen metaphors Yingtai used to hint at her love for him. "Meeting at Yingtai's Chamber" and "Crying at Shanbo's Bier" depict the lovers' passion and desperation.

The rich local oral tradition was most influential in the development of the Shengxian opera play. According to the recollections of veteran actors, "Eighteen-*Li* Farewell" and "Meeting at Yingtai's Chamber," the two most popular acts, took shape in Shengxian story-singing as early as the late nineteenth century. When Shengxian story-singing was turned into opera in the early twentieth century, these two acts were staged as independent pieces. It was not until the winter of 1919 in Shanghai, however, that the parts were united into an integral whole as described above.[66] In this early version of the play, folk superstitions, Daoist heavens, Buddhist notions of reincarnation, and peasant forms of sexually suggestive gestures and lighthearted flirtation are mixed with love motifs alluding to the May Fourth rhetoric of women's liberation and free love. Despite these mixed messages, the story of the butterfly lovers was best known in the early Republican era as a popular celebration of love and loyalty.

With these additions to its repertoire, the all-male Shengxian opera experienced a golden age in the 1920s. The rise of little opera in Shanghai was coterminous with the decline of Shaoxing major opera. As the native saying of the time put it: "The little brother defeated the big brother." In 1923, Shengxian little opera was performed at four permanent theaters, and by 1925, the number of venues had increased to more than fifteen, including amusement parks, large teahouses, native-place halls, inn lobbies, and new-style theaters. During the same period, the number of theaters that staged Shaoxing major opera declined from four to two.[67] Upon its initial success, little opera began to call itself "Shaoxing civil opera" (*Shaoxing wenxi*), claiming thereby to be the representative opera from Shaoxing prefecture, of which Shengxian was a part. The term "civil opera" (*wenxi*) indicates little opera's emphasis on love stories and the fact that love drama, not military romance—a particular strong point of Shaoxing major opera—was what made little opera popular in Shanghai.

Changing Gender Norms and Girls' Opera Schools

Sometime in the 1930s, the term "women's Shaoxing civil opera" (*nüzi Shaoxing wenxi*) began to appear frequently in advertisements, posters, and prints. Then, in the 1940s, "women's Yue opera", or simply "Yue opera," became the standard name for this newcomer to the Shanghai opera scene, signaling the coming of age of all-female Shengxian opera troupes and the passing of all-male troupes. The sudden rise of women's Shengxian opera and the disappearance of male actors around 1938 have been a mystery in Yue opera history and in the history of modern Chinese opera more generally. Moreover, that Yue opera was the only genre to evolve into an all-female theater, and one of the most popular theaters in modern China, begs for historical explanation. The official *Shanghai Yue Opera Gazetteer* (Shanghai Yueju zhi) devotes only one sentence to the decline of all-male troupes: "As actors became older and lacked successors, all-male troupes eventually declined and were finally displaced by all-female troupes."[68] Evidence suggests that men's Shengxian opera lost ground to women's opera on both artistic and institutional fronts. As the artistic transformation of Shengxian opera and the advantage of the all-female cast in this process are discussed in the next chapter, this chapter addresses the institutional aspect, focusing on girls' opera schools and changing gender norms in performance art in general.

The entrance of women into the entertainment market had a dramatic impact on gender arrangement in theatrical art in the early Republican period. In 1914, only two years after the founding of the republic, female performers made a powerful appearance in China's first modern theater, "new drama" (*xinju* or *wenmingxi*), which was imported from the West via Japan and prospered in China as "family drama" (*jiating ju*) and "live news drama" (*huobao ju*). Among some thirty new-drama companies, at least six were all female.[69] The all-female companies represented a break from the late Qing tradition of male-dominated theater but perpetuated the use of single-sex casts onstage.

Sex desegregation in theatrical arts was taking place in more traditional revues, first as a way of returning to a cross-gender acting tradition. In Shanghai's foreign settlements, women had begun performing Suzhou story-singing and "Shanghai storytelling" (*bentan*) in teahouses and Beijing opera in the late nineteenth century.[70] During the early Republican period, women performers became popular and fashionable; they took on both male and female roles and acted onstage with male as well as female partners. Cross-gender performance was common at the time for male and female actors.[71]

Gender-straight performance was first established in elite spoken drama in 1923. A coterie of avant-garde intellectuals, dissatisfied with the commercial and vulgar qualities of the new drama, formed the Popular Theatrical Association (Dazhong Jushe) in Shanghai in the early 1920s. The devotees called their new spoken drama "amateur theater" (*aimeiju*); the term uses a phonetic transliteration of the English word "amateur," rendered in Chinese characters that mean "love of beauty" (*aimei*) so as to emphasize its noncommercial character. These Western-influenced intellectuals considered single-sex theaters and cross-gender acting embarrassingly unrealistic and thought traditional theater's formulaic style was old-fashioned and feudal. In an effort to modernize Chinese theater, intellectuals adopted the

Western realistic mode of acting and initiated a gender-straight acting system by which men and women played the roles of their own sex. In 1923, the director and playwright Hong Shen staged *Marriage: A Lifelong Commitment* (Zhongsheng dashi), Hu Shi's influential May Fourth adaptation of Ibsen's *A Doll's House*, with a gender-straight cast. The next year, Hong Shen presented another gender-straight production, Oscar Wilde's *Lady Windermere's Fan*, which became one of the most frequently performed plays of the time.[72]

During the ensuing decades, the elite practice of gender-straight acting was to become the rule for all Chinese theaters, and although cross-gender performances continued to exist in various native operas, the practice became marginalized. Even Beijing opera could not escape when new generations of actresses eventually took over women's roles. Yue opera, like other native forms, freely adopted a variety of gender arrangements, from gender-straight to cross-gender and from single- to mixed-gender modes of acting. Significantly, when most native operas eventually were transmuted into gender-straight theaters, Yue opera evolved into a theater dominated by all-female troupes. Thus, the spectrum of possible gender arrangements displayed on Republican Shanghai's stage may be seen as a response to the rise of female performers and audiences, with women's Yue opera being a radical representative of this modern transition. Women's opera was, therefore, an exception in a general move toward gender-straight acting, one that proved the rule of the feminization of performing arts in the modern age. If the preference for gender-straight acting was much influenced by the West, then the rise of women's opera was evidence of various native and traditional influences in the shaping of China's modern theater.

Women's Yue opera was deeply connected with a cultural legacy of the region—the "all-girls training schools/troupes" (*nü ban*, also *nü xi* and *nü yue*), a tradition peculiar to the Jiangnan area that dated back to at least the Ming dynasty. The prosperous late Ming and early Qing literati in Jiangnan were fond of opera, and it was just as fashionable for men of means to train and keep private opera troupes as it was to build private scholars' gardens. Many of the best private troupes, such as those owned by Zhu Yunlai and Yu Shuiwen, consisted of women only.[73] During the late nineteenth century, after the government prohibited adult women performers, all-girls opera troupes, known as *mao'erxi* (lit., "children's opera"), emerged. The all-girls opera featured girls mostly in their early teens performing all roles in a highly professional manner, and the performers were known to be especially skilled in acrobatic fighting. All-girls opera enjoyed great popularity for a few decades and then disappeared completely by the end of the 1920s, when adult actresses reappeared in great numbers.[74] In the early 1920s, however, a combination of the popularity of female performers, all-girls opera troupes, and men's Shengxian opera seems to have inspired the idea of a girls' Shengxian opera.[75]

In 1923, a man by the name of Wang Jinshui, a Shengxian merchant sojourning in Shanghai, decided to create an all-girls Shengxian opera school in his hometown in order to prepare the girls for Shanghai's market.[76] Wang had been in the theater business for some years and had recently become manager of the Shengping Theater in Shanghai, one of the major theaters featuring all-male Shengxian opera. With three hundred silver dollars, Wang started an all-girls training school in early 1923 in Shi's Village (Shijia Ao), a poor village located in a mountainous area. Residents greeted him with suspicion, however.[77] Older moral imperatives and customs held sway there, and local people voiced a long-standing bias against the "three *zi*": "actors" (*xizi*), "soldiers" (*liangzi*), and "prostitutes" (*biaozi*). Taking up acting, they felt, was bad enough for men, let alone for women. Wang, however, had such confidence in Shanghai's lucrative market that he was determined to carry out his plan. He first recruited his daughter and his niece to demonstrate that he was serious and promised an attractive package for the students: free room and board and a gold ring, a dress, a pair of leather shoes, and one hundred silver dollars after three years of apprenticeship. In three months, Wang recruited about two dozen girls between the ages of nine and thirteen; daughters of peasants, artisans, and rural opera actors accounted for the majority of the apprentices, and many were family members, relatives, and neighbors of Wang and the instructors.[78]

Instruction began in the early summer. The school hired three teachers, all retired actors. Most girls were illiterate and had no previous acting experience, but they were nonetheless able to endure the arduous training program. The school safeguarded the girls' well-being in general, since most students had close ties to the men in charge, but the strict training program had the girls working day and night. Students got up early for physical fitness training before breakfast. Then they studied scripts and memorized parts of plays. In the afternoon, they studied performance skills until dark, and diligent students rehearsed additional work on their own by moonlight. The curriculum consisted of three basic training courses: "acrobatics" (*wugong*), "singing" (*changgong*), and "posture" (*zuogong*). Along with their basic training, they learned and memorized several plays. By the end of the third month, Wang was ready to put the girls onstage for a formal rehearsal.[79]

The first rehearsal was held in the open space in front of the school. The temporary stage was made up of several planks. The performance featured a costume play, *A Pair of Pearly Phoenixes* (Shuang zhu feng), a typical scholar-beauty love story, which begins with Wen Bizheng, a secondary-degree holder from Luoyang, seeing Huo Dingjin, the beautiful daughter of a high official, on his visit to a temple. He immediately falls in love but has no way to approach her. Wen goes off to a village to consult a go-between, and there he falls in love again, this time with the go-between's daughter. The go-between manages to sell Wen to the official's household as a slave-servant. While there, he finds an opportunity to meet the young lady he had seen at the temple and reveals his true identity and his love for her. At the end, Wen restores his status and happily marries both women. Although the stage and costumes were simple and the acting lacked sophistication, the villagers responded positively to the girls' efforts.[80]

Wang soon exhausted his initial investment of three hundred silver dollars and was eager to test the market in Shanghai. Early in winter 1923, he took his troupe to Shanghai and put on a show at the Shengping Theater. But the result could not have been further from the success he dreamed of. Three months of training proved insufficient, as the girls appeared technically inadequate as well as shy and immature. After few more tries performing without success at teahouses in Shanghai and Hangzhou, Wang brought the troupe back to Shengxian in spring 1924.[81]

The villagers welcomed the girls back with great enthusiasm. That the children had performed in Shanghai gave them a certain cachet in the minds of the villagers. The clansmen even defied rules and opened the stage inside Shenwu Hall, the Shi lineage hall, for the girls' homecoming show. The whole village was exhilarated. In the past, Shi's Village had not had the resources to invite opera companies; now the village had its own opera troupe, and the native daughters put on shows for the community free of charge. Villagers invited relatives and friends from other locations and even slaughtered domestic animals so that there would be sufficient provisions to treat their guests. On the day of the show, Shenwu Hall was packed with enthusiastic peasants. The program consisted of typical scholar-beauty love stories, including *A Pair of Pearly Phoenixes*, *A Pair of Jade Bracelets* (Yu lianhuan), and *Pearl Pagoda*. The girls were also excited. They had become more experienced during their several months of performing in big cities, and the warm and eager welcome they received helped mitigate any residual shyness. The girls put on a bold and lively performance and greatly pleased the audience. The troupe then performed a few successful shows in nearby towns.[82]

In the autumn of 1924, the school undertook a long-distance tour in the eastern Zhejiang countryside. On land, they traveled by foot, but most of the journey was on water, by raft and "riverboats covered with black awning" (*wupeng chuan*). Such tours became routine over the next few years. In 1927, when the school's four-year contract with the students expired, Wang turned the school into a professional troupe, adopting a salary system that put the leading actresses at the top of the payroll. By the late 1920s, the first all-girls Shengxian opera troupe had become a fixture in Shaoxing and had acquired name recognition in Ningbo and Hangzhou, replacing the declining all-girls Beijing opera.[83] The popularity of three leading actresses, known as "the three flowers" (*san hua*)—Shi Yinhua and Zhao Ruihua, who specialized in young female roles, and Tu Xinghua, who specialized in young male roles—marked the commercial success of the girls' Shengxian opera troupe. A 1927 article in the *Shaoxing Evening News* (Shaoxing wanbao) noted: "[The girls] performed in the Juemin Theater. Shi Yinhua and others already had great marketing power to attract audiences. The audience was reluctant to leave after the show was over, and the opera got a nickname, *diaojiaoxi* [lit., 'the opera you are not able to walk away from']. Shi Yinhua's salary was as high as nine hundred yuan [per month]."[84] In 1929, the first all-girls troupe came to a glorious end when the actresses left the troupe one by one for marriage. Among the first to leave, in 1928, was Shi Yinhua, who married the son of a rich family in the market town of Chongren. Wang Jinshui took the remaining twelve girls back to Shi's Village, where rural people had long been awaiting the troupe's return. During the troupe's last year of operation, people from near and far came to Shi's Village to contract with Wang to bring the troupe to their villages and towns. In one incident, the owner of a cloth shop in the market town of Huangze sent five sedan chairs to bring the actresses to perform at his mother's birthday celebration. The troupe traveled, or rather paraded, about twenty-five miles in sedan chairs, stopping to perform at several places and creating a sensation along the way. The troupe's splendid end instilled a dream in the minds of many young girls and also effectively demonstrated to the country folk that being an actress might not be such a bad idea after all.[85]

All-girls schools proliferated, however, only in the 1930s when the Great Depression began to take a toll on China's silk economy. Shanghai and Zhejiang, with silk industries closely linked to the international market, were hit hard. Sericulture and the silk industry had been an important part of Zhejiang's economy for centuries. The northern Zhejiang area (mainly the Hangzhou-Jiaxing-Huzhou plain) was the leader in the province's silk industry, supported by eastern Zhejiang's sericulture and cheap labor. Shengxian's mountainous terrain was unsuitable for agriculture, and as the economy relied heavily on sericulture, the area was especially affected. In the early 1930s, Shengxian endured a lasting depression.[86]

Economic disaster impoverished local families and changed the lives of many native daughters, inadvertently contributing to the rise of women's opera. Sericulture had been an important source of cash income for peasant households in Shengxian, and peasant girls traditionally labored alongside adult women in raising and harvesting silkworms, all the while dreaming of becoming wageworkers in the silk mills of Hangzhou and Shanghai. The outcome poor peasant girls most feared was being sold or given away as child brides by desperate parents, a common practice in eastern Zhejiang's poor countryside. Ironically, in the face of the bankrupt rural economy, a daughter's cash-earning ability became increasingly important to rural families. All things considered, opera singing suddenly did not look like such a bad alternative for a little girl whose family desperately needed her to bring in cash.[87]

Thus, just as a local natural disaster in the early twentieth century had pushed the development of Shengxian little opera, so an international disaster in the early 1930s resulted in the phenomenal growth of all-girls opera, first in Zhejiang and then in Shanghai. In 1929, a second all-girls school, Xinxinfeng Theater, was established in Huangze township. Then, from 1930 to 1934, at least thirteen girls' schools came into being in Huangze alone. In Shengxian as a whole, major schools during the period between 1930 and 1937 numbered at least forty, while smaller schools were even more numerous. Girls' opera schools also appeared in great numbers in such nearby counties as Xinchang, Xindeng, Lin'an, Shaoxing, Sanmen, Yuyao, and Longyou.[88] Girls' schools and subsequent all-female troupes vastly outnumbered men's Shengxian opera troupes; moreover, with their highly competitive fees and the quality performances presented by a cluster of well-known stars, girls' Shengxian opera marginalized all other genres active in the province, including the long-standing Shaoxing major opera, Hangzhou opera (Hangju), and Beijing opera. Like men's Shengxian opera, girls' Shengxian opera was deeply rooted in the peasant culture of Zhejiang's countryside and bespoke the general lack of entertainment in rural life. Backed up by the vast rural market, all-female troupes were able to test the waters at urban centers from time to time and eventually emerged as powerful contenders in the entertainment markets of Ningbo, Shaoxing, Wenzhou, Hangzhou, and, finally, Shanghai. Girls' troupes began to frequent Shanghai after 1935 and already enjoyed better market value than all-male and mixed-gender Shengxian opera troupes. In the meantime, all-male and mixed-gender troupes were demoralized by their declining market value and lack of new recruits.

The institution of the girls' opera school was vital to the success of women's opera for several reasons. The school gave its students systematic technical training in acting, singing, and acrobatic fighting, a benefit many peasants who became minor-opera performers never had. The school-trained troupe also enjoyed a strong institutional and technical structure with a team of well-trained long-term partners in all roles, crucial for a well-balanced troupe. Moreover, girls who lived, traveled, and worked together for months and years developed a sense of belonging that kept them going and overcoming all sorts of hardships in their career. Finally, the sheer number of girls' schools and women performers overwhelmed existing male performers and discouraged boys from taking up acting careers, effectively making Shengxian opera a women's realm.

The outbreak of the War of Resistance against Japan in 1937 gave women's Shengxian opera troupes one final push toward establishing themselves permanently in Shanghai. In August 1937, Japanese forces attacked the city, and the Battle of Shanghai began. It lasted for three months, and most Shengxian opera troupes left Shanghai to continue their performances elsewhere. When peace returned to the fallen city, entertainment quickly picked up in "island" Shanghai, which became crowded with refugees from the surrounding areas. On January 31, 1938, the lunar New Year's Day, the Yuesheng Theater, the first all-female troupe to arrive in the city after the Battle of Shanghai, successfully staged a performance at the Commercial Inn (Tongshang Lüguan), a hostel owned by a Shengxian native where many sojourners from Zhejiang congregated. Within two months, the troupe moved to a real theater, the Old Dam Theater (Laozha Xiyuan), where an enthusiastic audience filled the three hundred seats. On the day of the Lantern Festival (the fifteenth day after the lunar New Year), another all-female troupe arrived and performed at the Shanghai Little Theater. In April came the third troupe, which performed at the Empire Theater. Encouraged by the success of these pioneers, more troupes and actresses followed suit; as women's troupes moved into the city one by one, male performers and all-male Shengxian opera disappeared from the scene.[89] Within a few years, women's Shengxian opera had managed to become the city's most popular theater, while creating a distinctly women's culture in the city's public space.

清白

Chapter 2

The Rise of Feminine Opera

The story of women's Yue opera is primarily a story about the actresses. At the beginning of 1938, when the historical stage was set for the rise of women's Yue opera in Shanghai, it was the many young peasant girls from Shengxian who made it happen, but not without casualties.

It was February 21, 1942. In a funeral parlor at 838 Xujiahui Road in the former French concession, people from all over Shanghai came to watch the funeral ceremony for Ma Zhanghua, a twenty-one-year-old women's Yue opera star. Ma died of tuberculosis, but rumor attributed her illness to melancholy brought on by slanderous allegations of promiscuity. It was commonly believed that the slander was spread by Lu Gendi, boss of the Dalai Theater where Ma performed, in angry response to Ma's recent marriage and retirement.

Five years later, when another tragic death of a popular Yue opera star, Xiao Dangui, captured the headlines, some twenty thousand Yue opera fans crashed the Leyuan Funeral House, where the funeral ceremony was held. Xiao had committed suicide when her boss Zhang Chunfan accused her of having an affair with her male director. Xiao had lived with Zhang for many years, ostensibly as a concubine. Before she committed suicide, Xiao Dangui is reported to have stated to a friend: "My body is pure and clean" (Wode shenti shi qingbai de).[1] This statement reminded the public of the suicide of Ruan Lingyu, a popular movie star, which occurred in 1935, also amid a sexual scandal.

Ruan Lingyu's suicide was one of the first instances in modern Chinese history of a famous actress's tragic death becoming a topic of widespread public interest. Ruan's personal life became the subject of gossip when her ex-husband filed a lawsuit against her and her second husband, accusing them of adultery and of misappropriating his property. Newspapers published stories portraying Ruan as a playgirl who had abandoned her ex-husband for a wealthier man. On March 8, 1935, International Women's Day, one day before she was scheduled to appear in court, Ruan committed suicide, stating in a suicide note: "Gossip is frightening" (Renyan kewei), and "I cannot wipe out the wrong done to me if I do not die."[2]

Public fascination with the lives and deaths of actresses involved in "peach-colored news" (*taose xinwen*), or sexual scandals, was common to the cultural scene of Republican era Shanghai. Gossip, as well as reports on actresses' personal lives, filled the pages of tabloids and mainstream newspapers, feeding the curiosity of a large urban public. Subject to such exposure, actresses often went out of their way to defend their good name and, sometimes, died for it. If Ruan Lingyu's statement that "Gossip is frightening" was a protest against the public's scrutiny of her personal life, then Xiao Dangui's *qingbai* (purity and cleanliness), the description she applied to her body, represented a moral quality that actresses wished to cultivate as their public image.

The concept of *qingbai*, as a moral imperative of female bodily practice, was derived from a Confucian discourse on female chastity prevalent during the Ming and Qing dynasties. It was commonly used to describe women of good families, but rarely, if ever, public women who worked as prostitutes or entertainers.[3] The gender system during the Ming–Qing periods formally restricted a woman's role to provider of reproductive and sexual services to men, while a corollary concept of chastity valued female bodily purity as opposed to promiscuity. The virtuous woman remained in the inner chambers, her body belonging only to her husband; public women who offered sexual services and entertainment as consumable goods were at the other end of the spectrum. Yet, even among public women, there was a moral hierarchy structured according to the criterion of chastity. It is not difficult to find, for example, literary descriptions of morally superior courtesans who remained loyal to the dynasty and faithful to their literati lovers.[4] Since *qingbai* was traditionally reserved for certain categories of women, a woman's capacity to invoke this notion became a mark of her high social status in itself. In the 1930s and 1940s, however, female public entertainers became increasingly concerned with the idea of *qingbai*. Some even died after having been accused of being unchaste. This raises several questions: How did the notion of *qingbai* become central to the public image of the actress, a woman considered marginal in traditional social hierarchies? What social and cultural conditions of the Republican period rendered *qingbai* a desirable virtue for public women? And how did this notion affect the construction of women's Yue opera?

During the Republican period, actresses were caught up in the cultural conflict between traditional popular eroticism focused on the sexuality of public women and a reformist ideology that considered the cleansing of this popular eroticism to be part of the task of building a modern nation. The new ideology, which called for a redefinition of women's social role in general, required that women in theater be redefined as art workers who would move audiences to contemplate the well-being of the nation, instead of sexual objects indulging viewers with titillating entertainment. This cultural conflict was intensified by the emergence of mass media that provided a public domain in which the city's culture was being formed and re-formed.

The actress was a new type of woman born in the Republican period, an era with the slogan of women's liberation painted on its banner. Although, historically, there had been numerous female public entertainers, the Qing state adopted a strict Confucian gender ideology and excluded women from public entertainment. Female performers of the early Republican period came from a wide spectrum of social backgrounds, ranging from revolutionary new women and vocational performers to courtesans and prostitutes. While female students acted out revolutionary ideas in the form of Western drama, and upper-class ladies spent their time as Beijing opera amateurs, for lower-class women entertainers, the stage, only recently made accessible to them, presented a new opportunity to earn a living. In the 1920s, female entertainers began to reappear in numbers in teahouses, on stages, and on screens, adding a new category of performer to the two traditional types of entertainers, the actor and the prostitute. Despite territorial boundaries and sexual differences between actors and prostitutes, both provided similar services for their male customers. While young male actors often served as prostitutes, courtesans generally performed music and dance as well as provided sexual services. The new female actors occupied a niche between the traditional categories of male actors and female prostitutes, but they were easily viewed as a mixture of the two. Weikun Cheng, in his article on actresses in Republican Beijing and Tianjin, has also noted: "Contemporaries more or less understood stage performance by women in the early twentieth century as a form of urban amusement associated with erotic indulgence and immoral lifestyles, and believed acting to be a profession full of abuse, exploitation, and social control."[5]

Moreover, historically and also in the case of women performing in foreign settlements during the late Qing period, the line separating female performers and courtesans was ambiguous, as public women's sexuality was customarily considered part of their vocation, available for sale alongside their other entertainment skills. The Republican rhetoric of women's liberation may have opened a new niche for vocational female performers, but it hardly gave them a wholly new, ready-made social status. Centuries-old images of female entertainers were easily invoked to define public perceptions of these new actresses. Traditional gender-role ideas persisted as well.

The traditional consuming public's voyeuristic gaze, which manipulated female entertainers' sexuality, intensified dramatically in the first half of the twentieth century with the emergence of mass media. Newspapers, magazines, and tabloids filled Shanghai's streets, carrying, among other things, gossip about female stars. If female entertainers' performances and sexuality were consumable goods available only to a limited number of people before the emergence of mass media, they were now for sale as a commodity to a large urban audience. In a sense, the actress became an object of public erotic fantasy whose sexuality was the business of anyone with access to media-created gossip.

Being such a heavily eroticized commodity, the actress could not help but feel the gaze of her fans and the tabloid-reading public in general. Admittedly, this phenomenon is not uncommon to urban popular cultures elsewhere. Yet it remains important to inquire into the ways in which China's traditional gender system yielded different expectations of actors and actresses during the Republican period. Since the traditional Chinese family system was polygamous, multiple sexual relationships were considered normal for men. By contrast, women in the traditional family system were expected to be monogamous. Thus, while actors could engage in multiple sexual relationships without being stigmatized, the public imagined the actress as if it were involved in a love affair with her and therefore had a claim on her sexuality and loyalty.[6] In other words, the public paradoxically demanded chastity from its favorite actresses as it simultaneously consumed their sexuality.

The public further demonstrated its gender bias in its refusal or failure to distinguish between an actress's stage role and her real life. While an actress's alleged promiscuity could ruin her reputation and her professional career, her stage persona as an amorous character could irreversibly damage her personal reputation, making her more vulnerable to slander. Actresses who played loose characters were somehow more vulnerable to public gossip about their personal lives than were those who played righteous roles. This pattern is evident in many cases, including those of the three actresses whose deaths were described at the beginning of this chapter: Ma Zhanghua was famous for impersonating amorous young men; Xiao Dangui was known for playing erotic women; and Ruan Lingyu began her screen career playing loose women, and many considered her role as a prostitute in *The Goddess* (Shen nü), released in 1933, her most successful. The onstage persona of an actress often influenced public perception of her personality in the real world. In a sense, for the public, the actress became the characters she performed. The actress was therefore considered a sexual object during the early Republican period not only because of the traditional confusion between the actress and the courtesan but also because of the sexually suggestive performances she often gave.

These actresses, most of whom came from lower-class backgrounds and struggled to make a living, had little control over the program and roles they performed. The basic fact was that they were hired by their male superiors—a boss, teacher, or employer—for the sole purpose of pleasing a predominantly male audience. Thus, the relationship between the theatrical representation of women and the alleged moral character of actresses was embedded in a power relationship informed by class and gender inequality. The social position of female entertainers is thus articulated by the visually based, erotic public culture prevalent in early Republican Shanghai that made female sexuality a commodity for sale in theaters and mass media.

This public culture of erotica was, however, challenged by a rival intellectual ideology of social and cultural reform. During the early Republican period, a reformist discourse, supported to a large extent by the Nationalist Republican government after the May Fourth period, elevated theatrical performance to the status of art while degrading prostitution to the level of a social disgrace.[7] Within this discourse, the victimized Chinese woman, typically portrayed with bound feet and a weak body, represented the weakness and suffering of the Chinese nation, while the bodies of prostitutes and female entertainers symbolized the degradation of Chinese society. Liberating the female body therefore became a central metaphor of a Chinese revolution aimed at transforming the old society and building a wealthy and powerful modern nation.[8] The bound female body had to be emancipated in order to make healthy women, who would then plant the seeds of a healthy nation. Traditional eroticism, materialized in the bodies of prostitutes and female entertainers, in theaters and in print, had to be suppressed so that public morality could be attained.

Moreover, the theater itself became a vehicle by which enlightened intellectuals could educate the masses with messages of reform and modernity. Intellectuals in the early twentieth century experimented with spoken drama and initiated theatrical reform in Beijing opera. They scripted, directed, performed, and produced plays in both new and traditional theaters; many made a name for themselves as performing artists, the most famous being Ouyang Yuqian, Hong Shen, and Yu Shangyuan.[9] Intellectuals' participation in the theater enhanced the status of theatrical performance and exemplified the ideal of the Republican actor who not only entertained the like-minded with pure art but also enlightened the masses with messages of national salvation and social reform. Thus, although actors in the past were placed in the same debased social category as prostitutes, a reformist discourse now elevated these performers to full social status, while reducing prostitutes to the level of a social disgrace.

The actress thus occupied a particularly ambivalent position between vocational actors, who were striving to achieve higher social status as professional artists, and prostitutes, whose livelihood still depended on selling sexual services. As a commercial performer who needed to make a living, the actress had to seek favor from a general audience. Yet, at the same time, she had to reject the public's voyeuristic gaze, habitually cast on the traditional female entertainer, which dragged her down to the prostitute's level. She was caught between the conflicting demands of a public culture of erotica, which viewed her as a sexual object, and a reformist discourse that would grant her social status only if she could clearly distinguish herself from the prostitute.

Ruan Lingyu's suicide in 1935 and the media event around it illustrate the dilemma of the Republican actress and the environment Yue opera actresses were discovering. Ruan Lingyu entered China's young film industry in the mid-1920s. The daughter of a poor commoner family that had barely been able to put her through middle school, Ruan grew up with the industry under the guidance of her directors. She began her career playing prostitutes and "loose women" in films such as the 1927 *A Nominal Couple* (Guaming de fuqi), directed by Pu Wancang. During the early period, sensational themes dominated the film industry, but with the establishment of Lianhua Studio in 1929, a group of reform-oriented directors and screenwriters shifted to new themes of social-realistic critique. The film industry, as a form of modern art, was then much influenced by reformist intellectuals in the 1930s. Perhaps because of her lowly family background, Ruan Lingyu responded positively to the reform rhetoric. In 1932, she successfully played the role of a factory worker in *Three Modern Women* (Sange modeng nüxing), directed by Pu Wancang. Over the next two years, she continued to create images of new women in several other movies. Her last role, in *The New Woman* (Xin nüxing), directed by Cai Chusheng, was that of a progressive journalist who was slandered by the tabloids and ultimately committed suicide. Ruan's best performance was arguably in the 1933 film *The Goddess* (Shen nü), directed by Wu Yonggang, in which she played a young woman forced into prostitution, after being abandoned by her boyfriend and rejected by family and society, in order to provide for her son's education. Her sympathetic portrayal of the prostitute illustrated the reformist construction of "the prostitute" and presented a criticism of the social system that produced such unfortunate women.[10]

From *A Nominal Couple* to *The New Woman*, Ruan's popularity increased; her art matured, and she became a superstar in Shanghai's film culture. A pioneer in creating images of new women on-screen, Ruan began to develop the identity of the professional artist—a female artist who had emerged from the murky milieu of prostitution to become a new woman. At the same time, however, gossip about her two marriages and her ex-husband's lawsuit against her became a familiar feature in tabloid and newspaper headlines. Tabloid writers, irritated by the criticism of tabloid journalism in *The New Woman*, took revenge on Ruan by producing even more damaging gossip. Somehow, she came to be portrayed as a loose woman who lived with or abandoned men for their money, and who did not care about formally marrying either of her two husbands. These stories created a sensation among movie fans and sold well to the tabloid-reading public. Shanghai's shining star fell into moral disgrace. Certainly, her court appearance, scheduled for March 9, 1935, would have created an even bigger stir in the mass media. But in the early morning of March 8, International Women's Day, Ruan swallowed an overdose of sleeping pills. On that very day, most of which she spent barely alive in hospital emergency rooms, she had been scheduled to meet with a group of middle-school girls to talk about the meaning of Women's Day and how to become a new woman. She died later that day.

Ruan's death shocked the public. A sense of loss and sympathy for her dominated public attention and sparked a debate on who was responsible for her death. Seizing the opportunity, Shanghai's sympathetic liberal intellectuals launched an attack on the public culture of erotica, blaming a vulgar tabloid culture and old-fashioned gender biases for Ruan's death. Throughout the debate, liberal intellectuals represented Ruan Lingyu as not only a typical suffering Chinese woman victimized by a lingering feudal culture but also a talented artist who exemplified a new professionalism among actresses. "Ruan Lingyu's death was not a suicide but a murder," one writer asserted. "The gun that killed her may have been made of Zhang Damin's [her ex-husband] lawsuit and Tang Jishan's [her second husband] deception. But the ones who pulled the trigger were China's backward (not progressive) audience members, the old feudal society, and the restorationists who preached the return of the ghost of Lady Meng Jiang[11] urged concubines to follow a deceased husband by killing themselves, and cursed women who remarried."[12]

Another commentator pointed out that Ruan's death was a tragedy characteristic of the age, an age of transition. Living in this transitional age, Ruan was a victim of lingering feudal values, stigmatized by her remarriage and alleged loose lifestyle, and a victim of capitalist materialism, betrayed by her own material desires and seduced by Tang's wealth. Perhaps more important, the author went on, Ruan herself was in a process of spiritual transition. Just before her death, she had become enlightened through her participation in social-realistic films. This new consciousness created tremendous tension between old and new within her, and, according to this commentator, her weak character failed in trying to deal with the assault of external forces and influences.[13] For Lu Xun and Cai Chusheng, director of *The New Woman,* in which Ruan had played her last role, it was the "obscene tabloid press" (*huangse xiaobao*) that stigmatized Ruan in the public eye and thereby killed a defenseless woman and a brilliant artist.[14]

These comments represent the liberal intellectuals' admonition of public morality and their reconstruction of the public woman. Reformist discourse linked the tasks of delivering the actress from the sexual gaze and turning her into a new professional woman, making them into one process. Theoretically, the reformist ideology that included the actor while excluding the prostitute opened the door to full social status for the actress, as long as her cause was to change the old culture. In reality, however, only when the actress could establish herself in the public eye as no *nü xizi*, the pejorative term for the traditional female entertainer/prostitute, would she be considered worthy by the reformist cause.

The actress's social status was therefore shaped largely by her public persona, and it was in this context that *qingbai*, or purity and cleanliness, as a moral description of strict female bodily practice became central to the actress who strove for high social status. The term *qingbai* became a trope describing an actress's morality and hence signified her relation to the reformist cause. The ability of an actress to appropriate this term became crucial to her professional career as an art worker as opposed to a traditional female entertainer. Failure to appropriate this term could sometimes be fatal, as the deaths of these three actresses testify.

Building a public persona of *qingbai*, however, required the actress not only to restrict her sexual conduct in her personal life but also to perform the idea of *qingbai* onstage. Although the two were related, the stage performance had more influence in constructing an actress's public persona, probably because stage performance was the most direct form of communication between the actress and the public. Thus, while Ruan Lingyu's vulnerability to tabloid attacks on her personal life stemmed to a large extent from her earlier loose-woman roles, the re-creation of Ruan Lingyu as a model new woman and artist after her death was also grounded primarily on the pro-reform new female images she had created on-screen. Performing *qingbai* thus became the focal point at which the actress's need to build her pure and clean public persona converged with the reformist cause of remaking the theater into an educational tool for nation building and a showcase of modernity.

This complex relationship among reform discourse, a public culture of erotica, and the actress's struggle for survival and status produced a dilemma that many actresses would not survive. But this situation was also an opportunity for the actress to rise out of the social and cultural gutter. The concept of *qingbai* as a traditional moral imperative of women's bodily practice had dogged many public women, but, for others, it also provided a strategic weapon they could use to improve their social status. Performing *qingbai* onstage, in the printed media, and in real life helped the actress preempt public fantasy about her sexuality, fend off unwanted sexual advances from men, distinguish herself from traditional female entertainers or prostitutes, and ultimately join with the mainstream reformist cause.

The concept of *qingbai* indeed played a crucial role in the rise of women's Yue opera in Republican Shanghai. During the 1930s and 1940s, an axiom circulated among Yue opera actresses: "Carry yourself pure and clean; perform honestly and earnestly" (Qing qing bai bai zuoren; ren ren zhen zhen yanxi). With this axiom, in the course of two generations of Yue opera actresses, a "traditional" lowbrow form was reshaped by modern conditions, and the traditional female entertainer was transformed into the legitimate public figure of the art worker. Although this dual process took place to varying degrees in many other minor-opera forms, including Shanghai opera and Huai opera, women's Yue opera, because it was an all-woman theater and greatly popular, most clearly illustrates the actress's struggle during this period of transition and the ways in which it informed the re-formation of modern Shanghai's public culture.

Yue Opera Actresses in the 1930s

In the 1930s, Yue opera actresses appeared to many as young peasant girls performing curious little shows to entertain a carefree metropolitan audience. The opera was becoming increasingly popular, especially as more women began to attend, but Yue opera's status did not compare to that of Beijing opera and spoken drama. Beijing opera was honored in reformist discourse as the national opera that symbolized a national cultural heritage.[15] Its patrons were largely members of elites, including government officials, military officers, businessmen, and intellectuals, while the famous Beijing opera stars, such as Mei Lanfang and Zhou Xinfang, were no longer mere actors in the traditional meaning of the word. These stars were enthroned as "artists," and they were also capitalists, in the sense that both owned their own companies; Zhou also held a long-term lease on one of the best theaters in Shanghai, the Grand Golden Theater (Huangjin Daxiyuan). Spoken drama was basically a theater by and for intellectuals. Women's Yue opera, in contrast, a theater by women and increasingly for women, was of marginal significance to male elites and was neglected by mainstream newspapers, intellectuals, and art critics.

The comparative status of the performers was similarly unbalanced. Yue opera's women were, in the eyes of the cultural elite, not artists but traditional entertainers earning a living. Most women's Yue opera actresses started in their early teens as apprentices at a training school.[16] During the apprenticeship, they received only meager stipends in addition to room and board. At the end of their apprenticeships, the school often turned into a company, and the girls became employees of the company owner. The owner paid the actresses small salaries and pocketed whatever fees he received from contracting with theaters in Shanghai and Zhejiang for performances. Toward the end of the 1930s, as large numbers of actresses emerged from training schools and women's Yue opera became a regular feature in theaters everywhere in the region, theater owners began to contract directly with actresses, replacing company owners and taking on the role of bosses. The traditional "company system" (*xiban*) was replaced by a system in which the theater owner took control of his own performing team by contracting with individual actresses for fixed salaries over a half-year period. The company was therefore no longer a financially independent entity but was on the theater owner's payroll.[17] Companies were organized around a few leading actresses, by the stars or by the theater boss, but few actresses had their own theaters and none owned her own company.[18]

Earning a livelihood was hard work for most Yue opera actresses, perhaps harder than for actors in Beijing opera and other traditional major operas. For one thing, unlike many Beijing opera actors, who inherited family traditions or had relatives in the vocation, most Yue opera actresses came from poor peasant families and had few family connections in opera circles. As first-generation immigrants from the countryside of Shengxian, Yue opera actresses also lacked family support in the metropolis. Most of them scraped by on low salaries, sending the little they could save back to their families in Shengxian. Those who managed to put together sizable savings usually brought their families—parents, siblings, and close relatives—to Shanghai. In order to provide for their families, they often pushed themselves to the limit. Yue opera theater, unlike Beijing opera, which usually had only night shows, offered matinee as well as evening performances every day, and each show regularly lasted three or four hours. This put actresses on a tight schedule and left them little time for other activities, such as going to night school or socializing. The majority of actresses were illiterate, while the most schooled among them could be considered only semiliterate (though many eventually learned enough to do some simple reading and writing).[19] Many actresses slept backstage in the theater for years after they arrived in Shanghai, in part to save rent but also because they generally did not know anyone who could take them in.[20]

This lack of social support networks, shortage of economic resources, and low literacy severely limited actresses' cultural and political horizons and left them with little power to negotiate with various social elements, such as theater bosses, hooligans, and tabloid reporters. Theater bosses, many of whom had ties to secret societies or were local bullies themselves, were the most powerful controlling element in an actress's life. Often, actresses were more than employees to their bosses; their bodies and private lives might also be subject to the control of these men. It was not uncommon for a theater boss to take a wife or a concubine from among the actresses he employed. Given the extremely imbalanced power relations between the boss and his female employees, a boss's control over a famous actress's sexuality often meant virtual ownership of her person and the opportunity to exploit her talent and labor for economic gain. An actress could be very popular among audience members, therefore, but still have no social status and little control over her economic and personal situations. Overwork and pressure often led to illness. The death of Ma Zhanghua is only one example among many.

Among the most important and worrisome matters for an actress was marriage. For a woman in traditional society, marriage was the most important event in her life, because the social system made her reliant on her husband and sons for her support and comfort. While this situation had recently begun to change during the Republican period, with the slow emergence of professional and working women, marriage was still more important than a career for most women, socially, psychologically, and practically. The Republican actress, one of these new professional women, enjoyed economic independence to varying degrees. This independence, however, was compromised by the lingering public culture of erotica, in which the voyeuristic gaze favored young female bodies, effectively making a performing career a young woman's privilege and a transitional stage that would invariably end with marriage. Marriage was also important because it gave the actress standing in social and familial institutions, redeeming her from her dubious status as a female entertainer. For all these reasons, getting married and marrying well when still young were priorities for most actresses. Ordinary actresses often found spouses among the male staff members of their company or opera circle, while popular actresses often became concubines of rich men, a traditional practice still common during the early Republican period. Yet, as the Republican era gender ideology slowly changed the social practice of marriage, many Yue opera actresses tried to maintain their financial vitality and shunned the status of the concubine. Popular Yue opera actresses who married during the 1940s, including Yao Shuijuan, Xiao-Bai Yumei, and Ma Zhanghua, made a point of not becoming the secondary wives of rich men. Both Yao and Xiao-Bai, as well as many other popular actresses, suffered varying degrees of abuse and exploitation at the hands of their husbands. Ma died young, and Yao and Xiao-Bai had unhappy married lives and raised their children without the presence of, or help from, their husbands.[21] Despite their financial comfort, these actresses suffered in their personal lives, unable to fully overcome the stigma attached to women entertainers that left them vulnerable to scorn and abuse from their often unruly and unreformed husbands.

The public image of Yue opera actresses was also unflattering. Portrayals of actresses as sexual beings subject to the whims of powerful men were common in contemporary popular literature. One such example is the character Shen Fengxi in Zhang Hengshui's novel *Fate in Tears and Laughter*, published in 1929. In this novel, a *dagu* (a form of story-singing in the Beijing area) singer, Shen Fengxi, is forced to become the concubine of a warlord, who tortures her until she goes insane and then abandons her. In addition, as the fates of Ruan Lingyu, Ma Zhanghua, and Xiao Dangui testify, real-life actresses also faced personal tragedies, which became fodder for literary portrayal and public gossip that further debased the image of the actress in the public eye.

The popularity of Yue opera and its actresses, therefore, appears in sharp contrast to their marginal social status. Insightful contemporaries were aware of this contradiction. In his comments on Ruan Lingyu's death, Lu Xun remarked that actresses were "very famous but had no power" in the face of slander and the tabloids.[22] Ma Zhanghua's death in 1942 only made her colleagues more acutely aware of their situation. A talented Yue opera actress who specialized in young male roles, Ma was on the fast track to fame after coming to Shanghai in the mid-1930s. Her handsome appearance, beautiful voice, and articulate performances quickly made her the leading actress at the Dalai Theater. In 1941, defying the will of her boss Lu Gendi, Ma married the son of one of her fans, a certain Mrs. Bao, and retired from the Dalai Theater. Ma's father-in-law, a businessman, soon organized a company for her, and she staged a few successful performances at the Tianxing Theater. Angered by the loss of his main source of revenue and the object of his sexual desire, Lu set out to destroy Ma's good name. He sent hateful letters to the Bao family and paid tabloids to slander Ma by fabricating stories about her having sexual relations with men prior to her marriage. Ma was deeply hurt but had no way of retaliating. Eleven months after her marriage, Ma died of tuberculosis. She was twenty-one years old. Although a causal connection between Ma's illness and her maltreatment by Lu was never clearly established, it was nevertheless popularly assumed.[23]

Ma's death, which caused a public scandal, saddened her colleagues and triggered Yue opera reforms led by Yuan Xuefen, Ma's stage partner at the Dalai Theater and one of the more self-aware and autonomous personalities among Yue opera actresses. Born in 1922, Yuan was the eldest child of a rural family in Shengxian. The family lived off the father's meager income as a primary-school teacher for a few years, but the father lost his livelihood when the Great Depression hit Shengxian's sericulture economy. Since the family did not have a surviving son, Yuan was expected to help the family as a son would. Her father thus took her to the school where he taught and made her study for a couple of years, preparing her for work in a silk factory in Shanghai. The young Yuan Xuefen, however, loved to sing opera and joined a girls' opera school at age eleven on her own initiative. Yuan's father objected, based on traditional views against female performers, but her mother backed her, hoping Yuan would eventually bring some cash income to the family. Yuan did better. After her success in Shanghai, she provided for the whole family back in Shengxian and properly buried her father when he died of lung disease in 1942. She then moved her mother and sisters to Shanghai to live with her and provided for her sisters' education and marriage expenses. The school Yuan joined in 1933 was called the Four Seasons Company (Sijichun Ban), and Yuan's basic literacy distinguished her among her classmates. Then, in 1938, Yuan came to Shanghai, her school having become a company, and performed as the second leading actress at the Dalai Theater. From 1938 to 1941, Yuan collaborated with the leading actress Ma Zhanghua in many plays on the Dalai stage.

Yuan practiced the axiom "Carry yourself pure and clean; perform honestly and earnestly." While Ma played amorous young male roles, Yuan refused to play loose women and consistently portrayed morally restrained maidens. In real life, Yuan joined a religious sect and was a declared vegetarian and celibate in order to avoid unwanted social and personal engagement. Ma's conflict with Lu and her subsequent death probably shocked Yuan more than any other Yue opera actress, as she had witnessed Ma's ill-fated attempt to control her sexuality, private life, and finances.[24] Eventually, it became clear to Yuan that actresses' ambiguous social status made them vulnerable to economic and sexual exploitation, and that this ambiguity was closely related to the low status of their opera, something for which they were partially responsible as purveyors of cheap eroticism. Yuan recalled:

> Everyone who is familiar with history knows that Yue opera at the time had no status to speak of . . . and could not claim to be decent entertainment let alone to have any positive social utility. Even in a well-developed traditional play such as *The Butterfly Lovers*, beautiful folklore was riddled with all kinds of feudal superstitions and fatalist trash. . . . There was also a lot of erotic material in the lyrics that I felt uncomfortable singing. In the widely circulated version of the story, a preponderance of dross overshadowed the essence. As early as the late 1930s, when Ma Zhanghua and I were stage partners, we agreed not to sing these obscene lyrics and did a preliminary cleanup of the play. . . . At the time, I could claim no enlightenment but simply felt deeply hurt having to put on a performance like this. It was humiliating to the actresses. If it was only for the sake of making a living, then

there were a lot of other jobs one could choose! This was one of the reasons why I felt reform was absolutely necessary.[25]

This passage speaks of the beginning of a historical process in which a generation of young Yue opera actresses took control of their lives and careers. By the late 1930s, as they established their star status, Ma and Yuan began to rebel against what they deemed to be humiliating performances, and in 1942, Yuan turned this spontaneous resistance into self-conscious theatrical reforms.

Like many other minor operas of the period, Yue opera production was rough around the edges, and its content was old-fashioned, replete with lighthearted flirtations and crude sexual jokes. The theater itself was a noisy place, and while actresses performed onstage, chaos unfolded in front of them. The audience chatted, laughed, and told jokes; waiters hurried about serving tea; and hot wet towels were tossed through the air. These familiar aspects of theater life now made Yuan uncomfortable, especially as she became aware of ongoing trends in theatrical reform and the connection between the low social status of actresses and the practices of their theater. In her memoir, Yuan wrote about her experiences in these few years leading to her decision on Yue opera reform in 1942. Of Shanghai in 1938, she recalled:

> The performances on the stage were nonsensical, badly organized, and without fixed scripts, while the atmosphere in the audience hall and backstage was simply foul. Patrons flattering their favorite actresses was a prevalent practice, and [Yue opera] company bosses regularly profited by making actresses perform at banquets and private homes. I regretted that I had stumbled into the wrong profession when I was young and naive, but it was very difficult to go back to school and change my career. Father was dying of lung disease, and the responsibility of my family's livelihood was so heavy that I had no choice but continued to perform while enduring great pain and self-sacrifice. In order to maintain a quiet and peaceful life, I became a Buddhist vegetarian and shunned social life. I thereafter changed from a merry and lively girl to a quiet person who paid attention only to the safeguarding of her own moral standard. . . . But bad news kept coming. First, talented Ma Zhanghua had to leave the Dalai Theater and stopped performing with me; then her separate performances lacked [personnel] support; finally, suffering from poisonous slanders, she fell ill and died in melancholy and bitterness. She was only twenty-one! When the bad news came, I was shocked,

sad, and full of bitter hatred! I was so angry and upset about Ma Zhanghua dying uncleared of a false charge that I suddenly began to vomit blood. At the same time, I could no longer stand the theater and company bosses and my uncle "protector"—all of them disregarded my illness and forced me to continue performing. I then asked a fellow townsman Liu Baoxiang to accompany me and traveled back home.[26]

While the recollection may have been neatened by the passage of time, and influenced by the socialist ideology that guided Yuan's career after 1949, it indicates many tensions she felt at the time. At home, Yuan rested for about half a year and kept her father company in his last days. When she returned to Shanghai, Yuan declared her intention to reform the Yue opera theater:

> The bosses who invited me [to perform] had ideas that were very different from mine. They would consider nothing but their profit. The most important question for me was, however, what had I gained in the past eight years of performing with the opera school/company? All these meaningless performances of nonsensical stories had given me nothing but hatred and loathing of the backward and dark institution. I therefore determined to leave the opera school/company and to start on a new path that would change my personal life and the destiny of the genre.[27]

Love Drama and the Rise of Women's Yue Opera

The reforms Yuan Xuefen inaugurated in 1942 should be viewed as a phase in an ongoing urban transformation of Yue opera that centered on two major tasks. The first was to cleanse Yue opera of the lower-class crude eroticism that had always been part of the minor-opera tradition and to replace it with a mode of intensified love drama prevalent in Republican Shanghai's popular literature. The second task, discussed in the next section, was to enhance the production values of Yue opera performances and remake a shabby peasant form into a dazzling urban spectacle.

Ridding Yue opera of the peasant eroticism typical of minor operas was a prerequisite to successful performing careers in urban centers. Performers not only were under pressure to capitulate to the elite demand for moral sanitization but were also seeking measures by which to cater to the tastes of an emerging urban middle-class audience, of which women composed the fastest-growing sector.

Historically, crude sexual themes, performed using a combination of sexually explicit lyrics and gestures, had been a standard feature of male-centered minor operas. In catering to a lower-class male audience in rural gambling halls and teahouses, the female body was often described at length, part by part, creating a visual image of a composite sexualized body. Examples of such eroticism are abundant in minor-opera repertoires. One piece of "Ningbo story-singing" (*Ningbo tanhuang*), predecessor of Ningbo opera, *Floating Boat* (Danghu chuan), describes a young man's overnight boat ride from Changshu to Suzhou, Jiangsu. Along the way, the young man and the two sisters who operate the boat each sing a folk song. The young man's song, "Eighteen Caresses" (Shiba mo), sung in plain local colloquial, describes a woman's body from head to toe, following the movements of a man's hand and emphasizing sexual organs.[28] Other examples are found in such works as *Little Cowherd* (Xiao fangniu), *Selling Coal* (Mai qingtan), and *Selling Straw Cradles* (Mai caotun), titles from the repertoires of various local minor operas and their story-singing predecessors. Crude eroticism featured not only in short pieces about peasant life but also in more developed narratives, such as *He Wenxiu* (He Wenxiu), *A Pair of Phoenix Jade Clasps* (Shuang zhufeng), and early versions of *The Butterfly Lovers*.[29]

Evidence shows that sexually explicit performances were regular features of minor operas during the 1920s and 1930s, and both actors and actresses in Shengxian opera performed sexual scenes in Shanghai as well as in towns and villages in Zhejiang. One good example is a scene from *Marriage as a Result of Three Smiles* (Sanxiao yinyuan), performed by women's Shengxian opera in Shanghai in the 1930s. Zhou, a young scholar disguised in women's dress, plays a trick on a young mistress and, successfully passing himself off as a woman, is allowed to sleep with her for the night. Zhou then delivers the following lines in speech and song:

> [Speech] Well, well, well. The young mistress has fallen sound asleep. Let me feel her body all over.
>
> [Song] One hand opens the blue cotton bed curtain, two eyes steal a look at the girl's pretty face; gently feeling her body inside three layers of quilts, from four directions to touch her breasts, five fingers reach her privates. Ya! So frightened am I that I lose control over my six senses, trembling as if I have gone mad.
>
> [Speech] Ah ya ya! Feeling my way around, I checked her privates for urine. Ha, ha, ha! Let me compose a poem: This part is truly amazing. Two

peaks on both sides of a little stream, spring water dripping from the inside of the cavity, lush grass outside the door. There is water but no fish; there is no wood, but the bird can rest. Even if you spend a thousand pounds of gold, it is not easy to get; many people lose their minds for it.[30]

Such passages were scattered throughout the pages of the cheap lyric books and scripts that recorded established stage performances.[31]

Educated men's bias against this kind of unrefined eroticism was common at the time. One contemporary commentator had this to say about Yuyao opera, a notoriously erotic minor opera developed a little earlier than Shengxian opera in the same region:

> Yuyao opera is the most spineless of all Shaoxing operas,[32] for its lyrics are the most crude, vulgar, and disgusting of them all. It does not care about costumes or makeup, let alone ideas, and it boasts no acting skills. Officials constantly ban it, but they cannot possibly eliminate it. The opera is greatly popular among the lower orders of society. They sing in small teahouses in poor parts of the countryside and remote areas and charge very little, almost nothing. After a whole day of hard labor, country bumpkins take it as their chosen form of entertainment and crowd teahouses to see it. The performers are mostly unemployed wanderers. The opera corrupts public morals beyond our imagination.[33]

Cleansing itself of crude eroticism was only the first step taken by any minor opera aspiring to raise its status in the urban market. The larger question was one of stylistic redefinition, or how to turn minor opera's plain, rough style into sophisticated expressions of love and desire that would appeal to urban tastes. Faced with this challenge, the male and female troupes of Shengxian opera departed, and their respective choices for achieving artistic sophistication resulted in the decline of all-male and the rise of all-female troupes.[34] Male Shengxian opera, upon entering Shanghai, followed the model of major operas, emulating the highly stylized movements of Beijing opera and Shaoxing major opera while copying their costumes and stage designs (see fig. 2.1). As one contemporary reviewer observed: "I have also seen *didu* opera performed by male actors. It seems as if actors like Wei Meiduo and Ma Chaoshui sing a little faster than is done in women's *didu* opera. The play they put onstage, the performance, and the stage effect look very much like that of Shanghai-style [Haipai] Beijing opera. I am

2.1 Stage photo of the all-male Shengxian opera *The King of Zhou and His Favorite Concubine, Daji* (Zhou Wang yu Daji), with Ye Qinfang as Daji (left) and Tang Degui as the King of Zhou, Shanghai, 1920s. In style, the all-male Shengxian opera is similar to Beijing opera but quite different from women's Shengxian opera, which developed in the ensuing decades. (*Shanghai Yueju zhi* 1997)

afraid that this will shake the very foundations of *didu* opera."[35] In hindsight, it is apparent that male Shengxian opera was going against the current of change, but at the time, the actors had few choices available to them, as major operas, especially Beijing opera, represented the most sophisticated forms of opera at a time when new forms had not yet been established. Moreover, male actors of minor operas looked to major operas for inspiration, because major-opera troupes also consisted mainly of male actors, having only recently admitted a few actresses. The problem was that the artistic style of major opera did not fit well with the content of minor opera. The highly stylized movements of Beijing opera, which portrayed the ritualistic and reserved manner of generals and high officials, were not effective when used to express passionate love by the young lovers featured in minor opera.

The all-female troupes, on the contrary, developed a new feminine mode of expressing sexual themes. Two mutually reinforcing factors affected the course of women's Yue opera in the late 1930s: changes in the composition of opera audiences and the maturation of all-female theater. The audience for Yue opera changed from a lower-class, male majority to one anchored in a growing core of upper- and middle-class women. While men of letters despised lower-class eroticism, educated women probably felt at least uncomfortable with the ways in which minor opera objectified the female body. Two points need to be made in analyzing the tastes of Shanghai's middle-class women audiences. First, the exploration of sexual and love relations in the framework of marriage and family proved more attractive for women, especially middle- and upper-class women, because women's sexuality had historically been constructed within the confined domestic settings of traditional patriarchal society. They could not, for example, take seriously a sexual encounter such as the one described in *Floating Boat* because it is so far outside the family and marriage context. In fact, the genre, Ningbo story-singing, which featured such pieces, was notorious for its low taste and was never popular among Shanghai's middle-class women audiences. In contrast, the play *Marriage as a Result of Three Smiles* was a popular women's Yue opera play largely because the sexual scenes are grounded in a complicated narrative of the traditional scholar-beauty love story that ends with happy marriage. Second, explicit sexual scenes, even those presented in the context of love stories, had to be replaced with more refined expressions of love and desire. Modern, educated middle-class women, especially those in Shanghai, the modern metropolis and center for cultural production and consumption, were trained by popular literature and Hollywood movies to appreciate romantic love and artful expressions of sexual desire.[36]

The rapidly maturing all-female theater met the demands of this new audience. Actresses, who had long suffered from traditional biases against women entertainers and the objectification of their bodies by the male erotic gaze, came to identify the sexual obscenities they had been performing as a major source of their own social degradation. As a single-gender theater, it was easier for women's Yue opera to replace crude, poorly integrated sexual jokes and gestures with a more sentimental form of expression capable of conveying love and passion, as well as erotic desire, as part of the narrative of marriage and family. The contemporary commentator Xiao Wo compared the different acting styles of women's Yue opera and Beijing opera:

> With regard to singing, *didu* opera differs from Beijing opera. In Beijing opera, different voices are strictly defined for use by different roles, and all the actors who specialize in a particular role sing in the same voice. In *didu* opera, actresses sing with their own natural voices and thereby avoid such common drawbacks as exaggeration, overacting, and fabrication. On the Yue opera stage, there is nothing but self-expression of one's true nature, and the performers have freed themselves of the shackles of traditional artificial movements and singing styles.[37]

Zhang Linghui, a Zhejiang native who moved to Taiwan with the Nationalist government in 1949, recalled that, in the late 1930s and early 1940s, major women's Yue opera companies in Shanghai all trained in Zhejiang and periodically returned there to perform after settling in Shanghai. In light of the frequent interactions between Yue opera troupes in Zhejiang and Shanghai, Zhang's observation of women's Yue opera performances in the Zhejiang countryside should also hold true for women's Yue opera in Shanghai:

> Because it did not represent real life, Chinese opera often did scant work in portraying the details of human feelings. When a character was supposed to cry, for example, the actor would simply raise his arm and put his sleeve in front of his eyes a few times, indicating weeping. All local operas acted in this manner. When I saw Yue opera in the countryside, however, I found that the actresses were all able to put themselves into the shoes of the characters they were playing and convey the characters' inner feelings. In the case of a tragedy, they often performed the fictional plots with their own

true feelings and cried with abundant tears flowing down their cheeks, making the scene virtually real. Their earnest performances often won the hearts of rural women and made them cry along with the characters onstage.[38]

Feature films, especially Hollywood films, had much impact on minor operas in search of their own acting style, different from that of the major operas. Scenes common in these films—a handsome young man holding hands with, hugging, or kissing a pretty young woman, lovers exchanging affectionate looks—exemplified natural expressions of passion and intimacy to minor-opera performers as well as to Shanghai's romance-loving audiences.

The opera stage was, however, very different from the movie screen. It is one thing to perform before the camera, and it is another to perform passionate love before a live audience. It would indeed have been too embarrassingly real for both performers and audience members in a society in which free expression of passion and intimacy between lovers was more an ideal than a reality for most people. This gap between what people liked to see and what they could actually do in real life gave women's Yue opera a tremendous advantage over other operas with both male and female performers, because expressions of intimacy between women were commonly displayed in public. As an all-female theater, Yue opera could use a naturalistic acting mode and thereby be more expressive when performing intimacy and passion in love melodramas, because everyone in the theater knew that the performers were women (see fig. 2.2). The contemporary Yue opera critic Cai Yuying explained:

> Normally there is nothing surprising about men and women performing together onstage. But men and women still do not socialize openly in the countryside. As young girls in Shaoxing are shy when encountering [male] strangers, it is naturally impossible for them to perform with actors onstage. Even when they do, they merely perform their duty in a perfunctory manner.
>
> The essence of drama lies in the convergence of the performers and the roles they play. The story is fictional, but the performance has to be lifelike—that is what makes for an excellent show. The acting seems more earnest and real in all-male or all-female theaters. The plot almost always falls apart when men and women perform together. For the actress certainly wants to avoid getting too close to the actor she is performing with, and the actor is also too restrained by various considerations to guarantee a well-acted play. In the case of romantic love stories, the passion felt by the lovers is reflected in the story

2.2 Actresses Xu Yulan (left) and Fu Quanxiang in *Gold and Beauty* (Huangjin yu meiren), 1944. The display of intimacy between heterosexual lovers was tolerated in women's Yue opera but would have been scandalous in gender-straight theaters in Republican Shanghai. (*Shanghai Yueju zhi* 1997)

> line through flirtation, elopement, or sexual intercourse and has to be adequately performed in order to bring the play to a climactic ending. Look at the performance put on by gender-straight theaters: actors and actresses are indifferent, listless, and merely muddle through the show. That is why I always oppose gender-straight theaters. It is not that I am old-fashioned, but rather that the final product does not encourage gender-straight performances.[39]

Veteran Yue opera actresses support Cai's remarks. When asked why all-female Yue opera became more popular than gender-straight theaters, actresses who performed during that period, such as Xiao-Bai Yumei, Fu Quanxiang, and Xu Yulan, all gave similar answers: In a women's theater, they could act more naturally and passionately without restraint, while it was awkward to do so with male actors.[40]

Thus, under the elite directive to cleanse traditional sexual "obscenity" from minor operas, and in order to meet the demand of a changing urban opera constituency that increasingly consisted of upper- and middle-class female patrons, the all-female Yue opera developed a new mode of acting that replaced old-fashioned, crude sexual scenes with refined, sentimental expressions of love and desire.

Modernity as Respectability: The Making of New Yue Opera

If being an all-female theater gave Yue opera a natural advantage in performing the modern drama of love and desire, then it was the conscious reform efforts of Yue opera actresses in the late 1930s and 1940s that fully developed the potential of women's Yue opera and transformed it into a truly modern master theater of love drama. Before Yuan Xuefen initiated her reforms, leading actresses Yao Shuijuan and Xiao Dangui had already begun theirs. In 1938, Yao Shuijuan invited Fan Li, an unemployed former editor for *Dagong Daily* (Dagong bao), a mainstream newspaper, to create new plays for her. Around the same time, Xiao Dangui invited Wen Zhong, who had had a career in civil drama, to be her playwright.[41] Both actresses also experimented with the modern stagecraft of film and spoken drama. Yuan's reforms, however, consisted of a more conscious effort to make Yue opera into a meaningful modern theater, like spoken drama, and to modernize the Yue opera institution by establishing the opera's artistic staff.

More clearly than the reforms of Yao Shuijuan and Xiao Dangui, those of Yuan Xuefen took spoken drama as its model, as Yuan considered it the most respected theater in town.

> I went to see spoken drama and felt totally refreshed. First, the new plays: it was quite moving to see progressive spoken-drama workers put on educational, patriotic plays such as *Wen Tianxiang* [Wen Tianxiang], *Ge Nenniang* [Ge Nenniang], and *The Spirit of the Revolutionaries* [Dangren hun]. Second, the new forms: spoken drama used complete scripts, regulated rehearsals, realistic and earnest acting, and modern stage sets. All these revealed a new

horizon to me, a person who lived in isolation, as if an oasis suddenly appeared in the desert.[42]

Yuan had attended several spoken-drama shows, including *Wen Tianxiang*, a patriotic play about the great general of the Southern Song dynasty who fought heroically against invading barbarians. The play was staged a few months before the Japanese entered "island" Shanghai at the end of 1941, a heroic act given that the territory had been at the mercy of surrounding Japanese troops long before the actual takeover. Spoken drama appeared to Yuan to be a much more disciplined theater, as it produced progressive plays, its stage sets were realistic, its directors exercised control over all details of the production, its actors and actresses were serious performers, its audience was quiet and respectful, and it was devoid of obscenity and lighthearted flirtation. In short, the atmosphere in spoken-drama theater, in contrast to the chaotic situation in traditional theaters, commanded respect. Spoken drama had a small audience, but it had the social and cultural status Yuan hoped to bring to Yue opera and its actresses.[43]

Using her market power, Yuan cut a new contract with Lu Gendi, the owner of the Dalai Theater, and began to implement her reforms in late 1942. Since Yuan was one of the most popular Yue opera actresses, theater owners competed for her employment, and she agreed to return to the Dalai Theater only when Lu consented to her reform plan. Lu and other old-style theater owners had no interest in any substantial reforms, as they were content with Yue opera's current configuration, which placed them at the top of the system and made them the largest beneficiaries of the theater's popularity. As a local strongman, Lu also had little appreciation for the reformist rhetoric that characterized people like himself as "feudal" elements and saw reform as a threat to his power. But since he relied on Yuan Xuefen to bring in the profits, he compromised.[44]

Yuan's aim was to reinvent Yue opera as a serious modern art form, along the model of spoken drama. Her reforms were twofold—to create socially redeeming content centering on, if not limited to, anti-feudal love stories and to give the Yue opera stage a fresh appearance.

She began with three main changes. The first was to reorganize the structure of the theater and its backstage. During the nineteenth century, large teahouses had been the traditional venues for opera; they served a rich and powerful male audience who used the performances as occasions to socialize over food and drink. The traditional teahouse featured a three-dimensional stage extending outward into the audience's seats, which were set around tables, and interactions flowed in all directions on and off the stage. During the early Republican period, under the influence of various Western-informed theatrical reforms, large teahouses either closed down or restructured themselves in accord with Western-style theater forms; at the same time, new theaters were built to screen films and stage spoken dramas as well as native operas from the 1920s onward.[45] Designed to focus attention on the performance, new theaters featured a framelike stage and audience seats facing the stage in rows that discouraged disruption of, and distraction from viewing, the performance. These new structural features of theater design met with popular resistance, however, as native-opera actors continued to joke with the audience, while the audience chatted freely during the performance, and actors and non-actors alike streamed freely in and out of the backstage area during the performance. Theater owners set up tables in front of the first row of seats and attached wooden plates for teacups and towels to the backs of the seats.[46] In such a traditional theater setting, the performance was hardly the center of attention but only one of many things going on in the theater. For Yuan Xuefen, there would be no dignity for Yue opera and its actresses so long as they performed in such environments. She decided, therefore, that no one other than actresses and staff were to be allowed backstage during the performance, and the theater was to stop serving tea and distributing hot towels in the middle of a show.

Yuan's second change was to put the company in control of production and programming; the theater owner was not to intervene so long as ticket sales stayed high. The third was to hire literary men as directors and playwrights for the company. Lu agreed to the first two changes but refused to pay for directors, playwrights, or stage supervisors. From Lu's viewpoint, it was the stars that brought in the audience and there was no need for extra personnel. Yuan was determined, however, and decided to donate a large portion of her own monthly salary to pay for these men, whom Lu considered extra but Yuan considered essential.[47]

The establishment of a "staff" (*juwu bu*) composed of literary men was a crucial step toward modernizing the institution of Yue opera—its internal structure, production process, and productions. The staff served as an informal headquarters for Yue opera reform. Fan Ruijuan, a leading young male impersonator and Yuan Xuefen's stage partner, recalled the early reform period:

> During the 1940s, Yuan Xuefen initiated Yue opera reform and recruited many men of letters, the new-art workers [*xinwenyi gongzuozhe*]. These men brought new ideas and new knowledge to local opera. Their involvement

> greatly helped the reforms and pushed Yue opera into rapid development. . . . At that time, we actresses were mostly young girls from poor peasant families, and our literacy level was low. So we had great respect for the cultured people in the staff. We addressed them as "teacher" [*xiansheng*] and referred to the staff collectively as the "headquarters" of reform.[48]

Most staff members were drawn from the ranks of the so-called new-art youths (*xinwenyi qingnian*)—young high-school and college graduates, mostly from lower-middle-class families, who were deeply influenced by the May Fourth New Culture and New Literature movements and who held a left-leaning liberal outlook. They were fascinated with motion pictures and actively participated in amateur spoken drama, but they were also exposed to traditional Chinese forms, such as Beijing opera. When leading intellectuals and activists left the falling city before the outbreak of the Pacific War at the end of 1941, these talented petty intellectuals and veterans of the amateur scene, lacking the financial means and personal connections to flee, stayed behind and became invaluable resources for Yue opera reform. During the heyday of the amateur spoken-drama movement, from 1937 to 1941, patriotic young intellectuals and students took amateur spoken drama to the streets in an effort to mobilize the general population for national resistance.[49] Their involvement, both as actors and as audience members, in no small part created the spoken-drama boom. After the fall of "island" Shanghai, however, the spoken-drama mass movement in Shanghai came to a halt, and only a few professional spoken-drama companies were able to survive on commercial performances.[50] This initial contraction of the reach of spoken drama left many spoken-drama veterans unemployed and available to participate in Yue opera and other minor operas as directors, scriptwriters, and stage designers. They thus became a vital link between lowbrow operas and the New Culture theatrical reforms.

Han Yi (b. 1922) was among the first members of Yuan Xuefen's new staff.[51] His maternal grandfather, Ma Jianzhong, was the author of China's first modern grammar book, *Grammatical Dictionary by Mr. Ma* (Ma shi wentong), and a member of Prime Minister Li Hongzhang's staff. By the 1930s, however, the family had lost all its property, with the exception of some small estates in nearby Kunshan County. When Han's parents died in 1937, his uncle absconded with what remained of the family property, and Han took an apprenticeship with the British-American Tobacco Company, where his father had worked. He joined a friendship association organized by underground Communist Party members seeking to involve young employees in the anti-Japan amateur spoken-drama movement. When the Japanese took over the company after the outbreak of the Pacific War, Han refused to remain and found a job as a makeup technician for a spoken-drama company, earning a small monthly salary of twenty to thirty yuan. He soon moved to Yuan's company when she offered him a monthly salary of more than fifty yuan. "To make a living was the first concern, and personal interest was the second reason," Han remarked, explaining why he became interested in Yue opera, a lowbrow women's theater that young literary men like himself generally looked down upon.

As Yuan initiated her reforms, literary men such as Han Yi became her indispensable lieutenants. "Yuan insisted on reform, and we pushed the transformation," Han stated. The main challenge of the reforms was, according to Han, to "modernize" the art of Yue opera; cleansing Yue opera of its feudal content had become such a natural task that it no longer required special deliberation. His first artistic reform was to replace the traditional water-based makeup, which tends to be compromised by sweat and tears, with Western-style waterproof oil-based makeup. Then, Han Yi and his colleagues studied the history of clothing and designed different costumes and hairstyles for characters of different dynasties. As both director and stage designer, Han Yi was most noted for his inventive use of small devices influenced by various Western aesthetic styles, which created a setting and atmosphere that highlighted rather than overshadowed an actress's performance. In *Sister Xianglin* (Xianglin sao), of 1946, for example, Han created a small half-bridge with an inclining streetlight standing next to it against the backdrop of a blue sky—a typical Shaoxing street setting within which the tragedy of Xianglin's widow reaches its conclusion. Han's designs were described variously as "novel and pretty," "fresh and imaginative," and possessing "a special beauty."[52]

Remarkably, most of the actresses and staff members involved in the reform process were young people around twenty years of age. "Big brother" Lü Zhong was only about twenty-six. It was a youthful group, full of energy, creativity, and a sense of mission. A cartoon appearing in a 1946 publication commemorating the founding of the Xuesheng Company, led by Yuan Xuefen, depicted the relationship between the star actresses and the new staff in terms familiar to urban youth: the cartoon, titled "Snow White and the Seven Dwarfs," shows Yuan Xuefen singing atop seven dwarfs—the seven core staff members (see fig. 2.3). Among the seven was Cheng Rong (b. 1922), the only woman playwright in the company. A high-school graduate, Cheng was the daughter of a lower-middle-class family from Ningbo.

Her father was a small merchant, and her mother, a housewife, loved Beijing opera and Yue opera. When Cheng was young, her mother often took her to Yue opera performances because the tickets were cheaper and admission was free for small children. In middle school and, later, in women's normal school (the equivalent of high school), Cheng read Lu Xun, Guo Moruo, Ba Jin, and other leading writers of the New Literature, but she also loved classical poems and prose as well as works in translation by well-known Russian and Soviet writers. She became a fan of spoken drama, participated in amateur performances, and stopped going to see Yue opera. For a New Literature student like Cheng, Yue opera appeared vulgar, old-fashioned, and hopelessly meaningless in content; it was remote from the ideals of China's progressive New Culture. After graduating, she took a teaching position in a primary school to support herself while attending Daxia University's night school, and eventually, her love of traditional opera and classical literature drew her back to Yue opera. Cheng and her mother once attended a show by Yuan Xuefen and were greatly impressed. Cheng became a great admirer of Yuan and in 1944 joined Yuan's company to become the first woman scriptwriter in Yue opera. In Cheng's eyes, Yuan Xuefen was no ordinary female entertainer. Unlike other Yue opera actresses, she asserted, Yuan was more like a female student who loved to read and keep company with female students, and her performance was earnest and socially meaningful.[53]

The company's only other female staff member, not pictured in the cartoon, was the radio announcer Chen Shulian (1921–2000). Chen's family was originally from Shaoxing prefecture, but Chen was born in Huzhou, which is also in Zhejiang. After high school, she became a primary-school teacher and later a radio announcer at the Soviet Union Radio Station (Sulian Diantai) in 1943.[54] In 1944, she met Yuan Xuefen when the actress came to the station for a radio program and immediately befriended her. While Chen still worked full-time at the radio station, Yuan enlisted her as a member of the Xuesheng Company, the first radio announcer in Yue opera. Each day, Chen hosted Yuan and other actresses on her radio program, broadcasting live from the theater or introducing new plays to the radio audience. Through her familiar voice and intimate approach, the audience was introduced to the story lines, music, and songs of new plays while learning about the technical innovations used in the staging. Listeners could also call in to comment, request a song, or reserve tickets. Chen's radio program became very popular among opera fans and provided an important new channel of communication between the company and its audience.[55]

Perhaps the most influential member of Yuan's staff was Nan Wei (1921–

2.3 "Snow White and the Seven Dwarfs," a cartoon depicting Yuan Xuefen and her staff, celebrates the fruitful collaboration between Yuan and new-art youths in furthering Yue opera reform. Top: Yuan Xuefen. From left: Xiao Zhang, Lü Zhong, Hong Jun (Han Yi), Zhong Mei, Zheng Chuanjian, Nan Wei, and Cheng Rong. (*Xuesheng jinian kan* 1946)

1989), a talented playwright and director. Nan Wei was a native of Changzhou, Jiangsu. His father, probably a small merchant sojourning in Shanghai, was fond of Suzhou story-singing. Nan Wei was familiar with the genre as a child and became a Beijing opera fan in his teenage years, only to shift his interest to motion pictures and spoken drama in the late 1930s. He trained and worked as an accountant, but his love for the theater led him out of business circles. Nan Wei first took part in amateur spoken-drama theater and later joined Yuan Xuefen's company in 1943. Within three years of joining the company, he had written and directed approximately thirty new plays, including *Sister Xianglin*, and rearranged many traditional ones, such as *The Butterfly Lovers*.

The reforms that began at the Dalai Theater in late 1942 led to a new production process, according to which the newly established staff—

consisting of playwrights, directors, and other technical support personnel for lighting, costume, and stage design—assumed responsibility for production, altering the traditional actor-centered system prevalent in lowbrow entertainments. In the traditional system, predicated upon the actors' illiteracy and lack of access to scripts, a "master of plays" (*shuoxi shifu*), usually an experienced actor or musician with basic literacy who was familiar with the repertoire of traditional plays, taught the performers the acts and plots of a play. He assigned roles among the actors, making sure they understood their roles and the timing of their stage entrances and exits. During the performance, the master posted an "outline of acts" (*mubiao*) backstage to remind the performers of the order of the acts. Because only a few frequently staged plays developed fixed lyrics (these were known as the "meat" [*rouzi*] and were taught to young actors), it was up to the actors to improvise onstage everything from singing and dialogue to acting. Without fixed scripts, the show's quality relied almost entirely on the performances of a few main actors. Talented actors were given the whole stage on which to show off their originality and creativity and might sing for what seemed like forever to those backstage, leaving little time for the others to act. Inferior actors often embarrassed themselves by running out of lyrics and devices when the more powerful star actors failed to appear onstage as scheduled. Stage productions were thus crude and unpredictable, and plays were rarely refined through the accumulated experience of several generations. In order to cater to the tastes of an increasingly literary urban audience, Yue opera reform in the 1940s sought to replace this actor-centered system with a director- and script-centered system modeled on film and spoken drama, at the expense of the traditional improvisation.

At first, the new scripts were little better than the outlines of acts. The playwright arranged stories and plots and wrote some lyrics and verses but left the rest for the actors to fill out. In the famous 1938 play *Tears Over the Lovesick Land* (Lei sa xiangsi di), Yao Shuijuan improvised eighteen lines in song to express the protagonist's extreme sadness, although the original script provided only four lines. In the mid-1940s through the late 1940s, and after staging many new plays, playwrights and directors slowly began to establish their authority over the actresses' habit of improvising onstage. But the authority of the script and the director would be firmly established only much later, as a cultural policy of the new PRC state.[56]

The staff also reduced the theater owner's power over stage productions. Theater owners were mostly Shaoxing natives familiar with the traditional Yue opera repertoire and were the ones to decide their theaters' programs.

With the establishment of the staff and the modernization of the production process, Yue opera companies began to obtain artistic autonomy vis-à-vis the owners.

The combined reform force of actresses and new-art youths resulted in the creation of a self-proclaimed New Yue Opera (Xin Yueju), which signaled a higher level of professionalism and literary sophistication. Actresses, with the help of the director, became self-conscious practitioners of modern artistic methods such as character development. Fan Ruijuan recalled how Nan Wei helped her in this regard:

> Nan Wei opened up the actresses' minds by telling us to learn about dramatic theories and cultivate our artistic elements. During the 1940s reforms, I heard that Stanislavsky's books specially dealt with theater direction. Having no idea how hard his books could be, I asked Nan Wei to get me a copy of *On Actors' Self-Cultivation* [Lun yanyuan ziwo xiuyang (in Chinese translation)] and started reading it. My literacy level was low, and theoretical works were difficult for me. From time to time, I sought Nan Wei's help. He was always patient. He taught us how to study, understand, and perform a wide range of characters, especially how to create various characters through our careful observation of people in real life.[57]

Under Nan Wei's direction, Fan played roles ranging from romantic young scholars to opium addicts, bandits, and simpletons and emerged as one of the best Yue opera performers of her time. Zhang Guifeng, another leading actress who specialized in old men's roles, at first hated memorizing lines and following a script but eventually came to terms with the new practice. When Nan Wei assigned her the role of Wei the Bald in *Sister Xianglin*, conventionally a clown's role, Zhang made two trips to a teahouse on a dock in Pudong to observe how hooligans acted and spoke and was able "to capture the essence" of her role.[58] With the director's encouragement, second- and even third-tier actresses also became concerned about better acting, and their efforts raised the quality of each play and the professional level of Yue opera overall.[59]

Though heavily influenced by spoken drama, New Yue Opera nonetheless also took inspiration from such traditional theatrical arts as Kun opera, another native opera of the Jiangnan region popular during the Ming and early Qing periods and known for its elaborate love stories. For the actresses, popular rejection of spoken drama in favor of Chinese operas made it clear that Yue opera should not become spoken drama plus singing.

While rejecting the highly formalized postures of the Qing major operas represented by Beijing opera, they found inspiration in Kun opera's fluid dance style. Yuan Xuefen invited the Kun opera master Zheng Chuanjian to be the company's director of choreography, and Zheng taught Yue opera actresses to use Kun opera postures in their performances. Kun opera's unique body movements and postures greatly enriched Yue opera body language and contributed to a fluid acting style that integrated song and dance. This particular mode of traditional stylistic acting fit well with the modern naturalistic expression of love and desire, as Yue opera actresses creatively used traditional singing and dancing to enhance the aesthetic intensity of the modern romance.[60] As a result, a native opera that combined a Chinese-influenced acting style with Western-influenced stage design and theater discipline appealed to metropolitan audiences by means of its refreshing modernity and familiar native sensibility.

With Yuan Xuefen's company leading the way, other major Yue opera companies implemented similar reforms, and New Yue Opera flourished.[61] During the 1940s, more than one hundred modern productions of anti-feudal love dramas enhanced by innovative stage sets and fluid singing and dance reshaped Yue opera into an exciting and respectable modern theater.

Patriotism, Eroticism, and Love Drama in Women's Yue Opera

The Yue opera repertoire formed during the late 1930s and 1940s contained four main thematic subgenres: patriotic and revolutionary plays, family morality plays, erotic plays, and romantic love plays. The development of this repertoire further illustrates a dynamic relationship among Yue opera actresses' struggle for survival, status, and respect; the elite rhetoric of theatrical reform; and the demands of a changing urban audience that transformed Yue opera into a key sector in Shanghai's popular-entertainment industry.

In order to enhance the status of Yue opera as a serious theater, actresses eagerly staged patriotic plays, though they often embellished these plays with love stories in recognition of audience tastes. The first patriotic Yue opera play was *Hua Mulan* (Hua Mulan), staged in 1938 in "island" Shanghai at the height of the resistance culture. Not incidentally, *Hua Mulan* was also the first women's Yue opera play that made use of a playwright and a director and thus marked the beginning of Yue opera reforms. *Hua Mulan* was based on a folk song that originated in the late sixth or early seventh century. In the folk song, Mulan, the daughter of an old village couple, disguises herself in men's clothing and joins the army in place of her aging father. When she returns triumphantly after twelve years on the battlefield, the emperor wants to make her a minister, but Mulan wishes only to return home. She surprises her fellow soldiers when she emerges from her home in women's dress. While the original folk song conveys close feelings between Mulan and her parents and praises her talents in a simple and joyful tone, subsequent renditions elaborated on Mulan's moral perfection, noting that she was both loyal to the state and filial to her parents.[62] In modern times, Mulan came to be portrayed as a heroic woman who defended her nation by fighting alongside men. In the wartime context of the late 1930s, such updated versions of the story of Mulan became popular, because they resonated with several concerns prevalent in "island" Shanghai: nationalism, patriotism, women's liberation, and, indeed, romantic love. The legendary female heroine, who dressed in men's clothing and fought against barbarian invaders, found her way into film, spoken drama, Beijing opera, women's Yue opera, storytelling, and many other forms of entertainment.

In 1938, two Yue opera companies staged the story of Mulan in "island" Shanghai. One version was adopted from Mei Lanfang's Beijing opera piece, while the other, more well-known version was staged by Yao Shuijuan, scripted by Fan Li, and directed by Zhang Zifan (see fig. 2.4). Fan Li was a native of Hangzhou and had been a local newspaper correspondent for the *Dagong Daily*. After Japanese troops occupied Hangzhou, Fan fled to Shanghai, where he was introduced to Yao Shuijuan, who was seeking a playwright to help her develop new plays. *Hua Mulan* was Fan's first play. Yao Shuijuan's show, which combined patriotism with romance, was well advertised by both tabloids and radio stations. Advertisements also ran in the entertainment section of the American-operated local English-language newspaper, *The China Press*, which published a brief introduction to the play alongside a photograph of Yao Shuijuan dressed as Hua Mulan in military uniform. The introduction reads: "Miss Yao Shui-chuan [Shuijuan], noted Chinese actress, who is known as the Queen of Shaoshing drama [Yue opera], will make her debut tomorrow in 'Hwa Mo-lan' [Hua Mulan], China's Jeanne d'Arc, at Tien Hsiang Theater, in the Coal Guild Building."[63] The Yue opera play opened on schedule and ran for about a month, with performances twenty-seven nights in a row. Given that Yue opera companies usually changed programs every two weeks—sometimes every week if ticket sales were slow—*Hua Mulan* was indeed a success. The play brought newfound status to Yao Shuijuan and to women's opera in general. By producing a patriotic opera, Yao Shuijuan and her actress colleagues demonstrated

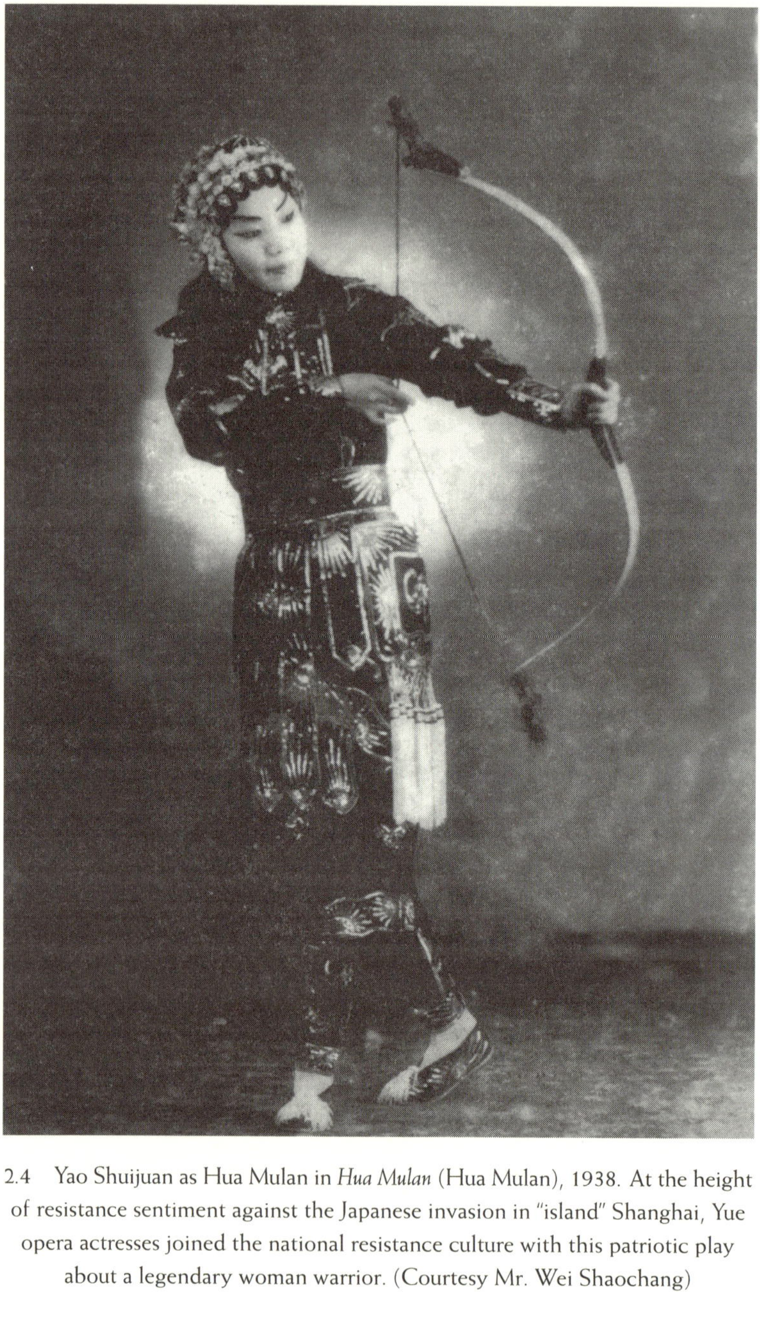

2.4 Yao Shuijuan as Hua Mulan in *Hua Mulan* (Hua Mulan), 1938. At the height of resistance sentiment against the Japanese invasion in "island" Shanghai, Yue opera actresses joined the national resistance culture with this patriotic play about a legendary woman warrior. (Courtesy Mr. Wei Shaochang)

2.5 Yuan Xuefen as Hua Mulan in *Mulan Joins the Army* (Mulan congjun), 1944. The staging of this patriotic play in occupied Shanghai hints at resistance on the part of Yuan and her staff but also suggests Japanese tolerance of popular culture. (Yuan 2002)

their patriotism and progressive ideas and hence distinguished themselves from old-fashioned popular entertainers (see fig. 2.5).

The Japanese occupation made it impossible to stage patriotic plays, but after the war, women's Yue opera troupes continued to produce plays that combined grand political narratives with love stories. For example, in *Sad Moon over the Liao Royal Palace* (Qiliang Liao gong yue), of 1946, Yuan Xuefen depicted a patriotic court maid who fought off evil officials for the good of the state. In 1947, *Prince Liu Chen* (Guopo shanhe zai), with Xu Yulan cast as Prince Liu Chen, criticized the corruption and decadence of the head of an ancient state. Yin Guifang, a leading actress specializing in young male roles who joined in the New Yue Opera reforms in the mid-1940s, created a series of images of revolutionaries, including Shi Dakai, the great general of the Taiping Heavenly Kingdom, in *Shi Dakai* (Shi Dakai), in 1946; the Guangxu emperor, the tragic reformist emperor of the late Qing, whose efforts were quashed by Empress Dowager Cixi, in *Emperor Guangxu and His Favorite Concubine Zhenfei* (Guangxu Di yu Zhenfei), in 1946; and Sun Kexian, the great Ming loyalist who fought the invading Qing army to his death, in *Ge Nenniang* (Ge Nenniang), of 1946. These plays, though usually not big hits, were noticed and warmly received by influential intellectuals.[64]

Family morality plays had been the mainstay of the Yue opera repertoire, and these included traditional plays such as *Pearl Pagoda* and *Emerald Hairpin* as well as such modern plays as *The Dark Family* (Hei'an jiating), of 1944,[65] and *The Prodigal Son* (Langdang zi), of 1947. These plays were intended to criticize social ills, such as drug abuse and gambling.[66] As most traditional family morality plays had a love story at their core and were organized within the structure of love drama, they may be considered a variation in the growing subgenre of the love drama.

The mainstay plays of the Yue opera repertoire developed around personal and private narratives centered on love and desire. The process went in two directions: one continued the traditional public culture of erotica by turning the "vulgar" (*su*) into the "refined" (*ya*), while the other displaced the earlier crude eroticism with a new mode of intensified love drama. While the refined eroticism maintained the prior emphasis on "sex" (*xing*), love melodrama made *qing*, or feelings of love, its focus and sex a subtext. The development of these two subgenres were, however, influenced by the May Fourth ideology of social and cultural reform that sought to eliminate the public culture of erotica but was friendlier toward love drama.

The subgenre of erotic plays in Yue opera, performed most notably by the famous actress Xiao Dangui, explored women's sexual desires. Xiao, an excellent singer, actor, and acrobatic dancer, became a Yue opera superstar around the same time as did Yao Shuijuan. Between the late 1930s and her tragic death in 1947, Xiao successfully played roles ranging from the female warrior in *White-Water Shore* (Baishui tan), to a medusa in *The City of Sizhou* (Sizhou cheng), to the cross-dressing figures Cai Lanying in *The Eaglewood Fan* (Chenxiang shan) and the title character in *Meng Lijun*. Her most acclaimed roles, however, were amorous women, such as the lonely and desirous Yang Yuzhen in *The Imperial Concubine* (Guifei zuijiu), the seductive Widow Ma in *Widow Ma's Inn* (Ma Guafu kai dian), and the oversexed Pan Jinlian in plays adapted from the Ming dynasty novels *The Water Margin* (Shuihu zhuan) and *Plum in a Golden Vase* (Jinpingmei).

In the early 1940s, Xiao was among the first women's Yue opera actresses to use playwrights and directors. She was slow, however, to incorporate such intellectual themes as nationalism into her plays. While Yuan Xuefen and Yin Guifang explored the path of Yue opera reform and cultivated a new constituency in female students and professionals with new-style love dramas, Xiao Dangui's repertoire, composed largely of sexually provocative plays, was popular among middle-class men and housewives. The female images she created onstage were of lustful, daring women seeking sexual satisfaction, and her performances explored a type of female eroticism focused on sexual desire as the basis for, not the result of, the sentiment of love. Her approach was thus distinguishable from both traditional crude eroticism focused on sex only and trendier sentimental love dramas. This kind of eroticism was common in women's Yue opera at the time. The following contemporaneous tabloid description of an erotic scene from a popular play put on by Xiao Dangui and her stage partner Zhang Xiangqing provides some idea of Yue opera eroticism of the 1940s:

> The famous Yue opera actresses Xiao Dangui and Zhang Xiangqing came to perform at the Zhedong Theater, and the audience in this middle district loved their shows, especially the two plays at which they especially excel, *Widow Ma's Inn* and *Stir Up the Sanya Garden* [Da'nao Sanya Yuan]. Tickets for these shows were always sold out. They are currently staging *Stir Up the Sanya Garden* again. Xiao Dangui is exceptionally beautiful and sexy in her bright red cheongsam and high-heeled leather shoes; Zhang Xiangqing, in her long white silken gown and Panama-style hat, deserves to be called a handsome young man. Their performance of the flirtation scene in the bedroom is really impressive; especially original is the way they take off each other's clothes. Xiao initiates it by taking off Zhang's coat, and Zhang then proceeds to take Xiao's clothing off, until they both are wearing only their underclothes. Even the queen of *ping* opera, Bai Yushuang,[67] would have to admit her inferiority before such a "bold" performance.[68]

The Yue opera fan Wu Ping saw similar performances of the famously, or notoriously, erotic *Widow Ma's Inn* in the 1940s, and she loved it.[69] In the story, Widow Ma desires a guest at her inn, Di Renjie, a young scholar on his way to the capital to take the civil-service examination.[70] At midnight, the widow, driven by uncontrollable desire, goes into Di's room and tries to seduce him—hence, the famous seduction scene.[71] Xiao Dangui was not the only actress to play Widow Ma, as the play was widely popular and was staged by almost every Yue opera company, but she was considered the best of them all—passionate and sexual, yet sensitive and dignified.

Explicit sexual expression was garbed in enhanced stage sets and costumes, exquisite performances, refined lyrics, and romantic settings, as seen, for example, in *Record of Retributions* (Guobao lu), with Mrs. Diao's desire for Wang Wen, a young scholar next door and a friend of her husband's. In the garden scene, Mrs. Diao, played by Xiao Dangui, sings refined lyrics expressing sexual desire and lovesickness while playing her lute, and Wang Wen, played by Jia Lingfeng, accompanies her on a *xiao*, a vertical bamboo flute, from the little hill in his own garden. Both sing of their desire in romantic but sexually explicit lyrics.[72]

Such explorations of female sexuality were very popular but ill fated in Shanghai in the 1940s. It was said that Xiao always had a full house whenever she performed *Widow Ma's Inn* and that she always performed it whenever box office sales were slow. *Widow Ma's Inn* and other similar plays prospered throughout the 1940s, with the support of Shanghai audiences and the absence of governmental attention: While the Japanese occupation authority simply did not seem to care, the Nationalist government of the postwar period was too busy cracking down on the Communists to clean up eroticism in popular entertainment.[73] The official ideology of the Nationalist government and the elite nation-building rhetoric of theatrical reform, however, deemed eroticism harmful to public morality. As the Republican discourse of women's liberation generally neglected the question of women's sexuality, paradoxically, the traditional virtue of *qingbai* continued to set the moral standard for good women.[74] Thus, in the late 1940s, both Republican government and elite leftist intellectual ideologies increasingly pressured Yue opera, and for that matter any lowbrow entertainment, to refrain from sexually explicit acting, be it crude or refined. This trend finally culminated in the banning of erotic plays after 1949 by the newly established PRC state.

Because patriotic plays relied on love stories to sell tickets and popular erotic plays gave Yue opera a bad name, love drama became the dominant subgenre during the process of Yue opera reform. In an article published in *Yue Opera World* (Yueju shijie), Xu Jin, a young Yue opera playwright, discussed three kinds of Yue opera plays. One was the conservative kind, which preserved the essence of traditional Yue opera but was behind the times. Another was the radical kind, which went too far toward making Yue opera into an art, neglecting the fact that Yue opera as a popular form was never just a showcase for "pure art." The third type of Yue opera play, Xu Jin wrote, catered to both audience tastes and the needs of the age. He asserted that it was wrong to say that catering to the audience meant that reform was not taking place: "Yue opera is gradually progressing, and its audience is growing—this is reform. It would be a failure if we raised artistic style to a level that the audience could not understand."[75] By "conservative" plays, Xu meant the refined erotic play represented by the famous Xiao Dangui as well as traditional lower-class eroticism; by "radical," he meant new plays loaded with too much political message. It is not surprising that, with such an understanding, Xu Jin became a master of the Yue opera love melodrama, contributing to the creation of several masterpieces, including *The Butterfly Lovers* and *Dream of the Red Chamber*. The lyrics he wrote and edited for these plays were among the best in Yue opera history—they were of high literary quality and were neither so refined that they intimidated ordinary audience members nor so vulgar that they repelled those who were better educated.

The leading actress Yin Guifang also spoke about the ways in which the relationship between ideological pressure and audience demands influenced Yue opera reform. To answer the call that Yue opera incorporate the nation-state narrative into its story lines, Yin placed patriotic generals, warriors, and scholars on Yue opera stages. In response to audience demands, Yin made her characters sentimental, caring, and loyal lovers. Yin Guifang's reforms stressed the importance of retaining the "essence" of Yue opera, as suggested in an interview with the mainstream newspaper *The New Citizen Evening News* (Xinmin wanbao) on August 22, 1947: "I am not only for reform but moreover hope to eliminate and not just amend the obscenities common in Yue opera. I uphold a principle, however, that the Yue-ness of Yue opera must be retained."[76] What was the "Yue-ness" Yin wanted to uphold? From her other writings, it is quite clear that she considered love stories to be the essence of Yue opera. Earlier that year, she had written: "Looking back, [I see that] the larger part of every play has always consisted of passionate love between young men and women. This is how Yue opera won a mass audience."[77]

Love stories were not necessarily conventional and were hardly meaningless, despite the opinion of the cultural elite. In fact, the fixation on love in modern popular culture reflected the psychological needs of an urban population witnessing drastic changes in gender and sexual relations. Contrary to the impression that love stories in women's Yue opera, or in all popular genres, were monothematic pabulum, the subgenre of love drama included varieties such as exotic plays, cross-dressing plays, and love tragedies.

The exotic play was often a mix of love story, patriotic theme, and adventure set in an exotic time and place. One of the most popular plays of this sort, *Desert Prince* (Shamo wangzi), of 1946, had a script by Xu Jin and was directed by Zhong Min. Adapted from a story in the Arabic classic *The Thousand and One Nights*, it tells the adventures of a young Mongol prince forced to flee into the desert after a rebellious tribal chief murders the king and usurps the kingdom. On his wanderings, the prince meets and falls in love with a young princess. But the tribal chief captures the princess and renders the prince blind by means of black magic. The prince then allies with the princess's father, another tribal leader, and eventually overcomes the rebels. As soon as he restores the kingdom, the prince gives up his crown to search for his lover. At the end, he finds her in the desert, and her passionate embrace restores his eyesight. The two live happily together thereafter, and there is great peace and prosperity under their rule. This play took Shanghai audiences to the Mongolian desert, displaying an exoticized Mongol people in colorful native costumes, all the while employing a fairy-tale love-adventure story line that was not so different from that of more conventional love stories. The images of the beautiful, passionate, and heroic Mongolian prince and princess that Yin Guifang and her partner Zhu Shuizhao created on the Yue opera stage were at once exotic and familiar, adventurous and conventional, and catered to the urban audience's passion for a combination of fantasy and comfort. By creating patriotic Mongol heroes, the play was also politically correct in terms of government policy regarding Mongolia and the multiethnic character of the Republican Chinese state. This was a love story that also spoke directly to the recent history of Japan's failed attempt to make inner Mongolia an "independent" state during the Second World War.

The Yue opera cross-dressing performance illustrates how love relationships are explored in the seemingly meaningless cross-dressing play. Cross-dressing, mistaken identity, and cross-gender acting are common to both Chinese and English theatrical traditions, the most notable English example being the plays by William Shakespeare that employed all three techniques. Women's Yue opera also used all three techniques, albeit with an all-female cast instead of the Shakespearean theater's all-male cast. Beijing opera, in contrast, featured female impersonators, but transvestite plays were few and represented a relatively insignificant part of its repertoire, as love drama was never a strength of Beijing opera. Transvestitism was not only a common device in Yue opera but also an essential part of the plot in several of its most popular plays, including two masterpieces, *The Butterfly Lovers* and *Meng Lijun*.

Although set in the Yuan dynasty, *Meng Lijun* was a modern play put together and produced by Shengxian opera in Shanghai for a modern urban audience. Shengxian opera first staged this play in 1921, at the height of the May Fourth New Culture Movement, when the discourse of women's liberation was still relatively new. Along with *The Butterfly Lovers* and *Emerald Hairpin*, *Meng Lijun* was instrumental in making Shengxian opera a presence in Shanghai's cultural market, and it became one of the most popular plays of women's Yue opera in the ensuing decades.[78]

Meng Lijun tells the story of a talented girl, Meng Lijun, who ventures into the world of men seeking justice and revenge for her father and her fiancé, both high officials persecuted by bad elements in the court of the Cheng emperor. Lijun disguises herself as a man, passes the civil-service examination, in which she takes first place, and becomes the emperor's trusted prime minister. During her tenure, she manages to rehabilitate her father and fiancé and punishes the wrongdoers. The emperor, however, comes to realize that Lijun is a beautiful woman and desires to make her his imperial concubine. Lijun remains loyal to her fiancé, however, and at the end, she resumes her life as a woman and marries her fiancé with the emperor's blessing.

In 1999, the Shanghai Yue Opera House staged a production faithful to a late-1930s audio recording of the play, employing an all-female cast. The double-layered sex play is intriguing: three actresses play out a heterosexual romance involving two men and a woman pretending to be a man. The production culminated in the act "Touring the Imperial Garden" (You Shanglin Yuan),[79] by which point the emperor, who has become suspicious of his minister's true gender, orders Lijun to accompany him on a tour of the imperial garden, where he tries to seduce her. As played by the actresses Zheng Guofeng (as the emperor) and Shan Yangping (as the transvestite minister), the emperor has the upper hand, and the minister must rely on her wit and moral courage to protect her chastity—the foundation of her dignity as a person. The young emperor is affectionate and lustful, and he genteelly seeks his objective by means of teasing, tricks, and a little coercion at times. Since the emperor is played by a woman, the character's desire for Lijun may be seen as same-sex as well as opposite-sex staging. The minister is shy and reserved, as is her nature as a woman, but at the same time brilliant and obedient, as befits her adopted nature as a male subordinate. Significantly, while her obedience also strongly suggests her femininity, when in masculine guise, her display of wit only highlights her desperate situation—she has no way out but to become the emperor's sexual captive. Lijun is rescued at the last moment when the emperor's mother puts a stop to her son's mischievous behavior and returns everything to order. The performance not only comforts audience members by driving home the traditional virtues of loyalty and chastity but also takes them into a fantasy world of dangerous pleasures, namely, seduction involving ambiguously gendered characters carried out according to the rules of intricate and fluid sex games (see fig. 2.6).

Love tragedies, represented by the three classic masterpieces *The Butterfly Lovers*, *Tale of the Western Chamber* (Xixiang ji), and *Dream of the Red Chamber*, were perhaps the most influential of Yue opera's love dramas. The remaking of *The Butterfly Lovers* illustrates the transformation of Yue opera into a modern master theater of love drama, which took place during the Yue opera reforms. In 1945, the Xuesheng Company restaged the story of the butterfly lovers as *The Tragic Story of Liang Shanbo and Zhu Yingtai* (Liang Zhu aishi), scripted and directed by Yuan Xuefen. The main modification was the use of modern stage design to enhance production values. The play was staged again in 1946 with further changes in content and lyrics.[80] As Yuan Xuefen explained:

> *The Tragic Story of Liang Shanbo and Zhu Yingtai* had been staged at the Nine-Star Theater [Jiuxing] last year. This new version of the play is again different. Last time, as we were in such a hurry, we only reformed the stage designs but left the lyrics and structure unchanged. I felt that further reform of many old elements was needed to make the play more ideal, and that is why I rearranged it again.
>
> It is hard to say if the new *Tragic Story of Liang Shanbo and Zhu Yingtai* is satisfactory, and I myself am not sure. But we tried hard to make the story more real and exciting, by eliminating many superfluous and obscene elements and by integrating new ideas into the play as much as possible.
>
> . . . If the story of Liang and Zhu were real, I believe people would most likely be sympathetic to their tragic story and lament the perils of arranged marriage.[81]

Emphasizing the theme of free love and marriage, the play eliminated such "feudal" elements as bawdy eroticism and plots related to reincarnation and other ideas from popular religions. It ended with an emotional climax, with Yingtai crying and pouring her heart out before Shanbo's bier.[82]

The play created an image not only of an independent-minded woman in Zhu Yingtai, played by Yuan Xuefen, but also of a woman's man in Liang Shanbo, played by Fan Ruijuan (see fig. 2.7). Fan came into her own as an

2.6 A scene in "Touring the Imperial Garden," from *Meng Lijun* (Meng Lijun), with Shan Yangping as Meng Lijun disguised as a man and serving as the minister (left) and Qian Huili as the emperor, Shanghai Yue Opera House, 1999. Multilayered cross-gender performances are a common technique in women's opera. (Courtesy Shanghai Yue Opera House)

2.7 Yuan Xuefen as Zhu Yingtai (left) and Fan Ruijuan as Liang Shanbo in *The Tragic Story of Liang Shanbo and Zhu Yingtai* (Liang-Zhu aishi), 1946. In the 1940s, Yuan Xuefen and her stage partners transformed this centuries-old folk story into a celebration of love and loyalty. (Yuan 2002)

artist when she reinterpreted the role of Liang Shanbo and subsequently became known for portraying sincere and kind young scholars. In folk versions of the story told during the Qing and early Republican periods, Liang Shanbo is comically cunning, salacious, and dull at the same time because his soul has been stolen from him by order of the Jade Emperor so that he will be unable to figure out Zhu Yingtai's true gender during the three years they study together and live in the same room. While the Xuesheng Company's 1946 version eliminated this premise, on the grounds that it was based on superstition, Fan Ruijuan transformed Liang Shanbo into a bookish young man, a little naive regarding women, but sincere, tender, and affectionate upon realizing his love for Yingtai. Fan's portrayal earned Liang Shanbo a nickname from the audience, "the adorable fool" (*keai de shagua*).[83]

In the 1949 version of *The Butterfly Lovers*, staged by the Dongshan Company, Fan Ruijuan, as Liang Shanbo, and Fu Quanxiang, as Zhu Yingtai, added a final act to their performance. On her way to Ma's household as the new bride, Zhu Yingtai stops at Liang Shanbo's tomb to mourn him one last time. As Yingtai weeps, heaven responds with a thunderstorm, and a bolt of lightning strikes the tomb and splits it open. As Yingtai jumps into the grave, Ma Wencai and others try to hold her back by grasping her skirt. After Yingtai disappears into the tomb, pieces of fabric torn from her skirt become a pair of beautiful butterflies (played by the two stars garbed in colorful butterfly dresses), happily courting each other under a rainbow in a graveyard of flowers in full bloom.[84]

The artistic achievement of New Yue Opera in the 1940s also laid the foundation for Yue opera's continuous development in the 1950s when, with the support of the PRC state, the genre gained national and international influence. At a 1952 opera conference held in Beijing, *The Butterfly Lovers* thrilled a national audience and brought home multiple awards for script, music, stage design, and best actress. In 1953, the play was made into China's first 35 mm color film, and its 1954 premiere in Shanghai attracted a record 1.55 million viewers. It won the award for musical film at the Eighth International Film Festival in Czechoslovakia in July 1954 and an award at the Ninth Edinburgh International Film Festival in Scotland in August 1955.[85] The film was distributed internationally and caused a sensation in Hong Kong, while the play toured nationwide and traveled to North Korea, the Soviet Union, and Eastern Europe as part of a mission representing theatrical arts from China. One performance in Berlin evoked such enthusiasm from the audience that the actresses had to answer twenty-eight curtain calls.[86]

過房娘

Chapter 3

Patrons and Patronage

The rise of Yue opera in Shanghai in the mid-twentieth century was not just a cultural phenomenon but also a social phenomenon that entailed the emergence of new social groups in the hierarchy of the city's public space. The opera's upward mobility was closely tied to its ability to build a core of upper- and middle-class patrons, and Yue opera grew by enlarging its audience base, keeping its lower-class audience while capturing rising numbers of urban middle-class men and, especially, women. These upper- and middle-class patrons of Yue opera were mostly from the rich Ningbo-Shaoxing area of eastern Zhejiang, the native home of Yue opera, in which Shengxian was a poor sibling.

Yue opera's ascent was thus closely related to the rise of three sometimes overlapping social groups in Republican Shanghai: an urban middle class that could include a wide spectrum of urbanites, from white-collar professionals, skilled industrial workers, and employees in service sectors to the self-employed and freelancers; Ningbo-Shaoxing natives; and female operagoers.[1] An investigation of the Yue opera constituency thus tells much about the social and economic formations of the city's population that fueled the rise of Yue opera as a women's culture as well as the stratification of the city's popular culture in general.

Venues, Patrons, and the Opera

In Republican Shanghai, a hierarchy of venues for commercial performance reflected the complex social stratification of the audience, opera genres, troupes, and performers. The various performance sites—teahouses, entertainment halls, and theaters—served people from various backgrounds and embraced different cultural atmospheres.

Westernization was part of modern theatrical reform in China. The first Western-style theater was perhaps the New Theater in Shanghai, built by reformist Beijing opera actors Pan Yueqiao, Xia Yueshan, and Xia Yuerun in 1908.[2] After the 1911 Republican Revolution, new-style theaters gradually spread across the country and became the mainstream venue in Shanghai. In the 1930s and 1940s, in the colonial downtown area, a handful of first-rate modern theaters hosted spoken drama, drawing a core audience of male intellectuals, while a score of large modern theaters featured major Beijing opera and Yue opera troupes, with audiences centered on rich, powerful male patrons for Beijing opera and upper- and middle-class female patrons for Yue opera respectively.

Less equipped medium-size and shabby small theaters in and on the peripheries of the city center, in Nanshi, Hongkou, and Zhabei, served as venues for all kinds of local operas, geared toward lower- and middle-class local audiences. Less prestigious Yue opera and Beijing opera troupes as well as other local operas regularly staged productions in these theaters, while itinerant troupes from nearby provinces and the countryside often took over during the regular troupes' summer and winter breaks. Teahouses in these areas remained popular for itinerant troupes, storytellers, and story-singers who entertained a mostly lower-class crowd.[3]

Entertainment halls represented another new development in Republican Shanghai's public space. During the early Republican period, entertainment halls provided a fashionable place for upper-class gentlemen to sample modernity, drinking tea while looking out on the city's skyline. Among the most famous of these were the Great World (Da Shijie) and the New World (Xin Shijie); both occupied multistory buildings in the downtown shopping area and were miniatures of Shanghai's entertainment world. Blinking neon lights illuminated the buildings' exteriors, while inside, many forms of popular entertainment could be found, from puppet and comic shows, to storytelling, to various native operas. But during the 1930s, as entertainment halls became increasingly popular among the urban masses, upper-class patrons escaped to modern theaters, cafés, and hotel lounges, leaving the entertainment halls to ordinary folks. A Shanghai municipal government survey in the early 1930s shows that, on average, one person from every working-class family in Shanghai visited the Great World once per month.[4] A 1939 Japanese travelogue describes the Great World's popularity: "The Great World in the French concession is a dream world serving as an entertainment institution for the commoners, mainly lower-class shop hands, laborers, and tourists. The entrance fee is twenty-two cents."[5] During the postwar period, entertainment halls declined sharply in number. The Great World was the only independent entertainment hall left, while a few others became attached to department stores and made hardly any profit.[6]

For opera troupes, decisions on where to perform and whom to entertain determined their social as well as economic status. While venues marked the status of the performing troupe and the genre it represented, opera troupes could advance along the hierarchy by performing at better places. The constant movement of opera troupes and audiences among various locations points to a dynamic structure of entertainment that was at once hierarchical and fluid. Beijing opera, for example, regularly occupied the most modern and grandest theaters in downtown but was also regularly featured at the open fairground and entertainment halls attended by lower-class urban crowds. While troupes performing in grand theaters for elite audiences certainly raised Beijing opera's cultural status, performances at fairgrounds and in entertainment halls inevitably imparted a lower-class character to the genre. Beijing opera was, therefore, both upper and lower class, depending on how and where one viewed it.

The rise of women's Yue opera exemplifies the correlation among an opera's venue, audience, and status in that it shows how Yue opera's entrance into better theaters helped expand its middle-class constituency and hence raised the genre's status from lower-class entertainment to middle-class pastime. Before the mid-1930s, all-male Shengxian opera companies were regular features in entertainment halls and medium-size theaters in the downtown area. In contrast, itinerant troupes and all-female troupes frequented small teahouses and shabby theaters in the river-dock section of Nanshi, where laborers and merchants from Ningbo and Shaoxing concentrated. Toward the late 1930s, as all-female troupes became increasingly popular, they moved out of teahouses and into theaters. According to the *Shanghai Yue Opera Gazetteer*, around and after 1936, all-female troupes performed mostly in small and medium-size theaters, all-male and mixed troupes in entertainment halls.[7] Then, after the Battle of Shanghai, all-female troupes soon moved into a dozen or so medium-size theaters, while all-male troupes disappeared.[8]

Upon entering medium-size theaters, the better all-female troupes were able to draw a large number of middle-class men and especially women, while the lower-class constituency remained in the teahouses with the itinerant troupes. Zhang Rongbiao and Zhang Yanqiu, an elderly couple living in Chongren, Shengxian, performed Shengxian opera in Shanghai during the 1930s until the outbreak of the Battle of Shanghai in August 1937. They both stated that roughly equal numbers of men and women attended the all-male or mixed Shengxian opera shows. Older people were the most frequent visitors, while large numbers of middle-aged men also attended. Zhang Yanqiu, who performed with both male-dominant and all-female companies, added that more men than women attended performances by all-female troupes. Why? Her explanation was that men wanted to take advantage of young actresses: "I had a husband and was thus spared. If not, men would probably have also come after me."[9] Other informants supported her description of the gender composition of audiences, although they did not necessarily give the same reason. Xiao-Bai Yumei, an actress who performed in place of her father with an all-male company in the New World entertainment hall in the mid-1930s, also described an audience of mixed gender and age.[10] This situation began to change with the rise of all-female troupes in the late 1930s. *Shaoxing Opera Daily* (Shaoxingxi bao), a tabloid published by a few Yue opera patrons, described the relationship between the popularity of all-female troupes, the places where they performed, and the growth of the female and middle-class audience in 1941:

> All-female troupes were active in small teahouses in the French concession, Nanshi, and Xiaonanmen districts. Seats were cheap, only one dime or two. Women went after all-female troupes like flocks of ducks. All-female troupes then swept through Shanghai. Although all-female troupes were popular, the pitiful fact was that they mostly performed in small teahouses and therefore lacked a respectable audience. To change this situation, they began gradual reforms while moving into performing halls in larger inns. The Commercial Inn in Nichengqiao was the first to host all-female troupes, and the Great Chinese Theater [Da Zhonghua] on Fuzhou Road was the second. The reformed theaters adopted a new seating system in which the viewer took a seat with a number that matched the number on the ticket; this practice attracted many upper-class spectators. Then theaters raised ticket prices to forty cents and competed for contracts with famous stars. New plays were staged, elaborate costumes were added, and the theater became full of vitality. The name of "*didu* opera" has since then been

imprinted on the minds of Shanghai residents. Now not only Shaoxing natives care about the opera; people of various native-place origins all love it and go to see it.[11]

The relationship between Shanghai's modern theater and the increasing number of women opera spectators described here is of special importance. The veteran Yue opera director Han Yi pointed out that there were few public places in Republican Shanghai where women could engage in social activities. Dance halls and popular music cafés that featured girls who danced with customers as well as female singers were designed to entertain modern men and were not appropriate for respectable women. Movie theaters were mostly a meeting place for young lovers, and teahouses traditionally were a place for men. Opera theaters therefore became one of very few public places for women and facilitated the increase in female operagoers by providing a venue where women could enjoy the opera and socialize while maintaining a sense of propriety.

During the course of reform in the 1940s, Yue opera became a regular feature of some first-rate large theaters, such as the Nine-Star Theater and the Star Theater, which both had about nine hundred seats, compared to the four hundred seats provided at the Dalai Theater. According to Han Yi and Cheng Rong, both members of Yuan Xuefen's reform staff in the 1940s, New Yue Opera attracted younger, better-educated, and increasingly female viewers. Cheng commented, "The core of the audience consisted of young housewives around forty. They were educated, financially well off, and had plenty of time. They often brought their daughters, friends, and mothers to the theater. Most men came as women's companions. Older audience members such as my mother had difficulty understanding the new plays we put on during the reform."[12] According to Han Yi:

> During the Japanese occupation [1942–45], the level of the audience was not high because of the low level of the venue [the Dalai Theater]. At the time, Yue opera had already established a stable group of female viewers, and middle-school girls were already a significant part of the constituency—a constituency of petty intellectuals began to develop. Shortly before the victory over Japan and through the late 1940s, as the company [Xuesheng Company] entered first-rate theaters, such as the Nine-Star, Star, and Grand Shanghai, the level of the audience rose further to include some college students. . . .
>
> A large part of Yue opera's audience at that time consisted of middle-school girls and some boys, middle-class housewives and concubines of upper-

> class men. Men were also many, mostly medium or small merchants, shop hands, office workers, and functionaries. . . . In the postwar period, large companies in Shanghai had a concentration of petty intellectuals who loved Yue opera.[13]

The testimony of Cheng Rong and Han Yi as well as other evidence indicate that Yue opera's constituency in mid-twentieth-century Shanghai was made up of the middle class, including lower-middle-class male clerks and upper-class housewives and concubines, and women across class lines. To put Yue opera's constituency in some perspective, the considerable number of upper-class women patrons gave the opera prestige vis-à-vis other local operas, such as Shanghai opera and Huai opera, but did not match the distinguished status upper-class men brought to Beijing opera and intellectual elite men brought to spoken drama. Compared to lowbrow entertainment such as Shanghai opera and Huai opera, on the one hand, and spoken drama, on the other, Yue opera was in the middle in terms of the educational level of its audience. Yue opera's directors and playwrights in the 1940s and 1950s were mostly petty intellectuals with high school educations, while its constituency had an average middle-school education. Although college students were more likely to be attracted to spoken drama, common folks with primary-school or lower educations made up the basic audiences for Shanghai opera and Huai opera, respectively.[14] Mainstream Yue opera thus can be characterized as a middlebrow entertainment for Shanghai's vast middle class, both men and women, with a medium level of education, while lowbrow troupes served a lower-class constituency, mostly at the city peripheries.[15]

The Native-Place Factor

Republican-period Shanghai was a rapidly developing industrial and commercial center with a swiftly growing population. Among the roughly four million people in Shanghai in the late 1930s, less than one-fourth were Shanghai natives. Immigrants from northern and southern Jiangsu, Zhejiang, and Guangdong constituted the majority of the city's population; the rest were from Anhui, Jiangxi, Shandong, and other provinces.[16] In big cities like Shanghai, which could be intimidating to newcomers from small towns and the countryside, immigrants from the same area tended to stick together on the basis of native bonds strengthened by shared local dialects, common customs and habits, behavior codes, and nostalgic sentimentality. For practical reasons, immigrants relied on native-place ties to help them operate in the city and to find friends, work, and places to stay. People from the same native place thus tended to hold similar jobs and congregated in the same areas.[17] Yet the uneven economic development in various regions of China meant that immigrants from better-developed areas, such as Zhejiang and southern Jiangsu, came more prepared to compete for jobs in the city compared to those from less developed areas, such as northern Jiangsu (Subei) and Anhui. Thus, native-place segregation compounded by class stratification informed a hierarchical structure in the popular politics of native-place identity, popular culture, and business operation that put Ningbo-Shaoxing natives at the top and Subei people at the bottom.[18]

Poor Subei immigrants typically took up coolie jobs in the city, such as rickshaw pullers, waste collectors, porters, and other types of low-paid workers. Because of this, Subei people were generally stereotyped, stigmatized, and discriminated against in urban Shanghai. Factory workers from Subei usually took up the lowest-paying and toughest physical work. Subei natives, for example, constituted the majority of the workforce in silk reeling mills[19] and performed the most menial jobs in cotton mills.[20] Even an educated Subei person found it difficult to locate a good job because of his easily identifiable accent.[21] Shanghai natives, generally speaking, were not highly represented in the middle and upper classes either. Many engaged in petty trade and odd jobs.

In contrast, a great number of immigrants from Guangdong, southern Jiangsu, and Zhejiang came with more financial resources and consequently were better educated and better situated in business, factories, government, public service, and educational institutions. While factory workers from these areas usually found skilled work at higher pay, such as silk weaving and knitting,[22] educated persons from these areas occupied the majority of white-collar positions. A 1941 survey of white-collar employees in the Shanghai Public Service Bureau shows only 16 Shanghai natives out of a total of 238, along with 44 Zhejiang natives, 85 Jiangsu natives, and 62 Guangdong natives.[23]

Zhejiang and southern Jiangsu immigrants composed the largest part of Shanghai's business class, intellectuals, and white-collar employees. Particularly well known was the near monopoly of the native banking business by the Ningbo-Shaoxing immigrant group, known as the Ning-Shao clique.[24] Several Japanese investigations pointed out the rapid growth of the Ning-Shao clique's financial power during the 1920s and 1930s in relation to the formerly dominant Guangdong group. By the late 1930s, the

Ning-Shao clique surpassed the Guangdong clique in its share of power to become ascendant in Shanghai's native banking system.[25] One study shows that, in 1941, among the larger native banks with capital in excess of 100,000 yuan, twenty-two belonged to the Ning-Shao clique, six belonged to the Shandong clique, five were Cantonese, and four were controlled by Shanghai natives.[26] The power of Ning-Shao immigrants becomes even more obvious when one realizes that three among the "four famous men in Shanghai" (*Haishang sida wenren*) were from the Ningbo-Shaoxing area. The godfather of the Green Gang, Huang Jinrong, was from Yuyao; the famous businessman Yu Qiaqing was from Ningbo; and the onetime president of the Shanghai Chamber of Commerce, Wang Xiaolai, was a Shengxian native. Only Du Yuesheng was a Shanghai native.[27]

Native-place economy and politics directly influenced the economy and politics of Shanghai's culture. Various native cuisines, dress, dialects, and operas competed with one another to define the city's cultural landscape. Not coincidentally, the rise of the Ning-Shao bankers paralleled the emergence of women's Yue opera. As Ningbo-Shaoxing economic and political power laid the foundation for its native opera, the success of the opera in turn symbolized Ningbo-Shaoxing hegemony in the city. Yue opera not only became the most popular genre in Shanghai but also came to represent Shanghai-Jiangnan culture in China, while neither Shanghai opera nor Jiangbei opera ever gained such national recognition. The modern Shanghai dialect was first influenced by the Suzhou dialect and later by the Ningbo dialect. The famous modern Shanghai term *ehle,* meaning "we," for example, originated in Ningbo dialect but has represented a proud Shanghainese identity since the mid-twentieth century.

The support of Ning-Shao immigrants was crucial to the increased prominence of women's Yue opera in "island" Shanghai in the late 1930s and early 1940s. With a steady influx of war refugees from adjacent areas, the population reached five million, and local operas—Yue opera, Shanghai opera, and Huai opera in particular—flourished.[28] As local operas drew audiences mainly from their native-place immigrants, the superior position of Ning-Shao immigrants gave Yue opera an edge. Ning-Shao immigrants promoted their native opera in several ways. Ning-Shao men of letters wrote new plays for the opera and put together tabloid publications and fan magazines to promote it, while Ning-Shao businessmen and their wives bought expensive stage costumes and paraphernalia for the opera's stars. Finally, a loyal cross section of the Ning-Shao audience paid for tickets that cost more than tickets for other local operas.

In 1939, Yue opera tickets were the most expensive among local operas, with the exception of Beijing opera. A ticket for a Yue opera show cost fifty cents, but one for Jiangbei opera was only ten cents; Shanghai opera performed in entertainment halls cost twenty cents plus the entrance fee, but admission to a Yue opera was an additional forty cents. Yue opera could charge more because its audience had a higher median income compared to audiences for Shanghai and Jiangbei opera, and it was also more popular. Especially important for women's opera was the large group of Ning-Shao upper- and middle-class housewives and daughters, who had both the time and the money to frequent the theater. The Shanghai-native middle class was proportionately smaller, and the Subei-native middle class was very small. This large core middle-class female audience steadily channeled the financial resources of Ning-Shao immigrants to Yue opera, providing the opera with a financial base that far surpassed those of other local operas.

Yue opera's superior financial situation enabled it to invest more in its productions, and higher production values in turn attracted more viewers. For example, Yao Shuijuan's 1940 play *The Romantic Death of Jiang the Fifth* (Jiang Laowu xunqing ji), scripted and directed by Fan Li and staged at the Queen's Great Theater, used realistic stage sets for the first time in Yue opera history, with an actual rickshaw and boat as well as realistic buildings appearing onstage. These unusual stage properties cost so much that the theater had to raise its prices by 20 percent. But the play was a sensation, and the first run lasted sixty-three performances.[29] A few such major productions were enough to establish Yao Shuijuan as the top star in Yue opera.

Similarly, Yue opera actresses had the resources to dress well onstage as a result of their higher incomes, which helped maintain their theater's higher value vis-à-vis other operas and their actors. During the Republican period, costumes were the responsibility and personal property of the actors. Actors had to make themselves appear attractive and dignified onstage; otherwise, they could lose their popularity or even their positions. The pressure to dress well onstage was high, and many ordinary actors were hard pressed to keep up with expectations. As Yue opera's popularity gave its actresses, especially the leading actresses, considerable incomes, they could afford such expenses, unlike their counterparts in other local operas. Revenues from ticket sales encouraged theater bosses to invest more willingly in improving stage properties and theaters as a whole.

All these factors added up to an enhanced outlook for Yue opera theater, which gained higher status in the public eye. Within a few years, Yue opera emerged as an urban modern theater and overtook Beijing opera to become the most popular opera in the region, attracting a mass urban audience that crossed native-place, gender, and class lines. In 1941, an observer pointed out in *Shaoxing Opera Daily*: "Now not only Shaoxing natives care about the opera. People of various native-place origins all love it and go to see it." Also in 1941, *Shaoxing Opera Daily* stated: "Before the war, 70 percent of the audience for Shaoxing civil drama [one of the many names for Yue opera] were Shaoxing natives and 30 percent Ningbo natives. After the war broke out, Shaoxing natives composed only 40 percent of the whole audience, and Ningbo natives 30 percent, while other natives increased to 30 percent. In this year, non-Ningbo-Shaoxing-native audience members have increased to 60 percent."[30] Though these statistics are difficult to verify, the Yue opera audience's historical expansion among various natives from the Jiangnan region is undeniable. Further evidence shows that Yue opera also began to attract attention from the mainstream media as, perhaps for the first time in its history, *Shanghai Newspaper* carried a positive commentary on Yue opera on May 3, 1941.[31] Initially an opera of Ning-Shao natives, Yue opera was being transformed into a general urban spectacle as it simultaneously grew into a distinctly women's opera in 1940s Shanghai.

Women Going to the Opera

Women made up the majority of Yue opera's audience in Shanghai in the mid-twentieth century. They were by far the most enthusiastic spectators, fans, and patrons. Although men constituted nearly half of the audience, it was the new female audience members who invigorated women's Yue opera and helped make it a great popular-culture phenomenon.

Going to the opera could be quite an urban experience for women who had not long ago achieved the right to enjoy themselves in the public space and view commercial entertainment. Besides their strong preference for romantic love stories, a specialty of women's Yue opera, women loved to attend Yue opera shows for a variety of social reasons. Going to the opera expanded women's horizons, exposing them to other sorts of urban experiences. Riding a trolley bus, rickshaw, or private motorcar, walking among the crowds on paved sidewalks between handsome high-rises, and passing through the urban scene represented quite an adventure. Operagoing, like shopping (and window-shopping) at downtown department stores, was recreation for urban women, a refreshing break in their routines. Opportunities for socializing were another benefit of operagoing, as women usually attended plays with female companions. Knowledge of the opera, the play, and the actresses provided good fodder for conversation; one could even show off if one's companions were less knowledgeable. Women also obtained a great deal of information from the variety of shows with themes ranging from contemporary social sensation (*The Romantic Death of Jiang the Fifth*, 1940), to patriotic epic (*Hua Mulan*, 1939), to the lives of workers in remote areas (*Daughter of a Border Town* [Biancheng nüer], 1943), to exotic ethnic subjects (*Desert Prince*, 1947) in addition to great love stories about famous historical and fictional personalities. Enthusiastic fans used the opportunity to try out their organizational skills with group activities and amateur performances. For the rich, patronage was a way of deploying their superior status and economic power in public. In short, going to the opera represented an opportunity for women to engage the world at large, to cross the boundaries of the family and the factory, and even to develop identities apart from their social stations.

The Economics of Viewing Opera

Women's Yue opera appealed to women from various backgrounds, including middle-class housewives and schoolgirls, factory workers, businesswomen and merchants, and, later, students and professional women. In other words, in the middle decades of the twentieth century, women's Yue opera attracted a broad cross section of the female population in Shanghai.

Factory workers made up a considerable part of the lower- to middle-class audience for Yue opera in entertainment halls and small theaters.[32] A 1939 study done by a group of communist labor workers, *Shanghai's Industries and Workers* (Shanghai chanye yu Shanghai zhigong), provides precious firsthand observations of workers' lives as well as valuable statistics.[33] The study states that among Shanghai's 600,000 industrial workers in 1939, cotton mill workers numbered more than 100,000, and silk-knitting and silk-weaving workers were estimated at more than 40,000 each.[34] The majority of these workers were women.

To understand the economics of viewing opera for lower- and middle-class audiences, it is helpful to put wages and opera ticket prices in perspective. The average wage of cotton mill workers was fifty cents (half a yuan) per day—certainly not a lavish sum. The workers were mostly from southern and northern Jiangsu, although some were Shanghai natives.[35] On weekends, workers went out for fun in groups. Many went to see Jiangbei opera in theaters where the price of a ticket was ten cents, about one-fifth an average daily wage; others spent twelve cents to see Shanghai storytelling.[36] Workers who earned less income could see the same entertainment for just a few cents at the West Shanghai Great World, an open-air fairground that regularly featured three Beijing opera troupes, two Jiangbei operas, one Shanghai local-dialect recitation, one magic show, two martial arts performances, and one storytelling show.[37] Yue opera was not performed there, indicating the lack of interest among cotton-mill workers, mostly non–Zhejiang natives, before 1939. By the early PRC years, however, cotton-mill workers composed a large portion of Yue opera fans, evidence of a growing interest in the genre among these non–Zhejiang natives during the intervening decade.

The factory workers among the Yue opera audience during the Republican period were predominantly from silk-knitting and silk-weaving mills, both among the better-paying industries. According to the 1939 *Shanghai's Industries and Workers*, workers' daily wages ranged from an average of forty cents in silk-reeling mills to ninety cents at the French-owned trolley bus company. An average daily wage for workers in silk-weaving mills was eighty cents, and workers in knitting mills earned sixty cents a day.[38] The study also reveals a significant correlation between workers' native places and their wages: the majority of silk-knitting workers were from Shaoxing and Ningbo,[39] while the better-paid workers in silk-weaving mills were natives of Zhejiang's sericulture area, including Shengxian, Xinchang, Dongyang, Hangzhou, and Shaoxing.[40] These workers enjoyed visiting entertainment halls to watch local operas, and their native Yue opera was their favorite entertainment. Many liked to sing, and some serious amateurs occasionally organized performances for their own and their fellow workers' amusement.[41] Workers generally were able to purchase access to some type of performance, depending on their personal budgets. In October 1939, one of the most popular shows, staged by the famous Xiao Dangui and her troupe in the Old Dam Theater, charged fifty cents a ticket,[42] while the entrance fee for the Great World was twenty-two cents.[43] It seemed that male workers found entertainment halls more attractive, probably for the dynamic atmosphere and varieties of entertainment, but female workers favored inexpensive seats in theaters, perhaps because they preferred to quietly enjoy the show.[44]

Shanghai's Industries and Workers does not mention gender differentiation among operagoers, which suggests that both male and female workers enjoyed local operas from their native regions. By the early PRC period, female workers had become the more enthusiastic fans of Yue opera. This conforms to other sources that argue for the growing portion of female, as well as non-Zhejiang-native, audiences in the 1940s and 1950s. Indeed, the increase in these sectors of the Yue opera audience made Yue opera the most popular opera in modern Shanghai.

Female domestic helpers and servants constituted another group of Yue opera's loyal customers. The writer Wei Shaochang, a Shaoxing native and the son of Wei Jinshan, the executive manager of the Zhonghui Bank owned by Du Yuesheng, recalled his childhood encounter with Yue opera in the 1930s. His nanny loved Yue opera and often made the little boy ask his mother for permission and money to go see the opera at the Great World so that she could go with him. Little Wei liked to go, too, for the excitement and the delicious snacks sold at the entertainment hall.[45]

Children also attended Yue opera shows. Unlike Beijing opera, Yue opera theaters admitted small children for free, perhaps a necessary accommodation to women spectators. Children exposed to Yue opera at a young age often carried their interest in the opera into adulthood. Wei Shaochang later became the editor of several Yue opera fan magazines and tabloids, including *Shaoxing Opera Daily*.[46] Wu Ping, a lifetime Yue opera fan who nurtured her granddaughter's interest in learning the art of Yue opera, had her own first contact with the opera in her preschool years as the companion of a young lady in her neighborhood. Later, during her adolescence, she often went to see Yue opera with a girlfriend. The two girls rode in one rickshaw and shared a seat in the theater—Yue opera theaters allowed two children to enter for one ticket.[47]

Middle-class housewives and daughters were the core audience for women's opera. Republican Shanghai's middle and lower middle classes consisted of roughly two groups: one was made up of self-employed merchants and shop owners, and the other of white-collar employees. Self-employed merchants were a traditional feature of the urban economic structure, and their numbers were great. Cheng Rong's father, for example, was a merchant whose income was sufficient to provide Cheng with an education through middle school, but her admission to teacher's college (equivalent to high school but subsidized by the government, which provided a small stipend plus a tuition waiver) no doubt relieved the stress on family finances.[48] For women from lower-middle-class families, attending Yue opera shows might require some special effort. According to Zhang Xingzhou, a merchant from Ningbo, the average Ningbo immigrant in Shanghai lived a frugal life. Though the women usually did not work outside the home, there was always plenty of work to do—cleaning, doing laundry, attending to sideline family businesses, caring for children, shopping, and cooking.[49] Ningbo immigrants were notorious for their miserly ways, and Ningbo women were discouraged from going out and spending money. The frequent Yue operagoers, Zhang remarked, were those who had both money and leisure. By this, he meant upper-class women.[50]

Shanghai's white-collar employees, according to *Shanghai's Industries and Workers*, outnumbered those in the rest of China—approximately 300,000 in three economic sectors. About 140,000 worked in traditional-style shops, about 100,000 in foreign-owned businesses, and about 50,000 in modern institutions owned by native capitalists. In the Chinese sectors, an average monthly salary for junior employees, who made up more than half the white-collar workforce, was between ten and twenty yuan, lower than the wages of average factory workers; an average salary for mid-level employees was about thirty yuan per month, except for some higher-paid employees in the financial sector. An average salary for mid-level bank employees, for example, was between fifty to sixty yuan per month. Employees of the Shanghai China Bank were by far the best paid.[51] The authors do not give a salary range for the one-third of white-collar workers who were employed in foreign-owned businesses; however, they clearly indicate that salaries in this sector tended to be higher than in Chinese sectors.

Another set of numbers from 1941 also helps us make sense of the economics of viewing Yue opera in wartime Shanghai. According to the Shanghai Public Service Bureau's annual report, the salaries for 232 white-collar employees in June 1941 ranged from 40 to 180 yuan per month, and 225 blue-collar employees earned from 22 to 60 yuan.[52] Meanwhile, Yue opera tickets ranged from 80 cents to 1 yuan and 20 cents in 1941. In either case, viewing Yue opera may not have been cheap, but at the same time, it was still affordable for middle-class families.

Middle-class men and women tended to have received better educations in modern schools, and the education gap between them and the lower class could not be ignored. The authors of *Shanghai's Industries and Workers* explain:

> China's modern industry has less than thirty years of history. As the rural economy disintegrated, blue-collar workers came mainly from poor peasant families, while white-collar employees came mainly from landlord and rich peasant families. The former were less educated and the latter better educated. In addition, in our country, industries that need skilled workers capable of handling complicated technologies are relatively few. This has

resulted in a big gap in educational levels between the white-collar and blue-collar workers and consequently divides them into two social categories.[53]

The two categories of workers corresponded with divisions in native-place origins. Natives of the Jiangnan region constituted a large proportion of Shanghai's college students and intellectuals as well as its entrepreneurs and white-collar workers. Although many white-collar men were not interested in Yue opera, they did not mind letting the women in their families enjoy it. The father of Yue opera fan Wu Ping, for example, was a college graduate who worked for the customs service during the 1940s. He had no interest in Yue opera or any other local operas, but he did not mind giving his daughter permission and money to attend Yue opera shows. According to Wu Ping, the four family members each had his or her own favorite pastime. Her father read, her mother played mahjong, her older sister loved pop songs, and she herself was crazy about Yue opera.[54] Middle-class women were fond of going to see Yue opera. A new bride in Wu Ping's neighborhood often went to see Yue opera, most frequently in the afternoons, when her husband was at work, but also sometime in the evenings, leaving her husband home alone. The well-known female writer Su Qing, a Ningbo native, admitted that attending opera was her favorite pastime.[55]

The Fans

Finally, later during the 1940s, a new group, and, in a sense, a new generation, of Yue opera fans appeared. They were schoolgirls, female college students, some female professionals, and new middle-class housewives, all educated in the modern school system with Republican ideas of equal rights for women, nationalism, and modernity. By the postwar period, the Republican educational system had made school education for middle-class girls commonplace and college education a possibility. This generation endowed the opera with new prestige as well as new stimulus for further reform. Cheng Rong, the first woman playwright for Yue opera, and Chen Shulian, the Yue opera radio announcer, both graduated from teacher's schools (equivalent to high school) and taught primary school before they joined Yuan Xuefen's company. Teng Jiazhen and her husband Song Zhiyou, both accountants and graduates of Dongwu University, were enthusiastic Yue opera supporters. During the late 1940s and throughout the 1950s, Teng held midnight snack parties at her home for actresses after their evening shows. She also taught them to read and write. As a professional, Teng emphasized in interviews that she was *not* an old-fashioned adoptive mother, nor one of the obsessed Yue opera fans. She just wanted to help the actresses. The actresses in fact addressed Teng as "teacher."[56] Many middle-school boys and girls as well as college students became Yue opera regulars; known as the "triangle brand audience," for they all wore triangular school badges, they were the pride of New Yue Opera as they embodied the opera's modernity.

Many of these young women were attracted to women's opera for reasons similar to those of their mothers' generation. Chen Shulian commented:

> At the beginning, I was not interested in Yue opera or any local operas [because local operas seemed vulgar and old-fashioned]. I had been a big movie fan. I became attracted to Yue opera after I befriended Yuan Xuefen, when she came to our station for a Yue opera radio program. The people from the Xuesheng Company were different from those of other local opera companies. Shanghai opera, Suzhou story-singing, and Shanghai comic shows all performed on radio programs at our station. Even well-known actors from Shanghai opera behaved just like lower-class folks in the marketplace, with cigarettes on their lips all the time. Only people from the Xuesheng Company looked respectable.[57]

That was how Chen got involved with the Xuesheng Company and fell in love with the reformed Yue opera.

Fan-club activities, which began in the early 1940s, reveal how Yue opera served young women's needs for socializing and personal development in the modern context. The appearance of several fan clubs in the late 1940s signaled young women's self-conscious efforts to forge a community. Through fan-club activities, women created a social space in which participants could express their individual opinions and make decisions regarding their clubs' affairs. Fans indeed openly criticized and argued with one another in tabloids, fan publications, and meetings, often unable to agree on what should be done and how. Although admittedly frustrated by this situation, members nonetheless took great pleasure in getting together with other women with the same interests, exercising control and influence at the same time. These fan clubs seem to have achieved very little of what the members wanted, but they provided a space where young women could develop a sense of their social selves while learning social and organizational skills.

One interesting feature of these fan clubs was the women's attempt to exclude men. Female fans' monopoly over fan clubs indicates not only their enthusiasm for Yue opera but also their desire for a social space of their own, free from male intervention. The women, consciously or not, tried to expand their horizon beyond the home and school and did so in defiance of male social dominance. It was to a certain extent a subversive practice, though it took place on the periphery of society and did arouse some male protest. One commentator, responding negatively to women's monopoly of fan clubs, wrote about the establishment of a fan club for Fan Ruijuan, a popular young male impersonator, in the weekly tabloid *Yue Opera News* (Yueju bao):

> According to the Founding Manifesto of the Fan Ruijuan Club [Juan She], it seems that the guiding principle is to support Fan Ruijuan, enhance Fan's art, and associate all the Fan fans in fellowship with one another. If this is to be the principle, then all the Fan fans, men and women, should be able to join the club. It goes without saying that it is contradictory for the club to limit its membership to women only. From this case, one can see how narrow-minded women are.[58]

Another interview with the club's president, Dong Qian, by a woman named Xu Fangfeng, probably a freelancer for the tabloid and a Yue opera fan herself, offers a general sense of the purpose and attitudes of these fan-club members. According to Dong:

> The Fan Ruijuan Club now has more than 120 members. There are fourteen volunteer workers; though the number is not great, we do not feel any lack of personnel because everyone works hard. Members go to see the shows on their own and convene when there is business to discuss. As for entertainment, members all suggest that I organize fan-club performances because everyone likes to sing. But organizing an amateur performance is not an easy thing. There are plenty of five-minute enthusiasts among Yue opera fans. In addition, we should not draw lines between one another if we want to perform together. In Shanghai, there are amateur performance clubs for Beijing opera; Yue opera as the local number one certainly should have these clubs. [I] am now writing a play for Miss Fan, tentatively titled *Lonely Figure under the Autumn Moon* [Qiuyue guying]. It's just an enjoyment for myself.[59]

Dong Qian is obviously a well-educated, young, single woman from a well-to-do family—typical of the new generation of middle- and upper-middle-class young women fans in Shanghai in the mid-twentieth century.

Republican Shanghai, largely due to its semicolonial economy and political system, was home to a large, mixed upper class composed of newly affluent entrepreneurs, high-ranking business professionals, high officials, the town strongmen, and the city's fading old aristocrats and rural magnates. During the turbulent years of the first half of the century, Shanghai's foreign settlements attracted rich aristocrats and modern intellectuals alike with its exotic and extravagant lifestyle while providing a safe haven for refugees fleeing political persecution, warfare, and famine. Many lived decadent lives, preoccupied with opium smoking and the company of courtesans and opera actors. The young novelist Zhang Ailing painstakingly describes in her fiction the lives of the declining elite in Shanghai's foreign settlements, witnessing the hopeless and self-indulgent existence of her father, stepmother, and other relatives.[60]

Patronizing and consorting with actors were traditionally prerogatives of upper-class men; the privilege was challenged during the Republican period when women entered into the practice. With the rise of minor operas, especially women's Yue opera, a new gendered division of upper-class patronage appeared. While upper-class men customarily attended Beijing opera and patronized famous Beijing opera actors, the women socialized with Yue opera actors and actresses. Upper-class women's patronage of Yue opera began in the 1920s with the establishment of the all-male Shengxian opera in Shanghai and became a popular-culture phenomenon with women's Yue opera during the middle decades. Thus, for example, while Huang Jinrong, the king of Shanghai's Green Gang, was a great patron of Beijing opera, his daughter-in-law was the adoptive mother of Xiao Dangui, the famous Yue opera star. As housewives who did not have independent social status apart from that of their husbands, these women did not have a formal role to play in the public domain. Thus, for them, more than for men, going to the theater and patronizing actors were not merely entertaining activities but also a means of socializing, crossing boundaries, and empowering themselves.

Women transgressing gender boundaries in modern Shanghai was a favorite topic of public gossip. During the late nineteenth and early twentieth centuries, when women were not supposed to appear in public entertainment venues, courtesans attended Beijing opera plays in foreign settlements; many became romantically involved with famous actors, while some caused scandals. Even though the male-centered public culture rendered them objects of male sexual desire, courtesans were able to turn the tables by making actors the targets of their own sexual desire, often at the expense of their male customers.[61] During the early Republican period, when operagoing became a legitimate pastime for women, upper-class wives—mostly courtesans who had become concubines—also began to have sexual liaisons with actors. When all-male Shengxian opera became popular in Shanghai during the 1920s and 1930s, upper-class women from the Shaoxing-Ningbo area did indeed take advantage of the naive young actors from the countryside.

In interviews, the Yue opera actress Xiao-Bai Yumei emphasized that her father, a famous female impersonator and renowned as Mei Lanfang in the all-male Shengxian opera, was never corrupted and stated that he was unusual in this regard.[62] Xiao-Bai Yumei inherited the famous name of her father when she took over his role in 1933 at the age of twelve and performed with popular actors of the time. Many famous actors smoked opium and had liaisons with rich concubines, and some became victims of their own decadent lifestyles. Xiao-Bai Yumei recalled a young man named Gao Yuesheng, a popular star specializing in young male roles and Xiao-Bai Yumei's stage partner. Gao was at the peak of his career when the two performed at the New World in the mid-1930s. Gao, however, indulged himself in liaisons with rich men's concubines. Every day, as soon as the show was over, there was always a car awaiting him outside. He obviously had more than one lover. As time passed, the quality of his performance and voice deteriorated, and eventually he had to quit. He died at the age of twenty-seven. Xiao-Bai did not see how it could have been possible for an actor to perform two shows every day while entangled in an excessive sexual life. She was not specific about the cause of Gao's death, perhaps because it was obvious to her that he simply overextended and exhausted himself.[63]

Gao's story provides an interesting case in which multiple transgressions of class and gender boundaries occurred. On the one hand, the actor undermined the elite's supremacy by seducing their women and consuming their wealth. The concubines, on the other hand, ridiculed male sexual dominance and male authority by enjoying the actor's sexuality at their husbands' expense. Concubines were able to engage in such sexual activity behind their husbands' backs largely because it was common Republican era practice to maintain concubines in separate dwellings, away from principal wives and children. Young concubines who had been courtesans and did not have children were most likely to initiate extramarital affairs.[64] A principal wife usually shunned sexual escapades, perhaps because her stake in the family was greater.

Defiance and transgression always had their limits and were subject to punishment in Republican Shanghai. Unlike rich courtesans, who had more autonomy over their own sexuality, concubines as well as principal wives owed their status and financial well-being to their husbands, who possessed certain prerogatives with respect to the women's sexuality. Thus, when women's opera and its actresses became publicly accessible, both concubines and principal wives turned to these sources of legitimate involvement. Concerned primarily with the well-being of the familial and social structure, the Chinese patriarchal system was largely silent on intimate relationships between women, which seemingly posed no threat to patriarchal authority. As Xiao-Bai Yumei explained, husbands were not worried when their wives became passionate about women's Yue opera and close to the actresses because these were "just women's things." Nothing serious could happen between women—meaning there could not be a scandal resulting from public misbehavior or pregnancy. Homosexual relations were rare and of little concern, she believed. In fact, husbands were at ease when their wives and daughters were attending women's opera and consorting with opera actresses.[65]

Women's opera also attracted upper-class wives because of the absence of male performers. In most other performing groups—such as other local operas, cinema, and spoken drama—actors and actresses worked and sometimes lived together day and night. This was to some extent a professional imperative, often compounded by financial necessity, that provoked titillation regarding modern lifestyles and suspicion of promiscuity among the public. Sexual relationships between male and female stars were a never-ending topic of tabloids and gossip, invoking the centuries-old stereotype of actors as promiscuous. In contrast to the perceived promiscuity of other performing troupes, women's Yue opera companies appeared pure and clean, with a hint of virtue and chastity. Actresses, mostly unmarried girls around twenty years of age from the countryside, looked as though they were begging for protection from potential patrons, if not waiting to be claimed.[66] Furthermore, the very absence of male actors backstage was convenient for women patrons, permitting them to move in and out freely and appropriate it as a woman's space.[67]

Adoptive Mothers and Sisters

"Adoptive motherhood" (*guofang niang*) is a peculiar institution related to wealthy women and their patronage of Yue opera actresses in modern

Shanghai.[68] It began with the appearance of women performers in Yue opera in Shanghai in the 1930s and ended in the mid-1960s with the Cultural Revolution, roughly the golden period of the opera in the city. An obscure practice among Shanghai residents, adoptive motherhood became an institution within the context of Yue opera patronage. Generally, when a rich patron decided to take her favorite star as an adoptive daughter, she would select a date on which the ritual was to take place. For the ritual, which was usually held at the adoptive mother's home, the adoptive mother would be seated when the adoptive daughter was brought in and knelt down before her. The daughter kowtowed three times, thereby formally establishing adoptive relations. The mother then presented the daughter with "gifts of the first meeting" (*jian mian li*), which could include dresses, accessories, stage costumes, or expensive jewels. Sometimes, the adoptive family would even host a banquet to announce the adoption. Adoptive relations were public and usually carried much prestige for both the mother and the daughter. For the mother, it was a way of showing off her wealth and status by playing the role of protector of a star; for the actress, the relationship symbolized access to the wealthy and powerful. Underneath the public and symbolic meanings of the institution, the relationship itself could be as complicated and diverse as any other.

Upper-class patronage of Yue opera was important in shaping the opera. Female patrons would take one or sometimes several of their favorite actresses into adoptive relationships, showering them with gifts ranging from cash, jewels, and offstage dresses, to stage costumes and decorations made of embroidered brocade bearing the actresses' names. The better and more expensive the stage sets and costumes, the more prestige the adoptive mother gained in the public eye. Adoptive mothers also took care of the actresses to varying degrees. They often took their adoptive daughters home after evening performances and provided food for them, and actresses sometimes stayed at their adoptive mothers' homes for a few days or even weeks. Some adoptive mothers even invited actresses to move in with them. Often, an adoptive mother would buy a dozen or more front-row tickets and invite friends and relatives to the actress's show. Adoptive mothers could also show off by taking their adoptive daughters, usually famous stars, to perform at private gatherings.[69]

The most exciting occasions, however, involved grand charity performances, opportunities for adoptive mothers to show off their wealth and power and for adoptive daughters to enhance their fame, financial situations, and social esteem.[70] Charity performances were always held in first-rate theaters with larger stages, more seats, and, most important, an esteemed audience of celebrities who did not usually go to Yue opera theaters. Tabloid coverage and advertising for these charity performances were profuse. As adoptive mothers called in to reserve tickets in the names of their adoptive daughters, tabloids updated ticket sales daily, listing actresses' names in order of the yuan amount and making the event into a public pledge competition. The larger the yuan amount pledged to the star, the more prestigious the star and her adoptive mother became. The rivalry continued onstage when actresses tried to display themselves at their best, in terms of costumes and paraphernalia as well as performing skill. For these reasons, both adoptive mothers and actresses considered participation in a charity performance to be an honor and a chance to gain public exposure while supporting a lofty cause.

The careers of the noted actresses Xiao-Bai Yumei and Yao Shuijuan illustrate how the adoptive mother system worked. Xiao-Bai Yumei's adoptive mother was the wife of He Lunzhang, a Ningbo native and comprador for the American-owned Xinfu Trade Company. Xiao-Bai was introduced to her adoptive mother by the woman's daughter, a great fan of Xiao-Bai's who attended her performance every day after school. The family had three private cars and employed seventeen domestic servants. Xiao-Bai's adoptive mother was the principal wife, which explained why she could spend so much money on Xiao-Bai. It seemed to be a point of pride for Xiao-Bai that her adoptive mother was the principal wife. The adoptive mother was very fond of the young Xiao-Bai Yumei, who was still a teenager. At the adoption ritual, Xiao-Bai recalled, "My adoptive mother was so happy when I called out loud 'Mma!' For that, she gave me a pearl necklace."[71] Xiao-Bai Yumei recalled with pride that, in the late 1930s, when she triumphed in a charity performance, her adoptive mother gave her seventeen taels of gold, which Xiao-Bai used to purchase a long-term lease on a house for her family.

Unlike Hollywood stars or a few Beijing opera superstars at the time, actors in Republican China were never rich, no matter how famous they were. Xiao-Bai Yumei's father, one of the most popular actors in all-male Shengxian opera, earned sixty yuan monthly, which was enough to keep a family of five comfortable. Xiao-Bai Yumei, however, earned in women's opera much more than her father did. Her income not only made her family comfortable but also paid for her three brothers' education. According to *Shaoxing Opera Daily*, the highest monthly salary for Yue opera stars was two hundred yuan in 1938 and six hundred yuan in 1940.[72] A reasonable extrapolation would indicate about four hundred yuan per month in 1939. Compared to the earnings of factory workers and white-collar employees, actors' salaries may look high, but only a few famous Yue opera actresses actually earned that much. Moreover, the money quickly disappeared—to pay for costumes and daily expenditures for families living in the city and relatives who remained in the countryside. There was always the question of saving for the summer and winter off seasons, when actresses did not earn salaries, as well as for the years after retirement, which usually occurred when actresses were in their late twenties. Thus, for actresses, gifts from adoptive mothers represented a source of income that contributed significantly to their personal finances.

Adoptive mothers helped Yue opera actresses not only financially but socially as well. The patronage Wei Shaochang and his parents bestowed on Yao Shuijuan is a good example, illustrating how the rich and powerful Ning-Shao immigrants helped make successes of an actress and an opera. When Yao Shuijuan made her debut in Shanghai in early 1938, a young female fan introduced her to Wei Jinshan and his wife, who subsequently took Yao as an adoptive daughter and deluged her with generous gifts, from professional to personal items. Yao's extravagant stage costumes and paraphernalia, along with her performing skill, became a subject of public gossip. It was said that she changed costumes eighteen times in one play. She had, it was rumored, the most gorgeous brocade stage curtains with her name embroidered on them; she was, in fact, the first Yue opera actress to use expensive logo curtains.[73] In 1939, with the backing of Wei Jinshan, Yao Shuijuan obtained a lease on the Queen's Great Theater and became the first Yue opera actress with her "own" theater, although it was actually controlled by the Weis.[74]

Wei Shaochang, then in high school, also became a fan of Yao Shuijuan's. He and two other Shaoxing natives published a couple of tabloid fan magazines, *The Song of Yue* (Yue ou), and *Shaoxing Opera News*, to promote Yao Shuijuan and Yue opera in general. Inspired by patron publications in honor of famous Beijing opera female impersonators such as Mei Lanfang and Cheng Yanqiu, Wei and his colleagues also published a special issue dedicated to Yao and her art, the first publication of the sort for a Yue opera actress.[75] These publications were filled with photos of Yao and articles and reports that praised the actress and her art, portraying her as a modern conscientious actress and her art as the best of its kind. The book also contains a line of calligraphy by Mei Lanfang for Yao Shuijuan, which reads: "The queen of Yue opera." Mei had not yet met Yao, and he crafted the calligraphy for

Wei Jinshan, who had requested it on Yao's behalf. It was a smart idea that helped lift the cultural-social status of Yao Shuijuan and Yue opera by equating Yao Shuijuan with Mei Lanfang, the "queen of Beijing opera."[76]

Patrons provided a social network, a sort of social protection, for actresses faced with the theater owner's monopoly of their trade. Actresses, who were rural girls newly arrived in Shanghai, lacked experience and social networks that might help them counter the power of the theater boss, who tended to take advantage of his employees' vulnerability. With powerful patrons such as the Weis, however, Yao Shuijuan secured a long-term lease on the Queen's Great Theater, hence becoming somewhat self-employed. Within a few years of her arrival, Yao Shuijuan became the most noted Yue opera actress and a star in Shanghai's public culture, or so it seemed. A December 1940 survey by *Drama Semi-monthly* (Banyue xiju) indicates that Yao Shuijuan's shows had the highest viewing rate, with Xiao Dangui second, and Ma Zhanghua third.[77] In fact, Xiao Dangui was at least as popular, as suggested by a saying of the time: "The three flowers were surpassed by the graceful; the graceful was surpassed by a laurel." The three flowers were Shi Yinhua, Zhao Ruihua, and Tu Xinhua, the very first generation of women's opera actresses; the "graceful" (*juan*) was Yao Shuijuan; and the "laurel" (*gui*) was Xiao Dangui. But Xiao Dangui and Ma Zhanghua were not as lucky as Yao Shuijuan. Both died young and tragically, after each tried to break free from her boss's control.

Even now, Wei Shaochang felt compelled to give credit to the adoption practice by comparing the different situations of Yao Shuijuan and Xiao Dangui: "Try to imagine," Wei commented, "with a devil like Zhang Chunfan following Xiao, how could decent adoptive mothers and sisters dare to get close to her? In contrast, Yao Shuijuan had the most powerful patrons and was friendly with tabloid writers. The different situations of the two stars could not but affect their careers and lives."[78] Self-promotion notwithstanding, Wei Shaochang's story is not without merit. Actresses must have found that the social and financial support provided by adoptive parents could be of some significance. What is important is not that Zhang Chunfan was a devil but that he alone controlled Xiao's life and career.

The adoptive parents system continued into the early PRC period. One interesting example involves the actress Gao Jin, a promising actress in the mid-1950s specializing in young male roles. Her family was quite poor, and her brother was in the laundry business in Hong Kong. Gao wanted to join her brother and could not obtain permission. But she knew a young girl who admired her and her art and whose mother held a position of some responsibility at the local police station. The girl introduced Gao to her mother, and the mother took Gao as her adoptive daughter and helped her obtain permission to go to Hong Kong.[79]

Patrons, of course, were not altruists. Some were suspected of being involved in activities deemed indecent or deviant, such as suspicious adoptive father-daughter relationships or homosexual adoptive mother-daughter relationships. An interesting commentary in *Yue Opera News* had this to say about patrons and patronage:

> Patrons all aim to satisfy their own desires. Their explicit purpose is to boost the actresses' popularity, but their implicit purpose is to appropriate the actresses. What patrons do is merely flatter the actresses, to win their favor. The great patrons flatter the great stars, and small patrons flatter small stars. To flatter an actress, a patron has to give costumes and paraphernalia as gifts, manage theaters, organize opera companies, publish special issues, and everything else necessary to gratify the star. There are also some people who join the claques as a favor to their friends.
>
> As for female patrons, they also have their purposes. Some want to be respectable senior adoptive mothers, others want to find concubines for their husbands, still others are interested in homosexual relations with the actresses. We find no concrete evidence of homosexuality in Yue opera circles, but we know it certainly exists.
>
> The formulae are as follows: male patrons (*yang*) flatter young female characters (*yin*), and *yang* plus *yin* equals neutrality. Female patrons (*yin*) flatter young male impersonators (*yang*—though fake *yang*, better than nothing).

The author declared, "I think the most loyal patron is every 'pure and clean' audience member in every theater." And he ended his comments with the question: "Does the development of Yue opera rely on flattery?"[80]

The author was certainly critical, but actresses generally condoned the practice of patronage and acknowledged that they benefited from it. Xiao-Bai Yumei as well as other actresses did not have many complaints about adoptive mothers, even though the adoptive mother system has received much criticism and negative portrayals in the official history and discourse on Yue opera after 1949. During the Republican and early PRC period, all popular stars had their loyal patrons, many of whom took the role of adoptive mother. A star usually had more than one adoptive mother and many more special patrons. Xu Yulan, for example, had at least two adoptive mothers, Zhao Naixue and the wife of Xu Datong, popularly known as "the king of paper manufacture." Xiao-Bai had three adoptive mothers; one was the wife of a comprador, and the other two were wives of Ning-Shao bankers. When asked why women's opera had such success in Shanghai, Xiao-Bai Yumei responded with one sentence: "That's because of the adoptive mothers."[81] Xiao-Bai might have had her personal success in mind with that answer, but indeed the success of many top actresses like Xiao-Bai ensured the success of women's Yue opera as a whole.

Another type of patronage involved women professionals and emerging entrepreneurs in Republican Shanghai, who aided their favorite actresses with their professional expertise and social experience. Zhao Naixue, an excellent tailor and the adoptive mother of Xu Yulan, not only took care of Xu's life but moreover was responsible for many of Xu's specially designed stage costumes. Xu Yulan moved in with Zhao in 1946 and lived with her for many years, until Xu got married in 1954. During Xu's sickness in 1946, Zhao acted as the actress's parent, caring for her at her bedside and also defending her against her boss Zhang Chunfan's demands that she perform.[82] Xu's own mother later came to Shanghai and lived with her, but as a rural woman, her mother could not give her the kind of social support that Zhao was able to provide.

Tang Diyin, owner of the Green Jade Pen Company, was a special patron of Yuan Xuefen's and supported many of the actress's activities through her business expertise, although Yuan was not exactly Tang's adoptive daughter, and the two probably had a more equal relationship than most others. Yuan met Tang at the Soviet Union Radio Station through Chen Shulian, the radio announcer. Yuan agreed to advertise for Tang's pens, not for money, but because she supported hardworking independent woman like Tang.[83] According to Cheng Rong:

> Tang Diyin's success came from her hard work. Her parents discriminated against girls and gave her no support. Tang was strong willed and managed to become an apprentice in a stationery shop after graduating from primary school. When I saw her in 1945, she wore very short hair and a straight cheongsam. She had a lot of ideas, very experienced and with a strong concept of women's independence. All of us four sisters [Yuan, Tang, Chen, and Cheng herself] were like that—we all wanted independence, not reliance on men.[84]

Tang's was a small factory that employed about ten workers. It was set up in two living rooms of a three-story townhouse on a lane that branched off the main roadway, a type of housing known as *shikumen*. Tang was not really rich, and she supported Yuan with her expertise and connections rather than financially. During the Civil War period, between 1946 and 1949, Tang acted as Yuan's trusted representative, and Yuan relied on Tang during these eventful and sometimes very difficult days.[85]

It should be noted that even though rich patrons adopted only popular stars who specialized in young male and female roles, other actresses, with little access to this institution, were not critical of it. Zhou Baokui, a well-known actress specializing in elder female roles, remarked, "Only big stars had adoptive mothers. Others did not have this benefit. We had to spend much of our monthly pay on buying stage costumes for ourselves." She may have been a little envious but certainly was not critical.[86]

The adoptive mother system lingered into the early PRC period but ended with the beginning of the Cultural Revolution in 1966. With the revolution, a totally different sociology and political economy replaced those of the 1930s and 1940s, which had encouraged the development of upper-class women's patronage of Yue opera.

Yue Opera in the Mass Media

In Shanghai in the 1940s, Yue opera's influence was not limited to operagoers. Modern means of mass communication, such as radio, the phonograph and audio recordings, and motion pictures, plus cheaply produced lyric handbooks (see fig. 3.1), made Yue opera a pervasive influence in urban society and beyond in the early Chinese electronic age.[87] Shanghai's residents, men and women, old and young, even if they did not attend the performances in person, were all exposed to Yue opera—constantly hearing its lyrics and music played on radios and phonographs, reading its gossip in the tabloid press, and seeing its images in theatrical posters, newspaper advertisements, lyric handbooks, and photographs displayed in downtown photo studios. Many lower-class women who could not afford to attend performances by major troupes before 1949 and many white-collar men who did not care to attend Yue opera were nevertheless familiar with it through hearing gossip about its stars as well as through its famous plays, lyrics, music, and character modeling.

The relationship between the new high-technology media and popular entertainment in mid-twentieth-century Shanghai was one of mutual reliance, not much different from that of our day, in which high-tech media depended on popular programming in order to develop, while popular forms

3.1 Cheaply produced Yue opera lyrics handbooks and popular promotional publications for Yue opera fans in the 1930s and 1940s. (Preserved at the Shanghai Municipal Library)

used high-tech means to spread beyond the limits of traditional venues. The most popular programming of the time included Suzhou story-singing, Yue opera, Beijing opera, Shanghai opera, and comic shows, with the story-singing and Yue opera being perhaps the most commercially viable. The story of Yue opera reveals much about the formation of a mass-mediated popular culture in modern Shanghai.

Radio appeared in Shanghai in the 1920s and became popular during the 1930s. Private ownership of radio sets was already prevalent in middle- and upper-class households, and women in these families were avid listeners, since they spent the larger part of the day at home.[88] But the influence of radio broadcasting went far beyond the ownership of radio sets. For one thing, Republican Shanghai was already a very crowded place. Most of Shanghai's commoner population lived in *shikumen*, three-story townhouses located on the narrow lanes that branched off the main streets.[89] A radio playing in one household could easily be heard by a dozen or so neighbors. Moreover, there were always some neighborhood shops as well as department stores, restaurants, and teahouses playing radios to attract potential customers off the streets. Movies made during the period often tried to create a lively atmosphere by playing radio shows, popular songs, Suzhou story-singing, or Yue opera in the background. The Yue opera fan Wu Ping remarked that when she was in primary school, she was always distracted by Yue opera broadcasts forever playing in the department store across the street from her classroom. "I was listening to the radio across the street from my school all the time. I didn't care that much about my math. But I could tell which actress was on as soon as I heard the *huqin* playing the opening scores, even before she started to sing."[90]

The first Yue opera radio show went on the air in July 1939, performed by Ma Zhanghua with Fu Quanxiang and later with Yuan Xuefen.[91] Sanyou Enterprises, a pharmaceutical company, sponsored the show in order to advertise its products. Ma Zhanghua's fame quickly spread via airwaves throughout the city. She soon became known as "the lightning young male impersonator" (*shandian xiaosheng*). The word *shandian*, "lightning," connotes speed while alluding to electronic devices, a perfect description of Ma's sudden success boosted by the radio program. Because she advertised a tonic product for Sanyou Enterprises, Ma got another nickname, a more cynical one perhaps, "the tonic young male impersonator" (*buwan xiaosheng*), vividly illustrating how much her fame was associated with the radio advertising.

Sanyou Enterprises, moreover, published a special issue accompanying its radio program, *Yue Opera Special Issue* (Yueju zhuankan), which was printed on cheap paper and distributed free of charge. The booklet of about three hundred pages contains pictures of Ma Zhanghua, Yuan Xuefen, and other popular actresses as well as the lyrics of popular pieces from Yue opera plays, punctuated by advertisements for the company's products. In one typical example, Ma Zhanghua's and Yuan Xuefen's lyrics occupy the larger part of the two facing pages. Below the lyrics is a clearly printed line: "From 6:00 to 7:10 P.M. during Ma Zhanghua's and Yuan Xuefen's Yue opera, please call in and request your favorite pieces. Ma's and Yuan's women's Yue opera performs at the Dalai Theater in Hushe on Beijing Road; for reservations call 92205." And on the left side, an advertisement for Sanyou tonics catches the eye.[92]

In the ensuing decade, as with Xuesheng Company and the Soviet Union Radio Station (discussed in chapter 2), major Yue opera companies used radio to introduce new plays, enhance their public visibility, and promote sales. Actresses made themselves available to listeners and answered their questions during the fixed daily programs, which usually ran one to two hours.[93] Live broadcasts from the theater were another regular feature. Yue opera companies contracted directly with radio stations for broadcasts; the two parties usually did not pay each other for these programs, but advertising revenues went to the stations.

The phonograph played a similar role in enhancing Yue opera's popularity. A phonograph was a luxury item owned mostly by upper-class families; in movies made during the 1940s, the presence of a phonograph indicated an upper-class lifestyle. The influence of phonographs and records, however, extended beyond the upper-class living room through a market network of phonograph and recording companies, radio stations, theaters, bookstores, publishing houses, department stores, radio equipment and repair stores, and even watchmakers' shops. A contemporaneous lyric pocketbook, *Complete Book of Lyrics from Shaoxing Opera* (Shaoxing xikao quance), testifies to a marketing network centered on Yue opera. The book was published in 1939 and cost sixty cents, roughly the price of a ticket to a Yue opera show. It contains seventy-nine pages of lyrics from various Yue opera plays, about twenty pages of pictures of Yue opera stars, and many pages of advertisements. This lyric pocketbook reveals an interconnected world of entertainment, commerce, and the media. One page has a chart listing radio stations along with station symbols, wave frequencies, phone numbers, and addresses. The other side of the page is an advertisement for a phonograph company. The first page contains two coupons from a phonograph company, which the reader could use to request that the designated radio station play two Yue opera pieces from the company's records. The next two pages list major Yue opera theaters, with phone numbers and addresses, and display an advertisement for another phonograph company. On the inner back cover is a list of distributors of the book, some of which appear to be retailers of phonographs and records. The distributors in Shanghai include four Yue opera theaters, four phonograph companies, three radio stations, a radio repair shop, and a bookstore. Distributors outside Shanghai include phonograph stores, watchmakers' shops, radio equipment shops, department stores, and various retail stores.[94]

Compared to radio, the phonograph had its advantages—it could play a recording over and over again, and it helped spread the influence of Yue opera far beyond Shanghai's radio boundaries. Qiu Wenguang, a Shengxian native and a lifetime Yue opera fan who has lived in Taiwan since 1949, recalled how young girls in Shengxian learned Yue opera by singing along with phonograph and records:

> My most vivid memory goes back to 1943, when I finished the fourth grade and returned home from my grandma's place to go to Chongren Senior Pri-

mary School. Almost all the twenty or more girls in the school were members of an opera school. As soon as they joined the opera school, they sat around a table, holding a piece of paper with lyrics in their hands, and sang together loudly with great concentration. . . .

During these two years, I had a classmate by the name of Qiu Chutao. Chutao's family and mine were on the same street, less than one hundred meters away from each other. We thus played together even after school. His family owned a phonograph, and his older sister Xingyun and cousin Aining (who was also called Yuxuan) often sang along with the records, assisted by a palm-size lyric book. As I had heard them singing all the time in these years, I had these lyrics down pat.[95]

Yue opera actresses began to produce records as early as 1936, when Yuan Xuefen made her first recording for the French-owned Baidai Recording Company.[96] After that, hundreds of recordings of numerous well-known Yue opera actresses appeared in the marketplace. Printed lyrics and scripts, used in conjunction with the phonograph and records, helped listeners better understand and appreciate the opera and aided amateur artists in improving their skills.[97]

Shanghai's press also played a role in creating a mass opera culture. Printing shops could be set up in a downstairs living room, and cheap, recycled paper could be used to produce low-cost handbooks, which could then be sold at bargain prices for a few cents to maybe sixty cents each.[98] Most of these publications were printed in a small, thin format so that they could easily be carried around in a pocket or a woman's purse. They were mass-produced to feed a large urban public interested in the opera. Fans collected these pocketbook lyrics, and amateurs used them as scripts when putting together shows for themselves.

Other publications included tabloids, Yue opera company promotional issues, and fan magazines. During the New Yue Opera reforms, companies began to put together playbills that were sold at theater entrances before each performance. The playbill included introductions to the plot and cast, information on new features in stage scenery and costumes, and incidental details about the stars and the production process. These playbills sold so well that they generated a considerable side income for the editors, usually company staff members.[99] Yue opera fan Wu Ping loved the playbills so much that she saved all the ones she bought at performances and carefully preserved them in a wicker suitcase along with many lyric scripts.[100] These publications connected a visual and audio world to a printed world, blurred the territorial boundaries of different regimes of mass communication, and helped diffuse the culture of Yue opera in Shanghai's public space.

Finally, it was the cinema that made Yue opera one of the most influential arts in the nation. Motion pictures acquired a mass audience in Shanghai during the Republican period. As a 1936 essay, "The Development of Shanghai's Cinemas," noted:

> Motion pictures . . . as a new form of art indeed won lots of people's interest and appreciation. The movie business developed rapidly. As time passes, it not only comes to share the entertainment market with China's traditional operas but tends to surpass them in popularity. Right now there are between thirty-three and thirty-six cinemas in Shanghai. Last year a movie revue, *Diantong Pictorial* [Diantong huabao], charted all the cinemas on a Shanghai street map and topped the map with a large-character headline, "Places Where a Million People Spend Leisure Time Everyday!"[101]

A decade later, a tourist book published in 1947 listed thirty-four movie theaters, while the *Shanghai Gazetteer* (Shanghai zhi) listed forty "noted" cinemas in Shanghai.[102] "A million people" is certainly a gross exaggeration, and statistics indicate that the cinema shared the entertainment market with other popular forms. Unlike local operas, however, the cinema drew a general audience from the city's young professionals and office workers as well as students, an audience that cut across native origins yet was characterized by its youth and modern-style education.

During the postwar period, Yue opera actresses began to look at the cinema as a means to expand the horizon of their art and reach out to the general public. The first to act in films was Yuan Xuefen, and the first Yue opera film was *Sister Xianglin*, produced in 1948 by the Qiming Studio. In the same year, this studio also produced the noted dramatist Hong Shen's *Hope for the Day at the Dawn When the Cock Begins to Crow* (Jiming zao kantian), directed by Ying Yunwei and starring Yuan Xuefen among others. *Sister Xianglin* opened in September 1948 in four downtown cinemas, and copies of the film were distributed outside of Shanghai. The September program at the Great Shanghai Theater (Da Shanghai Daxiyuan) featured the film *Sister Xianglin* in the afternoon and the Yue opera *Coral* (Shanhu yin), scripted by the famous playwright Tian Han, in the evening. Both were productions of Yuan Xuefen's Xuesheng Company.[103] Another example shows how cinema helped promote reformed Yue opera outside of Shanghai, even exporting it back to its native province of Zhejiang. In early 1949, Xiao Yueying, a leading Yue opera actress with a rural itinerant troupe in the Hangzhou-Jiaxing-Huzhou area, watched the film. Xiao was so impressed that she decided to adapt the film for the stage. Working solely from memory, she and her troupe put together the play and performed it successfully for her rural audience.[104] The most influential Yue opera films, however, were made in the 1950s and early 1960s and include *The Butterfly Lovers* (1953), *Emerald Hairpin* (1962), and *Dream of the Red Chamber* (1962) plus *Sister Xianglin* (1978).[105] These Yue opera movies were popular and attracted a nationwide, cross-gender audience; many of these people never attended Yue opera shows.

Women's Yue opera permeated the mass media and, through them, penetrated modern China's cultural consciousness. Radio, the phonograph, the printing press, and film together transformed an urban women's culture—Yue opera and its love dramas—into a media phenomenon with a lasting influence on modern China's cultural formation in the mid-twentieth century.[106]

祥林嫂

Chapter 4

Staging in the Public Arena

One evening in May 1946, the atmosphere in the Star Theater was unusual, as a special rehearsal of the New Yue Opera play *Sister Xianglin* was about to begin. The play had been adapted from the great modernist and left-wing writer Lu Xun's 1924 short story "The New Year's Sacrifice" (Zhufu). Well-known intellectuals and dramatists occupied almost the whole balcony, among them Tian Han, Hong Shen, Huang Zuolin, Shi Dongshan, Fei Mu, Zhang Junxiang, Li Jianwu, Bai Yang, Ding Cong, and Hu Feng. For the first time in its history, Yue opera had the honor of entertaining the cultural elite as a group.[1]

Sister Xianglin tells a tragic story of an unfortunate peasant woman who has married twice and been widowed twice. Both of her husbands died in sickness and poverty, and wolves consumed her only son, Ah Mao. Local superstitions have convinced her that she is to blame for her loved ones' misfortunes, because of bad karma from her previous lives. At the household of Master Lu, where she works as a domestic helper, a fellow servant tells her that the king of the underworld will cut her into two halves after her death so that she may serve her two husbands in the other world. Villagers scorn her for bringing bad luck to whatever she touches, and Master Lu eventually dismisses her for this reason. Wandering in the streets with a beggar's stick and basket in her hand, she asks passersby: "Tell me, will the soul continue to live after a person dies? Does hell exist?" No one seems able to answer her question, and people try to avoid her. Rejected by all, having no place to go, cold and hungry, she perishes in the streets one New Year's eve.

Lu Xun's work had rarely been adapted for the stage, due both to its political sensitivity and to the difficulties of translating his artistry—its nuance and rich meaning—into performance. This was the first time since the mid-1930s that a story by Lu Xun was performed onstage, an extraordinary time when his work had become even more politically sensitive than before in the eve of an all-out civil war between the Nationalist Party and the Chinese Communist Party. It would have been impossible for left-wing intellectuals to produce Lu Xun's work on a Shanghai stage under the Nationalist government's watchful eye. The leading cultural personalities were surprised that Yue opera—a local opera largely by and for women, featuring "conventional" love stories, and of little political significance—was doing what they could not do. The intellectuals had come to watch the play after being invited by Xu Guangping, Lu Xun's widow, and out of respect for the master. Hardly expecting that a "vulgar" local opera would be able to do justice to Lu Xun's work, they were nonetheless impressed by the show. Tian Han, for example, profusely praised the performance: "This is from real life, humane, accurate, and convincing."[2]

The play also caught the attention of the Nationalist government and eventually made Yue opera a site of contention between the two political rivals during the ensuing civil war, from 1946 to 1949. Out of this conflict, an unlikely alliance emerged between Yue opera actresses and CCP left-wing intellectuals: intellectuals, with their pens and networks, helped create positive modern images of Yue opera actresses in the city's mainstream media and began to penetrate Yue opera companies, through which they were able to influence a large population characterized by relatively low literacy, political apathy, and indifference to intellectual discourse.

The staging of *Sister Xianglin* in May 1946 set in motion a chain of landmark events in the ensuing years that culminated in the media drama in the wake of Xiao Dangui's tragic death. Unwittingly involved in the politics of the Civil War, the actresses fought their own battles and emerged during this conflict-ridden period with a newfound identity and status.

Politics and Culture in Postwar Shanghai

The post–World War II period in China witnessed another round of competition between the two rival parties on all fronts. While the two sides engaged each other ferociously on the battlefield, they also fought an ideological war on the urban front, competing to control or influence public opinion. On August 31, 1945, two weeks after Japan surrendered, the Nationalist Executive Committee issued guidelines for regulating the mass media. In September, the Nationalists ordered the confiscation of all newspapers, news agencies, magazines, and movie studios owned by Japanese and puppet-government institutions or related individuals. From September 17 to 22, the government reorganized the two major privately owned Shanghai newspapers, *Shanghai Newspaper* (Shen bao) and *Daily News* (Xinwen bao), taking control of their editorial boards.[3] On April 2, 1946, the Shanghai municipal police issued a directive, "Censorship of Shanghai's Broadcast Programs (Draft)," ordering that "all radio stations in the city, privately or publicly owned, should submit their broadcast programs to this bureau for review two days in advance."[4] Also in 1946, the Social Affairs Bureau of the Shanghai municipal government ordered all theaters and opera houses to register with its office as a prerequisite for licensing. It then ordered all actors, singers, dancing girls, and prostitutes to register, a policy deemed humiliating by all actors and threatening by left-wing intellectual actors active in film and spoken drama. The government also took steps to organize Nationalist-controlled unions in the entertainment business as well as in factories. At the same time, secret police relentlessly cracked down on CCP activities, arresting and executing the Party's underground workers.

These government measures were, however, far from effective in checking CCP activities. The Party reestablished its Shanghai Committee after the Japanese surrender, led first by Liu Changsheng and then by Liu Xiao after he arrived in Shanghai from Yan'an in February 1946. In January 1947, the CCP Central Committee established its Shanghai Branch, which in May became the Shanghai Bureau, headed by Secretary Liu Xiao and Deputy Secretary Liu Changsheng. The Shanghai Bureau contained subcommittees charged with responsibility for Party activities related to factories, businesses, schools, women, and culture. The Committee on the Cultural and Commercial United Front was then established under Secretary Zhang Zhiyi and Deputy Secretary Sha Wenhan to lead and coordinate underground activities in the fields of publishing, literature, theater, and music; at the end of 1948, it became the Committee on Cultural Work, with Chen Yusun as its secretary.[5]

Under the leadership of the Shanghai Bureau and its subcommittees, numerous grassroots cells were established in all walks of life, directly implementing the Party agenda in the local environment. Systematic party building aside, CCP cadres founded, penetrated, and controlled many civil organizations, such as teachers' associations, student unions, associations for film industry artists, and women's organizations, using them as legal venues for subversive activities against the government. The CCP's cultural activities incorporated a wide variety of artistic forms, including the popular sing-along movement, cartoon satire, and grassroots amateur performance.

The mass media—the press and the film industry—remained the priority of the Party's cultural work. As early as September 14, 1945, Mao Zedong and Zhou Enlai, in the middle of peace negotiations in Chongqing, sent a telegram to the CCP Central Committee in Yan'an and top leaders in the central China base area with the following instructions: "The Shanghai *New China Daily* [Xinhua ribao] and other Party-controlled newspapers published under the aegis of non-Party associates should be published in Nanjing, Wuhan, and Hong Kong as soon as possible. According to Nationalist regulations, newspapers can be published first and register later. Act quickly—the quicker, the better. Or we will get the worst of it."[6] From August 1945 to June 1946, before the outbreak of civil war, a large number of left-wing publications appeared. In Shanghai, CCP members published more than a dozen newspapers and periodicals, including *Times Daily* (Shidai ribao), *Weekly* (Zhou bao), *People's Weekly* (Renren zhoubao), *United Daily* (Lianhe ribao), *Free Man* (Ziyou ren), *The Renaissance* (Wenyi fuxing), *Literary Gallery* (Wencui), and *National Reconstruction Daily* (Jian'guo ribao). The Southern Committee of the CCP's Central Committee, for example, secretly sponsored *United Daily*, although the registered publisher was an American. The government shut down the newspaper on November 30, 1945, but the same staff managed to publish *United Evening News* (Lianhe wanbao) on April 15, 1946, secretly sponsored by the CCP's Shanghai Committee, only to have the paper banned again on May 24, 1947. In mid-1947, the government forcefully asserted control over the left-wing press as the military conflict between the two parties escalated and began to turn in the CCP's favor; by the end of the year, critical left-wing periodicals had virtually disappeared from the public domain.[7]

Left-wing intellectuals, however, also infiltrated the editorial boards of privately owned mainstream newspapers, the most famous of which were *Wenhui Daily* (Wenhui bao) and *Dagong Daily*; the editors in chief of both papers were CCP members.[8] CCP members and left-wing intellectuals moreover worked as editors, reporters, and columnists for major newspapers while contributing to government-controlled media such as *The Central Daily* (Zhongyang ribao), *Shanghai Newspaper*, and *Daily News*.

The CCP's presence in the print media was a highly motivated, organized, disciplined, and effective force consisting of capable young men and women. These journalists skillfully provided media support for student demonstrations and popular unrest and influenced public opinion through criticism of unpopular government policies. To a certain extent, CCP underground journalism was able to coordinate what in normal times would be routine scrutiny of the government into an opposition front and reoriented public sensibilities to the CCP's advantage.

Likewise, the CCP and left-wing intellectuals, who had held irrefutable prestige in Shanghai's film industry in the 1930s, quickly regained their influence in the postwar period. In 1946, Yang Hansheng and other CCP cultural cadres returned to Shanghai and reestablished the Lianhua Studio, which was reorganized into the Kunlun Studio in 1947. This studio produced many popular movies such as *Eight Thousand Miles under Clouds and Moonlight* (Baqian li lu yun he yue), in 1947); *River of Sorrow Flows East* (Yijiang chunshui xiang dong liu), in 1947; and *Lights from the Windows of Thousands of Families* (Wanjia denghuo), in 1948. Between 1946 and 1949, by the CCP's account, two dozen "progressive" and influential features appeared in Shanghai.

The Party was, however, slow in penetrating the world of popular entertainment in the city, as left-wing intellectuals who despised the commercial popular culture were in charge of CCP cultural operations. During the entire Civil War period, no CCP cell was set up in any popular entertainment form in Shanghai. Despite their low priority, entertainment forms were not free of CCP influence, and the staging of *Sister Xianglin* was partly a result of wide-ranging CCP underground grassroots activities.

Sister Xianglin *and the CCP's Underground Operation*

One day in April 1946, backstage at the Star Theater, Yuan Xuefen, the leading actress and head of the company, was putting on makeup while director and playwright Nan Wei read a story aloud to her. Nan Wei had recently read "Sister Xianglin—A Study of Female Characters in Lu Xun's Work," an essay in *Women and Literature* (Funü yu wenxue), by Ding Ying. The essay had introduced Nan Wei to Lu Xun's *The New Year's Sacrifice* and inspired him to adapt the story for the Yue opera stage. Yuan found herself becoming totally absorbed in the vivid scenery and characters of Shaoxing, which was so familiar to her, and as soon as Nan Wei had finished, she announced: "You write the play. I will perform it."[9] In little more than a month, the play *Sister Xianglin* was born.

Who was Ding Ying? Where did Nan Wei get the book? "Ding Ying" was one of the many pseudonyms Ding Jingtang used in the 1940s in order to protect his true identity. The following account is based on an interview (see fig. 4.1), his essays, and his book *Women and Literature.*[10] Ding Jingtang lost his parents when he was young. He left his hometown of Ningbo and moved to Shanghai to live with his aunt, who was married to, in Ding's words, a "medium-size capitalist." During his years at the Young Men's Christian Association (YMCA) high school, from 1936 to 1939, Ding and his fellow students worked with the Student Union (Xue Xie), a CCP-affiliated local association coordinating citywide student mobilization for the War of Resistance against Japan. Their duties included circulating the organization's journal *Student Life* (Xuesheng shenghuo), organizing study groups, and coordinating student activities in several middle schools along what is now Beijing Road. Ding joined the Party in 1938. "Comrades of our generation who joined the revolution during the War of Resistance almost all experienced a similar passage," Ding explained, "from reading the May Fourth New Literature, advancing to elementary Marxist readings and training in organizational activities, to joining the Party."[11] In 1939, Ding qualified to enter Dongwu University. In winter 1940, he became editor of *The United Voice* (Lian sheng), officially sponsored by the Association of Shanghai Christian Student Fellowships but actually under the direction of the CCP Committee on Student Activities. This and all other similar publications came to a full stop in December 1941, when Japanese troops marched into "island" Shanghai upon the outbreak of the Pacific War. Owing to the extremely dangerous situation in the occupied city, the CCP Shanghai Committee was disbanded, and in order to maintain some underground forces in the city, Ding and his comrades were instructed to lie low.[12]

As soon as the war ended, in August 1945, Ding Jingtang resumed his work of publishing journals propagating left-wing ideas. Within this context, he wrote and published his study on Sister Xianglin. Ding recalled in 1982:

> After the victory [over Japan], a former college classmate of mine asked me to contribute and organize articles for the journal *Progressive Women* (Qianjin funü) on behalf of the owners, Liu and his wife.[13] At that time, all the journals I was coordinating were student publications that lacked stable funding. These journals often appeared for a few months and disappeared whenever the funding ran out. Now, with this opportunity, I invited Tian Zhongluo (Yuan Ying), Zhou Jiling, Zhao Zi, and others to occupy this position. After the victory in the War of Resistance, I had planned to write a series of articles on female images in modern Chinese literature. At the time,

4.1 Ding Jingtang (right) and the author at Mr. Ding's residence, February 9, 1996. Ding and his CCP underground network facilitated the staging of *Sister Xianglin* (Xianglin sao) in 1946 by Yuan Xuefen and her staff. (Photo: Ding Yanzhao)

> I wrote two pieces. The first one was that very article, "Sister Xianglin—A Study of Female Characters in Lu Xun's Work," published in the second issue of *Progressive Women* [November 1945] under the pen name Li Yang. I had written it in October 1945. The article was later republished in a collection of essays titled *Women and Literature*, published under the name "Ding Ying" in February 1946 by the Shanghai Hujiang Book House.[14]

The Nationalist government shut down *Progressive Women* after four issues, when a member of the Nationalist Shanghai Committee accused the journal of printing CCP propaganda, and the Shanghai Hujiang Book House existed only as a name Ding had made up for the publication of his book. *Women and Literature*, not sold in bookstores owing to censorship of left-wing publications, circulated among friends and the like minded. Through a network of comrades, friends, and relatives, the book reached Nan Wei, and an accidental meeting between two high-school friends triggered the landmark production of the Yue opera *Sister Xianglin*.[15]

Ding Jingtang had a friend and comrade named Wu Kang. The two were classmates and fellow activists at the YMCA high school, and Ding brought Wu Kang into the Party in 1939. Wu qualified for entrance to Shanghai Zhijiang University, while Ding entered Dongwu University, and they both received YMCA fellowships for poor students. With his aunt's understanding, Ding offered his fellowship to Wu Kang; Wu was from a poorer family, one fellowship was not enough to support him through school, and, because he spent most of his spare time working for the Party, he was not able to work for money. Although classrooms for both Dongwu and Zhijiang Universities were in the same building of the Continental department store on Nanjing Road, the two friends nevertheless stopped seeing each other, following Party regulations on underground work. One day in 1946, Ding ran into Wu in the street. Told that Wu's brother-in-law Nan Wei worked for the Xuesheng Company, Ding handed Wu a copy of *Women and Literature* and asked Wu to give it to Nan Wei.[16] Hoping to draw his brother-in-law close to the revolution, Wu in turn asked Ding to send some friends to contact Nan. Ding recalled:

> At that time, I had already been transferred to work under the Shanghai [CCP] Cultural Committee [Shanghai Wenwei] and was in charge of the Party-led Shanghai Youth Association of Performing Arts. Many young Party members were engaged in various theatrical activities. So I sent Liao Lin to Nan Wei, with the introduction "Brother Ah Kang [reference to Wu Kang] asked me to come to see you." Liao Lin [pen names Luo Lin and Ye Ping] was an amateur spoken-drama veteran and a special correspondent in film and theater for the daily newspaper *The New Current Affairs* [Shishi xinbao].[17]

Liao Lin thereafter became a frequent visitor to the Xuesheng Company. Liao's girlfriend Tong Lijuan, also a Party member, was working with the Shanghai Women's Association, an organization headed by Lu Xun's widow Xu Guangping but in fact under CCP direction. In Xu's name, Tong Lijuan and another female CCP member acted as editors of the two daily newspaper supplements on women's issues, *Women's News* (Fuxun), for *United Evening News*, and *Women's Life* (Funü shenghuo), for *The New Current Affairs*. While Liao Lin made friends with Nan Wei, Tong Lijuan befriended Yuan Xuefen. The two young CCP cadres encouraged Nan and Yuan in their efforts to stage Lu Xun's work. Liao Lin told Nan Wei, "Putting Lu Xun's work on the stage will be a high point in your life." Tong Lijuan arranged for Yuan Xuefen and Nan Wei to meet with Xu Guangping, who gave the Xuesheng Company permission to adapt *The New Year's Sacrifice* for the Yue opera stage and also provided moral support. After the performance, Liao and Tong took Yuan Xuefen and Nan Wei to the home of Yu Ling, the playwright and head of the CCP underground Committee on Culture, where they met Tian Han and engaged in a serious discussion of local-opera reform.[18] Thus, although the production of *Sister Xianglin* was an autonomous decision made entirely by Yuan and her director, lower-level CCP cadres served as catalysts and guided Yuan and Nan to contact with top CCP intellectuals.

The staging of *Sister Xianglin* made Yue opera and its reforms a subject of discussion in the mainstream media. Left-wing journalists and commentators loudly applauded the play as a milestone in Yue opera reform and a turning point that marked the transformation of a "vulgar" local opera into a reputable and meaningful theater for social and cultural reform. These comments appeared not only in left-wing newspapers, such as *Wenhui Daily* and *The New Citizen Daily* (Xinmin ribao), but also in the Nationalist-controlled *The Daily News* and *The New Current Affairs*. Liao Lin, using the pen name Luo Lin, reported in *The New Current Affairs* a week before the opening of the play in an article headlined "Lu Xun's Famous Fiction Adapted for the Yue Opera Stage: Yuan Xuefen Plays *Sister Xianglin*, Setting a New Record in Traditional Opera Reform."[19] Three days after the play's premiere, Liao's article, titled "Tian Han Discusses Yue Opera Reform with Yuan Xuefen and Nan Wei," again helped draw Yue opera into mainstream culture.[20] In another article, using the pen name Ye Ping, Liao Lin wrote:

> The staging of *Sister Xianglin* is significant. No one can deny the fact that local opera is groping forward step by step. . . . We hope the staging of *Sister Xianglin* will influence various local operas and make them bear more responsibilities for the education of their audience.[21]

Wenhui Daily also published an interview with Yuan Xuefen by Mei Duo, a left-wing journalist. The article, titled "Sister Xianglin Backstage," cites Yuan:

> She [Yuan Xuefen] said that their Xuesheng Company has more than twenty members who have worked together for many years. The purpose for their getting together is not just to make some money but rather to reform Yue opera and make it progressive. . . . She said that because Yue opera (Shaoxing opera) traditionally presented stereotyped scholar-beauty love stories,

people naturally thought the opera worthless, but they can make the opera socially meaningful by changing the content of the plays.[22]

A commentary by Yu Ping in *World Morning News* (Shijie chenbao) reads:

> The conversion of *Sister Xianglin* for dramatic presentation opens a new path for Yue opera and gives the opera a new life. . . . Generally speaking, the conversion did not betray the spirit of Master Lu Xun's original work. Although the play emphasized a romance, it successfully manifested, through the romance, the suffering and misfortune of ordinary rural women in feudal society.[23]

Another commentary, by Yu Yu in *Daily News*, praised Yue opera reforms compared to the vulgarity of popular entertainment:

> While Beijing opera still ponders whether or not to reform, and when its "imperial capital style" [*Jingchao pai*] relies on *Break Open the Coffin* [Da piguan] and *Spinning Cotton* [Fang mianhua] [deemed representative of vulgar erotic plays], while the "vicious Shanghai style" [*exing Haipai*] relies on "striptease" to survive, the "*didu* opera" [Yue opera] that they viewed with contempt walks onto the great path of enlightenment one step at a time.[24]

The influential playwright Tian Han, in his article "The Path toward Popularization of Performing Arts," summarized the left-wing intellectual elite's view of Yue opera reforms and the staging of *Sister Xianglin*:

> *Sister Xianglin* moved me. I had occasionally seen *didu* opera, the so-called Shaoxing civil opera, in places like the Great World [entertainment hall] before the war. It did not catch my attention. Later, when I was in Chongqing [during the war], I heard friends returning from "island" Shanghai praising profusely the progressiveness of Shaoxing opera, saying that the opera had developed to the extent that it could stage many socially meaningful plays and that it now had its own opera houses. . . . Still, I did not hope for too much. Not until I attended the play *Sister Xianglin* was I convinced that the opera's achievement, due to its eight-year reform effort, has surpassed my imagination.[25]

Sister Xianglin moreover caught the attention of the top CCP leadership and ultimately inspired the Party to amend its underground cultural policy in

Shanghai. In October 1946, Zhou Enlai, then leading the CCP team in peace talks at Nanjing and spending a lot of time in Shanghai between meetings, quietly attended the Xuesheng Company's show *Sad Moon over the Liao Royal Palace*, performed by Yuan Xuefen. Zhou's family was originally from Shaoxing, and Zhou himself had been fond of performing onstage in his student years in Naikai High School in Tianjin. Impressed by Yuan Xuefen's performance and the size of the audience, Zhou summoned Yu Ling for an oral report on women's Yue opera and its reforms. Before he left for Yan'an, when the peace talks broke down in November 1946, Zhou twice discussed local operas with the Shanghai underground. He told Yu Ling and Liu Housheng, a CCP cadre and dramatist who later joined the Xuesheng Company as head of the staff, "You should pay attention to this [Xuesheng] company. I knew about Shaoxing opera, but I did not know that the opera had such a large audience and was so influential in Shanghai." He instructed, "You should send Party members to help them improve their arts and, through contacting them, respecting them, assisting them, patiently guide them toward the road of revolution. They have an audience, and that is power."[26]

Recognizing the popularity and hence importance of local operas in general, Zhou wanted them incorporated into the blueprint of the CCP's cultural work, instructing that Shanghai's underground work in the entertainment business should have a three-tier structure. The first tier consisted of overtly leftist spoken drama, which was entirely under Party control. The second tier was the Kunlun Studio and the Audience Drama Company, both in the hands of left-wing intellectuals but featuring more popular productions. And the third tier included local operas and privately owned movie studios, which indeed constituted the core of popular entertainment. If the government were to crack down on leftist spoken drama, as was almost certain to happen, then its personnel should move to the second tier and from there to the third tier. Zhou stressed that the Party ought to take local operas seriously because they had a considerable audience, but he cautioned the Shanghai underground to select upright and respectable cadres to work in local operas.[27]

Following Zhou's instructions, the Shanghai underground committee sent intellectual CCP members and affiliates to work with local opera troupes. Party member Qian Yingyu and Party affiliate Wu Chen joined Yue opera companies in 1947. Later, in 1948, Liu Housheng himself entered the Xuesheng Company as a director who also headed the staff. By 1949, almost all the five major Yue opera companies had one or two playwrights or directors who were CCP affiliates. Most of these men were veterans of spoken drama. As the spoken-drama market continued to shrink during the postwar period, and because the film industry could absorb only a limited number of new participants, some veterans found employment in local opera, calling this "jumping into the sea [of popular culture]" (*xia hai*). While spoken-drama veterans worked for Yue opera companies, left-wing journalists continued to support Yue opera reform and publicize new images of Yue opera actresses in the print media, gathering public opinion behind the actresses in a series of conflicts that followed the staging of *Sister Xianglin*. Moreover, cultural celebrities such as Tian Han and Yu Ling became friends and teachers of these young Yue opera reformers, providing much needed advice and moral support. Tian Han and his wife An E also began to write plays for Yue opera. The politically naive Yuan Xuefen and her colleagues at the time did not know that these respected "good-hearted masters" (*haohao xiansheng*) were associated with the CCP. In 1949, as the communist army approached Shanghai, Liu Housheng and Wu Chen called a few meetings with Yue opera actresses to discuss preparation for the imminent takeover. In May, when the People's Liberation Army (PLA) had overcome the last Nationalist resistance in Shanghai, actresses from five major Yue opera companies went on the air to welcome the PLA, telling Shanghai's populace to stay home and remain calm, as the PLA would not disturb the common people.[28] On June 5, after the CCP took over Shanghai, the Party convened a conference of the city's cultural elites. Major Chen Yi addressed the conference. The new government selected only two representatives from the field of popular entertainment: one was the famous Beijing opera actor Zhou Xinfang, and the other was Yuan Xuefen.

The Union Incident: Actresses in Local and National Politics

The staging of *Sister Xianglin* in 1946 also caught the attention of the Nationalist Shanghai government and made Yuan Xuefen and her colleagues targets of political surveillance. The incident that occurred in the wake of the show reveals how the national struggle between the CCP and the Nationalists affected local politics within the Yue opera trade in postwar Shanghai.

In July 1946, a group of Yue opera musicians, who were old masters of the actor-centered system, and backstage hands, mostly men with unstable employment or unemployed, organized the Yue Opera Workers' Union in the context of the government-sponsored union movement—a means of preempting the CCP's labor movement but otherwise having no obvious focus and hence badly organized. Although the Yue opera union was officially affiliated with the Shanghai General Union under the Social Affairs Bureau of the Shanghai municipal government, in reality it received little leadership or discipline from any of these entities. The union activists, the majority of whom were lower-class folks with little understanding of and no access to national politics, cared only for their own concrete interests. The union's purposes, its organizers declared, were to offset the power of theater bosses who had organized themselves into the Yue Opera Employers' Union, safeguard members' right to work, negotiate salaries on behalf of its members, and maintain its members' welfare. The union was instantly popular among most Yue opera employees because it promised to fight employers on behalf of union members. Actresses and staff in most Yue opera companies joined the union, and the unionists invited Yuan Xuefen to chair the board of directors. Suspicious that this might be just another way to squeeze money out of the actresses, Yuan declined to have anything to do with it. But other popular actresses, including Fu Quanxiang and Yin Guifang, were initially enthusiastic about the union and its ideas. Fu Quanxiang offered her home to serve as headquarters for the union, and Yin Guifang chaired the board with Fu Quanxiang, Zhu Shuizhao, Xu Yuexing (staff member), and Zhang Zifan (director) serving as board members. Unfortunately, Yuan Xuefen's suspicion was not without foundation. Before long, the union fell into the hands of some unscrupulous Shengxian-native men whose only concern was to collect money from actresses. They harassed companies with random demands for "membership fees," and the union's promise that it would protect the rights of employees turned out to be empty. The union quickly lost its popularity as people realized that it was nothing more than a charity for the unemployed former actors and a "rice bowl" for some local opportunists, as Fu Quanxiang put it.[29] Moreover, as money flowed into the pockets of the opportunists, the union's financial resources dried up, and the board members, most of whom were popular stars, ended up paying the union's bills out of their own pockets. Yin Guifang resigned on August 25, and other board members followed suit.[30]

The extortion of contributions from female stars by male associates—whether local troublemakers, retired actors, theater bosses, or members of male-dominated native-place organizations—was a common phenomenon of the time, according to Fu Quanxiang and other actresses. Female stars and their male associates were all part of a complicated native-place and professional network that obligated young actresses to contribute to the men's welfare on the basis of native-place ties and former teacher-disciple relationships. This moral pressure was often backed by the threat of vandalism or personal attack. No one liked to be squeezed, but actresses took different approaches to the situation. They usually had to accede to at least some requests—sometimes giving cash contributions and at other times performing for private parties or fund-raising events.[31] While Yin Guifang and Fu Quanxiang seem to have represented the attitude of many actresses in their willingness to negotiate and cooperate with the unionists, Yuan Xuefen refused to deal with them at all. Xiao Dangui and her Dangui Company, another major Yue opera company of the time, had nothing to do with the unionists, because Xiao and the company were firmly in the hands of Zhang Chunfan, a strongman in charge of the Employers' Union.

The unionists were angry. Not being in a position to harm Zhang, they blamed Yuan Xuefen for leading the rebellion against the union and plotted retaliation. On August 27, 1946, as Yuan rode in her personal rickshaw to the Soviet Union Radio Station for a regular broadcast program, a man ambushed her by pouring a bag of dung over her head. A few days later, Yuan received a threat instructing her to leave Shanghai within three days unless she wanted a taste of "peanuts" (the meaning of this term was made explicit by an enclosed bullet).

Yuan's persecution generated a wave of sympathy in both the mainstream and the tabloid press. On August 29, *Dagong Daily*, a left-inclined mainstream newspaper, reported these incidents with the headline "Refusing to Join the Opportunist Organization, Yuan Xuefen Execrated and Ambushed—Hit with Dung on Her Way to the Radio Station." According to the report, when the unionists insisted that Yuan head the board, she complained to the Social Affairs Bureau and refused to join the union, since its members were troublemakers, not Yue opera workers. The unionists tried to collect union fees from Yuan, even though she was not a member. Finally, decisively spurned by Yuan, the unionists resorted to base methods.[32] A *World Morning News* headline read "Let an Honest Person Live," and the headline in *The New Citizen Daily* was "Misfortune for a Progressive Actress of a Traditional Opera."[33]

Tian Han was indignant. Using his personal influence, he called a news conference to support Yuan and stage a general protest against government measures aimed at checking left-wing activities as well as cleansing obscenity in popular entertainment. About two hundred cultural celebrities, administrators of professional associations, and reporters attended, among them Guo Moruo, Hong Shen, and Xu Guangping, the linguist Zhao Jingsheng, the famous "butterfly" fiction writer and editor Yan Duhe, head of the Entertainment Association Dong Tianmin, and head of the Performers' Association Liang Yiming. At the news conference, held on September 10, 1946, a shy but determined Yuan Xuefen discussed her persecution in terms of women's liberation and theatrical reform. She described herself as a progressive actress devoted to Yue opera reform and complained that the unionists had attacked her because she refused to join their union. "I hope social celebrities and journalists will extend their righteous hands to me and uphold justice."[34] She also stated: " It is a small thing if it concerns only my career. But if this kind of behavior is allowed to continue, then what safeguard is there for other Yue opera actresses? Or for women's right to work in general?"[35] Xu Guangping also spoke about women's social status and encouraged Yuan and other Yue opera actresses to unite in seeking their own salvation.[36]

It is interesting to note that the celebrity status of left-wing intellectuals and their direct connection with top CCP leaders such as Mao and Zhou placed them outside the local Party network and allowed them to act freely without the Party's restrictions on underground work. It was, moreover, the duty of the Party's local branch to look out for the safety of these left-wing celebrities. While Tian Han and other celebrities relied on their personal influence to gather public support for Yuan Xuefen and used Yuan's case to highlight the general discontent of the actors as a whole, the Party's local branch had a different perspective and would not risk the underground network for such an event. Yu Ling, head of Shanghai's underground Committee on Culture, disapproved of holding a news conference for Yuan. Having learned that invitations had already been issued, he became concerned first with the safety of Guo Moruo and advised Yuan Xuefen to lie low and not to overstate her case: "You should be careful with your statement. Simply say that you are just an actress trying to make a living with your own labor, and you are persecuted because of this. Stop there. Do not make Guo Moruo speak, as everyone is watching him."[37] Yuan, as we have seen, developed her own strategy, but Guo indeed did not speak at the news conference.

While left-wing intellectuals gave Yuan tremendous moral support and helped her win the battle of public opinion, the unionists took advantage of the government's anti-leftist policy to avenge their grievances against her. Their persecution of Yuan was primarily a means of keeping their hold on the young actresses, but it was the government's anti-leftist stance that gave them a political pretext for their unlawful actions and allowed them to get away with it. The Shanghai edition of the Nationalist home newspaper, *Central Daily: Shanghai Edition* (Zhongyang ribao: Shanghai ban), engaged in a personal attack on Yuan as well as a general attack on her Yue opera reform. An article, "Yuan Xuefen Exaggerates a Small Incident" (Yuan Xuefen xiaoti dazuo), blamed Yuan for overreacting to these trivial incidents, accused her of staying out of the union merely to be different, and refuted her progressiveness with the claim that Yue opera "reform" was nothing but a gross deception.[38] The police conducted a halfhearted investigation of the case that yielded no satisfactory result, and the unionists continued to harass Yuan in the ensuing months.

If the left wing and Yuan won the battle of public opinion, then the unionists, though suffering bad publicity, managed with some success to continue to squeeze the young actresses. On October 8, 1946, the union sponsored a fund-raising performance for its welfare foundation. Yin Guifang, Zhu Shuizhao, Fu Quanxiang, and several other popular actresses formed the main cast.[39] Yuan Xuefen and the Xuesheng Company of course did not participate. Probably as a result, in November, three men intruded into Yuan's dressing room, demanding that she go with them to perform at a private party they had arranged. They informed her that if she refused to go, then they would claim one-third of her monthly pay as compensation for their "loss." In December, she received another threat demanding a cash contribution to the union.[40] By the end of the year, Yuan Xuefen resolved to retire. Left-wing intellectuals and journalists sent her off with a chorus of praise in the print media, honoring her achievements in Yue opera reform as well as her upright personality.

Though the exact reason for Yuan's retreat is not clear, it is possible to surmise several of the problems that faced her. Her ongoing conflict with the unionists certainly caused the theater bosses to worry about possible negative effects on the box office. It also seems to have caused friction among fellow actresses; some thought she was too harsh with the unionists, who were, after all, fellow Shengxian natives, while others disliked her simply because she was different. In addition, her reform agenda appeared too radical to Yue opera management and some of the other actresses. The New Yue Opera reforms seemed to have come to a crossroads. According to the recollections of Cheng Rong, who spent days and nights with Yuan during this time, Yuan took to heart the comments she received from the mainstream and left-wing media and carefully collected all the newspaper clippings on the topic.[41] She became even more reluctant to perform trite love stories as she was now subject to so much left-wing expectation after *Sister Xianglin*. But she was unsure of how to make Yue opera a vehicle of social reform while continuing to retain its audience.[42] Other reform actresses, including Yin Guifang, would not go that far.[43] Yin's attitude toward Yue opera reform, emphasizing the centrality of love drama in Yue opera, was probably more popular among Yue opera professionals, including most Yue opera stars and some playwrights such as Xu Jin. Yuan Xuefen's elitist inclinations not only caused her conflict with the unionists and theater bosses but also isolated her to some extent from her fellow actresses in and outside of the Xuesheng Company. In January 1947, Yuan retired and left the stage. Fu Quanxiang joined the company, which was renamed the Dongshan Company, in the main female role.

Looking back at the New Yue Opera reforms after more than half a century, Yuan still remembered the frustration she felt at the time and her dismay at the lack of a clear vision about reform among her fellow actresses, describing their mental status as *hunhun e'e*, meaning nonreflective or lacking in understanding.[44] Fortunately for Yuan, history would prove that her insistence on independence of and respect for the actresses and their professional work indeed provided the spirit as well as a clear vision for the New Yue Opera reforms. Her courageous rejection of the status quo, however unpopular at the time, demonstrated to her fellow actresses that resistance and change were possible.

The Ten Sisters of Yue Opera: Forging a New Collective Identity

During her retirement, Yuan reflected on the situation of Yue opera reform and concluded that the root of the actresses' vulnerability lay not so much in the harassment from the union opportunists but in the near monopoly exercised by the Yue opera management. In an article published in *Daily News*, she wrote:

> In Yue opera theater, the theater owners invest in the theater, managing the box office and paying the actresses' salaries. The employers also intervene in the production. They have their eyes on profit only and never care about social significance or the professional standards of the production. For them, a good play is one that sells well. Often, better plays are forced from the stage simply because the sales do not exceed 70 percent (since they prefer 100 percent ticket sales) owing to recession or bad weather. The theater owners especially like to stage traditional plays, because old plays sell as well as new plays while costing much less to produce. For traditional plays, actresses need only to put on ready-made, one-style-for-all costumes and go onstage, with no consideration for the particular historical setting of the

act; as such, employers need not pay for new costumes, stage properties, musical accompaniment, lighting, and other production costs, nor need they pay for the staff members. As the theater bosses aim entirely for profit, it is impossible for those of us who seek Yue opera reform to work with them.[45]

Besides greed and bias against Yue opera reform, theater owners were also pressed by financial difficulties resulting from the postwar recession. Theater bosses often threatened to break Yue opera contracts in favor of film screenings whenever sales were slow. The pressure from theater owners was intense, and actresses constantly worried about job security. Without job security, it was impossible for actresses to achieve artistic autonomy, and without reform, the status of Yue opera and its actresses could easily slide back to their previous low levels, and actresses would remain subjugated to theater bosses. Contemplating these issues, Yuan Xuefen began to entertain a bold idea—to build a theater of her own, a dream so ambitious that few actresses had ever imagined it. But why not? If none of them could create a theater on her own, maybe together they could.

Yuan's idea was that leading actresses would stage a grand show to raise funds for the creation of their own theater and a Yue opera school for young girls. They could experiment with reforms with the theater, which would attract a wider audience while further improving the status of Yue opera. The revenues would be entirely theirs, and they would use the profits to establish a Yue opera school, which would help secure their employment after they retired from the stage. When Yuan Xuefen shared her idea with other actresses, they all became excited and jumped into it immediately. After all, despite existing frictions, actresses faced similar problems and shared similar aspirations, and the need for collective action far outweighed their disagreements.

First came the announcement that the show was to open on August 18 and end on September 21. On July 29, 1947, ten leading actresses gathered at a Western-style restaurant on Fuzhou Road and produced a contract signed by all ten in the presence of a lawyer. The contract was indeed a manifesto and succinctly summarized the purposes and principles of the fund-raising production:

> After several meetings, we have found that we all share the same goals of sustaining the art of New Yue Opera and ensuring the welfare of our fellow actresses. We hereby decide to act together as cofounders in organizing a company for the construction of a new-style theater. From now on,

> cofounders shall be mutually responsible and do their best to ensure the smooth operation of the theater and performances, and so to forge a bright future for Yue opera. The cofounders of the organization have absolutely equal rights and responsibilities. With this contract signed, cofounders shall work to raise investment capital, either through personal connections or through collective fund-raising performances and radio broadcasting, and to attract shareholders. Each cofounder shall do her best to work toward these goals and shall not break the agreement or neglect her responsibilities.[46]

The ten leading actresses who signed the contract were Yin Guifang, Fu Quanxiang, Yuan Xuefen, Xiao Dangui, Fan Ruijuan, Zhang Guifeng, Xu Yulan, Zhu Shuizhao, Wu Xiaolou, and Xu Tianhong—now known as the "ten sisters" of Yue opera (see fig. 4.2).

Nan Wei, Han Yi, and Cheng Rong, in the meanwhile, scripted a new play for the fund-raising show, *For the Love of the Country* (Shanhe lian), which transposed the story of Alexandre Dumas's *The Three Musketeers* into an ancient Chinese setting drawn from the Ming historical novel *Histories of the States in the Eastern Zhou Dynasty* (Dongzhou lieguo zhi). The play tells a complicated story of desire, jealousy, conspiracy, and double crosses in a court struggle involving the king of Liang; his lusty minister; a beautiful princess and her lover, a prince of the Cao kingdom; an evil royal concubine; two righteous palace maidservants; and two righteous generals. The story had no obvious political message but instead focused on an intriguing good-versus-evil kind of melodrama played out on a grand scale (see fig. 4.3).

The play's greatest attraction obviously lay in its all-star cast and grandiose stage sets. The ten sisters dedicated themselves wholeheartedly to the fund-raising project and wanted the show to be a great event. They had often staged fund-raising performances for other organizations, but this was the first time such an event would benefit their own cause. Yin Guifang, for example, gave up a rare opportunity to make a Yue opera movie out of one of her popular plays. It would have been the first Yue opera film had Yin decided to participate. Yuan Xuefen voluntarily played the smallest role, in order to refute her critics' accusation that she initiated the production to enhance her own fame. The actresses were electrified and wanted everything to be perfect: the theater, the costumes and stage setting, and the media coverage.

The young actresses, however, underestimated the difficulties their project was to face. Yuan Xuefen had consulted Yu Ling, who had expressed doubts about the project's feasibility. But Yuan was too excited, and perhaps too naive, to heed Yu Ling's warning. For one thing, many sponsors

4.2 The ten sisters of Yue opera, upon deciding to launch a production to raise funds for a theater of their own, 1947. Front row, from left: Xu Tianhong, Fu Quanxiang, Yuan Xuefen, Zhu Zhuizhao, Fan Ruijuan, and Wu Xiaolou. Back row, from left: Zhang Guifeng, Xiao Dangui, Xu Yulan, and Yin Guifang. (*Shanghai Yueju zhi* 1997)

were interested in getting their hands on the money the actresses were expected to make. For many, it was simply unthinkable that these young girls could or should keep the profits for themselves.

The first major expense was to rent a theater. The actresses wanted a large theater for their event and decided on the Grand Golden Theater, which was unoccupied for the summer season. But the rental terms the actresses obtained from Zhou Xinfang, the famous Beijing opera actor who held the long-term lease on the theater, were harsh: the actresses not only had to pay a vast sum for rent but also had to furnish one month's salary

4.3 The ten sisters of Yue opera staged *For the Love of the Country* (Shanhe lian), 1947, to raise funds for building their own theater. Although the actresses did not achieve their goal, the performances deeply impressed audiences and the general public and did much to raise Yue opera's social status. (*Shanghai Yueju zhi* 1997)

for Zhou's entire company during the summer recess. The cost for the theater in the end amounted to one-fourth of the box office revenue for all the performances. Zhou certainly was a shrewd businessman and made a huge profit from the rental while depriving the theater employees.[47]

The actresses had another expense, to be expected in the case of such magnificent fund-raising, and that was to pay various native-place thugs so that they would not cause trouble.[48] The unionists, understanding that they were excluded from a share in this grand production, called a press conference to attack the actresses for having abandoned their teachers and "affronted their ancestors" (*qishi miezu*).[49] The Nationalist soldiers also wanted their share, and since they had not received free tickets, they rushed into the theater one day, expelling the audience and taking their seats. The actresses had no choice but to accommodate them.

The government and the CCP were both aware of the large sums of money the show was drawing into the theater. Yu Ling assigned two men to help Yuan Xuefen and the actresses with accounting and logistics, while the actresses, probably in an effort to avoid being squeezed by the government, also invited Wang Canzhi, daughter of the revolutionary martyr Qiu Jin and an official at the tax bureau of the municipal government, to head the proposed Yue opera training school. But this did not appease the government. Officials were skeptical that the young actresses—mostly illiterate, apolitical, knowing nothing but their trivial opera plays—could have come up with such an ambitious fund-raising effort solely by themselves, and they suspected that the revenue would flow into the hands of the CCP underground. Halfway through the show's run, the Social Affairs Bureau suddenly issued an interdiction, charging that the actresses had not properly completed registration procedures, and appointed a special board of trustees to oversee the funds raised by the production. The trustees included Wang Canzhi, Wang Xiaolai, and a few other government officials. The ban against the show was lifted only when the actresses agreed to place the funds under the trustees' control for three months.[50] Up until then, the show had stimulated public enthusiasm, and tickets were selling well. The government's disruption had a negative effect on the box office, and the second phase of the production did not go so well. Other elements may also have been at work. Not least was competition from the China Great Theater (Zhongguo Daxiyuan), where Beijing opera superstars—including Mei Lanfang, Meng Xiaodong, Zhang Junqiu, Ma Lianliang, and Zhou Xinfang—performed from September 3 to 13 in celebration of Du Yuesheng's sixtieth birthday; these dates coincided with the second phase of the ten sisters' production. Most Yue opera stars also performed at Du's private parties to show their respect for him. Yuan Xuefen, as usual, did not go.

When the performances concluded, the revenue was less than had been expected. After settling bills for costumes, salaries, and the theater rental, there wasn't much left. The trustees then froze the funds for a few months, while inflation mounted. When the trustees finally released the fund, after entertaining themselves with a banquet, the account was worth only ninety-six taels of gold. In the end, it was only enough for the actresses to rent a small two-story house with three rooms. They fixed up a small stage downstairs and put up a plaque that read "Shanghai Yue Opera Experimental School." The government never issued a permit for this school.

The fund-raising project, though it did not succeed as intended, was a big success in that it projected a positive, upbeat image of the Yue opera actress to the public. On August 11 and 12, a week before the opening night, the ten sisters launched a promotional radio campaign. Each went to the station to sing pieces from the new play and to answer calls from the audience. The two-day promotion climaxed with the ten actresses singing together in a chorus. Mainstream newspapers as well as tabloids covered the fund-raising show with eye-catching headlines, and the phrase "ten sisters of Yue opera" permeated Shanghai's mass media, marking the beginning of a new collective identity for the actresses.

The tabloid *Robin Hood* (Luobinhan), for example, first reported the ten actresses' initiative on August 5 in an article headlined "Ten Leading Yue Opera Actresses Successfully Cooperated." The report notes:

> This organization [Yuelian Company, founded by the ten sisters] is an innovation in any opera circle, for it is rare and precious that first-rate actresses might join hands like this.[51]

A few days later, another article in the tabloid praised Yue opera actresses and criticized Beijing opera:

> The Yue opera circle unites tightly under the leadership of Master [Xian Sheng] Yuan Xuefen (as everybody addresses her). The actresses are working hard to collect funds for a Yue opera school and a theater of their own. In contrast, Beijing opera, though esteemed as the National opera and with so many famous actors, does not compare. It is such a pity that famous Beijing opera actors all take care only of their own business; they cannot rival these young ladies full of progressive ideas and actions.[52]

On August 28, the tabloid carried a report mocking the unionists. According to the news, the Yue Opera Workers' Union convened a press conference on Teachers' Day to air its complaints that Yue opera had fallen under the spell of women. "Today is Teachers' Day, and everyone should promote respect for teachers," the union spokesman was quoted as saying. "But the younger generation of Yue opera performers pays their teachers no respect—they enjoy drinking the clear water but forget its source. We therefore ask you reporters to uphold justice for us." The article continues:

> The original purpose of this press conference was to ask the ten leading actresses, including Yuan Xuefen and Fu Quanxiang, to each hire one male Yue opera teacher for their companies, so as to help the teachers make a liv-

> ing. One of the union representatives' comments caused the assembled journalists much consternation. He said, "We are not as rich as Yuan Xuefen, and today's reception has not been easy for us to prepare. We have spent ten days collecting to make possible even these simple snacks." He even addressed the reporters as "comrades." Having heard him, the reporters could only smile at one another. Feeling sorry for the unionists, the reporters refrained from consuming the snacks.[53]

Mainstream newspapers reported this event differently. *The New Citizen Evening News* published interviews with each of the ten actresses. Yuan Xuefen was quoted as saying, "To accomplish anything requires cooperation and collective action. One person can do nothing. We all work for the future of New Yue Opera, not for personal fame."[54] Yin Guifang remarked, "I have been thinking about training more young actresses in this transitional period, when an older generation has already passed and the new is yet to come. But I cannot make it happen alone. So when Xuefen talked with me about the Yue opera school, I was really excited. This undertaking will fail, though, if it must depend only on us ten sisters. We need lots of friends to care for the school and to help. Support us."[55] An enthusiastic Tian Han published an article in *The New Citizen Evening News* titled "United, You Have Power!" in which he pointed out that it was already a great achievement for the actresses to have brought off such a production.[56]

Thus, in the process of this grand fund-raising, a new collective identity emerged among the leading Yue opera actresses, one of progressive, modern, and autonomous art workers. Correspondingly, this self-conscious identity was successfully projected in the news media in the image of the young, upbeat, and reform-minded actresses of Yue opera. It was also during this process that Yue opera actresses began to appear as subject-agents in the news media, making the news themselves and defining their own positions, rather than being reported and commented upon as before. In this context, Yue opera actresses took on a central role in the Xiao Dangui incident and staged a self-directed social drama in the public arena.

The Xiao Dangui Incident: Competing Narratives

On October 13, 1947, less than one month after the end of the fund-raising performances, one of the ten sisters, Xiao Dangui, committed suicide at her home. Xiao Dangui was from a poor peasant family in Shengxian.

4.4 Stage photo of Xiao Dangui in Qing-style dress. (*Zhongguo Yueju* 1989)

She was given away as a child bride at the age of eight and joined a girls' opera school, the Gaosheng Theater, at ten. Hardworking and talented, Xiao distinguished herself during her school years and took up a leading role immediately after her apprenticeship. During the 1930s, she performed with the Gaosheng Theater all over Zhejiang and made a good impression on Shanghai audiences as well. In early 1938, Xiao caused a sensation when she performed with the Gaosheng Theater in "island" Shanghai (see fig. 4.4).

Qiu Guangxian, owner of the Gaosheng Theater, was also a Shengxian native and the highly disciplined patriarch of the school. Qiu's admonition to the students may be summarized in the two sentences he often uttered: "Carry yourself pure and clean; perform honestly and earnestly." He not only hired the best teachers so that the students would receive good training in the operatic arts but also safeguarded the girls' moral and sexual purity. He set up strict rules forbidding socialization between men and women within the school and even hired a female manager to supervise the girls' everyday lives. When the school toured urban centers such as Hangzhou and Shanghai, Qiu always kept his eye on the students, not allowing them to socialize with local audiences lest they be seduced by money, sex, and the corrupt urban life, especially that of colonial Shanghai. In 1939, after a successful eight-month run in Shanghai and in the midst of a boom in women's Shengxian opera, Qiu decided to leave Shanghai. A strict disciplinarian, he could no longer prevent his actresses from becoming popular stars—the objects of public desire and the subjects of their own fates. Qiu applied a harsh punishment called "red all around," beating all the girls if one girl did something wrong. Even this could not stop the actresses from sneaking out of the dorm or receiving gifts behind his back. Losing control and fearing the consequences of the girls' behavior, Qiu took the troupe back to eastern Zhejiang to perform in Ningbo, Shaoxing, and Shengxian.[57] In 1940, Qiu retired and disbanded the Gaosheng Theater. At this point, Zhang Chunfan came and recruited Xiao and several veteran Gaosheng Theater actresses. Xiao returned to Shanghai and quickly became one of the most popular Yue opera stars in the city. When Xiao and her fellow actresses first came back to Shanghai, they all lived in the backstage area of the Zhedong Theater, where they performed. But before long, Xiao moved upstairs where Zhang Chunfan and his wife and children lived. Xiao and Zhang soon became sexually involved and lived together for about six years before Xiao's suicide.[58]

Zhang Chunfan, the defendant in the case, was also a Shengxian native. He came to Shanghai in 1930 to work in a silk factory and later became the manager of two small silk mills. In early 1940, seeing the boom in women's Shengxian opera in Shanghai, Zhang decided to seek his fortune in the opera business. He organized a troupe with Xiao Dangui as the leading actress and made a fortune in the next several years. Zhang was a capable man in his own way. By all accounts, he was greedy, controlling, and bullying, on the one hand, and generous, chivalrous, and useful to his friends, on the other. Zhang was a tough self-made local strongman with little education. He gathered a gang of followers who would not hesitate to use violence against his enemies and also organized and headed the Yue Opera Employers' Union. With his tough style and connections within the trade and through the Shengxian native-place organization, Zhang made himself one of the most powerful men in Yue opera circles.[59]

At first, Xiao's death seemed like just another sensational suicide of a popular female star. On the next day, October 14, the Leyuan Funeral House, which had held Ruan Lingyu's funeral twelve years before and where Xiao Dangui's body now lay, became the center of attention. While newspaper headlines were preoccupied with Xiao's suicide, tens of thousands of spectators crowded the Leyuan Funeral House. Press reports were eager to point out similarities between the two tragic deaths of famous actresses twelve years apart. *Dagong Daily* reported on October 15: "All the Yue opera stars in Shanghai went to mourn [Xiao]. The situation after Xiao's death is comparable to that after the death of the movie star Ruan Lingyu years ago. Both incidents created a public stir. For this reason, the police take the incident seriously and are investigating the cause of Xiao Dangui's suicide."[60] Mainstream newspapers, however, seemed unwilling to get into reporting on sex scandals, the so-called peach-colored news, as the despised tabloid press had done with the Ruan Lingyu incident. Trying to offer some explanation for Xiao's suicide, the *Dagong Daily* report came up with three points, most likely influenced by family members living with Xiao and Zhang. First, Xiao's business was losing money, and she was indebted for up to 400 million yuan, an especially heavy debt because she had quit performing after the departure of her stage partner Xu Yulan. Second, Xiao was frustrated because she felt that public reaction to her performance during the recent fund-raising show was not as favorable as for other actresses. And third, the report vaguely implied that she had some family trouble.

But events soon took a different turn on October 16, the day of Xiao's funeral, when the remaining nine Yue opera sisters charged that Zhang's abuse of Xiao was the cause of the actress's demise. Using their power as public icons, the actresses staged a social drama in which they were both directors and protagonists, setting up Zhang Chunfan as the defendant in a public trial. On that day, Yue opera theaters throughout the city canceled scheduled performances in solidarity in order to pay respects to the deceased Xiao. Many Yue opera actresses attended the funeral, where they became the main attraction for fans and the general public. About twenty thousand Yue opera fans and Shanghai residents once more crowded the funeral house; a few hundred of them broke into the funeral parlor, damaging the furniture, and a portrait of the deceased Xiao went missing.[61]

Focusing on the dramatis personae, represented as "the nine sisters of the deceased," media coverage quickly responded to the actresses and their charges against Zhang. *Dagong Daily* reported:

> Zhang Chunfan has now become the target of the people. The nine sisters met yesterday [October 16]. They request that no one cooperate with Zhang and that Zhang be thrown out of the Yue opera business. The Guotai Theater was bought with Xiao Dangui's personal savings, and therefore Zhang should not be allowed to manage its business. They [the nine sisters] should take charge of the business of the theater. The profits from the theater will be used to take care of Xiao Dangui's grave and annual memorial

> service, and the rest should go to her family [meaning her natal family in Shengxian] for their daily use.[62]

On October 18, *Shanghai Newspaper's* headline read: "Actress Xiao Leaves 2.1 Billion in Property, the Yue Opera Circle Makes Two Points—Suicide Had Nothing to Do with Financial Difficulties, Xiao Had No Dubious Sexual Relationship."[63] The article continued: "they [the nine sisters] will continue to press Zhang Chunfan and, at the same time, call for the support of the public in upholding justice in order to find out the real cause of Xiao's suicide."[64] As the actresses requested, Zhang handed an inventory of Xiao's belongings and property to the mediator, Huang Jinrong, the godfather of Shanghai's notorious Green Gang whose daughter-in-law was Xiao's adoptive mother. In the meantime, the nine sisters were reportedly planning a huge memorial service for Xiao, and a Yue opera play relating the story of her suicide was soon to open; according to the article, it was expected to cause another public sensation.[65] In fact, more than one Yue opera company staged the story. Xiao's suicide soon became a popular subject not only for Yue opera but also for other entertainment forms such as Suzhou story-singing and Shanghai opera.

On October 20, *Dagong Daily* published an interview with Leng Shan, Xiao's director, whom Zhang accused of having had a dubious relationship with Xiao. In this interview, Leng appeared as an honest intellectual who, accepting the suggestions of his friends in spoken drama, had entered Xiao's company to help reform Yue opera. Xiao was portrayed as morally scrupulous and an eager student of modern arts, unlike most other actresses in the company. The relationship between Leng and Xiao was purely one between a leading actress and her director, or between a student and a teacher. Watching movies and discussing performing skills were, according to Leng, part of Xiao's preparation for pursuing her goal of acting onscreen. In the evening of October 7, Leng recounted, he and Xiao set out to see a Hollywood movie. It was a little early, so they went for a walk. They became involved in a discussion about acting skill and never made it to the movie. The next morning, Leng told the reporter, he was summoned to Zhang's house, where Zhang demanded that he tell the truth about the previous night. Leng told the reporter: "I want to make a clear statement about my pure friendship with Xiao. But my sincere oath did not win understanding from a jealous Zhang, and in the end, a weak woman had to resort to suicide. I feel sorry and deep sorrow for her." Other newspapers also focused on Zhang's unfounded jealousy and his subsequent maltreatment of Xiao, which, according to popular belief, ultimately caused the actress's suicide. It seems that by this time Zhang was already presumed guilty in the public eye.[66]

As the social drama and the theatrical performance of Xiao's tragedy unfolded, the police were obliged to take action and arrested Zhang as "the main suspect in the case of Xiao's suicide."[67] On October 31, newspapers published excerpts from Zhang's lengthy statement of self-defense, written in police custody. Zhang described a nearly consummated affair between Xiao and Leng, portraying Leng Shan as immoral and Xiao as a confused woman who would have been seduced by Leng if not for Zhang's advice. But his self-defense had little impact on the police detectives. That same day, after more than ten days of investigation, the police charged Zhang as an accessory to Xiao's suicide and took him in handcuffs to the jail at the District Prosecution Office. The police spokesman made a statement at a news conference: "After Xiao Dangui committed suicide, the police took Zhang Chunfan into custody and investigated him in order to strengthen the law, reassure the public, and make the truth known." The main evidence of Zhang's offense, the officer said, was his refusal to accept Xiao's repeated avowal that her body was pure and clean and his subsequent maltreatment of Xiao. Zhang may have even told Xiao to kill herself, the police officer reasoned.[68] Then, on November 5, the trial opened, and the public prosecutor charged Zhang with abetting Xiao's suicide.

Since Zhang Chunfan had long been presumed guilty in the public eye, the court trial was at first presented in the daily newspapers much as the preceding newspaper trial had been—the same story told, and with the same witnesses. "Yuan Xuefen," a *Shanghai Newspaper* report on the trial read, "is an outsider. It is only because Xiao's death was so pitiable that she, as Xiao's sworn sister, appeals to the court to redress the injustice done to Xiao."[69]

The story was accompanied with a shot of a frustrated Zhang Chunfan, in long gown, walking into the court under police escort, and another showing Yuan Xuefen, wearing a plain cheongsam and smiling, posing for the reporter in front of the courtroom, with Leng Shan, wearing glasses and a Western-style suit, in the background (see fig. 4.5). The contrast is interesting. Leng Shan's appearance as a young Western-style intellectual is juxtaposed to the older Zhang Chunfan's traditional outfit and style, with Yuan Xuefen smiling confidently in the foreground.

檢察官懷疑三點
密告信敘述尤奇
署名「不平人」指張春帆謀害

4.5 A *Shanghai Newspaper* (Shen bao) article on the Xiao Dangui incident, November 5, 1947. Left: Yuan Xuefen in the foreground with Leng Shan to her right. Right: Zhang Chunfan under police escort.

On December 27, the district court acquitted Zhang, for charges against him did not constitute positive evidence, and released him soon after the verdict.[70] Zhang emerged from the jail after two and half months, to find himself disgraced in the public eye and deprived of a chance to benefit from the wealth that Xiao had left behind her. Xiao Dangui's older brother, from her hometown of Changle Township in Shengxian, was recognized as her legal heir and inherited Xiao's property and personal belongings.[71]

Throughout the incident, the nine actresses, cast as the nine sisters, assumed a central role in the public arena, affected the progress of events, and re-created themselves as powerful public figures in the mainstream media. Although their initial demand that they be permitted to take over the Guotai Theater, so as to realize the dream of having a theater of their own, soon proved without legal basis, they succeeded in compromising the prestige of theater owners, casting them in the image of a defeated Zhang Chunfan. How did this happen? How could these young actresses dare to pursue a local strongman like Zhang Chunfan? And what was their motivation? In a 1995 interview, Fu Quanxiang responded: "We were outraged. We just wanted to avenge the deceased Xiao Dangui [*da baobuping*]. I don't know where I got the guts. Zhang Chunfan's men threatened us, saying, 'Do you want to keep your hands? Do you want to keep your legs? Or do you care about your pretty face?' It was scary. We were really bold."[72] Yuan Xuefen, who assumed the leadership in this fight, and Xu Yulan, who had been Xiao's stage partner not long before Xiao's death, provided similar answers.[73]

The actresses suggested that they had no other motivation than to avenge the deceased Xiao Dangui. They had good reason to exact vengeance from Zhang Chunfan. One of the most powerful theater bosses in the trade, Zhang was monopolistic and ruthless and had no respect for the actresses. The actresses were also angry about the way Zhang had treated Xiao. As they saw it, Zhang, a married man, took control of Xiao's sexuality and used her artistic talent to advance his dominance in the Yue opera business. Moreover, the actresses believed that Zhang, while benefiting from Xiao's talent, abused her privately at home. It was quite obvious to the actresses that Xiao would not have resorted to suicide if Zhang had not humiliated her and treated her unjustly.

Many actresses had the impression that Xiao was an unhappy woman whose weak personality made her easy prey for Zhang.[74] They reasoned that Xiao had committed suicide out of desperation for several reasons: her popularity was in a decline, due to Zhang's hostility to Yue opera reform and his insistence that she play erotic characters; as her career drew to an end, she would become financially less useful to Zhang and thus subject to more abuse; and Zhang had already showed signs of disliking her. While it is not certain that Xiao had feared for her future because of tepid ticket sales for her shows, the actresses' reasoning was grounded in the reality of wife/concubine abuse permitted by the polygamous patriarchal system. To the actresses, Zhang appeared to be just such a local strongman who had no hesitation about abusing his power. Xiao's suicide once again confirmed him as a bully.

The actresses' enormous sympathy for Xiao and their anger with her abuser derived from their identification with certain tragic elements in

Xiao's case. The abuse Xiao suffered was, for the actresses, part and parcel of the more general abuse of women in the Yue opera trade and in society at large. Ma Zhanghua's distress at the hands of another theater boss, Lu Gendi, was still a fresh memory. Fu Quanxiang herself had endured misery in her first marriage as the second wife of the owner of the Shenzhou Inn, and she had recently initiated her own divorce. Yuan Xuefen was a self-proclaimed celibate. Xiao-Bai Yumei, Shi Yinghua, and Yao Shuijuan all had unhappy marriages.

In a broader sense, Xiao Dangui's tragic death became an outlet for women to speak their feelings through public agitation. When the nine sisters launched the public campaign charging Zhang Chunfan as Xiao Dangui's true murderer, they spoke not only for themselves, and for the deceased, but also to the sensibilities of many women. Yue opera fans, concubines as well as principal wives, knew their grievances, and some were able to identify Xiao's tragedy with their own suffering. During the uproar after Xiao's death, *Dagong Daily* reported an episode in which a Yue opera fan, Zhang Jinfeng, tried to kill herself. Zhang Jinfeng was obsessed with Xiao's case. She went to the Leyuan Funeral House to attend Xiao's funeral and followed the news passionately every day, so much so that she neglected her housekeeping chores. Her mother-in-law scolded her, saying, "If you are so concerned, why not go with Xiao yourself?" On the morning of October 26, Zhang Jinfeng drank a large quantity of gasoline in an attempt to kill herself. Her husband took her to the hospital, and her life was saved.[75]

The actresses won public support not only because they articulated women's sensibilities, elicited by Xiao's tragic death, but also because they succeeded in claiming the virtue of *qingbai*, or purity and cleanliness, through Yue opera reform. They had cleansed the opera of sexual obscenity and earnestly produced decent, sometimes socially meaningful, love dramas, and they had created a public image of themselves as respectable, modern art workers through the staging of *Sister Xianglin* and recent fund-raising events. If there was any doubt about Xiao's *qingbai*, Xiao had purified herself by giving up her life. The irony was, however, that the actresses were able to prevail as modern public figures only because they were firmly grounded in a traditional rendering of women's virtue. Zhang Chunfan, in fact, invoked the concept of *qingbai* to criticize Xiao's wrongdoing and justify the pressure he placed upon her. In his statement to the police, he stressed that he pressed Xiao because he was concerned about her *qingbai*, which was in jeopardy because of Leng Shan's seduction. Zhang's Shengxian supporters had even fabricated a sensational story of the alleged seduction.[76] Their story, like that of the unionists, was hindered by its outdated language and style to the extent that it sounds laughable to the modern reader. But in the end, only because the actresses *had* acquired the virtue of *qingbai* could they summon up enormous social sympathy, try the alleged abuser in the public forum, and turn a sexual scandal into a social drama of justice for women.

The Republican Actress Transformed in the Public Sphere

In May 1935, upon the death of Ruan Lingyu, Lu Xun pointed out with great pain the silence of the actress in the middle of the public uproar:

> "Gossip is frightening" is a sentence that we read in movie star Ruan Lingyu's suicide note, found after her death. After a lot of empty chatter, generated by the heartrending incident of her tragic death, public attention has gradually cooled. As soon as the drama *Fragrant Lingyu Vanishes with the Wind* (Lingyu xiangxiao ji) stops playing, the whole incident will fade away, leaving no trace, just like Ai Xia's suicide a year ago. Their deaths were a grain of salt dropped into the endless sea of gossip, adding some flavor. But soon, the gossip trade will be the same as before—tasteless and meaningless.[77]

Contending that the media's sensational descriptions of Ruan Lingyu's case were just another form of dalliance with women, Lu Xun continued:

> She [Ruan Lingyu] was slandered [by the media] with colorful inventions but had no way to clear herself. Couldn't she fight, some say? But since she did not have a home newspaper [*jiguan bao*], how could she fight? She had grievances, and injustice had been done to her. But since she did not have a clear enemy, whom should she fight? If we can put ourselves in her shoes, then we may understand the truth in her statement "gossip is frightening," as well as the truth in people's conviction that her suicide had to do with the media.[78]

Ruan Lingyu's words finally reached the public arena only after her lamentable suicide. A voice as weak as this, crying that "gossip is frightening," needed suicide to pierce indifference. Many died voiceless, only to excite even more sound and fury in the gossip media. Actresses served as the objects of a public culture of erotica—to be imagined, described, discussed, interpreted, and spoken for. If they were unfortunately entangled in sexual scandal, a favorite subject of the gossip media, the cost of their redemption was sometimes nothing less than death: only thus could they communicate protest and recover their innocence in the public eye, as we have seen repeatedly in the cases of Ai Xia, Ruan Lingyu, Ma Zhanghua, and Xiao Dangui.

Remarkably, the death of Xiao Dangui in October 1947 invoked a social drama that was very different from anything the public had seen. In 1935, male intellectuals seized on Ruan Lingyu's death to lecture the public and the gossip media on women's liberation and theatrical reform, but twelve years later, Yue opera actresses took center stage in the media to speak for themselves and seek justice for Xiao Dangui. This change clearly signaled the ascent of Yue opera actresses in the public arena, from silent objects of sexual scandals or reformist discourses to articulate subject-agents with full social status.

舞臺姐妹

Chapter 5

The Opera as History

On October 1, 1949, Yuan Xuefen climbed to the balcony of the Gate of Heavenly Peace (Tiananmen), along with a few hundred representatives to the First Chinese People's Political Consultative Conference, to witness Chairman Mao Zedong declare the founding of the People's Republic of China. Yuan was one of four actors selected to represent the local-opera profession nationwide; the other three were the famous Beijing opera masters Mei Lanfang, Cheng Yanqiu, and Zhou Xinfang (see fig. 5.1). Yu Ling, the former chair of Shanghai's CCP underground Committee on Culture and now head of the Division of Arts in Shanghai's new government, had sent Yuan, along with Zhou Xinfang, to Beijing as a special representative of local operas. From then on, Yuan's personal fortunes were tied to her relationship with the new government.

At first, Yuan recalled, she did not want to attend the meeting. She told Yu Ling that she was not interested in politics, because politics was dirty, and she wanted only to be a good actor. Unsettled by her sudden status as an equal of such important cultural figures as Mei Lanfang and Zhou Xinfang, Yuan told Yu Ling that she did not deserve the honor. Yu Ling simply asked, as Yuan recalled: "You say you don't like politics. Do you know what politics is?" Yu Ling continued: "Politics is first of all to make clear what is right and what is wrong." Once in Beijing and after being received by Premier Zhou Enlai, Yuan changed her mind. Zhou told her that he had secretly attended one of her performances in 1946 and had known of her for some time. She found the premier to be extremely nice and friendly, quite the opposite of what she had imagined high officials to be. She was equally surprised to discover that her old friends Yu Ling, Tian Han, and

5.1 Yuan Xuefen with three Beijing opera actors, representatives of the traditional opera circle at the First National Political Consultative Council, 1949. *From left*: Cheng Yanqiu, Yuan Xuefen, Mei Lanfang, and Zhou Xinfang. (Yuan 2002)

Liu Housheng had been members of the CCP underground and were now officials of the new government.[1]

Yuan joined the Communist Party in 1954. In 1955, she was appointed head of the newly established official Shanghai Yue Opera House. A decade later, she was persecuted during the Cultural Revolution, like many other officials, but her standing was restored immediately afterward, and she remained in the position until she retired in 1985. She was also a long-term representative to the National People's Congress and a member of its fifth, sixth, and seventh Standing Committees. In the meantime, she starred in a few New Yue Opera classics and two of the most influential Yue opera films, *Butterfly Lovers* (1953) and *Sister Xianglin* (1978).[2] Yuan and her colleagues at the Shanghai Yue Opera House performed internationally and entertained numerous foreign diplomats as representatives of China's traditional arts. Her political and artistic stature, combined with Yue opera's popular success, made Yue opera one of the most important in the nation.

Beginning in the late 1980s, however, Yue opera was caught in the trend of a general decline in native operas, suffered a sharp downturn in its popularity, and quickly lost its place in mainstream popular entertainment. In the ensuing two decades, Yue opera performances were few and the audience was small. The few remaining Yue opera troupes relied entirely or partially on government subsidies to pay for salaries and production expenses. By the end of the twentieth century, it became clear that Yue opera's glory as a shining popular-culture phenomenon had passed. Significantly, the rise of Yue opera actresses from lowly female entertainers/prostitutes to respected professional art workers, popular media icons, and even members of the cultural elite proved to be irreversible, despite the genre's decline.

How did the communist revolution and the PRC state affect Yue opera and its actresses? The vicissitudes of the opera and its actresses in the latter half of the twentieth century unfolded under the heavy-handed intervention of a socialist state during the early PRC period through the Cultural Revolution and within the context of waves of modern economic development and urban migration in the post-Mao era of "reform and opening [to the world]" (*gaige kaifang*) in the 1980s and 1990s. While the story of Yue opera and its actresses was still evolving, interpretations of this very story were put forward, seeking not only to define Yue opera's history but also to influence its future development. This chapter explores the dynamic relationship between the opera and its actresses, on the one hand, and the communist revolution and the PRC state, on the other, as well as the narratives about this relationship produced during the half-century after 1949. The discussion develops through a reading of two productions about the history of Yue opera: the 1965 film *Stage Sisters* (Wutai jiemei), directed by Xie Jin, representing a communist interpretation of Yue opera's history, and the Yue opera play by the same title, produced in 1998 by the Shanghai Yue Opera House, revealing an understanding of Yue opera's history and self-identity as defined by Yue opera people themselves.

Narrating the Yue Opera Story in Film

The film *Stage Sisters* tells the story of two Yue opera actresses from the Shengxian countryside who take different life paths after entering the dangerous metropolis of 1940s Shanghai. Zhu Chunhua chooses to abide by her teacher's admonition, "carry yourself pure and clean; perform earnestly and honestly," and she eventually joins the CCP-led "progressive forces" (*jinbu liliang*), a CCP term describing social forces sympathetic to the leftist agenda and critical of the Nationalist government in Republican Shanghai during the Civil War. By contrast, Xing Yuehong, longing for wealth and the status of a bourgeois housewife, marries a theater boss in order to secure her desired lifestyle. She ultimately falls victim to the evil theater boss, who soon tires of her and then sacrifices her, under order of Nationalist officials, in an effort to obstruct Chunhua's progressive activities. Finally, after Liberation, in 1949, the theater boss flees Shanghai for Taiwan, while Chunhua invites Yuehong to join the revolution and come back to the stage.

Conceived in 1957 and produced in 1964, *Stage Sisters* was a major success for the forty-one-year-old Xie Jin, the PRC's master film director of communist melodrama.[3] Like his *The Number Five of Women's Basketball* (Nülan Wuhao), of 1957, and *Red Detachment of Women* (Hongse niangzi jun), of 1960, *Stage Sisters* explores the fate of women before and after Liberation. Born and raised in Shangyu, a county adjacent to Shengxian, Xie Jin was familiar with the lives of Yue opera actresses of the past, and he was struck by the contrasts in the status and lives of these actresses before and after Liberation.[4] His two co-screenwriters, Xu Jin and Lin Gu, were also from Zhejiang, and Xu Jin was, as discussed in previous chapters, a master playwright of the Yue opera love drama. In *Stage Sisters*, as in Xie Jin's other two films, women's lives serve as vehicles for communist melodrama. Such stories typically start with oppressed, exploited, and victimized women before Liberation and end with "liberated" and happy women, who are grateful to the Communist Party and fully devoted to the revolution. The film *Stage Sisters* weaves the story of Yue opera and its actresses into this master narrative of the communist revolution, which in turn sets the framework for interpreting Yue opera's history. It should not be surprising that the film sought to construct and present the history of Yue opera as part of the melodrama of the communist revolution, for the new state emphasized the fundamental importance of ideology and propaganda, of which entertainment was an important aspect. Xie Jin clarified the main theme of the film:

> We heard many life stories detailing entertainers' struggles against the old ruling class—these were contradictions in life. The dramatic contradiction in *Stage Sisters* is manifested in the ideological conflict between the two sisters . . . , which to a certain degree reflects intense and complex class contradictions of the time. . . . This process of intensifying contradiction, in fact, tells us that people live in a complex class-stratified society and always have to choose between two paths—if they do not choose the revolutionary path, they will be used by the enemies, and their conduct will make the enemies happy and their friends grieved. . . .
>
> Local-opera singers in the old society occupied a low position and were

> called "tenth-grade humans." Thus, there is a certain amount of tragic elements in certain scenes; . . . the mood becomes exalted only after the appearance of the Party's leadership in the third chapter.[5]

The film opens with off-screen choral singing, alerting the audience to the film's main theme:

> The green water winds its way around the mountains,
> And the sound of opera singing fills the theatres.
> Tears and laughter are commonplace on the stage;
> Who would know there is real-life drama offstage?[6]

The scene is set in 1935 and focuses on a traditional stage built on a hillside in the eastern Zhejiang countryside , where a women's Shengxian opera performance is in progress. In front of the stage, various venders and gambling groups mingle with audience members, forming a typical performance scene. Suddenly, the audience is disturbed by a teenage girl running away from her pursuers, a man and a woman with rope in their hands. The girl is none other than Zhu Chunhua, escaping the fate of being a child bride, for she is scheduled to be sexually united with her "child husband" (*yuan fang*) that night. Teacher Xing of the troupe, Yuehong's father, pities the girl and takes her in as a student. Before long, the hardworking Chunhua proves herself to be a good actress, and she and Yuehong become stage partners and sworn sisters. A local wealthy landlord desires the two sisters, but he is soon put off by Chunhua's strong personality and her overt disgust at his sexual advances. Setting his eyes on Yuehong, the landlord conspires with the corrupt police force to storm the troupe's performance one day, under the pretext of banning the morally corrupt women's opera, and tries to kidnap Yuehong amid the chaos. Chunhua fights off the police and rescues Yuehong but is arrested in the end. Yuehong's father uses up his savings to secure Chunhua's release and, having been seriously wounded during the fighting, dies soon thereafter. His last words to the sisters are "Carry yourself pure and clean; perform earnestly and honestly." The owner of the troupe shrewdly sells the sisters into a three-year obligation to a theater owner in Shanghai. For this, he receives a large sum of money and tells the sisters he has used it all to pay for the burial of Yuehong's father.

In Shanghai, the two sisters soon emerge as rising Yue opera stars, but they then follow separate paths. Manager Tang, the theater boss, heartlessly abandons his lover, Shang Shuihua, the former queen of Yue opera, now overshadowed by the younger sisters, and takes Yuehong as his new lover. Humiliated and seeing no future for herself, Shang commits suicide.

The second part of the film depicts a struggle between the CCP-led progressive forces and the corrupt Nationalist establishment, as manifested in the struggle between Chunhua and Manager Tang over Yuehong's fate. Greatly disturbed that Yuehong has fallen into Tang's hands and by Shang's death, Chunhua adopts progressive ideas about right and wrong, as taught to her by the reporter Jiang Bo, a CCP underground worker under the leadership of Brother Lin. She decides to stage a production of Lu Xun's *The New Year's Sacrifice* in place of the traditional Yue opera plays, which she now considers obscene and meaningless. In cahoots with the Nationalist Social Affairs Bureau, which has banned the play, Tang cancels his contract with Chunhua's troupe. Chunhua counters Tang's effort to ruin her by organizing Yue opera actresses for a performance that would raise funds for building a theater of their own. The day before the performance, as Chunhua is walking home, a hooligan jumps out and throws lime powder on her face, damaging her eyes. The Nationalist commissioner Pan and the theater boss Tang name Yuehong as a coconspirator in an attempt to mislead the public into believing that the incident was part of a dispute between the two actresses. The trial is set in a clear-cut good-versus-evil format: Chunhua, the plaintiff, and Jiang Bo, who occupies the journalist's seat during the trial, represent the good, while the hooligan (the defendant), the Nationalist judges, Tang, and a Nationalist secret agent seated in the audience represent the evil. Yuehong, meanwhile, is caught in the crossfire; the trial ends in chaos when Yuehong faints.

At the end of the film, which is set in 1950, Brother Lin and Jiang Bo, both in army uniform, send Chunhua and her troupe off to participate in land reform in their hometown as part of an entertainment propaganda team. On the very stage where Chunhua and Yuehong performed fifteen years ago, Chunhua stages *The White-Haired Girl* (Baimao nü), an early Communist classic from Yan'an that tells the story of how the old society turned a woman into a ghost and how Liberation restored her. The story line thus parallels Chunhua's efforts to restore Yuehong to society, and the film ends with Chunhua vowing to perform revolutionary drama for the rest of her life.[7]

There is thus no doubt that *Stage Sisters* presents a Party version of the history of Yue opera and its actresses, a history that meshed closely with the Party's history of modern China in general. The director clearly expressed the film's overt political mission: "Through the vicissitudes of two stage sisters in a changing theatrical environment, through the different life paths Chunhua and Yuehong choose to take, the film conveys the love and hatred of the author and what the author wants the viewer to contemplate."[8] The film's author wanted to present an uplifting melodrama of the communist revolution and wanted the viewer to conclude that the history of Yue opera and its actresses was determined by a grand political struggle in the twentieth century.

How much of the film is based on real life and how much is self-congratulatory CCP propaganda? The story of *Stage Sisters* is based on Yuan Xuefen's experience during the 1940s, but it also draws liberally on the life stories of various people surrounding her, most of whom are discussed in previous chapters: fellow actresses Fu Quanxiang, Ma Zhanghua, and Xiao Dangui; theater bosses Lu Gendi and Zhang Chunfan; and CCP underground workers Yu Ling and Tong Lijuan.

Yuan and Fu entered the same all-girls training school in the Shengxian countryside in 1933, when Yuan was eleven years old and Fu was ten. Each recalled the other with great fondness, as a companion from school days. "I was very naughty, and Yuan Xuefen too," Fu confided. "While everyone could easily see my troublemaking, not everyone knew how mischievous Yuan was, because she was more thoughtful even when she was naughty. We were a good pair."[9] Yuan recalled with amusement her first meeting with Fu. Yuan's father would not give Yuan permission to join the opera school, but a stubborn young Yuan insisted and left home without any luggage. At the school, Yuan met Fu, who was from a nearby village. The two little girls struck up a conversation, telling each other their stories. When night fell, however, Yuan found herself without bedding. "Fortunately," Yuan said, "Fu offered to let me sleep with her under the same quilt."

After three years of study, the girls graduated in 1936; the school became a troupe and went to Shanghai to try its luck. As indicated in the film, the two friends followed different paths. While Yuan (Zhu Chunhua in the film) resisted the temptations of money and fame and conducted her life in a manner that was pure and clean, others were caught up in the tumultuous currents of city life. Fu had joined a religious sect with Yuan but could not adhere to the ascetic lifestyle. In 1941, at age eighteen, she quit the sect and became the second wife of the owner of the Shenzhou Inn, Zhu Xiangyun.[10] Five years later, after much hardship, Fu filed for divorce and ended the marriage.[11] The characters Xing Yuehong and Shang Shuihua also rely on the life stories of Yuan's stage partner, the famous "lightning young male impersonator" Ma Zhanghua, and the Yue opera erotic star Xiao

Dangui, both of whom suffered at the hands of theater bosses and died tragically while embroiled in sex scandals.

The character of Manager Tang is an obvious reference to the theater bosses Lu Gendi and Zhang Chunfan, who were implicated in the deaths of Ma Zhanghua and Xiao Dangui respectively and executed by the new government as counterrevolutionaries in 1951.[12] On the political left, the character Brother Lin is modeled after the playwright Yu Ling, chair of the CCP Shanghai underground's Committee on Culture during the Civil War and director of Shanghai's cultural affairs immediately after Liberation in 1949. Another important character, the reporter Jiang Bo, clearly represents a collective image of lower-level CCP underground workers who facilitated Yuan's staging of *Sister Xianglin* and supported her in the press during the union incident.

Though derived from real-life stories, the film politicizes and polarizes these stories in terms of the struggle between the two rival political parties, whereas the reality, as discussed in previous chapters, was more complicated. For example, Lu Gendi and Zhang Chunfan were not Nationalist officials or affiliates, and the man who attacked Yuan Xuefen with a bag of dung had nothing to do with Zhang Chunfan, nor was the attack ordered by Nationalist officials. The unionists had little political commitment and acted for personal revenge, although they did take advantage of the government's anti-leftist attitude. Such complicated everyday local politics are simplified in the film so that it fits into a grand narrative of the struggle of good versus evil, or the CCP versus the Nationalists. In fact, the film reflects the politicizing practice unfolding in real life in the early PRC period, as seen in the new government's execution of Lu and Zhang as class enemies, ostensibly in response to the request of Yue opera actresses who had held a public meeting complaining about Zhang's oppression.[13]

Yuan Xuefen, however, endorsed the film version of Yue opera history, or, rather, she helped create this particular version of history. For Yuan's career was completely tied to the Party after 1949, and her views intertwined with those of the Party to form the basis for an official interpretation of Yue opera history. During production, the film team consulted Yuan and her cohorts many times and, given Yuan's artistic and political stature and her status as the representative of the genre, any official interpretation of Yue opera history had to privilege Yuan's career and perspective.

The revolution reinvented Yuan as a member of the PRC political and cultural elite, not only occupying high official positions but also enjoying a personal relationship with Premier Zhou Enlai and his wife Deng

Yingchao. She was described by local officials as "someone who had direct access to top leaders in Beijing" (*tongtian*). Looking back, Yuan deemed the performance of *Sister Xianglin* in 1946 to be the turning point in her life and career. The play not only introduced her to the CCP before 1949 but also assured her career success after Liberation. Ideologically correct and artistically meritorious (thanks to Lu Xun's craftsmanship and Yuan's thoughtful rendition), *Sister Xianglin* showcased the best of Yue opera's revolutionary modern-attire plays and was bound to become a classic under the new government. The play not only exemplified Yuan's artistic achievement but also suggested her strong sense of right and wrong even before Liberation. The play was restaged at three politically significant moments: in 1956, on the twentieth anniversary of Lu Xun's death; in 1962, on the twentieth anniversary of Mao Zedong's talk on art and literature in Yan'an; and in 1977, shortly after the Cultural Revolution and on the forty-first anniversary of Lu Xun's death. Each restaging of the play in the PRC period reaffirmed Yuan's position in Yue opera circles and in national cultural politics.

In a sense, polarized interpretations of the initial staging of *Sister Xianglin* were inevitable given the life-and-death struggle between the two parties in these decades, and indeed, left-wing intellectuals began to politicize the show in the wake of the performance. The Nationalist Shanghai Social Affairs Bureau also became increasingly suspicious that Yuan was a CCP member and put her under surveillance, while tacitly allowing the unionists to blackmail and physically attack her. The bureau thought that the ten sisters were holding their fund-raising performances to raise money for Communist troops in northern Jiangsu and tried to block the project. Bureau archives show that, in 1948–49, Wu Kaixian, the head of the bureau, personally monitored the Xuesheng Company, while the bureau ordered the company to submit its program of performances for approval two weeks in advance.[14] Even in 1996, some Nationalist-affiliated Shengxian natives who moved to Taiwan in 1949 and who are now amateur Yue opera researchers in Taipei still believed that Yuan was an underground CCP agent.[15]

The State and Yue Opera in the Early PRC Period

The film's account of the history of Yue opera and its actresses was also informed by the complex transformations shaping the genre and the lives of the actresses in the early PRC period during which the film was produced. Having set itself up as the liberator of the masses, who were exploited and oppressed by the old ruling class, the CCP was, at least in theory, looking out for the good of the common people, and many CCP leaders were indeed sympathetic to the needs of disadvantaged, lower-class people. Unlike workers and peasants, whose status in the revolution was relatively clearly defined, lower-class actors and especially actresses were regarded by the CCP with both sympathy and suspicion and identified as people in need of both liberation and reformation. Zhou Enlai's view of Yue opera actresses, articulated in 1946, clearly reveals this approach:

> They [Yue opera actresses] were all children from poor families and became actresses because there was no other way to make a living. When they became popular in Shanghai, adoptive mothers and fathers all pursued them, and evil forces in society surrounded them and corrupted them. A few among them began to realize their status as the insulted and exploited and thus wanted to be progressive and learn from progressive spoken dramatists led by the Party's underground forces.[16]

Zhou accordingly instructed the Shanghai underground to help Yue opera actresses and draw them into the revolution.

Li Taicheng, an official at the Shanghai Cultural Affairs Bureau and later head of the bureau after the Cultural Revolution, had a similar perspective on the Party's attitude and policy toward actresses in the early PRC period:

> Actresses in the old society were the insulted and injured. In order to make a living and build a foundation for survival, actresses had to deal with hooligans, theater bosses, young mistresses, and rich concubines. Tong Zhiling [a noted Beijing opera actress], for example, had an unusual relationship with Dai Li [head of the Bureau of Investigation of the Nationalist Committee on Military Affairs, a notorious fascist organization], but we did not purge her for that. She was only an actress. If she were not, then it would have been a political matter. The Communist Party was in fact very sympathetic to these people. It was not that we had to use them to glorify the image of the Party—there were a lot of actresses with clean personal histories [who were willing to serve the Party].[17]

State policy toward popular entertainment in the early and mid-1950s sought to bring entertainment firmly under state control through the so-called three transformations (*san gai*), which applied to the entertainer, the structure of the industry, and the stage performance.

With entertainers, the state sought to educate them in socialist ideas and make them advocates for the new society. The lowly entertainer of the past now acquired the status of art worker and thereby not only became the equal of others in the new society but also was further honored as, in the state's term, an "engineer of the soul" who influenced people with powerful arts. In order to showcase this transformation, the state identified many figures similar to Yuan Xuefen in various local operas, such as Ding Shi'e in Shanghai opera, Chang Xiangyu in Henan clapper opera, Guan Sushuang in Hebei clapper opera, Hong Xiannü in Guangdong opera, and Mei Lanfang and Zhou Xinfang in Beijing opera, to name just a few, and made them part of the new cultural and political elite.

Within Yue opera, the state-run Shanghai Yue Opera House collected well-known actresses, such as Fan Ruijuan, Fu Quanxiang, Xu Yulan, and Wang Wenjuan. Most of them were given political status as members of the People's Congress or the Political Consultative Conference. After positions in Shanghai were allocated, other noted or even less well-known actresses moved out of Shanghai with the hope of acquiring similar status in other cities. In 1954, Zhu Shuizhao and her Yunhua Company became the Nanjing City Yue Opera Company,[18] and Gao Jianlin and her company settled in Xi'an,[19] while in 1959, Yin Guifang and her Fanghua Company relocated to Fuzhou.[20] The transformation of such actresses into members of state elites raised the status of entertainers in general and encouraged others to follow the Party as well.

In effecting structural transformation of the entertainment industry, the state sought to replace the old market-based structure with a centrally planned popular culture and economy. In Shanghai, the new entertainment industry was organized in tiers, with a few state theaters directly under the central government (*guojia juyuan*) at the top, followed by local state-owned institutions under provincial or municipal governments (*guoying jutuan*), state-run troupes collectively owned by the employees (*xin guoying jutuan*), and private troupes receiving state aid (*minban gongzhu jutuan*). The theaters were also placed under state ownership and tied loosely to various performance units. The government first created four state-owned institutions in major native-opera genres in the city: the Shanghai Yue Opera House, with the status of a state theater; the Shanghai Beijing Opera House; the Shanghai People's Shanghai Opera Company; and the Shanghai People's Huai Opera Company.[21] These state-owned companies were meant to showcase the best of each genre and lead opera reform in general. Before the Cultural Revolution, the field of popular entertainment included a planned entertainment culture represented by state-owned institutions and their productions along with the market-oriented popular entertainment provided by the collectively owned troupes. Employees in state-run institutions were on the government payroll and enjoyed a stable monthly salary and benefits, while those under collective ownership relied on the market value of their performances. Depending on the market and the quality of each troupe's performances, some actresses could enjoy a very good income, much better than those on the state payroll, while others had to rely on government-subsidized health care and welfare benefits when box office revenues were low.[22] In the mid-1950s, the government spent a considerable amount of money to safeguard the welfare of entertainers, providing everything from unemployment and health benefits to winter clothing and quilts.[23] At the same time, the state not only directly controlled the productions of state-owned companies but also asserted influence on collectively owned troupes by inserting administrators and Party cells in these troupes. Thus, before 1949, entertainers were largely on their own, and their livelihood depended on their ability to draw customers; after 1949, the state took responsibility for both the content of the production and the entertainers' livelihoods.[24]

Along with transforming the entertainer and the industry, the state sought to transform stage productions. According to Li Taicheng: "After Liberation, the administration exercised complete leadership over art and entertainment and did away with all social [market] influences."[25] Although the extent to which government control of entertainment was in fact "complete" is an open question, there is no doubt that during the early PRC period, state intervention had a great impact on stage performances as a whole. For the state, popular entertainment was to be reformed, along with the entertainer, so that it could educate the people with socialist ideas.

The new state took a populist stance toward local operas, promoting them as China's native folk arts and sending playwrights, directors, and composers as well as political leaders to native-opera troupes to help develop politically correct productions with high artistic values. While providing unprecedented intellectual, media, and financial support to local operas, and hence helping to raise their artistic sophistication to a new level, state intervention limited possibilities for exploring various subjects and styles. As the self-designated heir to the New Culture Movement, the state quickly banned plays it deemed morally corrupt or politically incorrect, including ghost horror stories and erotic plays such as the Yue opera *Widow Ma's Inn* and the Beijing opera *Break Open the Coffin*.[26] At the same time, it elevated and promoted revolutionary modern-attire plays conveying the Party line and propagating state policies on current affairs.

The state, however, was unsure about how to treat love drama. On the one hand, the new state sanctioned love drama with its strong pro-women position, which countered feudal remnants such as gender discrimination, arranged marriage, and the exploitation of women in the traditional family system. The constitution gave women rights equal to those of men, and in 1950, for the first time in Chinese history, the Marriage Law banned polygamy and granted women equal rights to family property and to divorce. The propaganda campaign launched in 1953 to promote the new law identified free love, as opposed to traditional arranged marriage, and women's liberation in general as fundamental components of China's socialist culture and the basis for forging a new socialist citizenry. The state's promotion of gender equality and free marriage gave love drama in Yue opera, and in popular entertainment overall, a great boost, as it granted political legitimacy to an already popular theatrical subgenre. On the other hand, the officially endorsed form of revolutionary heroism left no room for indulgence in the petty, bourgeois kind of love sentiment. Audiences, however, continued to support love drama and were uninterested in the new revolutionary plays. As revolutionary plays lacked popularity and erotic plays were banned, love drama thrived.

Yue opera love drama peaked both artistically and in popularity in the 1950s and early 1960s, a period that witnessed the production of several Yue opera masterpieces, including *Tale of the Western Chamber* and *Dream of the Red Chamber.* Just as the transformation of *The Butterfly Lovers* during the Republican period exemplifies the way in which folk traditions nurtured the opera's growth, so the staging of *Tale of the Western Chamber* and *Dream of the Red Chamber* shows how a mature Yue opera absorbed the cream of traditional literature and created theatrical masterpieces of love in the complex context of the early PRC period.

The Shanghai Yue Opera House's new rendition of *Tale of the Western Chamber* illustrates this process. Adapted from Wang Shifu's famous miscellany-opera play of the same title, the Yue opera *Tale of the Western Chamber* is a tragic love story about a talented young scholar, Zhang Gong, and Cui Yingying, the beautiful daughter of a late prime minister. The play was first produced in 1953 by order of Premier Zhou Enlai to entertain the visiting North Korean president, Kim Il-Sung, upon the signing of the Sino-Korean Treaty.[27] In the 1955 revision of the play, Yuan Xuefen depicted the character of Cui Yingying as a sensitive, lovesick maiden torn between her upbringing, with its Confucian notions of women's propriety, and her desire for love. Although Yingying's love for Zhang Gong eventually overcomes the constraints of

5.2 "Farewell," the last scene in *Tale of the Western Chamber*, with Zhu Dongyun as Cui Yingying (second left) and Cao Yindi as Zhang Gong (second right), 1960s. First produced in the early 1950s by the Shanghai Yue Opera House, the play has become a classic, staged by every generation of Yue opera actresses. (Courtesy of Shanghai Yue Opera House)

feudal morality, and the union of the two lovers defies feudal authority, their subsequent forced separation attests to the evils of feudalism.[28]

During the Qing dynasty, *Tale of the Western Chamber* was banned as an "erotic play" (*yin xi*), and in the Republican period, various local operas often performed it as such. It is said that Zhang Gong, as played by some rural or low-level itinerary troupes, extended his arm from behind the curtained bed, swinging egg whites on his fingers, a gesture considered extremely erotic at the time.[29] Other versions, including those in women's Yue opera and Beijing opera, had the character Hongniang, Yingying's maid, act out erotic gestures from her place outside the room where Cui Yingying and Zhang Gong are supposedly making love.[30] In the 1953 and 1955 Yue opera productions, all the explicit sexual episodes were eliminated, and romantic love governed the narrative. The strong subtext of the young lovers' erotic desire

5.3 Fang Yafen as Cui Yingying (left) and Zhang Yongmei as Hongniang in *Tale of the Western Chamber*, 1992. (Courtesy of Shanghai Yue Opera House)

for each other was veiled by the actresses' skillful depiction of the characters' emotional development (see figs. 5.2, 5.3).[31]

The state used Yue opera love drama to represent the achievements of Chinese native opera in the international community. Yue opera was the first native opera to be performed internationally. At the Geneva Convention in 1953, Premier Zhou Enlai entertained foreign diplomats and journalists with the new Yue opera color film *The Butterfly Lovers*. In 1955, the Shanghai Yue Opera House, touring as the Chinese Yue Opera Troupe, performed two Yue opera masterpieces, *The Butterfly Lovers* and *Tale of the Western Chamber*, in the German Democratic Republic and the Soviet Union.[32] These two plays and, after 1958, *Dream of the Red Chamber*, became internationally known through frequent performances overseas and at home for foreign guests. The Shanghai Yue Opera House became an important cultural ambassador for the PRC state. In 1962 and 1963, when a number of Yue opera plays were made into color films and screened nationwide and internationally, Yue opera's influence reached new heights. As the Yue opera playwright Cheng Rong remarked:

> Yue opera had always had low status and was not worthy of being talked about. As a Yue opera playwright, Xu Jin could not even find a wife before Liberation. He was married after Liberation. At that time [in the 1940s], we were all embarrassed to tell people that we were doing Yue opera. I thus eventually cut off communication with my former classmates, because they could not understand why I became involved in Yue opera—as if I were no good. Only after Liberation did Yue opera gain high esteem and come to be performed nationwide and even overseas, representing our country.[33]

Perhaps exaggerating somewhat, Cheng Rong nonetheless attested to the fact that Yue opera was at its political and artistic zenith during the 1950s and early 1960s. Although Yue opera had already been prominent in Shanghai's entertainment market before 1949, the new state acknowledged Yue opera's artistic achievements and further raised its status by making it into a national theater, widely known as China's second-largest native opera, second only to Beijing opera.

Most actresses felt optimistic and financially more secure under the new government. Wu Xiaolou, for example, had entered an all-girls opera school in 1934, when she was around nine years old, and joined the Shanghai Yue Opera House as a leading actress playing elderly male roles after Liberation. The youngest among the Yue opera ten sisters, she was enthusiastic about the revolution, and being part of the state-run Shanghai Yue Opera House was her way of joining the revolution. She willingly took a salary cut and never expected to receive such generous financial benefits in her retirement:

> Comparing the situations of actresses in the old and new societies, actresses now enjoy a higher political status and [level of] human dignity. Although we were very popular among audiences, we had no political status and were looked down upon by others. After Liberation, party leaders treated us so nicely, nicer than my own father. Moreover, when I joined the state-run institution, I was prepared to receive no salary. In the end, however, I received a monthly salary of three hundred yuan, plus free health care. Now, my retirement pension is more than one thousand a month plus free health care. I can be an in-patient whenever necessary. In the old society, I watched old Yue opera teachers dying in the streets.[34]

Wu's sentiment was shared by other elderly actors and actresses. The couple Zhang Rongbiao and Zhang Yanqiu, Yue opera performers in the 1930s, were comfortable, though not rich, living in retirement on government money in their hometown of Chongren, Shengxian, in 1995. Wu also alluded to another benefit Liberation brought to young actresses: they no longer had to deal with hooligans, theater bosses, and unscrupulous men trying to take advantage of them.

Not everyone, however, was initially as enthusiastic as Wu about the new government and state-run institutions and missed out on what the state had to offer. Jia Guilian, a member of the Yulan Company, led by Xu Yulan, refused to participate when Xu merged the company with the People's Liberation Army in Beijing in 1952; this was yet another way of joining the revolution and becoming nationalized. After two years of service, the Yulan Company was sent back to Shanghai and joined the Shanghai Yue Opera House. Zhou Baokui, who had spent her entire career with the Yulan Company, commented in 1996 that Jia had "calculated badly" and now lacked a stable salary and free health care.[35] This may not have been important at the time, as popular young actresses could probably make at least as much as the income offered by the state. But in the long run, those on the state's payroll could count on secure employment and better benefits, not to mention the status of being members of a national opera house.

The film *Stage Sisters*, made during this so-called golden age of Yue opera, reflected these positive changes in the status of Yue opera and the lives of its actresses. Indeed, it is indisputable that the communist revolution raised the status of local operas and benefited Yue opera actresses and entertainers in general by absorbing some entertainers into a national political and cultural elite while providing others with financial security and social standing.

Problems with Cinema's Master Narrative

Were there no problems, then, with *Stage Sisters'* communist melodrama and the polarization of good and evil manifested in its dichotomized representations of the CCP versus the Nationalist Party and of pre-Liberation society versus post-Liberation society? One problem with communist melodrama is that it denies agency to the people the CCP claims to have liberated from the evils of the Nationalists. It attributes agency only to the two battling forces, making objects of everyone caught between the two. In this way, it construes the relationship between the Party and Yue opera actresses as one between the liberator and the liberated and thus allows the Party to take full credit for the actresses' upward mobility. The melodrama therefore disregards the subjectivity of the people who created Yue opera as a popular phenomenon—their views and the strategies they adopted or forged in order to get through life. One striking example of this oversight involves the character Xing Yuehong, who is presented as a typically weak and misled woman, destroyed by evil forces and rescued only because of the triumph of good forces. By casting her as such a pathetic creature, the film does not give her credit for resistance or self-salvation. In real life, however, Fu Quanxiang, on whom the character is partially based, divorced her first husband entirely of her own volition. Like Fu, many other actresses managed to overcome adversity, one way or another, without the Party's help.

Significantly, the first draft of the film, titled *Detailed Outlines*, has a somewhat less clear-cut narrative and makes better sense of Yuehong's choices. Before taking his last breath, Yuehong's father tells her to find a good husband and quit this difficult acting vocation. Later on, disappointed in her marriage to Manager Tang, Yuehong returns to acting and tries to abort her pregnancy in order to free herself of Tang's control. At a crucial moment, Yuehong bravely, and also shrewdly, rescues Chunhua from the hands of Nationalist agents and helps make the fund-raising performance a success. The sisters are thus reconciled, and Yuehong joins the progressive forces before Liberation.[36] This early version of Yuehong's marriage to Tang reflects the ideals and life strategies common among Yue opera actresses at the time, and in portraying Yuehong's resistance to Tang, after she realizes the marriage was a mistake, it at least allows her some agency. After a subsequent editorial process that sought to "deepen the main theme" and "refine the plot line," however, Yuehong's marriage to Tang is recast as a categorical mistake, and the final production denied Yuehong any agency at all.[37]

Even the main character, Zhu Chunhua, is presented as a person who would be nothing without the Party. Chunhua's protests to Tang upon Shang Shuihua's death only help Tang boost his public image, while she is depicted as at her wit's end in fighting the dark forces. It is the left-wing journalist Jiang Bo who thereafter supports and guides Chunhua step by step, introducing her to Lu Xun's story about Sister Xianglin, writing articles supporting her in the news media, and guiding her through the complex courtroom battle. At the same time, the film tries to make clear that Chunhua's, or Yuan's, struggle would not have had a chance of success were it not for Liberation. As Jiang Bo tells Chunhua when the actresses are working on the fund-raising project for their own theater: "The Xinhu Theater is a small stage, and society is a large theater. There is a big boss behind Manager Tang, and behind the big boss there is the American. These people control the large theater. . . . If society remains the same and the big boss remains in control, we cannot possibly have our own theater."[38] Liberation becomes the only solution to all of the problems facing the actresses, rendering their spontaneous activities trivial.

In real life, Yuan Xuefen displayed an exceptionally strong will and stubbornly pursued her own agenda of making Yue opera and its actresses both modern and respectable. Yuan not only followed a lifestyle based on *qingbai* but also performed that virtue onstage. From the time of her youth, Yuan was reluctant to participate in what she considered lighthearted and obscene plays and chose instead to specialize in the roles of serious women. In 1942, when she started the New Yue Opera reform movement, she made it a principle not to sing at private parties. *Chang tanghui*, the practice of performing for rich, powerful patrons in their homes, was a tradition from imperial times and continued into the Republican period. For many popular entertainers, *chang tanghui* could be an important source of income, a way of exchanging favors with the host or go-between, and a chance to establish or renew ties with upper-class patrons. Under the influence of the Republican rhetoric of theatrical reform, and inspired by the model intellectual actors in film and spoken drama, some entertainers, such as Yuan Xuefen, began to see the practice as feudalistic and humiliating, contrary to their desired new status as art workers. Even when Madame Chiang Kai-shek (Song Meiling) invited Yuan in 1946 to perform at her house, Yuan declined, saying that Madame Chiang could see her performance in a theater; the invitation had come through Wang Xiaolai, former president of the Shanghai Chamber of Commerce and perhaps the most powerful Shengxian native in Shanghai. In Yuan's mind, her decision was not directed toward Madame Chiang Kai-shek but was a matter of principle and consistency in building her self-esteem and character.[39] Left-wing journalists found only political value in Yuan's action. The CCP-controlled newspaper *United Evening News* reported the episode, implicitly politicizing Yuan's refusal.[40] Three decades later, Yuan's biography presented this small episode as evidence of her political choice.[41]

While communist revolution was not her agenda, to some extent because she had no idea what communism was at the time, some of her undertakings inadvertently coincided with the interests of the left, such as her staging of *Sister Xianglin* and her refusal to be involved with the Yue Opera Workers' Union, which was sanctioned by the Nationalist Social Affairs Bureau. By making these two incidents the center of the Yue opera story, however, the film neglects the most important development of the time, one initiated entirely by the actresses themselves, namely the New Yue Opera reforms of which *Sister Xianglin* was a product. What mattered to Yuan at the time was not her "discovery of the Party," as she never discovered the Party until after Liberation, but access to the mainstream media and a powerful left-wing social network.[42] Because of *Sister Xianglin*, Yue opera made headlines in mainstream newspapers for the first time in its history, initiating a continuous stream of reportage about its reforms and its actresses over the next few years; coverage of Yue opera became a regular feature, making Yuan Xuefen a positive public figure in the mainstream press.

Sister Xianglin also introduced Yuan Xuefen and other Yue opera actresses to women's activist groups, members of the left-wing cultural elite, and high-level CCP Shanghai underground leaders. Yuan Xuefen established relationships with such influential individuals as Xu Guangping, Tian Han, and Yu Ling as well as with the young intellectuals Liao Lin, Mei Duo, and Tong Lijuan. This social network opened up a new world for Yuan and the other actresses. Yuan Xuefen and Yin Guifang were invited to attend seminars and tea parties for youth and women organized by Xu Guangping and performed twice for fund-raising events benefiting the Chinese Children's Foundation (Zhongguo Fuli Hui) sponsored by Madame Sun Yat-sen (Song Qingling). Yuan and the Xuesheng Company also participated in various leftist-sponsored activities. The Xuesheng Company, for example, sent representatives to the memorial conference for Tao Xingzhi, a well-known left-wing intellectual, and to the public memorial service for Wen Yiduo and Li Gongpu, both of whom had been assassinated by Nationalist special agents in 1946.[43] By participating in these functions, and providing popular material for left-wing media, Yue opera actresses also supported the left wing and the CCP underground, albeit unknowingly. The relationship between Yue opera actresses and the CCP was mutually beneficial and required continual negotiation after 1949. In any case, it was hardly a relationship between a liberator on one side and those waiting to be liberated on the other.

The film's communist melodrama also presents a one-sided view of how Liberation benefited Yue opera and its actresses, neglecting any possible negative effect the post-Liberation reform process had on the opera. After the government finished restructuring the entertainment system in 1958, it turned its focus to productions that would reflect the heroism and patriotism of the working people in building socialism during the Great Leap Forward. From 1958 onward, Yue opera was under great pressure to change the emphasis of its repertoire from costume love dramas to revolutionary modern-attire plays. Numerous plays about heroic struggles against the Nationalists and the Japanese invaders in the past and about ongoing class struggles were hastily staged to help disseminate government propaganda for political campaigns; these productions, however, attracted few viewers and usually ended after only a few performances.[44] The situation became increasingly tense when Mao himself delivered two speeches on culture, at the end of 1963 and in mid-1964. Mao's instructions were echoed by the radical leftist Zhang Chunqiao, then head of the CCP Shanghai Ministry of Propaganda, who instructed the art and entertainment industries to concentrate on the momentous achievements of the thirteen years since Liberation. As Li Taicheng, then deputy head of the Shanghai Cultural Affairs Bureau, recalled:

> We were so afraid when we heard of Chairman Mao's two instructions in 1963 and 1964. Mao also commented [on another occasion] on a report sent to him about the storytelling campaign that Beijing opera is all about emperors, kings, generals, and ministers, while Yue opera is all about scholar-beauty stories. . . . Because of Mao's instructions, the CCP Ministry of Propaganda was a little nervous, and Zhang Chunqiao thus declared "ten great merits for focusing on the thirteen years since Liberation.". . . Mao's instruc-

tions were [issued in] only a few sentences, but the wind began to blow. Wind coming from nowhere could become so strong that it would shake heaven and earth.[45]

In 1964, the recently released, instantly popular Yue opera film *Dream of the Red Chamber* was quietly recalled, signaling the end of good fortune for love drama and anticipating the great disaster soon to come. In fact, an increasingly radical state cultural policy had already damaged the popular-culture market. Even before the Cultural Revolution, most state-owned institutions, including the Shanghai Beijing Opera House, the Shanghai People's Shanghai Opera Company, the Shanghai People's Huai Opera Company, and major theaters, had been running deficits for several years, despite the tax exemption they received for staging modern-attire revolutionary plays.[46] The Shanghai Yue Opera House was perhaps the only state-owned institution that did not lose money, because of revenues from several popular Yue opera movies made during the 1950s and early 1960s. It, too, was losing money on stage performances of modern-attire revolutionary plays, and revenues from its limited staging of love dramas, with special permission from the Cultural Affairs Bureau, could not make up for the losses. The overall market for popular entertainment was shrinking.

In short, just as the Party assumed the role of liberator of the people, so it made itself a designer of culture, directing artists and audiences onto what it considered to be the right path. This elitist attitude again blinded the Party to the crucial roles artist agency and audience reception played in cultural development. The state's privileging of the communist revolution in *Stage Sisters* obscured many other forces at work in the history of Yue opera. The rise of women's Yue opera and its actresses was a ramification of several modern processes: the actresses' struggle for full social status, the formation of an urban bourgeois culture with a strong female component, and an urban-based theatrical reform in the context of nation-building rhetoric. The social, political, and economic upheaval that occurred from the early PRC period through the Cultural Revolution drastically altered Shanghai's bourgeois modernity, which had supported Yue opera's success, and the Cultural Revolution was the coup de grâce.

The Storm

Stage Sisters, along with the 1963 films *The Second Month in Early Spring* (Zaochun eryue), directed by Xie Tieli, and *Jiangnan in the Northern Country*

(Beiguo Jiangnan), directed by Shen Fu, had become an object of criticism even before its 1965 release. According to the Party's leftist radicals, led by Mao and his wife Jiang Qing, these films propagated not the heroic revolutionary spirit but bourgeois humanism, which had its roots in the bourgeois orientation of the early leftist films produced in Shanghai in the 1930s. *Stage Sisters* was thus a "poisonous weed" (*ducao*) threatening the garden of socialist art and entertainment with its bourgeois sentimentality, as expressed in the two sisters' deep feelings for each other. Mao and Jiang Qing used such cultural criticism to weaken rivals within the Party who were allied with Liu Shaoqi, then PRC president, who had been in charge of the Party's underground work in large cities in the 1930s and 1940s. *Stage Sisters*, they claimed, was guilty of propagating the wrong line, one that emphasized underground work, as opposed to Mao's correct line of building revolution in the countryside in order to surround and finally take over the bourgeois cities.[47]

These charges against *Stage Sisters* reflect an important division in approaches within the CCP: the Maoist rural-based, tough proletarian approach versus the urban-oriented, bourgeoisie-friendly approach advocated by Liu Shaoqi and Deng Xiaoping after the founding of the People's Republic of China. Though it had its roots in the 1930s, when Mao emerged victorious from intraparty struggles and the Nationalists' military campaign to wipe out the CCP, this division reemerged in the 1950s; it became increasingly clear in the early 1960s in the wake of the great famine that resulted from the Great Leap Forward. Mao had been forced to resign as president of the state in 1962, when the national economy hit rock bottom and twenty million to thirty million people died of starvation. Liu Shaoqi took over and consolidated ongoing economic adjustment policies, which were later labeled capitalistic by hardcore Maoists. On the cultural front, Liu's new approach encouraged the production of numerous sentimental revolutionary melodramas, including the three films noted above. Yet, as the economy was recovering, Mao was gathering his forces. He noted in his two directives on cultural affairs issued in late 1963 and mid-1964:

> There are a lot of problems that involve a lot of people in the various art forms—local operas, storytelling, music, painting, dance, film, poetry, and literature. Socialist reform has achieved very little in many institutions.
>
> The majority of [artistic] associations and their publications (it is said a few are good) basically have not followed the Party's policy over the past fifteen years. They have behaved like high officials and not tried to get close

to the workers, peasants, and soldiers so as to reflect socialist revolution and construction [in their arts]. In recent years, they have even fallen to the edge of revisionism.[48]

The rhetorical campaign Mao and his allies waged against certain films and operas between 1963 and 1965 was followed by the campaign criticizing the Beijing opera play *Hairui Dismissed from Office* (Hairui baguan), penned by the historian Wu Han, which became the prelude to the Cultural Revolution.[49]

During the Cultural Revolution, leftist radicals purged the entertainment industry of all "feudal" and "bourgeois" productions, leaving a handful of thoroughly revolutionary films and operas, mostly about heroes and heroines led by Mao in armed struggles against the Nationalists and Japanese invaders in the 1930s and 1940s. The radical state now asserted nearly complete control over cultural production and consumption, and all it could offer in performance art were the ten so-called model operas, which featured the same dry narratives of the heroic communist revolution. Yue opera was hard hit, as it focused on the bourgeois love stories and the feudal costume plays that ran counter to proletarian arts. Between 1966 and 1971, almost all Yue opera companies in Shanghai were disbanded, properties were disposed of, and artists were sent to labor in the countryside and factories or otherwise devoted themselves entirely to political activities. After President Richard Nixon's visit to China and the signing of the Shanghai Communiqué in 1972, the state slightly loosened its policy toward local operas. In 1973, the Shanghai Yue Opera House was reorganized into the Shanghai Yue Opera Company and staged its first public performance of a modern-attire revolutionary play, *Song of the Dragon River* (Longjiang song), copied from the model Beijing opera. Thus, less than a handful of gender-straight modern-attire revolutionary plays constituted the only Yue opera performances during the entire decade of the Cultural Revolution.[50] The damage done to Yue opera was so severe that the genre never recovered, except for a short period following the end of the Cultural Revolution.

Yuan Xuefen and many other well-known actresses were politically persecuted and physically tortured by the young rebels in the Shanghai Yue Opera House during the Cultural Revolution. In 1977, having barely survived, Yuan and the Shanghai Yue Opera House once again staged *Sister Xianglin*. At this moment of rehabilitation, Yuan reflected on her sufferings during the Cultural Revolution and waxed nostalgic about the passage of time. Sensing that this might be her last performance as Sister Xianglin, she wrote an essay recalling her first performance of the play thirty-two years before:

> At that time, I was young and naive, having never read Marxist-Leninist works. I did not comprehend the greatness of Lu Xun and had only vague feelings about the things I liked and disliked in society. I simply felt sympathetic to Sister Xianglin's misfortune. I had seen and was familiar with female figures like the character Sister Xianglin. I just wanted to adapt *The New Year's Sacrifice* for the stage. . . .
>
> The performance attracted considerable attention. The Nationalist reactionaries dispatched secret service agents to tail me, and they assaulted me with dung, libel, and other means. Reactionary newspapers threatened that if I "turned to the left, there would be no way out." But progressive forces of the time supported me and encouraged me, pointing out that the misfortune of Sister Xianglin was not simply a question of who killed her but a criticism of the social system. I then began to understand that the distress of Sister Xianglin in Lu Xun's story condemned the reactionary social system, the foundation of the old society. This theory enabled me to see the social origin of Sister Xianglin's tragedy. From then on, *Sister Xianglin* led me to progressivism and revolution.[51]

Yuan blamed the Nationalists for all her adversities in the three years before Liberation and did not doubt that the CCP underground supported her otherwise lonely struggle against all odds. Two Party scholars, Zhang Lihui and Gao Yilong, later elaborated on this theme in their 1984 biography of Yuan:

> After the staging of *Sister Xianglin*, progressive forces and reactionary forces both paid attention to Yuan Xuefen and the Xuesheng Company. During those turbulent and confusing days, the inevitable questions [Yuan and other actresses] faced were: Which path to take? And whom to follow?[52]

Yuan's statement and her biography are in line with the communist master narrative of Yue opera's history as featured in Xie Jin's film. At this time Yue opera was enjoying a huge but short-lived revival. The Yue opera film *Dream of the Red Chamber* was released in 1978 and instantly broke box office records across the nation, and the wide-screen color film of *Sister Xianglin* attracted numerous viewers throughout the nation and in Hong Kong. In Shanghai, enthusiastic spectators crowded theaters to see Yue opera classic love dramas. While the Shanghai Yue Opera House regained its prestigious title, several district-level state-owned Yue opera companies also revived. Then, during the late 1980s, Yue opera's market began to shrink, and the genre slid into the same desperate position as other local operas that had long been relying on government subsidies. The reason for this negative change, according to several Yue opera practitioners and scholars, was the lack of a new generation of operagoers due to the disruptions caused by the Cultural Revolution.[53] It seemed to many that the new state brought Yue opera to its glorious peak only to destroy it. When asked to assess the relationship between state control and the fate of Yue opera, veteran Yue opera director and reformer Han Yi responded:

> Before Liberation, there were many inadequacies in terms of funding, the quality of personnel, and internal organization. The most difficult problem was the lack of funding for artistic experimentation. After Liberation and with the state's support, artistic accomplishments reached to a new height, only to stagnate because artistic considerations had to be subordinated to bureaucracy and the Party's orders. . . . It is possible that Yue opera would be better off today if not for Liberation and the Cultural Revolution.[54]

Yue opera's downturn in the 1980s thus invited Yue opera people to reassess the genre's relationship with the communist revolution and to reflect on their hopes for the opera's renewal.

The New Context of the Post-revolution Era

After Mao's death, China's national objectives underwent dramatic changes. The landmark Third Plenary Session of the CCP Tenth Central Committee, held at the end of 1979, passed a resolution to stop considering "class struggle" the center of the Party's platform and to shift its focus to "socialist modernization."[55] The Party began to reinstate market-driven economies, slowly moved away from the Soviet model of a planned economy, and allowed a capitalist economy to coexist with socialism. In 1980, the CCP government established four Special Economic Zones—Shenzhen, Zhuhai, Shantou, and Xiamen—in which to develop a capitalist economy. In 1984, another fourteen large coastal cities, including Shanghai and Tianjin, were opened to foreign investment.[56] In 1992, during Deng Xiaoping's southern tour to Guangdong and Shanghai, his famous speeches finally crystallized the Party's determination to focus on economic development and the policy of "opening and reform."[57] Deng believed that China "should borrow and use all those advanced economic models that reflect the laws of modern mass production developed by countries around the world including developed capitalist countries."[58] His methodology blurred the line between socialism and capitalism and freed the government to use all available means for China's development. Deng's famous "cat philosophy"—"White cat or black cat, as long as it can catch the mouse, it is a good cat"—became the motto of the reform era, and the Maoist ideology and politics of class struggle crumbled.

Under the leadership of Deng Xiaoping and his successor, Jiang Zemin, economic development became the Party's focus, and ideology was assigned a supporting role. Reinstating a market economy was key not only for economic stimulation in general but also for cultural production. As the state now prioritized putting money into people's pockets over reforming their souls, artists and entertainers were released from their obligation to assist the state in this endeavor and could explore artistic themes that inspired them, as long as they posed no explicit challenge to the CCP leadership. The 1980s and 1990s witnessed the emergence of a lively entertainment market characterized by a diversity of cultural activities, including revived native-opera and story-singing performances, movies and television dramas directed by veterans and new generations of Chinese directors, and new cultural forms influenced by a globalized mass culture, such as rock and roll, karaoke and dance halls, and foreign films.

The entertainment market in the reform era differed from that of the previous decades in two ways. First, unlike during the early PRC period and the Cultural Revolution, productions featuring revolutionary and politically correct patriotic narratives, considered "main melody" (*zhu xuanlü*) works by the Party, no longer dominated; instead, along with main-melody productions, which represented the official ideology, the Party allowed the development of a diverse cultural market. Second, the later post-Mao years witnessed a general decline in "traditional" entertainment forms, such as film, native operas, and story-singing, following a brief boom when the entertainment market returned, and the rise of new cultural forms influenced by globalized mass entertainment that appeals to younger consumers. According to Li Taicheng, head of the Shanghai Cultural Affairs Bureau from 1977 to the mid-1980s:

> From the Bureau for Public Health, I was asked [by the Party] to go back and take charge of the Shanghai Cultural Affairs Bureau on January 10, 1977.

> I began by restoring some native-opera troupes, and Yue opera resumed performances initially with modern-attire plays, such as *Spring Tide* [(Sanyue chunchao), of 1978] and *Yang Kaihui* [(Zhonghun qu), of 1977]. By the 1978 Chinese New Year, tickets for native-opera and story-singing performances were no longer as coveted as before. Suzhou story-singing was the first to decline in popularity, because it was too slow and its audience was aging. There were still people attending shows in the daytime, but few showed up for the evening performances. On the other hand, libraries were full of people. In the latter half of 1978, Beijing opera took its downhill turn. But Yue opera, comic shows, and Shanghai opera were still popular. After 1979, many genres lost their appeal, including Yue opera. But dance and comic shows remained pretty popular. It is clear that there was a generational change in the audiences. Comedy became popular, film declined, TV drama entered people's homes, and newspapers became extremely popular. Later, pop songs, karaoke, dance halls, and television boomed, and native operas crashed.[59]

In Shanghai, although native operas no longer dominated the entertainment market, along with movies, as they had before, they still managed to survive, thanks in part to government subsidies that helped sustain a few state-owned institutions, including the Shanghai Yue Opera House, the Shanghai Beijing Opera House, the Shanghai Shanghai Opera House, the Shanghai Huai Opera Company, and the Shanghai Kun Opera Company. Facing increasing challenges from globalized mass entertainment and the demands of new generations of consumers, native operas were under great pressure to revive themselves and find their niches in the new marketplace or become museum pieces. Each of these genres has been trying in its own way to attract new audiences, but none so far has been very successful.

Yue opera in Shanghai has experienced perhaps the most painful downturn, given its tremendous popularity and national influence during the early PRC period and after the Cultural Revolution. The decade between the late 1980s and the late 1990s may have been Yue opera's most difficult and uncertain period, during which it had to rely on government stipends or corporate charity for survival. Only four Yue opera companies remained, the Shanghai Yue Opera House and three second-tier state-owned troupes in the Hongkou, Jing'an, and Luwan districts. According to Lu Shijun, a researcher at the Shanghai Yue Opera House and editor of *Shanghai Yue*

Opera Gazetteer, the decline in Yue opera was reflected in the "three fews": few operagoers, few performances, and few Yue opera professionals.[60] As Lu observed, the more performances the troupes put onstage, the more money the government lost on Yue opera, because box office revenues did not make up for the expense of each performance.[61]

How to revitalize Yue opera became a hot topic in Yue opera circles and concerned scholarly communities. Many symposia and conferences were held to discuss related issues, and conference volumes and anthologies were devoted to answering this very question. The title of one collection published in 1994, *Toward Glory Once Again* (Chungxin zouxiang huihuang), reflects the general aspirations of those who participated in these meetings and contributed to the publications.[62] There was, however, a range of opinion concerning the nature of the problem, and opera professionals and scholars, as well as the leadership of the Shanghai Yue Opera House, including Yuan Xuefen, put forth a wide variety of solutions. While many Yue opera practitioners welcomed the attention, they also felt overwhelmed by the sheer quantity of often contradictory opinions and expressed the desire to be left alone to work on their art. As one Yue opera director complained at a 1995 symposium: "No one seems to have a clear idea about the main theme [of Yue opera]. In the past, it was anti-feudal. What is it now? For example, the main-melody theme was thought to be not right for Yue opera, but later it was deemed right again. It is now both right and not right." He then pleaded with the various theorists: "Quality productions need time to mature. Please do not put too much pressure on the artists!"[63]

Quietly but consistently, in the midst of these heated debates, Yue opera practitioners have been making their own choices. They have selected topics that stray from main-melody themes and stuck with those that are more mundane, as reflected in a series of new productions such as *Xishi Returns to Her Home Country* (Xishi gui Yue), of 1989; *The Lotus Girl* (Lianhua nü), of 1991; *The Jade Hairpin* (Yuzan ji), of 1996; and *Cao Zhi and Zeng Luo* (Cao Zhi yu Zeng Luo), of 1996.[64] In the meantime, *Dream of the Red Chamber* continued to be the most popular Yue opera play. Then, in August 1999, the Shanghai Yue Opera House successfully staged a special production of this Yue opera classic for the newly constructed Shanghai Grand Theater. Yue opera was the first native opera to be performed in this palace of modern performing arts, itself a landmark of Shanghai's contemporary architecture. The play created a sensation; local audiences as well as people from Hong

Kong and other cities packed the eighteen thousand seats for every performance. The everlasting popularity of *Dream of the Red Chamber* helped Yue opera artists understand that Yue opera's artistic strength lay in its ability to explore love and passion, not grand nation-state narratives.

Same-Sex Love in Women's Yue Opera: Artistic Identity Redefined

The 1998 Yue opera play *Stage Sisters* was produced during this Yue opera artists' soul-searching process. Although represented as an adaptation of Xie Jin's 1965 film, from which it takes its title and basic story, the Yue opera play is in fact not at all like the film.[65] It tells a different story about Yue opera's history and the relationship between the two actresses. While the film derives its dramatic tension from conflicts framed in terms of good versus evil, or the CCP versus the Nationalist Party, the play does away with such political polarization and focuses instead on the theme of sisterly love. The theme song makes this clear from the outset and reminds the audience throughout the performance what the play is all about:

> Tough times are hard, they sing year in, year out;
> Homeless anywhere, yet they make their home everywhere.
> Exhausting tragic and happy stories on the stage,
> Never forgetting sisterly love in the real world.

Several important changes depoliticize the play's story. The two left-wing figures, Brother Lin and the journalist Jiang Bo, are eliminated and replaced by a secondary character, Ni Tao, a Shengxian native and progressive youth who loves his native opera and tries to help the actresses deal with the challenges and temptations of the metropolis. He introduces spoken drama and the patriotic play *Wen Tianxiang* to the actresses and later writes the play *The New Year's Sacrifice* for Chunhua to perform. The bad characters are also drawn in less political tones. While Commissioner Pan, of the Nationalist Social Affairs Bureau, and the Nationalist secret agent are eliminated, Manager Tang is rewritten so that he is no longer a character with direct ties to the Nationalists but a politically insignificant local strongman who bullies his way through social relationships and exploits actresses in his employ. The story line of the second half of the play is altered accordingly. Politically charged developments such as the staging of *The New Year's Sacrifice*, the fund-raising performance, the lime-powder attack on Chunhua, and the courtroom drama either disappear completely or fade into the background, given only a few lines of treatment. Perhaps the most important change between the film and the play is the ending. While the film ends with the Party returning the humiliated Yuehong to society after Liberation, the play conveniently ends in the winter of 1946, avoiding Liberation and its significance to the Yue opera story altogether.

By cutting out these political story lines, the play makes room for exploring the relationship between the two actresses. Certain long-standing Yue opera dramatic techniques are deployed to develop the theme of sisterly love. One central device is the "drama within the drama" (*xi zhong xi*), which is only hinted at but not fully employed in the film. The play makes excellent use of this device to develop a second theme of heterosexual love, intertwining the motif of the butterfly lovers with the main theme of sisterly love. The two themes work together extremely well in building emotional development, thanks to the peculiarly fluid cross-dressing plays of this all-female theater. The two actresses—Qian Huili, as Xing Yuehong, and Shan Yangping, as Zhu Chunhua—are both skilled performers of the cross-dressing plots seen in many Yue opera plays. While Shan Yangping specializes in young female roles and excels at playing cross-dressing characters, such as Zhu Yingtai and Meng Lijun, Qian Huili is a popular male impersonator noted for her performances of Jia Baoyu and many other young lovers. In *Stage Sisters*, the drama within the drama allows her to impersonate the young male lover and thus enriches an otherwise gender-straight performance.

The four scenes of the drama within the drama punctuate the structure of the typical love story: unity-split-unity. The play opens with the two actresses, Chunhua and Yuehong, on a traditional stage in Shaoxing in the early 1940s. They are performing the classic "Eighteen-*Li* Farewell," in which the cross-dressing Zhu Yingtai promises a happy Liang Shanbo her little sister in marriage; the sister looks exactly like Yingtai. Their lively acting wins an enthusiastic response from the audience. This scene not only helps set the temporal and spatial frame for the story but also introduces the emotional status of the two main characters, as a pair of young partners onstage and offstage. This union, however, breaks down, and the second and third dramas within the drama bring the emotion of the play to a double crisis. Chunhua and Yuehong go onstage for one last performance together after Yuehong announces her marriage to Manager Tang. The two have just had a fight, as Chunhua tried in vain to dissuade Yuehong. The program is "Meeting at Yingtai's Chamber," in which Shanbo comes to request Yingtai's hand in marriage, only to learn that he is too late. The heartbroken lovers then sing farewell to each other. In the course of their performance, the two actresses cannot help but improvise lyrics that comment on their own farewells to each other:

> *Chunhua:* Sending Brother Liang off to the door, I hold your hand, not letting you go. [*Pulling Yuehong into a kneeling position side by side with her.*] Don't you remember that we swore on the ancient theater that we would never separate?
>
> *Yuehong:* Not to separate, we still have to separate; you and I are not destined to be together for all our lives. [*Turning to face Chunhua and raising her hand to wipe Chunhua's tear, but Chunhua turns her face away in protest.*] Not letting go, I still have to go; there is never such a thing as sending off your Brother Liang to the door.
>
> *Chorus* [*from the side*]: It is impossible to tell if this is about the passion in the play or the passion between the sisters, and there is no way to keep the person who shares the same origin but turns out to belong to somebody else!

The act ends with an emotional climax: Liang Shanbo (Yuehong) bids farewell to Zhu Yingtai (Chunhua) and runs offstage, and while Yingtai cries out for Brother Liang, another voice calls out in a panic that Shang Shuihua has killed herself. Shocked by Shuihua's fate and feeling desperate about Yuehong's future, Chunhua collapses.

The third drama within the drama occurs when Yuehong is committing suicide after Manager Tang has accused her of being unchaste, locked her in her bedroom, and convinced her that Chunhua has betrayed her. Only after a desperate Yuehong has swallowed some poison does she receive a secret message from Chunhua warning her about Tang's trick and telling her that she, Chunhua, is coming to rescue her. The message comes too late, however, and a dying Yuehong sings "Shanbo at his last moments," interspersing her own lyrics about her longing for Sister Chunhua mixed with the original lines expressing Shanbo's longing for Yingtai:

> Having no chance to sing with Sister Chunhua again,
> I play the dying Shanbo by myself one last time.
> I request that my relatives bury me next to the ancient stage
> And erect two stone tablets inscribed
> With Sister Chunhua's name in red and Sister Yuehong's in black.

I cannot be with her again in this life,
But I will definitely be her sister in my next life.

For audiences familiar with the classic story of the butterfly lovers, these dramas within the drama—intertwining the beautiful love story of the heterosexual butterfly lovers, performed by two actresses, with a tale of same-sex love between two sisters—enhance and intensify the play's emotional effects.

In the last act, Chunhua searches for Yuehong, who is nowhere to be found in Shanghai. Sadly, Chunhua returns to Shaoxing to mourn Teacher Xing on the fifth anniversary of his death. Yuehong, who was rescued and has been recovering in hiding, appears when she hears Chunhua's prayers for her, and the two sing a happy piece from "Eighteen-*Li* Farewell" on the ancient stage of their hometown. The curtain falls at the end of the piece with the local audience applauding the two sisters. The play is thus primarily a story about the love between the sisters, the telling of which is enhanced by references to the classic love story of the butterfly lovers.

The play's depiction of sisterly love has its roots in the tradition of the same-sex culture of women's Yue opera. This culture may be understood along two lines: "homosexual relationships" (*tongxing lian*) and "sisterly love" (*jiemei qing*).

Homosexual relationships existed in the Yue opera circle, at least at the level of gossip and the so-called mosquito tabloids (*wenzi xiaobao*), cheap irregular publications featuring scandalous rumors and chitchat. Numerous allegations about homosexual relations surface to this day, and homosexual love is reported to have been quite common among such new professional women as nurses, doctors, and schoolteachers in Shanghai in the 1930s and 1940s. Reliable written documentation is lacking, however, in fan magazines, established tabloids such as *Shaoxing Opera Daily* and *Yue Opera News*, mainstream newspapers, and official documents. Homosexual relationships likely existed, not necessarily among actresses but rather between actresses and unmarried independent professional women from the audience. The general attitude toward such relationships was one of uncertainty, with neither strong support nor opposition.

While homosexual love existed in the twilight zone between rumor and actuality, sisterly love, or same-sex nonsexual relationships, was the main form in the culture of women's opera. Sisterhood first developed through the days of all-girls opera schools, when teenage girls slept under the same roof, ate from the same wok, trained and suffered disciplinary beatings together, and traveled and performed together. Sharing the same native-place origin, training background, and aspirations for a better life, these young actresses developed a strong sense of bonding after entering the metropolis of Shanghai. They addressed one another as "older sister" (*jie*) or "younger sister" (*mei*), and sworn sisterhood was common among Yue opera actresses. Other than the most famous Yue opera ten sisters formed in 1947, there were many sets of sisters in the Yue opera circle, and adoptive sisterhood was also common between actresses and young women in the audience. The closest relationships between actresses may have formed between long-standing stage partners, most well known among them being Yin Guifang and Zhu Shuizhao in the 1940s and Xu Yulan and Wang Wenjuan in the late 1940s through 1960s. Xu and Wang were perceived as very close to each other, even though both were married and had children.

Both nonsexual sisterly love and homosexual relationships were marginal in society at large and subordinate to the dominant heterosexual relationship. Yue opera actresses all wanted to get married and to marry well in order to have good standing in society, and some did so at the expense of sisterly love, as depicted in both the film and the Yue opera *Stage Sisters*. The relationship between Yin Guifang, a popular male impersonator, and Zhu Shuizhao, a specialist in young female roles, tells much about sisterly love crossed and destroyed by heterosexual relationships.

According to Yin Guifang's recollections, she and Zhu Shuizhao first met and became friends when they performed together in Shenjiamen, Zhejiang, in 1934. They performed together once again in 1937, after the outbreak of the War of Resistance against Japan. In Huangyan County, they were persecuted by the police and confined to the county jail for fifty-three days.[66] After being released from jail and before bidding each other farewell, the two became sworn sisters. Separately, each went to Shanghai, and they once again became stage partners in 1940. During the ensuing years, the two were close friends and well-established partners onstage. Together, they joined in the New Yue Opera reforms, performed numerous popular love dramas onstage, and participated in the Yue opera ten sisters' fund-raising performance in 1947. Yin Guifang wrote about her complex feelings toward Zhu Shuizhao:

> The director ordered me to be intimate with my lover—who, needless to say, is my only long-term stage partner Zhu Shuizhao. We are lovers onstage, and our feelings toward each other increase every day; as nine out of ten plays

> we perform are conventional love stories, we have come to forget that we are actually love sisters. This practice has been very helpful for our acting on the stage. . . . But because of this, naturally we grow affectionate toward each other. Zhu Shuizhao, my dear stage partner and lover, I am deeply in love with you. I forgive any possible shortcoming in my only stage partner and lover, so the sweet ambience on the stage would not be disturbed—for the body of the actress is in the arm of the stage! Looking back, the masses appreciated Yue opera because private feelings between men and women are always dominant in every [Yue opera] play.
>
> Many people, oh no, only those gossipers often intentionally create ridiculous rumors as if to tease me. Am I angry? No—because I have decided to treat these gossipers as characters in a play. Those who cannot tell the difference between onstage and offstage are just too nervous.[67]

In this seemingly confusing passage, Yin made it clear to people who speculated about homosexual relations between herself and Zhu that the relationship was one of nonsexual sisterly love. She also explained to readers that the director had demanded that she and Zhu become immersed in their roles and portray authentic heterosexual love onstage, and that performing love dramas with Zhu resulted in the growing affection between them. Obviously, the intense love dramas onstage combined with the intimate relationship offstage led to public speculation about a homoerotic relationship between the two actresses. Notice that while Yin tried to clarify the nonsexual nature of her relationship with Zhu, she confessed her deep love for Zhu, a same-sex love enhanced by the heterosexual love they performed onstage every day.

In 1947, Yin was engaged to a male patron who later decided that he really wanted to marry Zhu. Zhu married the man, and Yin remained single all her life. The two sworn sisters never performed together again: Zhu organized her own troupe and shifted her specialization to young male roles because it was easier to find a stage partner in young female roles, while Yin Guifang's career suffered from the lack of stable stage partners in young female roles.[68] In 1954, Zhu and her company moved to Nanjing, and she committed suicide when she was persecuted during the Cultural Revolution. Yin and her company moved to Fuzhou in 1958. She was tortured and became partially paralyzed during the Cultural Revolution but was rehabilitated and returned to Shanghai in the 1980s. Yin passed away in 2000 at the age of eighty. As in *Stage Sisters*, the actresses' intense sisterly love in real life was enhanced by the heterosexual love they played onstage, which was then destroyed by a heterosexual relationship. Unlike the story in *Stage Sisters*, there was no obvious reconciliation and reunion for the two actresses, aside from Yin's fond memories of Zhu, published in her memoirs after the Cultural Revolution.[69] Zhu Shuizhao, however, did not leave any words in print about her relationship with Yin.

For most Yue opera actresses in Shanghai in the mid-twentieth century, sisterhood was the primary relationship in their daily lives, and the struggle for a better life, respectability, and status was the major concern. The political struggle between the CCP and the Nationalists was in the background or, for many, simply irrelevant. For the creators of the Yue opera *Stage Sisters*, sisterly love emerged naturally as the main theme after they decided to depoliticize the original plot of the film. The shift in focus to sisterly love made the play truer both to Yue opera history and to the genre's artistic identity as a theater of love. As the composer Su Jinzou explained: "From the very beginning, we made the decision to make the political tone as light as possible. Everyone felt that the Yue opera *Stage Sisters* should have its own artistic characteristic and should emphasize sisterly love."[70] Scriptwriter Xue Yunhuang hesitated before identifying sisterly love as the theme, observing: "It was not the case that we set the main theme first and then developed the play around it. I started by thinking how to develop a main thread and a few characters. I concentrated on sisterly love because Yue opera was good at that." It is revealing that, unlike the director of the film version, who wanted to make sure the film's main theme was understood and properly expressed, the Yue opera producers focused on the opera's artistic characteristic, identified as the exploration of human emotions, and the main theme then emerged naturally. As Xue Yunhuang noted: "Everyone agreed that [*Stage Sisters*] was not a political play and should focus on sisterly love, and that there was no need to develop a political thread. . . . Moreover, the spectators would not be interested in politics. They would want to see sisterly love."[71] Su Jinzou similarly stated clearly that Yue opera's artistic characteristic is elaboration on human feelings, or *yanqing*.[72]

Neither Xue nor Su is in any sense a political radical or dissident. Both are Party members, and Xue once served as vice president of the Shanghai Yue Opera House. They are mainstream personalities representing fairly common views in the field of local operas. Moreover, the creation of the Yue opera *Stage Sisters*, as they and the two leading actresses emphasized, was very much a collective effort. The scriptwriter, the score composer, the director, and the leading actresses all actively participated in shaping the final product. Much was decided during rehearsals, rather than at the scriptwriter's or director's desk. "Usually, Yue opera is a synthesized art, and everyone participates in the production," Xue explained. "During the rehearsal, if one person dislikes a detail and others do not disagree with her or him, then the detail is gone." He gave two examples of the troupe's improvisational approach. Xue had tried to incorporate the courtroom scene, following Yuan Xuefen's suggestion, but without success, because no one in the rehearsal liked it. In contrast, everyone liked the drama within the drama, and so he replaced the courtroom scene with Yuehong's suicide, making for a third drama within the drama. Moreover, the first version of the play more closely resembled the film and retained such details as Chunhua's performance of *The New Year's Sacrifice*, the attack with lime powder, and Manager Tang's accusation that Yuehong was the instigator. Only after much feedback from both audiences and experts did the team settle on the final, 1999 version. Apparently, there was consensus among Yue opera artists and audiences as to what would make a good Yue opera play.[73]

Xue and Su, therefore, spoke not only for the artistic characteristic of the Yue opera *Stage Sisters* but also for the genre's distinctive artistic identity as a theater of love stories. In the reform era, Yue opera artists were able to reclaim the legitimacy of their theater's concern with the private and the everyday and refocus its productive energies on the love drama or, more generally, the genre of *yanqing*.

The state's new cultural policy endorsed the Yue opera artists' approach by showering awards on *Stage Sisters*. In 1998, the play was selected to participate in the First Shanghai International Festival of Arts and was one of three that won an Excellent Play award. At the end of 1999, the Shanghai Yue Opera House sent the troupe to Beijing to participate in celebrations commemorating the fiftieth anniversary of the founding of the People's Republic and to enter the competition for the Wenhua Awards sponsored by the Ministry of Culture, the most prestigious official performing arts awards in the nation. In 2000, *Stage Sisters* won the Ninth Wenhua Award for New Plays, and the two leading actresses won the Wenhua Award for Best Performance. The actresses also won the Plum Blossom Award for Chinese opera from the National Association of Dramatists.

Yue Opera History Reconstructed

The Yue opera *Stage Sisters* not only helped the genre claim an artistic position for itself in the cultural landscape of the new era but also aided it in distinguishing its history from the communist melodrama presented by the 1965 film and by Yuan Xuefen and her biographers. Both Su Jinzou and Xue Yunhuang considered the current version to be closer to "historical reality" (*lishi zhenshi*). To be sure, no one wanted to deny the facts of Yuan Xuefen's relationship with the CCP underground and left-wing intellectuals, but as Xue pointed out, "Yuan being attacked with a bag of dung was her personal fate, not political struggle. It was not a struggle between the two lines, and the class struggle interpretation does not accord with historical reality."[74] Xue and Su Jinzou both thought that the Party did not have the level of influence on Yue opera's development before 1949 that the film suggests; the play only softens this exaggeration while clarifying other facts in Yue opera history. The new character Ni Tao, for example, who replaces Brother Lin and Jiang Bo, is obviously a tribute to such historical personalities as Nan Wei, Han Yi, and Xu Jin, who were crucial to the Yue opera reforms of the 1940s.

From the vantage point of the post-revolutionary era, Yue opera practitioners were able to take a long view of their own history and place the communist connection in perspective. The Yue opera *Stage Sisters* is, in this sense, a story about Yue opera told by Yue opera people themselves. The director's notes, printed on the playbill, poetically describe this story:

> A pair of young sworn sisters leave their hometown in Shaoxing and come to blaze new paths for life in Shanghai, a place where "even the streets were paved with gold." They take care of each other and share the hardships of life—a story full of love and resentment, joy and sorrow, and partings and unions is unfolding. . . .
>
> People say that the rivers and mountains of Shengzhou [Shengxian] have spirit and are delicate, and that they have nurtured native daughters and a native opera as beautiful as themselves. Coming from her native land, Yue opera has overcome many hardships and absorbed many influences in the metropolis, now trickling like a rivulet, now flowing in waves. . . .
>
> Tough times are hard, they sing year in, year out;
> Homeless anywhere, yet they make their home everywhere.
>
> This is the song sung by the Yue opera people themselves—life is like a song![75]

This reading of Yue opera history emphasizes its native rural origin and the long, continuous process of urban migration and transformation, carried out generation after generation by native daughters. It is, in this sense, an ethnographic view of Yue opera history as a way of life maintained by a group of people, as well as an expression of their native culture, negotiated within the dynamics of a cosmopolitan urban society. As long as the dynamic tension between the Zhejiang countryside and Shanghai the great metropolis persists, Yue opera as a way of life will continue.

Yue opera was indeed an art developed by Zhejiang immigrants in Shanghai in the last century, and it still is today. From 1949 until the early 1980s, immigrant actresses such as Yuan Xuefen, Fan Ruijuan, Fu Quanxiang, Xu Yulan, and Wang Wenjuan dominated Yue opera. During this period, when the state prevented urban in-migration in order to control urban population growth, the locally trained younger Yue opera performers were largely overshadowed by their more successful seniors. The reinstitution of a market economy beginning in the 1980s has resulted in a new wave of urban migration, and Shanghai has once again become a popular destination. Significantly, new generations of immigrant Yue opera performers contributed much to the revival and maintenance of Yue opera in Shanghai after the disruptions of the Cultural Revolution. The last two decades of the twentieth century witnessed the rise of a new generation of Yue opera stars who were recent immigrants from Zhejiang and surrounding areas. The majority of the younger generation of ranking performing artists in the Shanghai Yue Opera House—including Zhao Zhigang, Fang Yafen, Wang Zhiping, Zheng Guofeng, Zhang Ruihong, and Zhang Hailing—were from Zhejiang and surrounding areas. The two stars of *Stage Sisters*, Qian Huili and Shan Yangping, were from Zhuji and Jiande, Zhejiang, respectively. Youngsters from Zhejiang composed the majority of Yue opera students in the Shanghai Native Opera School (Shanghai Xiqu Xuexiao) and were on their way to becoming the next generation of Yue opera stars in Shanghai.

While the pattern of urban migration and expression of native culture has remained a basis for Yue opera's development in Shanghai, the terms and conditions of that migration and cultural expression are very different from before. The generations of Yue opera performers that have grown up in the PRC period have had a much smoother experience than their predecessors did, thanks to the struggles and ground-breaking achievements of these predecessors and to changes in modern Chinese society since the early twentieth century. In the past, most entertainers came from poor families who chose their low-status professions only to make a living. Nowadays, entertainers in China are accepted members of society, and stars even enjoy unusually high status, as public idols and cultural celebrities, much like entertainers elsewhere in the world. Moreover, female entertainers now enjoy the same privileges as their male counterparts, as social celebrities and art professionals. The stigma that used to be attached to actresses is a reminder of how much the gender norm has changed in the past century. The Chinese state also grants many popular stars an elite political status; the young Yue opera star Qian Huili, for example, is a member of the Shanghai Political Consultative Conference and was appointed vice president of the Shanghai Yue Opera House in March 2003. Although Qian Huili, like Xing Yuehong, migrated from Zhuji to Shanghai, she asserted that she does not personally identify with the character. "Not at all. I have never had any hardship, as Xing Yuehong does. I have always been cheered, protected, and supported by everyone. My career has been smooth sailing all along."[76] By "everyone," she meant the government and the leadership of the Shanghai Yue Opera House as well as her colleagues. Shan Yangping, who plays Zhu Chunhua in *Stage Sisters*, however, had a somewhat different answer to the question: "Xing Yuehong is a prototype of immigrant actresses. Although the present-day society is perhaps different from before Liberation, the allure of the great metropolis is the same. America is also like that—very tempting. There are very few actually like Chunhua, and I cannot say that I stand on such a high moral ground as she does."[77] Indeed, the allure of a better life has always driven generations of Zhejiang's native daughters to other countries, but the desire for self-expression has been equally strong. Thus, during the difficult years of the 1980s and 1990s, some promising actresses, like Xing Yuehong, gave up their careers and moved to the United States and Japan. Many stayed, however, and worked to sustain Yue opera in Shanghai while making names for themselves, and some have returned from abroad to resume their acting careers.[78]

The new generations of Yue opera performers found employment in state-owned institutions stable and secure, although it did not necessarily make them rich. Under the current system, a considerable portion of the government's budget for culture is devoted to preserving and developing native operas as treasures of traditional folk arts, which are seen as endangered by a globalized mass popular culture. City and district governments underwrite the Shanghai Yue Opera House and a few district Yue opera companies, guaranteeing artists and administrators monthly salaries plus health and retirement benefits. This system provides baseline security to employees of these companies, and the diverse cultural market offers artists opportunities to earn extra income through various channels of production, to help support their companies and meet personal expenses. Shan Yangping,

5.4 Yuan Xuefen (right) gives her student Fang Yafen a lesson. (Yuan 2002)

for example, starred in a Yue opera television drama in 1991, financed jointly by Shanghai Television and China Central Television, and the first Yue opera karaoke video compact disc (VCD), "Song from the Heart" (Xinqu), in 1995, sponsored by Eastern Television.[79] Wang Zhiping, another noted young actress, with the backing of her home institution, the Shanghai Yue Opera House, invested her own money and collected private funds for the production of the 2001 hit *The Butterfly Dream* (Hudie meng).[80] Moreover, the government also allows private, independent studios for native operas. The noted Yue opera star Xiao Ya, who specializes in young male roles, for example, began her private studio in June 2002 and has already staged a number of successful productions.

Looking back at the end of the twentieth century, Yuan Xuefen and other senior Yue opera artists, now enjoying their old age, cannot help but feeling nostalgic about the good old days of Yue opera (see fig. 5.4) The younger generations, however, seem less sentimental and sometimes appear, in the eyes of their seniors, to be too content with the current situation. They, too, certainly would like to see Yue opera become more popular, but it is not entirely within their power to make this happen. Every era has its own popular culture, and as a social and cultural phenomenon, Yue opera belonged to the twentieth century. The opera will continue to exist as part of China's cultural tradition, as a representative genre of native opera, but it no longer represents significant social movements of the time.

陰柔

Chapter 6

A Feminine Aesthetics

Produced in 1958 and filmed in 1962, the Yue opera rendition of the eighteenth-century novel *Dream of the Red Chamber* was perhaps the greatest and most popular Chinese love story of the twentieth century. It is impossible to assess the impact of women's Yue opera in shaping a modern culture of love in twentieth-century Chinese popular culture without talking about the play. An incident in Shanghai in the early 1970s vividly illustrates the play's popular influence. A young man was running to catch a bus, but the bus conductor, a young woman, closed the door, and the bus pulled away without him. The young man cried out jokingly to the conductor, parodying a line from the popular Yue opera play: "Cousin Lin, I have come too late!" Bystanders all smiled, and the conductor blushed with embarrassment. The words the young man spoke are from a line delivered by the heartbroken Jia Baoyu when he arrives at his beloved Lin Daiyu's chamber shortly after her tragic death, and everyone on the street knew the scene by heart. That the Yue opera play was still very much alive in people's memories during the Cultural Revolution, even though the radical state leadership banned it, suggests just how popular the play must have been before the Cultural Revolution.

In August 1999, the Shanghai Grand Theater staged a new production of the play, starring Qian Huili and Shan Yangping, which turned out to be a rare commercial success at a time when the genre had long passed its golden age and native operas all faced declining popularity. Subsequent tours of the play in Beijing in 1999 and 2001 were equally successful. Again, in April 2004, the Shanghai Yue Opera House sent the play to tour several cities in the northwest and southwest, including Xi'an, Lanzhou, Xining, Chengdu, and Chongqing. Local audiences received the play with great enthusiasm, and many viewers sang along with the actresses during the performance.[1] The play's lasting popularity is a clear indication of the centrality of the love theme in modern China's popular culture and the strong influence of women's Yue opera in shaping the modern culture of love.

The Poetics of Yue Opera: Toward a Feminine Aesthetics

Women's entrance into the entertainment market as both actors and audience resulted in the feminization of opera content and style as well as of the operatic body. While major changes occurred nationwide, many developed first and most intensely in Shanghai, where modern Western ideas, traditional Chinese aesthetics, and the quickly forming metropolitan tastes of urban residents mingled, calling for new-style theaters. Every theatrical form in Shanghai answered this call in its own way and experimented with a variety of new strategies. Special effects and machine-operated stage props, first adopted by Beijing opera, new drama, and other local operas in Shanghai, created visual spectacles that catered to the tastes of a developing, curious metropolitan audience. An emphasis on visual effects and emotive acting, in contrast to the traditional emphasis on singing and restricted acting within a spare stage setting, became trademarks of Shanghai-style Beijing opera.[2] Shanghai opera responded to the need for theatrical reforms with modern-attire plays, in which actors and actresses appeared onstage in Western suits and cheongsams, with Western-style hairdos and leather shoes (the women in high heels), and performed amid modern living-room settings. The intellectuals' spoken drama, by contrast, rejected the popular taste for pure spectacle and adhered to its own ideas of social and theatrical reform modeled on Western drama.

Women's Yue opera emerged amid a variety of evolving theatrical forms as one of the most successful new theaters in the 1940s through the 1960s. Striking a balance between a naturalistic acting style and the modern love drama, and enhanced further by a feminized theatrical spectacle, women's Yue opera created a modern poetics of human emotions that helped set trends for theatrical renewal in general. Yue opera's feminized poetics—evident in the way it developed its music, stage design, singing, and acting style so as to best elaborate a feminized narrative of *qing*, or feelings—provoked a unique and intense sensibility in the modern urban audience, not only among fans but also among those who did not care much for Yue opera's love drama. Many middle-aged and older Chinese men who are not Yue opera fans have claimed that they like Yue opera because it is beautiful. For many from the north, the Yue opera film *The Butterfly Lovers* (1953) or *Dream of the Red Chamber* (1962) might be the only Yue opera play they have seen in its entirety. While many admitted that they had little patience for Yue opera's scholar-beauty cliché in general, they emphasized that Yue opera music and singing "please the ears" (*hao ting*) and its costumes and stage settings "please the eyes" (*hao kan*).[3]

Yue opera fans appreciated the opera for its feminine poetics and the love drama it elaborates. Fans of various ages give basically one reason for their appreciation of Yue opera: Yue opera is beautiful. Wu Ping, a lifetime Yue opera fan who began her association with the opera as a preteen in the 1940s, recalled that she was drawn to Yue opera by its beautiful actresses, costumes, and singing as well as its love stories.[4] A group of middle-aged women, the next generation of Yue opera fans, also emphasized Yue opera's beauty and its elaboration of human feelings. Li Jiang, who was born and raised in Beijing, was passionate about Yue opera, even though she was a northerner. She said repeatedly that Yue opera is "so beautiful"—the stage scenery, the costumes, the actresses, the singing and acting styles, and the music—all "so gentle and incredibly beautiful." Li Jiang's first encounter with Yue opera was in 1958 or 1959, when Fan Ruijuan and Fu Quanxiang performed *The Butterfly Lovers* in Beijing. At the time, she was impressed by the beautiful actresses and stage set but was too young to appreciate the art. Her real introduction to Yue opera occurred in 1962 through a cluster of Yue opera films, including *Dream of the Red Chamber* and *Emerald Hairpin*. Li used the word *yangpai* (foreign style), which Wu Ping also used, as opposed to *tuqi* (rustic) to describe Yue opera aesthetics. She explained that Beijing opera is too stiff and tough, and *ping* opera a bit too rustic and also a little tough for her taste, even though these operas are from her northern homeland. "I enjoy only Yue opera," she said.[5] Fans also indicated that they appreciated Yue opera's dramatization of *qing*, especially "human feelings" (*renqing*) and "affection," "passion," or "sentiment" (*ganqing*). The comments of these fans echo the remark of the popular Yue opera star Yin Guifang, who said in 1947 that "love and private feelings" (*er nü si qing*) would always be the center of Yue opera plays, because the audience appreciated it.[6]

The vocabulary Yue opera fans used to express their appreciation for the opera resonates with that used by Yue opera scholars and the performers themselves. Yue opera scholars and artists have consistently described Yue opera aesthetics as beauty (*mei*) that is soft, gentle, fluid, and flexible (*rou*). The word *rou* is often used with *yin* (feminine), as opposed to *yang* (masculine). The term *yin rou* (feminine and soft) defines Yue opera's particular kind of beauty, and its antonym, *yang gang* (masculine and tough) often describes the kind of beauty Beijing opera embodies. Indeed, soft feminine beauty has characterized the idiosyncratic Yue opera aesthetics since the 1940s.

Yue opera singing and character modeling are perhaps the two elements that contribute most to its softness. About Yue opera singing and music, the Yue opera director Huang Sha noted: "The softness of the tunes and melodies is a distinctive feature of Yue opera as a genre. It is the main element that contributes to the formation of Yue opera's sentimental poetic aesthetics."[7] Yue opera music achieved its softness by doing away with the deafening gongs and drums commonly used in Qing major operas and building on the pleasing folk melodies of the Jiangnan region where it had originated. Actresses sing with their natural voices, and their singing is like a natural extension of their speech; its purpose is not to display elaborative vocal techniques but to express a character's complicated emotions. Compared to vocals in Beijing opera and Italian opera, both of which involve complicated techniques and special training, Yue opera singing appears almost effortless and, accompanied by traditional *sizhu* (lit., "silky string and bamboo") instruments such as the bamboo flute and the *huqin*, a two-string instrument played with a bow, moves listeners with its unassuming intimacy (see fig. 6.1). The speech and singing use mostly Shengxian Mandarin (*Shengxian guanhua*), in which vowel sounds are close to those of standard Chinese (making it understandable for northern people as well) and consonant tones are softer. In the early stage of women's Yue opera, actresses mainly used the *sigong* scale system, in which the *huqin*'s two strings are treated as the sixth and third notes of the scale (somewhat similar to the Western system's A major) and defines the primary key area; this produces a lively, blissful tone but lacks a layer in the lower-note range. During the November 1943 premiere of *The Fragrant Princess* (Xiangfei), Yuan Xuefen and her accompanist Zhou Baocai created a *chai* scale system, or *chai diao*, in improvisation. Compared to the *sigong* system, the primary key area of the *chai* scale system is where the *huqin* strings are treated as the fifth and second notes of the scale (somewhat similar to the Western system's G major); this system has a lower-note area that enables the actress to elaborate on more dramatic changes in the character's emotions and sentiments.[8] Since then, the *chai* scale system has developed into a rich resource for Yue opera music and singing that are uniquely expressive of sentimental feelings. According to Yue opera musicologist Lian Bo: "The *chai* scale system took shape in Japanese-occupied Shanghai in the early 1940s. It mainly

6.1 Yue opera musical instruments. (*Shanghai Yueju zhi* 1997)

expresses the sad and plaintive feelings prevalent in a troubled time. The *chai* scale system, however, is also lovely, graceful, and charming, typical of Jiangnan folk tunes nurtured by the region's natural environment and cultural traditions."[9]

As it carries the lyrics, narrative, and emotions, singing is the soul of every successful Yue opera play of lasting influence. A 1983 statistic from the Chinese Record Company, which had a monopoly on the record industry until cassette tapes became popular in the late 1980s, attests to the importance of Yue opera music to the genre's popular identity: the Yue opera *Dream of the Red Chamber* was the best-selling record, with more than three million copies sold, and the Yue opera *The Butterfly Lovers* was the third-best seller.[10]

The creation of modern female images in Yue opera was another key element in defining the genre's feminine aesthetics. Traditional operatic images of women had been designed and defined by men in Beijing opera and other Qing major operas according to an orthodox gender system that prioritized women's virtue over their physical beauty. On the opposite side of this moralistic orthodoxy was a public culture of erotica that objectified women's bodies as sexual parts, as seen in numerous minor-opera productions in the late Qing and early Republican periods. These were two manifestations of the same misogynist system that subordinated women to men. The situation began to change during the Republican period, as actresses and female patrons became increasingly important. Minor operas had to cleanse themselves of their misogynist erotic performances, and major operas such as Beijing opera also began to reformulate their female images. Beijing opera critics have long celebrated the female images created by the four great female impersonators, such as Mei Lanfang's aristocratic beauties, Cheng Yanqiu's suffering but virtuous women, Shang Xiaoyun's righteous militant heroines, and Xun Huisheng's intelligent and lively maids. These female images, however, were created by men and more or less reflected men's ideas of women, and they never succeeded in attracting a female audience, as attested by the predominance of men in Beijing opera audiences throughout the Republican period.

Women's Yue opera set a new standard for operatic images of women. The female images in Yue opera embodied not only the new era's idea of autonomous women but also a modern urban fascination with female physical beauty, offering a variety of lively female characters enhanced by delicate ornamentations. Popular appreciation of decorated female physical beauty was especially well developed in Shanghai, which was located in a region renowned for producing beautiful women and proud of being called "the Paris of the Orient" in recognition of its leading position in China's fashion industry. Much talk within the Yue opera trade and among female spectators concerned ways of enhancing the actresses' physical beauty onstage.[11] Women's Yue opera used soft, fresh synthetic colors instead of the strong, dark primary colors that dominated Qing major operas. It also led the way in character modeling, using Western-style techniques such as oil- instead of water-based makeup to enhance the actresses' feminine beauty. Women's Yue opera was among the first to use silk extensively for its stage costumes. Silk was softer than cotton and came in more delicate colors. The Jiangnan-Shanghai area was the center of China's silk production, and Shengxian natives composed a large portion of the workforce in Shanghai's silk industry. Being expensive and delicate, silk costumes demanded great expertise in their care, and this expertise was more easily found among Zhejiang natives than among other native-place groups. Most stars could afford to have experts tend to their costumes, but since ordinary Yue opera actresses knew how to care for their own costumes, the use of silk was more common in Yue opera than in other operas.[12]

As women patrons competed with one another in costuming their favorite actresses, and actresses competed in creating enchanting female images, Yue opera directors were pressured to provide innovative stage designs that would set off the fresh female images.[13] New designs for stage sets, lights, and props in pinkish and greenish shades along with silk costumes evoked feelings of warmth, gentleness, and fluidity. This stage effect worked in concert with the actresses' naturalistic acting style to create a new aesthetic of theatrical presentation—a feminine representation of the sentiments of love drama.

Yue opera's new female imagery quickly won the hearts of a large audience, especially women. The Yue opera fan Wu Ping loved seeing actresses in beautiful costumes and enjoyed the eye-pleasing stage scenery. At the time, she recalled, acting skills were not as sophisticated as in later days, and audiences paid more attention to the overall appearance of the stage elements—the scene designs, the costumes, and the hairstyles. She especially enjoyed the performances of two actresses, Qi Yaxian and Zhu Shuizhao. Qi, said Wu Ping, was good at playing young tragic female roles and sang her lyrics very clearly, making it easier for the audience to follow the plot. Wu Ping acknowledged: "Tragedies were my favorite kind of story. Because I loved Qi Yaxian, I went to see her performances all the time. I followed her performance no matter what new play she put on the stage." She also idolized Zhu Shuizhao because Zhu had such a beautiful appearance and was a good performer. "Zhu Shuizhao *was* the [commonly acknowledged] queen of Yue opera at that time!" Wu emphasized, "She was very beautiful."[14] It is apparent that Wu Ping embraced Yue opera as a whole: for its visual presentation, its acting styles, and its sentimental love stories. Cheng Rong, another early Yue opera fan who later joined Yuan Xuefen's company, was drawn to the opera partly because its imagery of ancient women was so convincing to her—she had been collecting cigarette boxes with depictions of ancient beauties and felt as if these figures had come to life before her very eyes on the Yue opera stage.[15]

Wu Ping admitted that plays about peasant lives did not interest her. She considered them too rustic, and only well-composed stories with gorgeous stage sets appealed to her. For this reason, she was also attracted to Shanghai opera's modern-attire productions. She did not like Beijing opera, however, in part because it was difficult for her to follow the northern dialect and because of its emphasis on acrobatic fighting. But no less important, she deemed the characters "ugly" (*nankan*) or "not good-looking" (*bu haokan*). Her complaint: "The young female roles in Beijing opera wore dark-colored, old-fashioned clothes and sported depressing hairstyles and makeup."[16] Yue opera was totally different. Almost forty years later, the Yue opera's ten sisters' grand fund-raising performance of *For the Love of the Country*, in 1947, was vivid in her mind. Wu Ping recounted in considerable detail the plots and characters, and who played which roles. She recalled the spectacle with relish, with all the popular stars appearing onstage together in their best costumes. Like many Shanghai women then and now, Wu Ping's tastes may be summed up in two opposing terms: *yangpai*, meaning "foreign style" with the implication of being modern and urban, and *tuqi*, or "rustic," which suggests backward and provincial. Not surprisingly, she used the term *yangpai* for Yue opera and the term *tuqi* for Beijing opera.[17] The next generation of Yue opera fans, such as Li Jiang and her friends, expressed similar views.

Yue opera's aesthetics began to gain nationwide influence during the early years of the People's Republic. At a 1952 national opera conference, about two dozen local operas, including Beijing opera, *ping* opera, and Shanghai opera, presented as many as one hundred of their best productions.[18] Yue opera playwright Cheng Rong, who attended the conference, recalled: "All the local operas had almost the same appearance. They all looked like one another, as they all imitated Beijing opera. You had no idea what opera it was until the actors opened their mouths [to sing or speak]. [But] when Yue opera went onstage, you saw the stage suddenly illuminated. It was so fresh and so beautiful. The stage design, hairstyles, and costumes were all so different and nice looking."[19] Despite Cheng's clear partiality with regard to her own opera, her comments contain an important element of truth. Beijing opera, by virtue of its status as the opera of the capital and its historical influence, served as a model for numerous local operas. Beginning with the 1952 opera conference, however, Yue opera's fresh style and feminine aesthetics began to make a nationwide impact on other local operas, through many national and regional opera conferences, numerous nationwide tours, and, most important perhaps, films of such masterpieces as *The Butterfly Lovers* and *Dream of the Red Chamber*. Many local operas, especially minor operas, learned from Yue opera's stage design and character modeling and enhanced their own production values. Within a few decades, local operas began to look somewhat similar again, and audiences could not readily distinguish one opera from another until the actors spoke or sang—all local operas resembled Yue opera, with soft, fluid costumes, refreshing stage colors, and delicately ornamented characters.

Male Impersonators: Women's Ideal Men

The "young male impersonator" (*nü xiaosheng*) arguably made the most important contribution to the femininity of Yue opera aesthetics. The opera theorist Gong Hede suggested:

> Yue opera is a soft and beautiful feminine opera . . . that is performed by women and is good at telling women's stories. It is women's favorite opera. The key to the establishment of this feminine opera is the young male impersonator. The standard male impersonator should be handsome, delicate, and bookish and have a natural grace and elegant bearing. . . . The fact that the young male role is played by women determines that Yue opera's main theme is the love story and soft beauty is its main style.[20]

Contrary to Gong's claim, the male impersonator did not "determine" the love story as the main theme of Yue opera; historically, as discussed in previous chapters, it was the love drama that facilitated the rise of women's Yue opera. There is no doubt, however, that the young male impersonator has shaped the distinctive feminine aesthetics that made Yue opera the master theater of love drama. More specifically, young male impersonators in Yue opera embody women's ideal men—elegant, graceful, capable, caring, gentle, and loyal.

The male impersonator began to take leading roles in women's Yue opera in the late 1940s and soon thereafter became the biggest attraction for Yue opera fans. Li Huikang, a retired Yue opera playwright and researcher at the Shanghai Institute for Research in Arts, considered the rise of the young male character to be an indication of the maturity of women's Yue opera,[21] but Lu Xun's comments on the gendered spectatorship of Mei Lanfang's performances are perhaps more useful for understanding the Yue opera case. Men and women, Lu Xun noted, saw different things in Mei's performance: men observing the women created by men, and women observing men playing women. Similarly, in Yue opera, it may be said that women observed the men created by actresses, while men watched women performing men. The theory remains simple: just as Mei Lanfang and his cohorts created women more or less from a male perspective and on the male body, so Yue opera's male impersonators created men more or less from a female perspective and on the female body.

Yin Guifang, as Li Huikang pointed out, was, at the end of 1946, perhaps the first performer to establish the young male role as a lead in Yue opera, having just founded the Fanghua Company. Yin was an excellent actress who successfully created numerous well-known representations of men, including Prince Luolan in *Desert Prince,* Jia Baoyu in various theatrical adaptations of *Dream of the Red Chamber,* and Jin Yuqing in *The Prodigal Son* (Langdangzi) of April 1947, with script by Xu Jin and directed by Yan Jin (see figs. 6.2–6.4). Yet, while Yin created women's ideal men in Prince Luolan and Jia Baoyu, she also staged a criticism of the kind of men who disappoint women. In the modern-attire play *The Prodigal Son,* for example, the young schoolteacher Jin Yuqing meets and falls in love with Li Ping. The two get married and establish a nice family. Yuqing unfortunately begins to spend time with a playboy and ends up falling into traps of the urban underworld. He becomes involved with a prostitute, Yang Liusi, and spends days and nights in her brothel, which also features a gambling hall, a bar patronized by alcoholics, and an opium den. Yuqing eventually runs out of money and is thrown out of the brothel. Meanwhile, Li Ping has had to take work as a domestic servant in order to provide for her father-in-law and daughter Xiaoqing. One day, their house catches fire and burns down. That night, an exhausted Yuqing finally comes home, only to see Xiaoqing crying alone amid the ruins of the house. He takes Xiaoqing to an abandoned hut and tries to make a living by begging and by gleaning and reselling scrap. Then the daughter falls ill, and Yuqing has no money to buy her medication. Desperate, he steals a small amount of cash from a woman outside a pawnshop, but the woman turns out to be his wife, who has just pawned her coat to buy medicine for his father. Yuqing is greatly ashamed. As he walks along the Huangpu River, Yuqing decides that he can no longer bear to recall what he has done. Just as he is about to jump into the river, he encounters an old friend, Zhu Fuhua, and Zhu helps Yuqing get back on the right track. The production hit the theater world with a bang and ran two shows every day for a full month. The last song Yuqing sings on the bank of the Huangpu River became a popular piece.

The play spoke a truth for women, that men's selfish and irresponsible behavior was the direct cause of many broken families and destitute women. While echoing government propaganda against drug abuse and gambling, Yin's play put forth a gendered critique of the situation faced by many struggling Shanghai families. The ending in particular reflects women's views, as Jin Yuqing repents of his past wrongdoings and comes back to restore his family. For most middle-class women at the time, divorce was debilitating because women still lacked independent social status outside of marriage as well as the means to achieve financial independence;

even for working-class women, who earned their own wages, divorce was the last resort in dealing with an alcoholic or gambling-addicted husband. The best women could hope for when their husbands abused drugs or took up gambling, therefore, was that their men would one day find help, repent, and come back to them.

Xu Yulan was another influential male impersonator. Her debut as a young male impersonator was in the 1947 comedy *It's My Fault* (Shi wo cuo), with a script by Tao Xian and directed by Shi Lei, about two childhood sweethearts, Zhao Wenjun and Li Yuzhen. The parents of both families agree on a marriage contract, but Wenjun later changes his mind, when he decides that Yuzhen is not an adequate match and wants a daughter from a wealthier family. His mother, however, cannot wait for the marriage to take place and for grandsons to be born. On the wedding night, Wenjun says to Yuzhen that they should be like brother and sister, rather than husband and wife. Li Yuzhen then suffers considerably from her husband's coldness and her mother-in-law's complaints about her failure to produce a grandson. During the civil-service examination year, Wenjun leaves home for the capital and earns a *jinshi* degree. Meanwhile, Yuzhen, who can no longer bear her mother-in-law's ill treatment, decides to end her life. At the moment when she is about to jump into the river, Yuzhen unexpectedly encounters her long-lost birth father, who takes her to the capital city. On the night of the moon festival, Wenjun hears a woman's voice chanting poems. When he climbs up the wall to take a peek, he discovers that it is a beautiful young lady; he instantly feels respect for her and falls in love with her. He sends a go-between to the young lady to arrange a conference with her, and to his great embarrassment, the lady he meets is none other than Li Yuzhen, his wife. Overcome with regret, Wenjun kneels down before Yuzhen, apologizes, and asks for her forgiveness. The play, ending with their happy reunion, reflects at once women's criticism of men's disloyalty and their readiness to forgive the men when they return home. The song Zhao Wenjun sings when he apologizes to Li Yuzhen, "It's My Fault," which became quite famous, praises Li's, and hence women's, virtue while criticizing and making fun of his own mistakes with humorous lyrics.[22]

In their long careers as young male impersonators, Yin Guifang and Xu Yulan created many women's men on the Yue opera stage and attracted thousands of female fans. Fans developed crushes on their favorite actresses and sometimes confused their love for the actresses with their feelings for the characters their favorite actresses created. They wrote hundreds of letters to their idols, some of which found their way to tabloid newspapers, while

6.2 Yin Guifang (1919–2000), 1959.
(Li Huikang 1995)

6.3 Zhu Shuizhao as Li Ping (left) and Yin Guifang as Jin Yuqing in *The Prodigal Son* (Langdangzi), 1947. (Li Huikang 1995)

6.4 Yin Guifang as Prince Luolan (left) and Zhu Shuizhao as Princess Yili in *Desert Prince* (Shamo wangzi), 1946. (Li Huikang 1995)

others appeared in companies' promotional publications and fan publications. A letter addressed to another popular male impersonator, Fan Ruijuan (see fig. 6.5), published in *Yue Opera News*, reads:

> When the curtain rose for the show *Coral* at the Great Shanghai Theater, Miss Fan Ruijuan, who had stolen my heart, appeared before my eyes. My heart boiled with excitement. I forgot about everything and anything. All my heart and mind was concentrated on her. I could stop eating and sleep-

> ing, but I had to see her performance. For she alone occupied my whole heart. I didn't know anything else other than her.
>
> In this state of mind, I have passed a short few months.
>
> *The Butterfly Lovers* is such a sad drama. But who could make a clear line between life and drama?
>
> Her farewell show was *The Tragic Story of the Butterfly Lovers*. I felt too sad to attend. But I had to go see it. After today, there would be no tomorrow. When I walked into the theater, the play had already proceeded to the scene "Meeting at Yingtai's Chamber." This seemed to give me a warning that after this meeting, more tragic moments were to come.
>
> "Shanbo's Last Days," "Yingtai Mourning at Shanbo's Bier"—one act follows another. The show was now over. The viewers all left with smiles of satisfaction. Everything was over. Dragging my heavy legs, depressed, I returned home, bringing back a broken heart. So long, Ruijuan! Lying in bed restlessly, I could not fall asleep. From that night on, I have become an absolute insomniac.[23]

And as another reader wrote: "Ruijuan is a handsome man. It is a pity that she is only a cross dresser."[24]

In the mid-1950s, the Fanghua Company staged *Baoyu and Daiyu* (Baoyu yu Daiyu), starring Yin Guifang. The play created a sensation everywhere it went, and Yin Guifang's Jia Baoyu was a big hit. In 1959, when Yin Guifang and the Fanghua Company were leaving Shanghai and relocating to Fuzhou, Fujian, thousands of her fans packed the Shanghai railway station to see her off. Many were in tears, and as the train was about to depart, people jumped onto the tracks to form human barriers and blocked the train for some time.[25] Some fans missed her (or perhaps the Jia Baoyu she created) so much that they took trains to Fuzhou just to see her and her performance in *Baoyu and Daiyu*.[26]

During the opening run, in 1958, of the Shanghai Yue Opera House's *Dream of the Red Chamber*, in which Xu Yulan played the affectionate Jia Baoyu, fans called out for her every night outside the backdoor of her house: "Jia Baoyu, Xu Yulan, come out. Please let us see you, please."[27] Later, after the premiere of the 1962 film version, Xu Yulan became a nationwide popular heroine whose appeal went beyond the women who were her fans and reached out to men. "It was said," Xu recalled, "that the film was usually only shown at county-level cities. But for some reason, my hometown Xindeng township also screened it. There was a rumor circulating in town that

6.5 Fan Ruijuan as the office worker in *Happy Family Reunion* (Hejia huan), 1947. (Courtesy of Shanghai Yue Opera House)

the CCP Central Committee approved the screening after Xu Yulan wrote a letter of request."[28] Then, in 1979, after the film was rescreened nationwide, Xu Yulan went to Yunnan to perform for soldiers fighting in the Sino-Vietnamese War. The young soldiers were overjoyed to see Jia Baoyu with their own eyes. They were not alone in their excitement; a local girl threw herself into Xu's arms upon recognizing the actress's Jia Baoyu.[29]

Explaining her interpretation of the character Jia Baoyu, Xu wrote: "Jia Baoyu's love for Lin Daiyu contains his respect for women, his pursuit of the ideal, and his encompassing concerns for his lover's well-being. . . . He is indeed an elegant, graceful, and talented young master above the masses."[30] Such a young man became an ideal type not only for women but also for men desiring to find true love in their lives.

One important function that Yue opera's male impersonators perform is to make young female roles even more feminine. The typical lovers on a Yue opera stage, both male and female, are beautiful, delicate, and graceful, and their speech and singing are soft and sentimental. If Yue opera male impersonators feminized the male role, then the young female roles are unmatched in their softness and grace, setting up the standards for modern femininity. Wang Wenjuan, who played Lin Daiyu in the Shanghai Yue Opera House production of *Dream of the Red Chamber*, won the hearts of millions of viewers as she brought Cousin Lin to life. In the novel, Cousin Lin, an incarnation of a celestial, possesses unearthly frail beauty. When she sobs in the Grand View Garden, the scene and the sound are so sad that birds and flowers cannot bear it—birds fly away and flowers fall like snow.[31] When Wang Wenjuan shed tears onstage or on-screen, thousands of viewers could not stop themselves from crying along with her. There is no way to quantify how many tears the Yue opera *Dream of the Red Chamber* has earned from its audiences. The image of the Yue opera Cousin Lin materialized on Wang Wenjuan's body has since set the standard for later theatrical and filmic recreations of this popular fictional beauty.

Feminine Cast, Feminine Opera

But how "feminine" could women's Yue opera be if the company and theater owners, directors, and playwrights were mostly men? The answer lies in the ways in which performance art is materialized on the performer's body. Generally speaking, any theatrical production is as the performer presents it onstage at that particular moment. On a more particular level, actor-centered performance was characteristic of all native Chinese operas. In the early period of women's Yue opera, for example, most actresses were illiterate and there was no director or playwright. For the actress, preparation for a performance involved learning the rough story line and her part and memorizing some basic lines. Most of the performance was improvised onstage, through spontaneous interactions with stage partners coupled with an awareness of the audience's reactions. In the old "improvised performance" (*lutou xi*) system, common in local operas, actors were free to perform anything their way as long as the audience liked it. Talented actors could carry an audience for a long time with their singing and acting without exhausting the lyrics and thus dominated the stage, while less experienced or less talented actors often ran out of lines and devices quickly and could not keep themselves onstage long enough to make an impression on the audience.

The role of the actor was so important that even when modern theater professionals entered Yue opera troupes in the 1940s, the actor-centered system of performance did not change. Women's Yue opera continued to grow around a constellation of superstars in the 1950s and early 1960s, each of whom developed her personal style of singing and acting through long-term improvisational experience and attracted her own set of loyal fans. Even though the authority of the director and playwright has become more firmly established in the past few decades, it has not deprived actresses of their personal style and their power of final interpretation.

In the final analysis, then, the all-female cast was the basis for Yue opera's unique femininity. The peculiar feminine aesthetics of Yue opera are indeed built on the bodies of the actresses, just as the all-male cast of the late Qing period Beijing opera embodied a masculine aesthetics. The point is not simply that gendered qualities are constructed; it is, rather, a question of who constructs what and out of what materials. Thus, if the femininity projected by the four great female impersonators of Republican era Beijing opera was largely a male construction of the female that helped define the masculine, then Yue opera's construction of the male on the female body yielded a kind of masculinity that served women's interests and helped define the feminine. In a general sense, the all-female cast was the key to Yue opera's creation of a feminine dynamic onstage.

The importance of the all-female cast becomes clearer when women's Yue opera is compared with *ping* opera in Tianjin and boy-singers' opera in Taipei, on the one hand, and gender-straight performances within Yue opera itself, on the other. *Ping* opera and boy-singers' opera also featured young male impersonators, but male actors always were a strong presence in the cast and dominated male roles in general. Although actors in young male roles adopted a rather feminine style and young male impersonators were popular, these theaters still fell short of establishing the dominance of feminine aesthetics on the stage, owing to the presence of male bodies.

Gender-straight Yue opera, in contrast, never fully caught on with national and international audiences, despite the CCP's long-term support for gender-straight performances. The first gender-straight Yue opera troupe was born in the Siming Mountain area in eastern Zhejiang, as part of the CCP-led New Fourth Army's propaganda team, during the War of Resistance against Japan. The Siming Mountain Yue opera focused entirely on revolutionary and war themes, and its repertoire of predominantly modern-attire plays, as well as the CCP's modernist ideology, required gender-straight performances in which men and women played the roles of their own biological sex. The Siming Mountain Yue opera was in fact a very different opera that developed in parallel with women's Yue opera, which was centered in Shanghai and spread throughout Zhejiang during the same period. Except for their common origin and use of the same native Shengxian Mandarin, the two operas had little in common, for they developed very different melodies, musical accompaniment, costumes, stage sets, performance styles, and content. In the early PRC period, Siming Mountain–style Yue opera troupes spread rapidly across the province in coordination with political campaigns such as land reform, implementation of the New Marriage Law, and the Cultural Revolution, staging such revolutionary, modern-attire plays as *The White-Haired Girl*, *Sorrow of the Poor People* (Qiongren hen), and *An Antique Coin* (Luohan qian). This Zhejiang tradition of gender-straight Yue opera was quickly pushed to the sidelines after the Cultural Revolution, when political propaganda went out of fashion, and was overshadowed by a popular revival of women's Yue opera. As the "little flower" (*xiao baihua*) troupes, featuring only young actresses, mushroomed throughout the province, only one or two government-supported gender-straight Yue opera troupes remained at the official Zhejiang Yue Opera House.[32]

In Shanghai, women's Yue opera has dominated since the late 1930s, and experiments with gender-straight Yue opera proved even more difficult and unfruitful. During the latter half of the twentieth century, the official Shanghai Yue Opera House followed the state's lead and invested a great deal of resources in developing gender-straight Yue opera. The opera house produced a number of revolutionary modern-attire plays and trained several generations of actors, though with limited success. Only a couple of costume plays were somewhat popular, and a handful of actors achieved name recognition among audience members, with only two, Shi Jihua and Zhao Zhigang, acquiring significant numbers of fans.[33] Created by state ideology but never really embraced by audiences, male Yue opera actors remained marginal in a genre dominated by women. It is no accident that the most popular actor, Zhao Zhigang, is also the most feminine, and his popularity owes not only to his excellent acting skills but also to his relatively small build and feminized singing and acting style, which make him more acceptable to Yue opera fans. Li Jiang and Cheng Liping liked Zhao precisely for his femininity, and although others did not care for him, Li Jiang and her friends agreed that Yue opera is all about the young male impersonators and the all-female cast.[34]

Complete feminization of male roles materialized on the female body in women's Yue opera has resulted in an even deeper feminization of female roles, making Yue opera performance exceedingly soft, and created a unique environment that nurtured an exquisite feminine performance of heterosexual love that has no match in gender-straight or mixed-gender theaters. Commenting on the women's opera of his time, the Ming dynasty literati Zhang Dai, an opera connoisseur, remarked: "Though not perfect, women's opera charms people as it is so pretty and coquettish, easy and relaxed, and soft and enchanting."[35] Although Zhang Dai was referring to Kun opera, his description easily fits the feminine beauty of women's Yue opera. Zhang Dai's appreciation of the feminine beauty of women's opera as well as his reservations on the art of women's opera found echoes in the opinions of contemporary Chinese male intellectuals, as discussed earlier in this chapter.

This feminine beauty of women's opera, combined with the modern urban sophistication nurtured by the city of Shanghai, became the trademark of Yue opera and gave the genre its unique artistic and aesthetic identity. With these characteristics, women's Yue opera, as distinct from gender-straight Yue opera, won a significant place in China's theatrical traditions.

Women's Voices, Women's Narratives

As women's Yue opera developed a distinctive modern feminine aesthetics on the bodies of its actresses, it also represented a distinctive woman's voice speaking to the public through the opera.

During the early Republican period, the intellectual and political elite, mostly men, dominated the discourse of women's liberation and gender equality, making it part of nation-building ideologies, while women's voices, expressed by a handful of women writers such as Ding Ling, Bin Xin, and Lu Yin, sounded weak and uncertain. In her discussion of women writers during and after the May Fourth period, the literary scholar Wendy Larson thus concluded that by the early 1930s there was no subject position available for women, and distinctive women writers, such as Ding Ling, began to shift the focus of their writing "from love to revolution," or from a more feminine to a more general (read "masculine") leftist discourse.[36] Women's voices became loud and clear in wartime Shanghai, with best-selling women writers, such as Su Qing and Zhang Ailing, as well as the so-called young lady writers of popular literature. But the wartime boom for women writers did not endure in the postwar period. From the early PRC period up to the end of the Cultural Revolution, women writers and women's writing were framed within a general communist ideology and assumed little gender-specific characteristics. Larson's study further shows that literature in contemporary China has retained its "traditional masculine prestige."[37] Contemporary women writers such as Wang Anyi and Dai Qing, Larson contended, were not able to take a distinctive women's position, and those who did, such as Can Xue, were then marginalized for it.[38]

If well-educated women writers largely echoed dominant masculine ideologies, as Larson argues, then it should come as no surprise that actresses did so all the more, for in general they had less literary education than women writers and were thus less prepared to create their own rhetoric. As Yin Yicui, the former head of the CCP Shanghai Ministry of Propaganda, has remarked: "Among the branches under the Ministry of Propaganda, the print and electronic media often have reservations about Party's policies, while the entertainment circle is most willing to follow the Party's directions."[39] She failed to point out, however, that popular-culture artists have always both used and misused Party rhetoric to advance their own agendas.

While feminist scholars such as Wendy Larson are dismayed by women's lack of a subject position from which to speak, women may be seen as having adopted various subject positions as necessary strategies for asserting themselves, taking, shifting, and, whenever possible, creating new positions in search of a better place from which to speak. Thus, what matters is that women did make themselves enunciating subjects and tried to occupy meaningful positions in the public space.

The performing women of twentieth-century China constituted a new type of enunciating subject whose speeches broke the male monologue in the realm of public culture. Because of the increasing presence of women in public culture, and as female voices became stronger and more assertive over time, women's performances were likely to produce new meanings pertinent to female experiences. This is perhaps most apparent in the case of women's Yue opera, but even during the Cultural Revolution, when women's Yue opera was temporarily sidelined, revolutionary heroines figured prominently in model operas and films. Although they may not have developed their own grammar and rhetoric, women in entertainment spoke for themselves by taking advantage of various existing rhetorical strategies and by engaging in a dynamic dialogue with mostly male elite discourses. From wartime through the early 1960s, Yue opera actresses managed to tell their stories onstage with borrowed languages ranging from the traditional rhetoric of womanly virtue to modern discourses of nationalism and Marxism. These narratives were as varied as women's experiences and their relationships with different rhetorics.

In the play *Widow Ma's Inn*, for example, the performers used several rhetorical strategies in rendering a well-known character. Originally a *chuanqi* story from the Tang period, by the early twentieth century, *Widow Ma's Inn* had become a typical misogynist play that portrayed women as seductive, dangerous, irrational, stupid, driven by uncontrollable sexual desire, and possessed of a weak sense of morality. Women, the play suggested, should therefore be contained, controlled, and educated by men. In an opera script printed in the 1930s or 1940s, Widow Ma's attempt to seduce Di Renjie meets with Di's firm rejection and results in Di lecturing the widow on female chastity. An ashamed Widow Ma then becomes determined to remain chaste and to raise her son properly. Her son eventually passes the civil-service exam and marries the daughter of the minister, who invites Widow Ma to the capital for the wedding. When Widow Ma arrives at the household of the minister, she realizes that he is none other than Di Renjie. She is so ashamed that she wants to commit suicide, but Di is able to persuade her to stay. He then memorializes the emperor, and a memorial board is bestowed upon Widow Ma in recognition of her having safeguarded her chastity and properly raised her son. Di thus once again saves the widow from falling into disgrace.[40] In the early 1950s, the PRC government banned the play as "obscene theater," but then, in 1956, a new edition of the play, produced by the Hezuo Company, turned the story into an overt criticism of Di Renjie, the hypocritical Confucian moralist who betrays his lover, Widow Ma, because of his political ambition.[41] Three discourses underlie these two versions of the story: a traditional misogyny that makes women sexual beings for men to desire and to control at the same time; a leftist discourse of women's liberation; and a Neo-Confucian puritanism shared by moralists from the Qing to the PRC periods.

In her performance in the 1940s, Xiao Dan'gui vividly portrayed the young widow's strong sexual desire, her longing for love, and her sense of shame when rejected. Xiao, however, made the widow commit suicide upon recognizing that the minister and father-in-law of her son is Di Renjie, the young scholar she encountered twenty years before.[42] In China's long history, female suicide was, as summarized by Margery Wolf, "the weaker's weapon," a socially acceptable way for a desperate woman to protest against and take revenge on the ones who had wronged her, or to clear her good name when it was compromised by rumors and accusations.[43] Particularly in the context of chaste widows in the late imperial period, as pointed out by Susan Mann, women's suicide as an autonomous action was respected and dignified.[44] With her suicide, Xiao's Widow Ma ultimately rejects Di's patronage, implicitly implicates Di, and transforms herself from a pathetic widow into a dignified person. Xiao's portrayal of Widow Ma reveals not only her appropriation of the May Fourth rhetoric about the suffering Chinese woman in the old society but also her struggle to give human dignity to women's sexual desire and the sexually desiring woman in the face of the old misogynist demand for women's chastity and the new reformist purge of eroticism. Sadly, the tension in Xiao's treatment of Widow Ma mirrored the tension in her own life and anticipated her tragic death. Her sexual relationship with her boss Zhang Chunfan put her in an ambiguous and shameful status between an old-fashioned concubine and the illegal lover of a married man, which made her vulnerable to charges of moral depravity. Her performance of supposedly obscene plays, moreover, made her appear unclean and unprogressive to the modernist intellectuals who otherwise felt sympathy for her as the victim of the feudal evil man Zhang Chunfan. Ironically, Zhang accused her of being unchaste when she tried to develop a relationship with modern forces through her director Leng Shan. In the end, Xiao died to restore her dignity.

Yuan Xuefen, perhaps the most intellectual among Yue opera actresses before 1949, represents a different case. Yuan passionately echoed the leftist rhetoric of women's liberation and gender equality in her quest for independence, equality, and respectability for women. Writing in the mid-1940s, she noted:

> Women are unfortunate, especially women in our country. Having suffered feudalism and experienced extreme pain in human life for thousands of years, women still get the worst of it even today when the rhetoric of gender equality is bandied about. . . . Don't you see that only women are asked to be virtuous wives and good mothers? Men are never asked to be "virtuous husbands and good fathers." Why is that? Being respectful should be mutual and equal [between husband and wife], and sacrifice should also be worthwhile. The so-called "virtuous wife and good mother" is only a lofty phrase men use to make women their slaves.[45]

Apparently, Yuan found in the discourse of women's liberation and gender equality powerful articulations of her personal struggle for independence and respectability, and the characters she created on the Yue opera stage, such as Sister Xianglin and Zhu Yingtai, reflected her understanding of women's liberation.

Fu Quanxiang, another actress, was inspired to express her life experience through her portrayal of courtesans. Fu's first marriage to Zhu Xiangyun, owner of the Shenzhou Inn, in 1941, was certainly not a happy one. For this marriage, Fu called an end to her three-year commitment to a religious life, alienated her good friend and colleague Yuan Xuefen (with whom Fu had joined the sect), and earned herself a bad name. Tabloids accused her of breaking her religious vows and of marrying for money, interpreting her marriage as another example of an innocent girl being corrupted by the evils of urban society.[46] When asked about her personal life, Fu simply replied: "Actresses all had similar experiences in their personal lives in the past, and there is no special value to discussing these things now. . . . I don't want to think about these unpleasant things in the past, and they have all gone after I cried myself out at my meeting with Master Chen Letian.[47] Now, I care only to leave my art with the younger generation, and my reflections on life have been crystallized in the theatrical images I have created."[48] Her goal, she said, was to convincingly portray a few courtesans. Fu has created several courtesan characters, including Jiao Guiying and Du Shi'niang, who suffer humiliation and betrayal at the hands of their lovers and kill themselves in protest. Another character, Li Wa, destroys her beautiful eyes to make her literati lover focus on his book, not her beauty, so that he will pass the civil-service examination.[49] Using the May Fourth rhetoric of the suffering woman in feudal society, Fu managed to register her own grievances against male exploitation of women and their love, sex, and labor.

Qi Yaxian's story provides yet another example of women shaping their own narratives by appropriating various discourses. Qi was born into a poor family in Shanghai.[50] According to Qi's recollections, her father picked up petty jobs only now and then and failed to take responsibility for supporting the family; he was the kind of person who would lend the family's last few dollars to other people while allowing his own family to go hungry. He also had a bad temper and beat his wife and children when he was unhappy. About her mother, Qi wrote:

> My mother was an ordinary housewife: hardworking, diligent, and frugal, embodying many of the traditional virtues of the old generations of Chi-

nese women. She was skinny but could bear a great deal of hardship in life. She gave birth to five children. I am the fourth, with three older brothers and one younger sister. Married to such a man, with such a heavy family burden, Mother raised us children one by one, with tears in her eyes, enduring hardship with a dogged will.[51]

Because of the family's poor financial situation, Qi Yaxian never had a chance to go to school, and her brothers all started to work as apprentices at a young age. As the elder daughter, little Yaxian helped her mother with housekeeping and contracted needlework to add to the family income. When Qi was twelve, her mother got her a position as a utility girl in a Yue opera company, as she did not want the child to toil in factories or work in a dance hall serving male customers, and that was the beginning of Qi's Yue opera career. Qi recalled:

> [Mother] was poor all her life. In her suffering and hardships, the only thing that could console her was to attend women's opera performances. Paying a few cash for a seat far from the stage in a small, run-down theater, she enjoyed performances of familiar scholar-beauty stories. She cried for the people of the past, sympathized with female characters' misfortune, and cheered for happy marriages at the end. With these performances, Mother could, for a moment, forget her worries and her family's miserable condition. She was certainly delighted that her daughter was now to join the opera.[52]

Qi eventually became a popular star whose specialty was "tragic female roles" (*beidan*) in "bitter plays" (*kuxi*). She explained her personal relationship with tragic roles:

> In my childhood, there were more tears than joy. Tragic plays composed the largest group of the plays I learned in girls' opera school. The plays I performed after my apprenticeship were also mostly tragedies. Because I had suffered poverty and struggled in my life, and because I was particularly familiar with the bitterness in women's lives, my acting in tragic plays was vivid and quite moving.[53]

Two May Fourth themes ran through these various narratives in Yue opera. First, women are almost always suffering, and even Yuan Xuefen's generally more assertive characters cannot escape it. While the elite discourse on women's suffering in imperial China's patriarchal system was one obvious origin of this narrative, it is imperative to take note of another source—a folksong form popularly known as "crying tone" (*kuku diao*) sung by women throughout China's countryside in olden times, from which sprang a number of minor operas including Yue opera, boy-singers' opera, and flower-drum opera. Qi Yaxian's remarks about suffering women in bitter plays, therefore, should be understood not simply as echoes of the elite discourse but also as a women's narrative rooted deeply in women's historical experiences.

Second, most Yue opera plays took the form of the scholar-beauty love story. As Zhang Ailing and Su Qing argued during the 1940s, women artists tended to focus on love stories because a woman's real-life drama had always centered on her marriage. However, by using the framework of the love drama, women's Yue opera also offered multifaceted narratives pertaining to women's experiences. While Beijing opera's imperial narratives reflected traditional elite (male) views and tastes that neglected women's experiences, and spoken drama exemplified modern intellectual (again mostly male) constructions of nation-state ideology that subordinated women's concerns to national interests, women's Yue opera became a vehicle by which women could tell their own stories and create their own public expressions in the scholar-beauty formula. If the May Fourth intellectuals appropriated the popular crying tone within a traditional women's culture, then the scholar-beauty formula appears to have been the opposite case, in which women took on the May Fourth construction of women's liberation and free love in order to articulate their particular aspirations.

Intellectuals were critical of this appropriation. Women, they claimed, needed to be freed from feudal bonds so that they could better serve the cause of national salvation and help build a strong nation. In his 1945 essay "Old and New Women in Chinese Theater," the leftist writer Yang Hansheng presented a review of changing theatrical representations of Chinese women over time, from the feudal era, through the May Fourth period, to the time of the War of Resistance against Japan. Yang noted that in operas during the Yuan, Ming, and Qing dynasties, Chinese women suffered all kinds of hardship and oppression. After the Republican Revolution, however, women rose up under the banners of "science" and "democracy," and the new women appeared onstage. Yang listed several female characters featured in scripts by famous elite writers, such as Hu Shi, Tian Han, and Guo Moruo, that exemplified women's struggle to liberate themselves from feudal bonds and embrace free love and marriage.

Yang went on to describe the female characters produced within the war culture of the 1930s:

> After September 18th [1931, when Japanese troops occupied Manchuria] and before July 7th [1937, the official outbreak of the War of Resistance], the new women of China appeared onstage as heroines.
>
> We all remember the play *Seven Women in a Thunderstorm* [(Baofengyu zhong de qige nüxing), by Tian Han]. The women protagonists in this play were no longer vexed by love questions centered on their personal lives but concerned with national salvation and resistance to the Japanese invasion. The goal of their effort is no longer free love but national liberation. Compared to the heroines of the May Fourth era, these women have clearly made a great leap forward. . . .
>
> After the war broke out on July 7, China's new women all stood up and rushed to take up various forms of work for the divine cause of resistance. For this reason, a great number of heroines and women warriors appeared in our wartime theaters. . . . Today's Hua Mulan, for example, does not need to go home; she probably would have already dispatched herself heroically to the occupied area to fight the enemy.[54]

To Yang's dismay, his model Hua Mulan soon disappeared from the stage, and love drama once again dominated wartime Shanghai's popular culture.[55] The intellectual and political elites were apparently not able to impose their agenda on Yue opera and other popular genres. Even during the early PRC period, Yue opera continued to produce women's narratives built around their mundane experiences, and audiences continued to prefer Yue opera love dramas to dry state-sponsored revolutionary plays.

Yue Opera's Dream of the Red Chamber: *A Feminine Reinvention*

The Yue opera *Dream of the Red Chamber* is a telling example of women's influence on the novel's reinvention as a great love story that defined the popular sentiment of love in the twentieth century. Cao Xueqin's eighteenth-century novel *Dream of the Red Chamber* is an important part of China's cultural heritage and has influenced many aspects of modern Chinese culture, from specialized scholarship to popular entertainment. The novel gained fame among literati men and women immediately after its creation and remained popular throughout the eighteenth and nineteenth centuries, even though the Qing state tried to ban it.[56] The novel's reputation continued to grow during the twentieth century, when literary and scholarly interests made its study a specialized field of inquiry known as Redology (Hongxue). It was considered one of the "four great novels" (*sida qishu*) of the Ming and Qing dynasties, the other three being *The Water Margin*, *Romance of the Three Kingdoms*, and *Journey to the West* (Xiyou ji). Unlike the other three novels, however, *Dream of the Red Chamber* was not successfully integrated into popular entertainment and did not reach a large illiterate or semiliterate population until the 1940s. Yi Bing, a Yue opera playwright and administrator, was part of the leadership of the Shanghai Yue Opera House in the early 1950s. He observed in 1959:

> Many stories from *Dream of the Red Chamber* had been staged in Kun opera, Beijing opera, and other local operas. But they were not as fortunate as plays adapted from *Romance of the Three Kingdoms*, *The Water Margin*, and *Journey to the West*, many of which have been reworked by generations of artists and are still an important part of the contemporary stage, attaining immortal artistic status. But most plays adapted from *Dream of the Red Chamber* were forgotten [until recent times].[57]

Yi Bing attributed this past lack of success in adapting *Dream of the Red Chamber* for the opera stage mainly to the inability of theatrical arts to capture the "rich and broad social content" of the novel. For a Marxist like Yi Bing, the phrase "rich and broad social content" referred to Mao Zedong's instruction that the novel be read as a textbook of China's feudal society.[58]

A more convincing explanation, however, may be found in the dominance of love drama in Republican Shanghai's popular entertainment, for it was within this context that the novel became a popular modern love story. Beijing opera and other male-centered major operas from the Qing period had little interest in the novel's focus on domestic affairs and love relationships, or the tedious details about court politics; in contrast, they drew widely on stories about the Monkey King in *Journey to the West*, the rebels in *The Water Margin*, and the great military strategist Zhuge Liang in *Romance of the Three Kingdoms*. It was only in the twentieth century, with the growing interest in themes related to love and women's roles in society, that popular entertainment began to draw on stories from the novel *Dream of the Red Chamber*. The Beijing opera master Mei Lanfang was among the first to stage Lin Daiyu, the novel's female protagonist, but his solo piece, *Daiyu Buries Flowers* (Daiyu zanghua), was based on traditional elite male interpretations of a young lady saddened by the sight of falling flowers, a metaphor of her own passing beauty. It was certainly not one of Mei's more successful plays, despite his graceful singing and dance. In the 1940s, the novel gained increasing favor with popular-entertainment genres and was adopted by Suzhou story-singing, Shanghai opera, Yue opera, and film. A contemporary source pointed out: "1944 is the year of Lin Daiyu. The whole city is staging *Lin Daiyu*, from Beijing opera and film to the Yue opera *Lin Daiyu*, which finally opens at the Nine-Star Theater!"[59] Together, these productions made the novel a popular love story.

Women's Yue opera troupes began to stage solo acts drawn from the novel in the early 1940s. Zhi Lanfang's *Daiyu Buries Flowers*, recorded around 1941, appears to be the earliest extant record of such performances.[60] Yuan Xuefen staged *Lin Daiyu* (Lin Daiyu) in 1944, and Yin Guifang and her stage partners first performed the story in 1945.[61] In the mid-1950s, Yin Guifang and her Fanghua Company put on *Baoyu and Daiyu*, which immediately became a big hit in Shanghai and Beijing. In Shanghai, the play was sold out for one hundred consecutive days, with two shows daily. During its Beijing tour, the company had to move the performance to the Labor Theater, a four-thousand-seat open-air theater, and extended the show for several days.[62] Over the course of her acting career, Yin Guifang played the protagonist Jia Baoyu many times, in four different versions, and was remembered as one of the most successful Jia Baoyus. Her portrayal transformed the character from a lighthearted playboy, as he was commonly perceived at the time, into a caring young man noted for his passionate and tender feelings for women and his loyalty to his lover.[63]

In 1958, the Shanghai Yue Opera House produced a new version of the story penned by Xu Jin, with Xu Yulan as Jia Baoyu and Wang Wenjuan as Lin Daiyu. This version was also a hit. It toured widely within and outside of China, greatly enhancing Yue opera's national and international reputation. Then, in 1962, the play was made into a color film that, perhaps more than anything else, helped popularize both Yue opera and the novel, making Jia Baoyu and Lin Daiyu household names throughout the nation.

Cao Xueqin's *Dream of the Red Chamber*, as many scholars have noted, is much more than just a love story, as it deals with many different aspects of human life, such as religion, politics, money, disaster, sex, marriage and family, and fate as well as love and desire. It is monumental as both a political novel and a *yanqing* novel containing 120 chapters and featuring more than seven hundred characters ranging from monks and nuns, slaves and entertainers, peasants and servants to merchants, officials, aristocrats, and imperial concubines. In addition, another two hundred or so names are mentioned in the narrative.[64] Two main themes run through the book: the political and the emotional. The political theme develops around the vicissitudes of the Jia household, whose rise, fall, and revival within a span of several generations are contingent upon court politics and the emperor's unpredictable temper but are also affected by corruption and power struggles within the complex multigenerational household. The other theme develops around the emotional world of Jia Baoyu, the teenage son of the Jia family, contrasting his appreciation for young, unmarried women and their pristine world inside the Grand View Garden with his disgust for adult men and their dirty, competitive world outside.

In the novel, Lin Daiyu and Jia Baoyu are human incarnations of two celestial beings. Baoyu is, as his name indicates, a precious stone that was left unused by the legendary figure Nü Wa when she finished repairing the fallen sky. The stone was first assigned a position as the "divine companion of heavenly flowers" (*shenying shizhe*), flowers being a common metaphor for young women in Chinese literature. While wandering along a heavenly river, he saw a lonely little herb. He took a liking to it and nurtured it with sweet dew, the cream of heaven and earth, and the herb grew, day by day, into a female celestial being. She used to say that she had nothing like sweet dew to give him in return for his favor, but should he decide to visit the earth, she would certainly accompany him and pay him back with all her tears. Baoyu is thereafter born with a piece of jade in his mouth, and Lin Daiyu, her surname composed by two "wood" radicals indicating her herbal origin, turns into the most beautiful, delicate, and sentimental of all women. Xue Baochai, another celestial being, is born with a golden lock that matches Baoyu's jade. When Lin Daiyu and Xue Baochai move in with Baoyu's family, a romantic triangle forms among the three protagonists, and the stage is set for a love tragedy to unfold. Lin Daiyu sheds tears for her love all her life as she can never be sure that she will be united with him in marriage, owing partly to her powerless position as an orphan and partly to Baoyu's love for Baochai and the pleasure he takes in the company of young women in general. After Daiyu has exhausted her tears, she returns to heaven, and Baoyu eventually returns as well after completing his earthly duty to the Jia household, having passed the civil-service examination and fathered a son with his wife Baochai.

Although the relationship between Jia Baoyu and Lin Daiyu serves as the emotional center that helps hold the numerous threads together, it is only one part of Baoyu's love, which covers at least two dozen young women and a couple of young men, that is fully described in the novel, reflecting the male-centered polygamy common in traditional Chinese society. Only about a dozen chapters, eight of them in the first thirty-four chapters, feature details of Baoyu's relationship with Daiyu. Lin Daiyu dies in the ninety-seventh chapter, and, before and after, each of the lovely young women living in the Grand View Garden leaves, one after the other, to meet her own, in most cases tragic, fate. Near the end of the story, as the world of the Grand View Garden crumbles, Jia Baoyu deserts it and disappears into the world of the Buddha. The novel, however, ends with the beginning of a revival of the Jia household as Baoyu's young nephew, Jia Lan, passes the first level of the civil-service examination and the new emperor revises the late emperor's punishment against the family.

The Yue opera *Dream of the Red Chamber* elects to focus on the Baoyu-Daiyu love story, knitting together details from the dozen or so chapters that specifically feature the relationship between the two, while the political fortunes of the Jia household fade into background and most of the other important characters are not even mentioned. It is interesting to note that Cao Xueqin, likely being limited by his male perspective, never described female homosexual relationships in the Grand View Garden, where many beautiful young women and only two young men, Jia Baoyu and his preteen nephew Jia Lan, lived closely together. Baoyu, who loves and is loved by these women, is the center of this feminine world, and Baoyu's love for Daiyu is the most intense but not the only and exclusive love. Taking a woman's perspective, the Yue opera play elevates Lin Daiyu to a position comparable to that of Jia Baoyu and makes the love relationship between the two equal and exclusive. The feminine perspective of Yue opera thus helps reinvent the novel as a modern love story in two ways: first, by focusing on the emotions unfolding in the feminine world of the Grand View Garden while treating the masculine world outside only as background and, second, by focusing on, hence promoting, a monogamous love relationship between Baoyu and Daiyu while omitting, hence demoting, the traditional male-centered polygamous system of love relationships as well as the male same-sex love relationships described in the novel.

In the 1958 version of the play, Lin Daiyu, played by Wang Wenjuan, is still quite young when her mother, the sister of Jia Baoyu's father, dies and her maternal grandmother, the matriarch of the Jias, has her delivered by boat to the Jia household. Daiyu has no siblings, and her father dies soon thereafter. Living alone in the rich, powerful, and complex household of her uncle, Daiyu is sensitive about her vulnerable situation. Jia Baoyu, played by Xu Yulan, in contrast, is the only surviving son by the principal

6.6 Xu Yulan as Jia Baoyu (left) and Wang Wenjuan as Lin Daiyu in *Dream of the Red Chamber* (Honglou meng), Shanghai Yue Opera House, 1958. This Yue opera masterpiece re-created Cao Xueqin's eighteenth-century novel as a love drama for millions of modern Chinese. (*Shanghai Yueju gaige wushinian tekan*, 1992)

wife of his father, a high official and master of the household. Unusually good-looking and intelligent, Baoyu is the prince of the household, spoiled by his grandmother and mother and indulged in the company of his beautiful sisters and cousins. Growing up together and sharing unconventional views, Baoyu and Daiyu develop a deep affection for each other (see fig. 6.6). But the adults choose Xue Baochai, daughter of the sister of Baoyu's mother, as Baoyu's bride because they consider Baochai to be a better influence, somebody who can help them in their efforts to curb Baoyu's "wild" behavior and set him on track to prepare for the civil-service examinations. Knowing that Baoyu will not agree, the adults tell him that he is marrying Cousin Lin and conceal their real plans from Daiyu. On his wedding night, Baoyu collapses when he sees that his bride is really Baochai and learns that his Cousin Lin has died. A few days later, a heartbroken Baoyu visits the Bamboo Lodge and pours his heart out before Daiyu's bier.

Keeping his promise of eternal love to Cousin Lin, he walks out of the prosperous Jia household, abandoning this dirty world once and for all.

The play depicts the development of love between the two protagonists in a series of episodes organized into several main acts including "Daiyu Enters the Jia Household" (Daiyu jinfu), "Reading *Tale of the Western Chamber*" (Du *Xixiang*), "Daiyu Buries Flowers," "Daiyu Burns Poems" (Daiyu fengao), "The Perfect Gold-Jade Marriage" (Jin-Yu liangyuan), and "Baoyu Mourns for Daiyu and Leaves Home" (Kuling chuzou).

Baoyu and Daiyu are awakened to their love for each other when, surrounded by flowers in the Grand View Garden, they break the taboo and steal a reading of the forbidden love story between Cui Yingying and Zhang Gong in *Tale of the Western Chamber*. Then, left in a powerless position by the death of her father, Daiyu becomes worried about the future of her love for Baoyu and "sheds tears from winter to spring, and from summer to autumn," as the lyrics describe it.

In "Daiyu Buries Flowers," one of the most poetic scenes, Daiyu collects and buries fallen flowers amid a gorgeous spring scene in the garden and is saddened as she thinks of her own fate. She sings:

> Within the broad expanse of heaven,
> Where could I find a tomb for the blossoms?
> Better to shroud the fragrant remains in silk
> And bury the beauty with a handful of clean earth.
> Pure you come and pure you go,
> Not stuck in the ditch and getting mired.
> People consider me silly burying flowers,
> But who will bury me when I die?
> When spring leaves and takes youth away,
> Who would notice the fallen blossoms or the dead maid?

When Daiyu overhears the wedding plans for Baoyu and Baochai without knowing the details, she collapses at the thought that Baoyu has betrayed her. Throwing her poems into the brazier, Daiyu sings her last words:

> All my life
> Poems and books are my close friends in the inner chambers;
> Brushes and ink are my blood and flesh.
> . . .

These poems are not fishing for fame and compliments;
All I hope is to find a soul mate who can appreciate them.
But now that the soul mate has gone away,
How can I still keep these poems?
Have all heartbroken poems burned in the fire!
This handkerchief with poems on it used to be carried by him all
  the time;
It has wiped so many of my tears in the past.
Who would know his heart has changed while the poem handkerchief
  is still new?
What a pity my devotion has been repaid with his hypocrisy.
If I had known human feelings were thinner than paper,
I wouldn't have kept the poem handkerchief till now.
Today sees the end of all my love;
Only a crescent moon witnesses the burial of the soul of poems.

Daiyu dies as the wedding music makes its way into her lonely chamber in the Bamboo Lodge. At the same time and in another place, a happy Baoyu gently sings to the person he thinks is his dear Cousin Lin, her face covered by a red bridal cloth:

Now I can marry you;
My heart brightens like wedding candles.
Past illness and worry have all gone away;
The future will be filled with endless happiness.
From now on,
I will get up early and help you wear flowers in the spring,
Stay up late to guess at riddles in the winter,
Light incense to take pleasure by your side in calligraphy and paintings.
From now on,
The room will be full of witty words in soft voices;
Like water, which cannot be cut by a knife, we cannot be separated.
It's proved true that the expansive Milky Way has a bridge after all;
The Cowherd and the Weaving Girl, though separated, can still meet in
  July.

Baoyu cannot believe his eyes when he takes off the red cloth and sees Baochai's face. When he finally understands what has happened, he immediately cries out for Cousin Lin, singing in tears: "Where are you, Cousin Lin? You must be seriously ill and dying, your heart tortured and your tears flowing endlessly!" He implores the matriarch:

> Both Cousin Lin and I are painfully ill,
> And our illness comes from the same source.
> I beg you to let us stay in the same room.
> Let the two lovesick ones sympathize with each other, heart to heart,
> So that we may see each other every day when we are alive,
> So that we may be buried in the same tomb when we die.
> My dear Grandma!
> There is nothing in the world I want to have
> Except to live and die with Cousin Lin.

Seeing that his pleading has no effect on the matriarch, who has always let him have his way till now, Baoyu soon realizes that everybody is in on the plot. He rushes out to find his Cousin Lin, only to collapse when Baochai announces that Daiyu has died.

The last act, "Baoyu Mourns for Daiyu and Leaves Home," is set in the Bamboo Lodge, several days after the wedding. Walking into Daiyu's chamber and faced with her bier, Baoyu is immediately overcome by a wave of sadness and cries out: "Cousin Lin, I have come too late!" Only Daiyu's faithful maid, Zijuan, stands by the bier as Baoyu pours his heart out. Looking around the once familiar place, now so empty without its mistress, Baoyu is making up his mind:

> A mistake is made firm with all the irons in the world;
> A wrong marriage is made by a single red rope.
> The broken sky could be fixed by the Goddess Nü Wa,
> But it is impossible to repair broken hearts.
> Having left this filthy world,
> You are as clean as snow and ice.
> How then could my clear conscience compromise with these
> vulgar minds?

Sobbing, Zijuan says softly: "Young Master, please go back now. It is late." The temple bell tolls in the background. Murmuring, "Yes, go back now, go back now," Baoyu walks out, throws his jade to the floor, and disappears into the twilight. The curtain falls as the chorus sings: "He throws away the jade and rids himself of gold; he gives up this dirty world and leaves behind the prosperous nest built upon bloody competition."

In the novel, scattered throughout the last thirty or so chapters after Daiyu has departed are descriptions of Baoyu's desperate efforts to communicate with Daiyu, waiting for her every night in his dreams and visiting Zijuan at the Bamboo Lodge to ask about Daiyu's last days. He needs to find meaning in Daiyu's death and in his love for her. The bond between the two lovers is finally resolved only when Baoyu awakens to the Buddhist truth that all worldly desires are but illusions that bring only suffering. In fact, the Buddhist theme is so strong that it was possible for the classical scholar Wang Guowei to read the novel as a Buddhist text that points out the vanity in human affairs and shows that deeply felt loss can awaken people to the Buddha's truth. The Yue opera play, however, makes Baoyu's mourning for Daiyu a simple display of his unfailing love and casts his abandonment of the world as an act of loyalty to his lover. As the scriptwriter Xu Jin suggested, the emotional journey on which the play takes the viewer will be completed only if Baoyu can convince the viewer of the sincerity of his love and matches Daiyu's sacrifice with his own.[65] Indeed, not until Baoyu throws away his jade and walks out into nothingness is the great love tragedy born.

Significantly, almost all renditions of the novel in popular forms in the 1940s and 1950s focus on a monogamous love story and depict a feminine world centered on Jia Baoyu, the feminine teenage boy. For example, Huaying Studio's 1944 film *Dream of the Red Chamber*, written and directed by Bu Wancang and starring Yuan Meiyun and Zhou Xuan, has a similar plot and character development as those in the 1944 Yue opera *Lin Daiyu* and the 1958 *Dream of the Red Chamber*. The film also centers on the domestic and feminine world of the Grand View Garden and features a group of predominantly female characters, with only the minimal presence of male characters including Baoyu's father and a few male servants. Furthermore, as in Yue opera, the character Jia Baoyu is played by a woman, the noted actress Yuan Meiyun. This feminization of Cao's novel in Shanghai's popular entertainment of the mid-twentieth century provides yet more evidence of a general trend that is most clearly manifested in women's Yue opera.

It was the unique feminine aesthetics developed in women's Yue opera that gave the feminine narrative of *Dream of the Red Chamber* its perfect form. Yue opera's actresses fleshed out, on their own bodies, a constellation of enchanting female figures and the feminine Jia Baoyu, and these images were so popular that they became standard portraits of these characters. Yue opera renditions of the novel, with the fluid operatic acting style, body posturing, and cutting-edge character modeling, helped bring Cousin Lin and Jia Baoyu to life. Moreover, the beautiful arias featured in the Yue opera play, enhanced by lyrics drawn from the novel's poems, carried the audience through an intense emotional journey with the protagonists. If these hundreds of poems in the novel define the work's poetics, then Yue opera's arias fully bear this poetics. The arias circulated across the nation, through the 1962 film and millions of records, and came to symbolize what the story was all about. The 1944 film, limited by its realistic style, had no such feminine operatic aesthetics in place to help enhance the feminine narrative, to articulate the complexity and intensity of the characters' emotions, or to bear out the special and traditional poetics of the novel. Thus, as the 1944 film quietly faded into the past, the movie industry was content to simply film the 1958 Yue opera play rather than make another film.

The Yue opera film was immensely popular. It attracted four hundred thousand viewers when it was first released in Hong Kong in 1962. It was an instant success in Mainland China, but the film was quietly removed from circulation soon after its premiere as the radical leftist leadership tightened its grip on the cultural market. When it was rereleased in 1978, however, it set a box office record nationwide. Across the country, many places showed the film around the clock for several days in order to make maximum use of their copies within their limited time slots.[66] Large numbers of viewers watched it several times and shed tears in the theaters. One Yue opera fan went to see the film every day after work until the local run was over, and many collage-educated young men living in and outside of Shanghai began to appreciate Yue opera after viewing the film.[67] The Yue opera play also brought the story to millions of the illiterate and semiliterate, and numerous people read the novel after viewing the play in the theater or on the screen.

The Yue opera *Dream of the Red Chamber* greatly popularized the novel while increasing the genre's influence and prestige. Yue opera's remaking of the novel into a great love tragedy helped shape the popular reception of Cao Xueqin's novel in modern China more than any other interpretation or scholarly work. Even Chairman Mao's instruction to read the novel as a textbook on the feudal society has had less effect on the book's popular reputation. Known as a master theater of the love drama and with a cluster of popular plays such as *The Butterfly Lovers*, *Tale of the Western Chamber*, and *Dream of the Red Chamber*, women's Yue opera inscribed its feminine imprint on the culture of love and instilled a feminine sentiment into popular sensibilities regarding gender and sexual relationships in modern China.

Conclusion

For at least five hundred years, from the mid-Ming to the last decades of the twentieth century, local operas represented a prominent part of popular culture and an important aspect of Chinese life, and their transformations were integral to epochal social and political upheavals. In the twentieth century, the massive entrance of Chinese women into the public realm and their active participation in popular culture resulted in a profound transition of opera culture, from the realm of men to an artistic and social world in which actresses and female spectators figured prominently. The feminization of the operatic body gave rise to a distinct feminine opera culture of the twentieth century. While the transition was a general process, it was manifested most intensely in the phenomenon of women's Yue opera in Shanghai.

The early development of Yue opera comprised two major transformations—from rural to urban and from all male to all female—which occurred in the late nineteenth and first half of the twentieth centuries. The increased prominence of Yue opera, and of minor operas in general, may be seen as an expression of many modern processes, such as the deterioration of the rural economy, the rise of treaty-port cities as industrial and commercial centers, and mass urban migration. Major political and ideological revolutions of the period also facilitated the transformation of Yue opera and of minor operas more generally. The 1911 Republican Revolution lifted the ban against women in the entertainment market that had been imposed by Qing law and custom; the subsequent May Fourth New Culture Movement promoted ideas of women's liberation and free love and marriage as opposed to arranged marriage and hence sanctioned love themes that were central to minor operas. The emergence of Yue opera as a female opera, then, should be viewed not as a special case in cultural development that ran contrary to the trends of the time but as a phenomenon that most intensely expressed the gendered nature of these historical processes.

The success of women's Yue opera in Shanghai was a ramification of the city's social formation, characterized by key factors of gender, class, and native-place ties, and revealed the city's basic cultural characteristics—bourgeois, colonial (domestically as well as internationally), and feminine. Yue opera's constituency came mainly from three powerful new groups in Republican Shanghai that helped define the city's social landscape: an urban middle class; Zhejiang, more specifically Ningbo-Shaoxing, immigrants; and women. First, as the largest industrial city and the most important commercial and financial center, Shanghai was home to a great number of capitalists, modern businessmen, and white-collar professionals as well as apprentices at printing houses, shop hands in modern stores, and industrial workers. The concentration of these new groups in Shanghai nurtured China's first generation of the urban middle- and lower-middle class. These wage earners or wives of wage earners made up the majority of Yue opera's audience. Second, Shanghai was a city built by settlers.[1] Divisions among various immigrant groups from different native places, though not necessarily always so clear-cut, were a basic factor in the city's social life and political economy. If most Subei natives and many Shanghai natives composed the lower layers of society, members of the new bourgeoisie were mostly natives from the more economically developed Jiangnan region. More specifically, the powerful Ningbo-Shaoxing business group and intellectuals strongly backed Yue opera, and the opera's success in turn symbolized the rising power of this native-place group in the city. Third, Shanghai had a high, perhaps the highest, concentration of new types of women, which included factory workers, shop assistants, domestic helpers, middle-class housewives, students, office workers, and professionals such as accountants, teachers, nurses, doctors, and actresses. Mostly young immigrants in a young metropolis marked by a semicolonial cosmopolitanism, these women found unprecedented, though still quite limited, freedom in pursuing their personal interests, among which was the choice to patronize public entertainment. During this important period of transition in gender norms, women's Yue opera provided opportunities for various women to expand their lives beyond their social stations.

When historical conditions were right, the actions of young actresses made it all happen. When a group of girls from the poor countryside of

Shengxian joined the first all-girls opera school in 1923, when female Shengxian opera troupes frequented Shanghai in the mid-1930s, and when female troupes joined refugees flowing into the falling city in the late 1930s, they probably did not think they were making history. But their struggle for economic survival, human dignity, sexual autonomy, and social status against all sorts of gender- and class-based exploitation constituted an important dimension of China's modern history. Key to the actress's struggle was the need to rescue herself from a traditional public culture of erotica that had fixed its voyeuristic gaze on her sexual body and to transform herself from the lowly female entertainer into a modern artist. This would be possible only if she could transform her opera from a bawdy peasant form into a refined and socially meaningful urban theater. Fortunately, the actresses' struggle converged with two modern processes: the formation of an urban bourgeois culture with a strong female component and the dissemination of elite nation-building rhetoric in theatrical reform. Through a series of efforts to reform Yue opera, actresses turned the opera into a master theater of the modern love drama and an urban theatrical spectacle. While Yue opera's romanticized and dignified love stories appealed to middle-class and female audiences, the patriotic message attached to the principal love drama won political legitimacy for the opera.

As Yue opera actresses remade the opera into a decent theater, they simultaneously achieved the status of art workers. Their quest for respect, dignity, and full social status won the support of a large middle-class female audience, left-wing intellectuals, and a new public educated in the rhetoric of women's liberation. Actresses' struggle against class- and gender-based traditional contempt toward the female entertainer culminated in a series of public events in the late 1940s. *Sister Xianglin*, the union incident, the collaborative fund-raising performances, and the Xiao Dangui incident, staged in both the theater and the mass media, were all part of a public drama that discursively transformed the public definition of the actress. The dramatic transformation of Yue opera and its actresses was a central event that took place in the limelight, and the resulting prominence of a women's culture gave the city's modern culture a strong feminine flavor.

Feminine Value

Romantic love and love drama had dubious reputations in modern China's public culture. While they dominated popular literature and entertainment, they occupied a lower position in the overall cultural hierarchy, looked down upon by elitist artists and cultural connoisseurs as trite and criticized by intellectual and political elites as self-indulgent. Various male authorities since the Qing period thought that the emotions of personal love belonged to the feminine, private sphere and were hence trivial matters. From such an elite male perspective, it is easy to dismiss the feminine opera and its love drama as insignificant and inconsequential. Educated elitist women struggling to break conventional gender norms also tended to sideline Yue opera as a women's cultural ghetto in which self-indulgent female fans enjoyed actresses performing stereotypical feminine clichés.[2] This bias against the feminine opera culminated during the Cultural Revolution, when women's Yue opera was banned, and the Maoist notion that "times have changed, men and women are the same" tried to make women like men.[3] Opposition to feminine opera continued in the post-revolution era. A recent commentary, provoked by two Yue opera productions—*The Butterfly Dream*, of 2001, and the Shanghai Grand Theater version of *Dream of the Red Chamber*, of 1999—provides a clear example of how disturbing Yue opera's femininity can be to its critics. The author, displaying a superficial and impressionistic knowledge of Yue opera, attacked the opera, from its music to its male impersonators, and denounced it with indignation:

> Yue opera is simply the sediment of the dirty and rotten elements in the long river of Chinese opera tradition, and it brazenly exhibits and elaborates the decadent and frivolous sentimentality from the Five Dynasties [907–60] to the present. . . . Yue opera distorts the true character of many intellectuals in history as it depicts them in a sickly manner. Yue opera castrates traditional intellectuals' innate unswerving determination, as expressed in the motto that scholars can be killed but cannot be humiliated, and steals their aspiration to bring peace to the world starting from self-cultivation and ordering the family and the state [*xiushen qijia zhiguo pingtianxia*].[4]

Combining an old Confucian discourse on gentlemanly conduct with the more recent discourse of nation building, the author expresses an unreflective male elitist prejudice against Yue opera's femininity, contrasting it to the masculine tradition in Chinese opera represented by Beijing opera. As harsh as it is, there is nothing new in this commentary.

Yue opera has been loved and censured for its renowned femininity ever since the 1940s. As a feminine theater featuring emotionally intense feminine narratives, Yue opera provoked strong emotional reactions in viewers, and where its admirers saw beauty, its critics saw decadence. Yue opera fans were notorious for their unrestrained public expressions of love for their icons, while critics expressed scorn for the opera and its fans. It is remarkable that despite such elitist masculine prejudices and political efforts to shape Yue opera into a revolutionary theater, women's Yue opera thrived as a master theater of the love drama. Its aesthetics and narratives were articulations of modern urban feminine aspirations that helped set the fashion for popular entertainment in twentieth-century China. The opera was, therefore, an expression of the rise of feminine power in Shanghai and in Chinese society in general.

Despite many differences, both women's Yue opera and Western "chick flicks" (films that appeal especially to women, often focusing on romance or relationships) are energetic, melodramatic, urban, popular, and feminine, and both have provoked unsettling feelings in elitist feminists as well as in masculine mainstreamers. Moreover, both clearly symbolize the growth of feminine power in public culture, a kind of self-authorized female representation that embarrasses various (including feminist) orthodoxies and defies simple definitions.[5] In Yue opera, as in chick flicks, we see women's aspirations for the right to agency, independence, respect, and love as autonomous human beings. Through the opera, Chinese women refuted traditional misogynist views that subjugate them to men while they simultaneously negotiated with the modern revolutionary rhetoric that subjects them to the nation. The main political and intellectual discourses on women's liberation criticized the feminine *yin* as being traditional (read "backward"), soft, weak, and small-minded and tried to subordinate women to the masculine *yang* nation-building causes, but the women of Yue opera sought to rectify and lift the feminine as equal to the masculine. In this way, the women of Yue opera used seemingly conventional feminine values to challenge male dominance and to empower themselves.

The theory of performance and subject formation articulated by Judith Butler is useful in explaining the construction of femininity in Yue opera. As Butler argued when discussing the construction of "sex":

> Crucially, then, construction is neither a single act nor a causal process initiated by a subject and culminating in a set of fixed effects. Construction

> not only takes place *in* time, but is itself a temporal process which operates through the reiteration of norms; sex is both produced and destabilized in the course of this reiteration. As a sedimented effect of a reiterative or ritual practice, sex acquires its naturalized effect, and, yet, it is also by virtue of this reiteration that gaps and fissures are opened up as the constitutive instabilities in such constructions, as that which escapes or exceeds the norm, as that which cannot be wholly defined or fixed by the repetitive labor of that norm. This instability is the *de*constituting possibility in the very process of repetition, the power that undoes the very effects by which "sex" is stabilized, the possibility to put the consolidation of the norms of "sex" into a potentially productive crisis.[6]

Butler's argument for the construction of "sex" as a performative process in everyday life sheds light on how women could change gender norms while seemingly acting to affirm them. Instead of following the male elite's denial of feminine value, the women of Yue opera exercised considerable self-authorization in exploring feminine aesthetics and women's narratives in the form of love drama. With the opera's popular success, the women of Yue opera helped establish private feelings and mundane experiences as major themes in artistic representations of modern life, making the "feminine" concerns of the everyday as important as the "masculine" public discourse of nationalism and modernity, as represented by spoken drama and Beijing opera. Thus, the women of Yue opera advanced the modern process of signification of the feminine, making it equal to, yet still different from, the masculine.

The Revolution

This urban process, however, was met with the rural-based communist revolution that came to dominance after 1949. To be sure, many different forces helped shape Yue opera's vicissitudes before the Communist Party's left-wing intervention of the late 1940s. Riding on the trends of industrialization and urban in-migration, women's Yue opera quickly established itself in Shanghai in the 1930s and 1940s with the support of an emerging middle-class, especially female, audience, at a time when women's education and careers outside the home had already begun to change gender mores. Yue opera's rise in Shanghai can be understood only within these urban-centered fundamental social and economical processes.

Actresses' struggle for survival and respect, however, converged with the left-wing program for social and gender equality, and their relationship with the communist revolution was for the large part mutually beneficial. The CCP underground forces aided Yue opera actresses' struggle in the 1940s, and during the PRC period, the state elevated the status of entertainers to engineers of the soul, admitted their representatives into the new cultural and political elite, and made entertainment a lofty profession while providing financial security for entertainers. Most actresses welcomed the social changes brought about by the new state and supported it with their performances. Although the CCP cannot be credited as the sole liberator of the suffering actresses, there should be no question that the PRC state, and the communist revolution, had a positive impact on the actress's transformation from member of the underclass to full member of society.

The PRC state's intervention in the arts, however, had more questionable effects on the genre's development. In restructuring the entertainment business in the 1950s, the state pulled together intellectual and material resources and produced a cluster of Yue opera masterpieces of love drama, which boosted the opera's national and international influence. This development rested, however, on the artistic foundations laid by Yue opera reforms of the 1940s and should not be credited solely to state intervention. In the long run, the state's ideological and administrative control of art production was detrimental to Yue opera, and to performance art in general, as it limited artists' creativity and their ability to respond to their audiences. As state control of art intensified during the Cultural Revolution, allowing only one kind of revolutionary heroic art, art and entertainment withered. Even when the state shifted to a laissez-faire policy during the reform era that began in the 1980s, Yue opera and other native-opera genres were not able to reclaim their dominant position in the entertainment market.

Neither Yue opera's glorious achievements in the 1950s and 1960s nor the genre's waning popularity in recent decades was due entirely to the PRC state, although in both cases, the state and the communist revolution were contributors. Several developments in the late twentieth century sent Yue opera and other native operas into decline. First, a globalized mass-entertainment culture captured the imaginations of younger generations after China reopened itself to Western influence in the 1980s. The freshness of things Western seems to have rendered traditional art forms obsolete in the minds of young people. Second, thanks to economic and social development, there were no longer as many desperate people relying on grassroots low-brow performances as a way of making a living. Third, the Shanghai municipal government imposed regulations on free-flowing troupe formations and performances in an attempt to maintain minimal control over anti-government or pornographic revues. Thus, while Yue opera continued to be part of the entertainment scene in Shanghai, it was no longer as bustling as it had been in its golden period (1930s–60s), when the opera rallied novel artistic imaginations and tremendous youthful energies.

Thus, the impact of the communist revolution on Yue opera, especially the 1949 Liberation and the Cultural Revolution, is only of historical significance but is not historically significant (to borrow a Joseph Levenson expression) because it was not the decisive factor in the rise and decline of Yue opera.[7] The communist revolution and the story of Yue opera are better understood as two separate phenomena that interacted with each other, both shaping and being shaped by fundamental historical transformations in social, economic, and political systems in twentieth-century China. Moreover, in the long run, the urban-centered primordial modernity, as reflected partly in Yue opera, is no less a revolution than the rural-based grandiose communist movement.

Periodization

Yue opera's history, as a process separate from national revolution, suggests a periodization different as well as independent from the division in political history marked by the founding of the People's Republic of China. Until recently, the 1949 divide has been taken as a standard in modern Chinese history, reflecting the tremendous impact of the regime change on the lives of the Chinese people and on the international order. This division, however, has been increasingly problematic since the 1990s, as the People's Republic became a subject of historical inquiry and as China entered a post-revolution period amid the global post–Cold War period. Reassessing the role of the communist revolution in China's modernization process, China scholars questioned the usefulness of the 1949 divide. Political historian Nishimura Shigeo, for one, argued that the regime change of 1949 did not interrupt the process of building a modern nation-state in China.[8] William Kirby and his students pointed out, from an economic history angle, continuities in the building of state-sponsored and state-controlled large-scale industries across 1949.[9]

Similarly, Yue opera also shows continuities across 1949 in modern developments in cultural and social aspects, indicating the necessity of treating the period between the 1920s and the 1980s as a coherent temporal framework defined by several particular social and cultural processes. Of primary importance in this regard is the prominence of a public women's culture centered on Yue opera, a phenomenon that epitomized the contradictions and conflicts in the rise of women in urban society. The Yue opera phenomenon emerged during a period when the new gender ideology had just begun to transform traditional gender praxis, hence the necessity for women to carve out a separate space of their own in which their new experiences in public life would be comfortable. The home base provided by women's Yue opera was an open space, and the actresses and female audiences were highly visible figures who moved publicly in and out of theaters and produced various social dramas in the mass media. The cultural activism of the women of Yue opera as a social/cultural group was unprecedented, and it helped normalize women's presence in social life and remake gender norms in the city's public culture.

The trend of women going outside the family and into the public realm in urban society received a big boost after 1949 when the state mobilized women to join the workforce. The new state's intervention further expanded and legitimated women's activism in the public domain, and the subsequent Cultural Revolution pushed this trend to a climax. Partly because women all over the country became increasingly active in public life, the popularity of women's Yue opera expanded beyond the city limits and became a national phenomenon. However, having grown strong in conjunction with the general trend of women's entrance into social life, women's Yue opera began to lose its grip on younger women and rather suddenly lost popularity in the 1980s, signifying the end to a phase in the cause of women's liberation, and a positive end it is. Younger generations of women, growing up in a society in which women performed public duty alongside men and gender equality was the norm, no longer shared the experiences and aspirations of their predecessors; they saw in Yue opera a women's culture that was outdated and embarrassing, which reminded them of women's lowly status in the past.

More broadly, Yue opera's history was part and parcel of the modern transformation of popular entertainment in Shanghai that began in the 1930s and ran across 1949 and through the Cultural Revolution, despite the increasingly dominant leftist radicalism of the early PRC period. This period, from 1949 to 1976, witnessed a revolutionary state pushing the entire society into an all-around socialist transformation. The construction of a socialist culture was of paramount importance in this ambitious plan, and the socialist transformation of popular entertainment was a key element in the state's effort to disseminate its ideology to the grassroots. In 1951, the state announced the policy of three transformations—which applied to the entertainer, the structure of the industry, and the stage performance—and launched an all-out operatic reform campaign. The state's effort to gain full control of the entertainment industry culminated during the Cultural Revolution, when the industry was allowed to offer only a dozen or so state-approved theatrical productions. The radical ideology and praxis of this period gave the impression of a total rupture in cultural development. Interestingly, however, the perceived rupture may be viewed as an extreme push in the same direction. Close examination of the situation reveals that, underneath the surface of radical rhetoric and practice, several threads of cultural modernity ran through the early PRC cultural restructuring, including institutionalization, the push for professionalism, and citizenry building.[10]

Institutionalization in popular entertainment developed in two ways: market self-ordering, through competition and negotiation, and government-imposed regulation. Shanghai's popular-entertainment market grew rapidly with the influx of immigrants and the city's expansion in the early twentieth century. There was not, however, much institution building to speak of up to the period of the War of Resistance against Japan because local opera troupes were unstable in terms of formation and movement, and the split sovereignty in semicolonial Shanghai compromised governmental efforts to regulate the market. Real institution building took place in the 1940s, especially after the end of World War II. As China regained full control of the city and the foreign concessions were abolished, the Nationalist Shanghai municipal government set out to regulate the entertainment market. It issued a series of laws and regulations requiring performance companies, theaters, and dance-hall entertainers to register with the Social Affairs Bureau. The government also censored pornographic and politically dangerous performances and attempted to control unionization in the industry. Meanwhile, through a process of fierce competition and constant negotiation, the entertainment market matured and stabilized; order began to emerge, with star troupes and performers becoming established in various trades while the less successful were pushed to the periphery. In the Yue opera trade, for example, a cluster of such superstars as the so-called nine sisters and five large companies (Xuesheng, Fanghua, Yulan, Dongshan, and Shaozhuang) dominated the market. Meanwhile, interest groups within the trade took advantage of the government-directed union campaign and set up the Yue Opera Workers' Union and the Yue Opera Employers' Union in order to increase their power through institution building. This trend of institutionalization continued after 1949, refashioned completely within a framework of socialist ideology and centrally planned culture. The thorough socialist reorganization of the entertainment business represented radical measures of modern institution building beyond political and ideological differences between the Nationalists and the CCP. By the end of the Cultural Revolution, the landscape of Shanghai's entertainment industry had stabilized, albeit in a socialist fashion, with regulated performance companies, venues, professional organizations, and educational units as well as governmental administrative organs. In the post–Cultural Revolution era, when the government saw the need to reinstate an entertainment market, the successful institution building of the previous period made it much easier for the government to open and control a market. The open market of popular entertainment, in which spontaneous street performances and itinerant troupes and performers moved freely, had become a memory of the "premodern" past.

Professionalism was another important aspect in the continuous process of cultural modernization in the 1950s. Most important in this regard was the development of a script-based, director-centered system in theatrical production that gradually replaced the previous mode of production centered on actors' unscripted improvisational performances. This process began in the late 1930s and developed throughout the 1940s within local opera troupes active in Shanghai. In the 1950s, the state sent professional scriptwriters, directors, and stage designers to every opera troupe and made sure that every production followed a standard procedure, starting from a complete script that was actualized onstage under a director. This greatly enhanced professionalism and modernized aesthetic standards in local operas and led to a cluster of masterpieces in the early PRC period, including the Yue operas *Tale of the Western Chamber*, *Dream of the Red Chamber*, and *Pursuing the Carp* (Zhui yu); the Shanghai operas *An Antique Coin* and *The Slave Mother* (Wei nuli de muqin); and the Huai operas *Qin Xianglian* (Qin Xianglian) and *The Blue Bridge* (Lanqiao hui). The push for professionalism was so strong that general improvement in the artistic quality of local-opera productions was achieved at the cost of the actors' creativity and their ability to give their roles individuality through idiomatic singing and acting. Today, talented self-authorizing actors of the past are legendary figures, and improvisational performance has become a legacy of the premodern tradition of native operas.

Citizenry building was an integral part of modern China's nation building and another aspect of the continuous development of a modern culture in the early PRC period. Despite political and ideological differences between the Nationalists and the Communists, both worked to forge among the people a sense of one nation and one people—an understanding of the correlation between personal and national interests as well as the urge to take on one's duty to the nation. The Republican effort at citizenry building is easily identified in various versions of the New Life Movement, patriotic discourses against foreign invasions, and nationalistic rhetoric against the warlords and the Communists. School education and the mass media served as the primary channels for such construction. During the early PRC period, however, the state made popular entertainment another important venue, pushing the traditional idea of "education through entertainment" (*yu jiao yu le*) to the limit. By means of a centrally planned culture, the rhetoric of revolutionary patriotism permeated all media and most theatrical productions, helping to create a uniform socialist language for the nation's unified citizenry. Through the socialist transformation of stage performances and performers—two of the three transformations in 1950s operatic reform—the new state not only made the lowly entertainers members of the citizenry but moreover constructed an imagined national community of citizens as reformed entertainers popularized state ideology through the staging of socialist arts. This radical citizenry building reached its climax during the Cultural Revolution, when revolutionary heroic arts encouraged citizens to work and die for the country. At the end of this period, the idea of China (Zhongguo) and Chinese (Zhongguoren) had taken root in the common people's political consciousness and informed their identity formation.

The New Century

Around the turn of the twenty-first century, Yue opera began to experience a small revival with a few well-received productions by the Shanghai Yue Opera House, including *Stage Sisters* in 1998, *The Meilong Township* (Meilong zhen) in 2000, and *The Butterfly Dream* in 2001 along with the special production of *Dream of the Red Chamber* for the Grand Theater in 1999. This is part of a revival in the cultural market for performance art in Shanghai that began with the opening of the Grand Theater in 1998. Supported by a powerful economic upturn in the 1990s, Shanghai once again aspires to rebuild a cosmopolitan spirit and restore its leading position in making culture. The Grand Theater and a group of landmark buildings, including the Shanghai Museum and the Museum for Urban Planning, erected at the center of the city around the People's Square, symbolize this ambition. In recent years, the Grand Theater has contracted with many international companies as well as first-rate troupes nationwide to perform on its stages, and its calendar is nearly full year-round. Citywide, about two dozen venues feature a variety of performances ranging from acrobatic displays, comedy shows, Yue opera, Beijing opera, and dance, to pop, rock and Western music concerts, Russian ballet, Irish folk dance, and Broadway musicals. Yue opera was the first among local operas to stage at the Grand Theater, with the ever popular *Dream of the Red Chamber*, indicating that the genre has retained much of its charm for many people in the city and around the nation. Playing up the cultural aspirations of the city, Yue opera artists made it their goal to restore the brand name "Shanghai Yue opera" nationwide. Between 2002 and 2006, the Shanghai Yue Opera House has accordingly organized several well-publicized performance tours to Zhejiang, the southwest, the northwest, and the northeastern regions showcasing a sophisticated modern urban culture as well as the special charm of women's opera.

The reform era has also witnessed a new wave of urbanization and urban migration. As Shanghai becomes increasingly open to new immigrants, many Zhejiang natives have once again found in Yue opera a desirable career in the metropolis. This trend will continue into the conceivable future, since the government has made urbanization a strategic goal for China's development in the decades to come. Thus, the same dynamics between the Zhejiang countryside and Shanghai that supported the twentieth century's Yue opera boom in Shanghai are once again working to revitalize the opera (see figs. 7.1, 7.2).

Moreover, economic development in the past quarter century created a sizable population of young professionals and entrepreneurs in the city, many of whom are women. Contemporary female fans of Yue opera are found not only in theaters but also on the Internet. College students and white-collar workers have created at least two dozen Web sites devoted to Yue opera in general or to specific leading actresses. One such Web site,

7.1 A middle-aged Yue opera fan rehearses at a party at Xiao-Bai Yumei's residence, 1996. (Photo by the author)

Shan Yangping Forum (Yangping Luntan), a lively chat board devoted to the beautiful actress Shan Yangping, is filled with young women's unrestrained expressions of love for her and for one another as Shan fans.[11] Another Web site devoted to the handsome male impersonator Qian Huili is similarly filled with young women's confessions of love for their idol.[12] This group of well-educated fans, like those of the past, is the most vocal and visible group among all Yue opera fans, but the majority of the Yue opera audience is still composed of middle-aged women. It remains to be seen whether Yue opera will be able to expand its influence among this younger group and how the new generation of Yue opera fans and actresses will shape Yue opera (see fig. 7.3).

At the beginning of the twenty-first century, women's Yue opera is enjoying a small revival, and not much seems to have changed: the same

7.2 A young Yue opera fan learns to perform at a party at Xiao-Bai Yumei's residence, 1996. (Photo by the author)

patterns of love drama persist, and the opera has never tired of telling women's narratives presented in exquisite feminine aesthetics to a predominantly female audience. Relationships between audiences and stars also remain more or less the same: fans fall in love with their idols because of both artistic and sexual attraction. Adoptive mother-daughter relationships are no longer as formal and ostentatious as before, yet it is common knowledge within Yue opera circles that most leading actresses have special patrons, mostly overseas Chinese businesswomen and businessmen. The most obvious difference is the changing status of Yue opera actresses.

7.3 The Yifu Tianchan Theater, a major stage for native-opera performances in contemporary Shanghai. (*Yue yuan shen yun* 2001)

The old stigma attached to female entertainers belongs firmly in the past, and for Yue opera performers today, acting not only represents job security but also is a respected profession that provides fame and celebrity status for the stars.

Thus, the social and economic processes that once supported Yue opera seem to have been revived in the last quarter century of the reform era. Especially since the 1990s, Shanghai has once again emerged as the center of China's modern economy. A new middle class is developing as immigrants flow into the city, and female white-collar workers symbolize the new women of Shanghai. The question is, Will women's Yue opera thrive once again in the new century?

The answer is probably negative, for the social context is very different from that of the early twentieth century. During the first four decades of the People's Republic, Shanghai grew into a huge residential city, with older generations of settlers becoming Shanghainese and the newcomers being shaped by the city rather than shaping it. At the same time, society has become so open to women that women in Shanghai no longer need Yue opera to help broaden their social horizons. In short, members of the new bourgeoisie in Shanghai have found less sociological and emotional connection with the opera, although they may deem it aesthetically and perhaps sexually attractive. As Yue opera makes itself a permanent feature of Shanghai's cultural scene, it no longer has the glamour and popularity of its heyday, as popular-culture preferences have shifted to a globalized mass entertainment represented by domestic and international rock and popular-music stars and, most recently, such pop-culture representatives as Chinese rappers. Thus, although Yue opera will continue to be a highly developed art form in the city's entertainment scene, it is no longer an important social phenomenon.

In today's China, when native operas are reduced mostly to relying on government subsidies in order to survive, Yue opera has joined Beijing opera as a representative of China's living cultural tradition. Both operas, however, still claim the loyalty of a small segment of the population made up mostly of the middle aged and elderly. The divide along gender lines between Beijing opera and Yue opera, in terms of content, style, and audience, is still apparent. Yue opera continues to produce love dramas, while Beijing opera retains its focus on grand imperial or nation-state narratives. This is evident in several new productions by the Shanghai Beijing Opera House, such as *Cao Cao and Yang Xiu* (Cao Cao yu Yang Xiu) and *The Prosperous Reign of the Taizong Emperor* (Zhenguan shengshi). In Lu Xun Park, in northeastern Shanghai, on a sunny weekend, coteries of Yue opera fans, mostly retired women, gather at the pavilion on top of the hill and rehearse their favorite pieces; down the hill, across the lake, Beijing opera fans, mostly elderly men, get together at the corridor and entertain themselves by singing well-known pieces. Beijing opera and Yue opera, the products of two differently gendered cultures in two different eras, have left deep marks on China's history and, as living traditions, continue to offer entertainment for the population and inspiration for artists around the world.

Appendix

Interviews and Informants

Name	Sex	Birth Date	Occupation	Place	Time	Method
Chen Shulian 陳疏蓮	F	1920	Radio announcer	Shanghai	Dec. 6, 1995	Tape
Cheng Liping 承立平	F	1943	Yue opera fan	New York	June 21, 2002	Notes
Cheng Liping,	F		Yue opera fans (group interview)	New York	July 13, 2002	Notes
Li Jiang 李江,	F	1948				
Zheng Yinyin 鄭銀銀	F	1941				
Su Jinzou	M					
Cheng Rong 成容	F	1922	Yue opera scriptwriter	Shanghai	Nov. 9, Dec. 5, 1995	Tape
				Telephone*	Mar. 29, May–July 2002	Notes
Dai Xinghuang 戴行煌	M	1927	Yue opera agent and administrator	Shanghai	June 13, July 2001	Notes

Name	Sex	Birth Date	Occupation	Place	Time	Method
Ding Jingtang 丁景唐	M	1920	Writer and PRC official	Shanghai	Feb. 9, 1996	Tape
Fu Quanxiang 傅全香	F	1923	Yue opera actress	Shanghai	Dec. 26, 1995	Tape
Han Yi 韓義	M	1922	Yue opera stage designer, director, and scriptwriter	Shanghai Telephone*	June 1, 5, 2002 Sept. 16, Nov. 25, Dec. 28, 2002	Tape Notes
Li Taicheng 李太成	M	1921	PRC official	Shanghai	Feb. 15, 1996	Notes
Lu Shijun 盧時俊	M	1935	Yue opera actor and researcher	Shanghai	Jan. 19, 1996; June 28, 2001	Notes
Qian Huili 錢惠麗	F	1963	Yue opera actress	Telephone*	Dec. 26, 2002	Notes
Qiu Yawei 裘亞衛 Qiu Wenguang 裘文光	M M	1932 1935	Taipei Shengxian Native-Place Organization activists and Yue opera researchers (group interview)	Taipei	Aug. 10, 1996	Tape
Shan Yangping 單仰萍	F	1962	Yue opera actress	Telephone*	Dec. 29, 2002; Jan. 14, 2003	Notes
Su Jinzou 蘇進鄒	M	1941	Yue opera music writer	New York	July 13, 2002	Notes

Name	Sex	Birth Date	Occupation	Place	Time	Method
Teng Jiazhen 滕家振, Song Zhiyou 宋之由	F M	1916 1910	Yue opera audience members (couples)	Shanghai	Jan. 29, 1996	Tape
Wang Zhiping 王志萍	F	1966	Yue opera actress	Telephone*	June 8, 2003	Notes
Wei Shaochang 魏紹昌	M	1922	Writer	Shanghai	Jan. 7, 11, 1996	Tape
Wu Ping 吳萍	F	1936	Yue opera fan	Shanghai	Jan. 28, 1996	Tape
Wu Xiaolou 吳小樓	F	1926	Yue opera actress	Shanghai	Jan. 10, 1996	Tape
Wu Yanli 吳燕麗, Gao Jin 高瑾	F F	1923 1941	Yue opera actresses (group interview)	Taipei	Aug. 11, 1996	Tape
Wu Zhaofen 吳兆芬	F	1937	Yue opera scriptwriter	Telephone*	June 4, 2003	Notes
Xiao-Bai Yumei 小白玉梅	F	1921	Yue opera actress	Shanghai	Dec. 28, 1995; Jan. 30, 1996	Tape
Xu Yulan 徐玉蘭	F	1921	Yue opera actress	Shanghai	Dec. 27, 1995	Tape

Name	Sex	Birth Date	Occupation	Place	Time	Method
Xue Yunhuang 薛允璜	M	1938	Yue opera scriptwriter	Telephone*	Dec. 22, 2002; Jan. 5, 2003	Notes
Yuan Xuefen 袁雪芬	F	1922	Yue opera actress	Shanghai Telephone*	Dec. 23, 1995; May 30, 2002; Jan. 1, 2003	Tape Notes
Zhang Rongbiao 張榮標	M	1913	Yue opera actor	Chongren, Shengxian, Zhejiang	Nov. 24, 1995	Tape
Zhang Yanqiu 張豔秋	F	1923?	Yue opera actress (couples)			
Zhang Xingzhou 張行周	M	1918	Board member, Taipei Ningbo Native-Place Association	Taipei	Aug. 10, 1996	Tape
Wang Xiongfu 王雄甫	M	1915	Chairman of the Board, Taipei Ningbo Native-Place Association (group interview)			
Zheng Zhongmei 鄭忠梅	F	1928	Yue opera actress	Shanghai	Nov. 13, 1995	Tape
Zhou Baokui 周寶奎	F	1920	Yue opera actress	Shanghai	Jan. 13, 1996	Tape

Name	Sex	Birth Date	Occupation	Place	Time	Method
Zhu Juxiang 竺菊香,	F	1923	Yue opera actress	Shanghai	Nov. 13, 1995	Tape
Zhou Baocai 周寶財	M	1912	Yue opera musician (couples)			

*Telephone interview, New York to Shanghai

Notes

Preface

1. As Wendy Larson argues in her study of modern China's women writers. Larson 1998.

2. Fuller 1980, 235.

3. Hall 1980.

Introduction: Opera, Gender, and the City

1. "Mandarin ducks and butterflies" fiction is a subgenre in Republican period popular literature that focuses on love stories. At first, the term was pejorative and referred particularly to love stories written in classical Chinese in the 1910s and early 1920s; eventually, it came to refer to all popular love stories of the Republican period.

2. Link 1981; Wei 1962, 1984, 1990; Wang Dewei 1988; Zhang Gansheng 1991; Yang Yi 1993; Wu 1995; Pickowicz 1993; Yingjin Zhang 1996; Lee 1999; and Poshek Fu 2003.

3. Furth 1999; Mann 1997; Hershatter 1997; and Ko 1994.

4. Frith 1988.

5. The other important form of popular entertainment comprised local storytelling genres, akin to local operas in the sense that both were grounded in local dialects.

6. For example, the authoritative *Dictionary of Chinese Opera Genres* (Zhongguo xiqu juzhong da cidian), published in 1995, lists 335 genres that existed in the past 150 years up to 1985. *Zhongguo xiqu da cidian*, 1995.

7. For Beijing opera, *Shanghai Jingju zhi* 1999; for Huai opera, *Shanghai Huaiju zhi* 1998; for Shanghai opera, *Shanghai Huju zhi* 1999; and for Yue opera, *Shanghai Yueju zhi* 1997.

8. Gao 1991; and Ying 2003.

9. In a more general sense, I have benefited from reading a wide range of scholarship

on Chinese opera. In Japan, there are some very interesting studies of Chinese operas, such as those by scholars Tanaka Issei and Ōki Yasushi. See Tanaka 1985 and Ōki 1989. Although I occasionally draw on these works, I do not attempt to discuss these studies here mainly because most are concerned primarily with operas in history, while my focus is cultural history manifested in one particular opera.

A small number of works of history and comparative literature have recognized, to varying degrees, the importance of studying local operas as a means of gaining access to popular mentality and sociality in China. In his study of the Boxers, Esherick astutely noted the ways in which rebel heroes from opera repertoires provided local peasants with role models, as well as the inspiration to rebel, in a time of crisis (Esherick 1987), while Mackerras devoted a book to the social organizations of Beijing opera in the late eighteenth and nineteenth centuries (Mackerras 1972).

There is also a group of important articles scattered in various journals and collections, including Tanaka, "The Social and Historical Context of Ming-Ch'ing Local Drama" (1985); Ward, "Regional Operas and Their Audiences" (1985); Arkush, "Love and Marriage in North Chinese Peasant Operas" (1989); Bensen, "The Manipulation of *Tanci* in Radio Shanghai during the 1930s" (1995); Stock, "Huju and Musical Change" (1997); and Bender, "Shifting and Performance in Suzhou Chantefable" (1999).

Other modern scholars of Chinese culture and society have studied the Chinese elite's use of opera as a means of transmitting elite messages; see, for example, Hsiao-T'i Li, "Opera, Society, and Politics" (1996), and Hayford, *To the People* (1990), 127–32. Rebecca Karl used the case of Jingju reform in Shanghai in the 1900s to illustrate features of Chinese nationalism in the late Qing in *Staging the World* (2002), while Joshua Goldstein discussed the "nationalization" of Beijing opera in the Republican period in "Theatrical Imagi-nations" (1999a) and "Mei Lanfang and the Nationalization of Peking Opera, 1912–1930" (1999b).

10. My background as a Shanghai native made my investigations much smoother, as my interviews with Yue opera actresses and audience members were all conducted in various Shanghai versions of the Wu dialect of the Jiangnan region, which includes the northern part of Zhejiang, part of Jiangsu south of the Yangzi River, and Shanghai. My conversations with the Yue opera fan Li Jiang, from Beijing, were an exception, since she does not speak the Wu dialect although she understands it through her appreciation of Yue opera.

11. For research on the foreign settlements in Shanghai, see Xu and Qiu 1933; and *Shanghai gonggong zujie shigao* 1980. A classic work on Shanghai's development as a treaty-port city and its role in China's economic modernization is Murphey 1953.

12. Chen Zhengxiang 1970.

13. Tang 1989.

14. A 1996 exhibition of Republican posters in Shanghai included a picture of the movie star Li Lihua wearing a cheongsam made of mandarin blue cloth. A caption signed by Li reads: "Mandarin blue cloth is my favorite material for a dress" (*Liujin suiyue* 1996).

Another example pictured in Leo Lee's *Shanghai Modern* shows the movie star Ruan Lingyu in a mandarin blue cheongsam on the cover of the popular *Young Companion Pictorial* (Liangyou huabao), published in Shanghai in the 1930s and 1940s. See Lee 1999.

15. Zhang Gansheng 1991.

16. For a detailed discussion, see ibid. See also Link 1981.

17. Zhou Shoujuan, "Chatting about *Saturday*," quoted in Zheng Yimei 1987. *Saturday* was published from June 1914 to April 1916 and from March 1921 to February 1923.

18. Zhang Ailing 1943. Also in Zhang Ailing 1945, 56.

19. The hierarchy of theaters, audiences, and opera genres and troupes is discussed in detail in chapter 3.

20. For a detailed discussion of the connections among various popular-entertainment forms and popular literature, see Wei 1990, 264–71. For example, Wei wrote: "'Mandarin ducks and butterflies'–style fiction and authors were first staged in civil drama [*wenmingxi*]. Bao Tianxiao's *The Fall of the Plum Blossom* [Meihua luo] and *Orchid in a Deserted Valley* [Konggu lan] were staged by the Shanghai New Citizen Society in March 1914. Zhou Shoujuan published a review in *Shanghai Newspaper* [Shen bao], and even participated in the performance himself. Early film was in fact civil drama plays on screen. The three tycoon directors of the Mingxing Studio—Zhang Shichuan, Zheng Zhengqiu, and Zhou Jianyun—all had experience with civil drama. Actors of silent feature films produced in the early 1920s were almost all from civil-drama companies. During the middle and later years of the 1920s, many 'mandarin ducks and butterflies' fiction masterworks were made into films, including *Spirit of the Jade Pear* [Yulihun], *The Tide of Guangling* [Guangling chao], *Fantastic Marriage Bond* [Xiafeng qiyuan], *Orchid in a Deserted Valley*, *The Fall of Plum Blossom*, and *Flame on Honglian Monastery* [Huoshao Honglian Si]."

21. For one example, see Ma Weishi 1935.

22. "New drama" was also known as "civil drama" (*wenmingxi*).

23. Huayan Yigai, "All about *Tears and Laughter*." Quoted in Wei 1990, 103–4.

24. Yang Yi 1993, 335. The concept of Haipai, or Shanghai-style, culture is elusive and difficult to define, and much has been said about it since the 1930s when some Beijing-based elite writers led by Shen Congwen criticized the commercialization of Shanghai writers such as Shao Xunmei, Mu Shiying, and Shi Zhecun, labeling them "Haipai" writers. The term then became a pejorative description of things and styles of commercialized Shanghai until after the Cultural Revolution. In recent decades, with the rapid economic development of the city, the term "Haipai" has gained more prestige than it ever enjoyed, and a few serious scholarly works appeared to rectify Shanghai-style culture. For recent discussions on Shanghai-style literature and the Beijing-Shanghai debate in the 1930s, see Wu Fuhui 1995. Hanchao Lu also briefly discusses Shanghai style and its commercial, modern characteristics in comparison with "Beijing style" (Jingpai) as a more conservative, hinterland culture of China. See Hanchao Lu 1995. Other important works on the topic include Yang Dongping 1994; Yang Yi 1993; and Zhang Gansheng 1991.

25. Pickowicz 1993, 301. For Brooks's ideas on melodrama, referenced by Pickowicz,

see Peter Brooks, *The Melodramatic Imagination: Balzac, Henry James, Melodrama, and the Mode of Excess* (New York: Columbia University Press, 1985).

26. Pickowicz 1993, 301.

27. Link 1981, 8.

28. Ibid., 9.

29. Leo Lee has a passing discussion of this concept in his *Shanghai Modern*. See Lee 1999.

30. Li Zhi was the most prominent spokesperson for gender equality and intellectual-spiritual freedom within the Taizhou School. See Jin Jiang 2001.

31. For an English-language study of the scholar-beauty fiction of the seventeenth century, see Qingping Wang 1998.

32. Sometimes, parents also lived with the family. But unlike the traditional multigenerational, multifamily household, although grandparents could still live with a family, they were not the head of the household. In 1947, the average size of a Shanghai household was five, which was standard for Shanghai's nuclear or extended families. Chen Zhengxiang 1970.

33. Xu Dafeng 1939.

34. Pickowicz 1993.

35. Quoted in Gao Yilong 1991, 65.

36. Wang Changnian 1947, 202–11.

37. The population of "island" Shanghai tripled. Before the war broke out in 1937, the population in the foreign settlements was about 167 million, and it reached more than 4 million in late 1938 and 5 million in the early 1940s. See Shen, Jiang, and Zheng 1996, 120.

38. By the end of the war, Shanghai's population had dropped to around 300 million; it began to rise again after the war and reached 337 million by the end of 1945. See Chen Zhengxiang 1970.

39. Chen Qingsheng 1995; Ke 1994.

40. On intellectual attitudes toward the Japanese occupation, see Poshek Fu 1993.

41. See *Gaimushō kōbun*, no. 52189 (April 1, 1941) and no. 24719 (July 27, 1939).

42. See Ke 1994; and Tao Juyin 1979.

43. For example, Lu Xun's widow Xu Guangping and the left-wing intellectual Ke Ling were arrested and tortured by occupation forces.

44. *Gaimushō kōbun*, no. 55955 (July 17, 1942) and no. 56270 (July 28, 1942).

45. For a discussion of the wartime cinema in Shanghai, see Poshek Fu 2003. Also see Liu Qikui 1987 for discussions on cultural activities led by the Wang Jingwei collaboration government in wartime Shanghai.

46. Many critics as well as the political and intellectual elite interpret this saddened sensibility as a revival of the "mandarin ducks and butterflies" style of literature. My reading suggests, however, that wartime literature represents a deepened modern urban aesthetic more articulate than its "butterflies" predecessors and more grounded than that of the Modernists in the 1930s. For discussions on the "butterflies" style of spoken drama

in "island" Shanghai, see Zong Fei 1940; on the "butterflies" style of film, see Bai Mao 1940; and on the "butterflies" style of literature, drama, and film in occupied Shanghai, see She Ren 1943.

47. Women's Yue opera enlisted popular writers, including Yan Duhe and Zhou Shoujuan, to support and help establish its status in the city's booming popular-culture market. A chronicle of events reported in the tabloid *The Song of Yue* (Yue ou), for example, hints at the interaction between Yue opera actresses and writers of romantic fiction. On May 24, 1939, well-known drama critics attended Yao Shuijuan's performance of *Embroidering the Mandarin Ducks* (Xiu yuanyang). On May 31, "Shanghai's artists and drama critics, including Yan Duhe, Zhou Shoujuan, Wu Chengda, Huang Jiping, Luo Quyuan, Huang Yuzhai, and Master of the Plum Blossom House [Meihua Guanzhu], presented at the Tianxiang Theater and watched Yao Shuijuan's *Emerald Hairpin* [Biyu zan]." "In June," the tabloid reports, "Ma Zhanghua invited journalists for a banquet at Da Jiali Restaurant. With Mr. Fan Jugao invited on behalf of Ma Zhanghua, Misters Zhou Shoujuan, Hu Hanzhu, Wang Xuechen, Chen Xiaodie, Master of the Plum Blossom House, She Yu, Chen Chanweng, and Xu Zhuoai were in attendance." See *Yue ou*, vol. 1 (July 1, 1939).

48. While Zhang Ailing created a variety of female characters in her best-selling fiction, Su Qing, the period's foremost feminist writer, published two best-sellers in 1944: *Ten Years of My Married Life* (Jiehun shinian), an autobiographical novel describing the collapse of her marriage, and *A Collection of Essays from Huanjin* (Huanjin ji), which includes numerous essays reflecting on her life and related women's issues. In late 1942, Su Qing began publishing one of the period's most successful literary magazines, *Heaven and Earth* (Tiandi), which carried articles about women, men, love, marriage, family, women's rights, men's attitudes, food, housing, and travel. In 1944, *Miscellany* (Zazhi), a best-selling literary periodical, organized and later published a roundtable discussion by female writers, including Su Qing and Zhang Ailing. In March 1945, *Miscellany* featured a conversation between Zhang Ailing and Su Qing about women, family, and marriage. *Zazhi*, vol. 13, no. 6 (March 1944), and vol. 14, no. 6 (March 1945). For studies of women writers of the period, see Nicole Huang 1995; and Hamada 1993.

49. Su Qing 1944a, 1–4. Also in Su Qing 1995, 503–6.

50. *Zazhi*, vol. 13, no. 1 (April 10, 1944), 53.

51. Susan Glosser discusses the changing discourses of women and family in Republican China in *Chinese Visions of Family and State, 1915–1953* (Berkeley: University of California Press, 2003).

52. Zhang Ailing, "Huali Yuan," 1947. See Zhang Ailing 2006, 147–58.

53. Su Qing became a professional Yue opera playwright in the 1950s and created many Yue opera plays. *Shanghai Yueju zhi* 1997, 342–43.

54. As described in MacPherson 1998; and Zheng Wang 1999.

55. *Jingu qiguan* is a collection of stories handed down in the storytelling tradition of the late Ming dynasty. Compiled by Baoweng Laoren from Gusu (present-day Suzhou).

56. Zhang Ailing 1944. Quoted in Wei 1990, 35–36.

57. Tao Lanying 1943.

58. Hanchao Lu 1999; Hershatter 1997; Henriot 2001; Honig 1986, 1993; Mann 1994; Goodman 1995; Wakeman 1995; Lee 1999; Jones 2001; and Perry 1993.

1. *The Origins of Yue Opera*

1. The cult of *qing* prevailed in late Ming and early Qing intellectual discourse. See Ko 1994.

2. See Wang Xiaochuan 1958.

3. Ko, in her story about a late Ming woman poet, Huang Yuanjie, provides a succinct discussion of a pair of "age-old attributes for women: respectable/mean, defined according to a woman's distance from the family system." See Ko 1994, 119–23.

4. See Lu Xun's recollections of going to opera shows when he was a child visiting his grandmother in the Shaoxing countryside. Lu Xun 1922.

5. While the origins of the practice remain obscure, it is common knowledge that this had been the general practice since the eighteenth century. See Qi Rushan 1964, vol. 2: 7. Evidence indicates that there were some exceptions in the late nineteenth and early twentieth centuries. First, women began to appear in opera theaters as both performers and spectators in foreign settlements in treaty-port cities such as Shanghai and Tianjin in the late nineteenth century. Second, in the couple of years immediately after the Allied occupation of Beijing following the Boxer Rebellion in 1900, theaters in Beijing admitted women spectators in designated areas. And it is also possible that a few prestigious women might be admitted to semicommercial performances held in native-place facilities in urban centers.

6. Wang Xiaochuan 1958.

7. Private female troupes of rich household and inner court actresses were still allowed, but they were not involved in public commercial performances.

8. See Sun and Xu 1995; and Mackerras 1972.

9. *Pi* stands for *xipi*, and *huang* stands for *erhuang*—two local melodies from the area where Hubei, Jiangxi, and Anhui meet.

10. "Laolangmiao beiji" (Tablet of Laolang Temple) in Suzhou. *Jiangsu shen Ming-Qing yilai beike ziliao xuanji* (A collection of stone inscriptions in Jiangsu since the Ming and Qing dynasties). Quoted in Sun and Xu 1995.

11. Time and again, the Manchu court had banned Manchu officials from being involved with opera and opera performers. But these bans never seemed to last long, and the Manchu court was often the most generous patron of popular opera.

12. See Qi Rushan, "Tongzhi hou wushi nianjian Beiping hengyan jumu" (A list of plays often staged during the fifty years after 1883). In Qi Rushan 1964, vol. 4. The last three are stories from the popular Ming novel *Romance of the Three Kingdoms* (Sanguo yanyi).

13. Chinese opera scholars have done a great deal of research on numerous local operas

and their histories in the past two decades, including Wang Lin's work on *ping* opera in Tianjin (Wang Lin 1991), the work on Hebei clapper opera by Ma Longwen and Mao Dazhi (Ma and Mao 1982), Zeng Yongyi's work on boy-singers' opera in Taiwan and Fujian (Zeng 1988), and Luo Di's work on opera and Zhejiang (Luo Di 1991). Japanese and Western scholarship on Chinese opera and opera history has focused largely on Beijing opera and paid very little attention to other local operas and even less to folk operas. Except for a small number of articles and chapters, I am not aware of substantial research on the history of minor operas and local major operas other than Beijing opera outside Mainland China and Taiwan. Drawing on the example of Shengxian little opera, the forerunner of Yue opera, and an extensive reading of scholarly works in Chinese on various minor operas, I offer an overview of the origins and growth of minor operas in the late nineteenth and early twentieth centuries.

14. For dictionary definitions of *daxi* and *xiaoxi*, see *Zhongguo xiqu quyi cidian* 1981, 68.

15. For studies of *ping* opera and boy-singers' opera, see Hu Sha 1982; Wang Lin 1991; and Zeng Yongyi 1988.

16. On the transformation of *yangge* from a folk art to a modern drama in the 1940s in Shaanxi and other parts of the north, see Jack Chen 1949. For a discussion of *yangge* in Dingxian, Hebei, in the 1920s, which also describes some characteristics of *xiaoxi*, although the author seems unaware of this term, see Arkush 1989.

17. See Zhang Jishun 1992a.

18. Zhang Jishun 1992b.

19. On the official prohibition of minor operas, see Wang Xiaochuan 1958.

20. Qi Rushan, "Xijie xiao zhanggu" (Anecdotes of the opera circle). In Qi Rushan 1964, vol. 4: 86–88.

21. Mei Lanfang 1954, 128.

22. For details about Mei Lanfang's reforms, see Mei Lanfang 1954, 221; also see Xu Chengbei 1990.

23. Sanshiliu Yuanyang Guanzhu, "Ziyou lianai Zhuo Wenjun" (The free-love Zhuo Wenjun). In Xu Hansheng 1935, 8.

24. Zhang Dezhi, "Wo suo renshi de Cheng Yanqiu" (My understanding of Cheng Yanqiu). In *Cheng Yanqiu zhuanji* 1938.

25. See *Xiqu jingying* 1989, vol. 1; and *Zhongguo xiqu quyi cidian* 1981.

26. Mei Baojiu, the son of master Mei Lanfang, may be the only exception, as the PRC government strongly supported Mei Lanfang's desire to see his art carried on by his son. Brief information about these early female performers can be found in *Zhongguo xiqu quyi cidian* 1981.

27. *Zhongguo xiqu juzhong da cidian* 1995, 129–34, 44–54, 455–63.

28. Ibid., 18–19, 379–81, 129–34, 44–54, 455–63.

29. Ibid., 882–83, 1058–59, 1092–93. After 1949, as the PRC government devoted considerable energy and resources to salvaging disappearing Qing major operas, Beijing opera continued to enjoy its high political and cultural status, but it, too, survived only on government subsidies after the 1950s.

30. "Didu" was a phonetic imitation of the beep produced by knocking a small stick at a piece of wood to keep the rhythm for singing and acting in Shengxian little opera.

31. Xiao Wo, "Shaoxing diduban de jiantao" (A critique of *didu* opera from Shaoxing). In *"Shaoxing shangbao" liangzhounian jinian tekan* (A special issue for the second anniversary of *Shaoxing shangbao*), October 1935.

32. *Yue ou*, vol. 1 (July 1, 1939).

33. For more on *ping* opera, see Wang Lin 1991; and Hu Sha 1982.

34. Ma Chaoshui 1960.

35. Zhang Jishun 1992a.

36. In the *sigong* scale system, the primary key area is around the sixth and third notes of the scale, somewhat similar to A major in the Western system.

37. Ren Wensi 1992.

38. See Ma Chaoshui 1960.

39. Ibid.

40. Ma Chaoshui 1960; and Ren Wensi 1992.

41. Ma Chaoshui 1960.

42. Ma Chaoshui 1960; and Ren Wensi 1992.

43. Zhang Jishun 1992a.

44. *Zaoqi Yueju fazhan shi* 1983, 31. For more examples of stories about peasant life, see Zhang Jishun 1992a.

45. *Shanghai Yueju zhi* 1997, 135.

46. For a discussion of "precious volumes" (*baojuan*) and women's relationship to them, see Overmyer 1985.

47. Ding Yi 1992a. Also see *Zaoqi Yueju fazhan shi* 1983.

48. Ma Chaoshui 1960, 6.

49. Ibid., 7.

50. For a study of this elite idea, see Hsiao-T'i Li 1996.

51. Ma Chaoshui 1960, 5–6.

52. *Zaoqi Yueju fazhan shi* 1983, 48.

53. Ibid.

54. Ma Chaoshui 1960.

55. Ibid.

56. Ibid. Also see Qian Yonglin 1992; and *Zaoqi Yueju fazhan shi* 1983.

57. For details, see *Zaoqi Yueju fazhan shi* 1983.

58. *Liang Shanbo and Zhu Yingtai* has been known internationally as *The Butterfly Lovers* since the 1950s, after the Yue opera play's international tour and the release of the color film of the same title in 1953.

59. She Huimin 1992.

60. Ma Chaoshui 1960.

61. She Huimin 1992.

62. This discussion of the butterfly story draws upon a variety of opera and story-

telling scripts. See these titles, which all begin with "Liang Shanbo," in the references section.

63. Lu Gong and Ding Yi believe that the tale is in Zhang Du's *Collections of the Xuanshi Studio* (Xuanshi zhi), of the Tang dynasty. I cannot find the tale in that book and suspect the record may have a later date. The story, however, does make sense. Minister Xie An, a native of Shangyu, retired to his hometown, which was only seven miles away from the Zhu Family Village. Xie was known for teaching literature to his niece, the famous poet Xie Daoyun, which might explain Xie An's interest in the legend of Zhu Yingtai. See Lu Gong 1955, 10; and Ding Yi 1992b.

64. See Lu Gong 1955, 10–11.

65. Early versions of the play were based on the Buddhist idea of retribution and reincarnation, a framework inherited from oral traditions within folk culture. Liang Shanbo and Zhu Yingtai, as the play and other folk traditions had it, were in fact reincarnations of Golden Boy and Jade Girl, who served the Jade Emperor in his heavenly court. The two had fallen in love with each other at a party given by the Heavenly Empress (Wangmu Niangniang) and had accidentally broken the Glazed Cup. The angry Jade Emperor punished them by sending them down to suffer three lives on earth (in some versions, they have seven lives), separated from each other and devastated by lovesickness. According to this framework, Liang Shanbo and Zhu Yingtai were the last incarnations of Golden Boy and Jade Girl. After Zhu Yingtai and Ma Wencai jump into Liang Shanbo's grave, the three take their dispute to the court of the King of the Underworld (Yanluo Wang). Checking his *Book of Life and Death* (Shengsi bu), the king discovers the true identities of Liang and Zhu and sends them to the Jade Emperor, as they have now completed their three incarnations on earth. Ma Wencai is sent back to earth, where he happily marries his predestined bride. *Liuyin ji* [1930s?]; and *Liang Shanbo baojuan* 1924. Also see Ding Yi 1992b.

66. Ding Yi 1992b.

67. *Zaoqi Yueju fazhan shi* 1983.

68. *Shanghai Yueju zhi* 1997, 2.

69. Quoted in Zhou Huiling 1996.

70. For a discussion of Shanghai's entertainment market in the late nineteenth century, see Luo Suwen 1993.

71. For a discussion of cross-gender performance and performers in ancient China, see Zeng Yongyi 1976.

72. For a discussion of gender and performance in early Republican China, see Zhou Huiling 1996.

73. Zhang Faying 2002, 206–10.

74. For details on all-girls opera in the Jiangnan region, see Luo Suwen 2005.

75. In 1916, Zhang Zaiyang, a Shengxian native who became governor of Zhejiang in 1922, organized an all-girls Beijing opera troupe in Hangzhou, the provincial capital. When he brought the troupe back to his hometown, Chongren, to celebrate his father-

in-law's birthday, the rural town was astir with excitement. The governor's patronage of all-girls opera may have encouraged other Shengxian natives to organize their own all-girls troupes. *Zaoqi Yueju fazhan shi* 1983.

76. This account of the first girls' training school in Shi's Village is based largely on Jin Xiangyin 1992; *Zaoqi Yueju fazhan shi* 1983; and research at the Yue Opera Museum in Shengxian in 1995.

77. Wang was not a native of Shi's Village but came to live with his wife's family. His status might have given him less credibility than a native villager would have enjoyed in the same circumstances. It is not clear whether or not his sojourn in Shanghai added to or reduced his credibility in the eyes of the villagers. See Jin Xiangyin 1992.

78. Ibid.

79. Ibid.

80. Ibid.

81. Ibid.

82. Ibid.

83. The decline of all-girls Beijing opera and the rise of girls' Shengxian opera were captured in a book published in 1928, titled *Hangsu yifeng buji* (Supplement to *Old Folk Customs in Hangzhou*). Quoted in Jin Xiangyin 1992, 62.

84. *Shaoxing wanbao* July 1, 1935. Quoted in Jin Xiangyin 1992, 62.

85. Jin Xiangyin 1992.

86. See *Zhejiang sheng nongcun diaocha* 1934; and *Shaoxing shangbao niankan* 1935.

87. An article in a local newspaper reads: "Why is *didu* opera developing so well at a time of rural bankruptcy? . . . Peasant women in general have no work to do because of the decline of sericulture in the countryside, . . . and this is why there are so many *didu* opera troupes nowadays." Quoted in Gao Yilong 1991, 57.

88. See *Zaoqi Yueju fazhan shi* 1983.

89. *Xinwen bao*, entertainment advertisement pages, 1930s. Also, interview with Zhang Rongbiao and Zhang Yanqiu, 1995.

2. *The Rise of Feminine Opera*

1. This was a way of saying that she did not have a sexual relationship with her director, thus of defending herself against Zhang Chunfan's accusation. *Xinwen bao*, December 21, 1947.

2. He 1935, 34.

3. Ko 1994, 119–23. See chapter 1, note 3.

4. A specific example is that of Li Xiangjun, the courtesan heroine in Kong Shangren's renowned seventeenth-century drama *Peach Blossom Fan* (Taohua shan). Other courtesans in traditional literature who kept their bodily purity for their loved ones include Li Wa and Du Shiniang, among many others.

5. Cheng 1996.

6. Even getting married could hurt an actress's popularity. Several retired Yue opera

actresses I interviewed in Shanghai in 1995 and 1996 told me that fans did not like their favorite actresses to be married or have affairs with men, and the careers of many well-known actresses went downhill after they married. There are also many whispers about homosexual relationships among Yue opera practitioners and audience members, and those affairs also hurt the actresses involved. In these cases, it seems that what mattered was the fact that an actress was taken away from the public by an individual.

7. For a discussion of this reformist discourse on theatrical reform, see Hsiao-T'i Li 1996. For studies of Shanghai prostitutes and the discursive formations of the concept of "prostitutes" (*jinü*) in the Republican period, see Hershatter 1997, part 2.

8. The conception of victimized Chinese women advocated by May Fourth New Culture intellectuals continues to dominate various understandings of Chinese women up to the present time. Dorothy Ko was among the first to challenge this May Fourth discourse. Ko 1994, "Introduction." More recently, Wendy Larson offered in-depth analyses of how the female body was made to carry various meanings for male elite discourse in the early Republican period. See Larson 1998.

9. Hsiao-T'i Li discusses the intellectuals' use of Beijing opera as a means of imparting reform ideas to the masses. See Hsiao-T'i Li 1996.

10. For detailed examination of the reformist construction of the idea of the prostitute, see Hershatter 1997, part 2.

11. A popular Chinese folk tale about Lady Meng Jiang is representative of a large repertoire of folk stories with similar plots and images. Lady Meng Jiang's husband was drafted by the First Emperor to build the Great Wall and never returned. He was believed to have been buried underneath the Wall. Lady Meng Jiang was so sad that she wept day and night beside the Great Wall for forty-nine days. Her endless tears flowed like a river and eventually brought down the Wall.

12. He 1935.

13. Ibid.

14. See Cai's scrolls for Ruan Lingyu's funeral in He et al. 1986, 46; and Lu Xun 1935.

15. For a representative publication about the making of Beijing opera into a "national opera," see Yu Shangyuan 1927; and Qi Rushan 1964, vol. 3: "Guoju gailun."

16. The following brief account of life in an all-girls training school and a school that became a company is based on a variety of sources, including *Xuesheng jinian kan* 1946; *Fanghua jukan* 1947; *Yueju suyuan* 1992; and *Zaoqi Yueju fazhan shi* 1983. I also relied on my 1995 and 1996 interviews with many retired actresses, including Zhang Rongbiao, Zhang Yanqiu, Xiao-Bai Yumei, Yuan Xuefen, Fu Quanxiang, and Xu Yulan.

17. *Shanghai Yueju zhi* 1995, vol. 1.

18. In her heyday, Yao Shuijuan, a Yue opera star, bought a lease of the Queen's Great Theater with the help of her wealthy patron Wei Jinshan, manager of the Zhonghui bank owned by Du Yuesheng, and operated it for a short period of time.

19. Yuan Xuefen attended the village primary school for one or two years and achieved basic literacy, while Zhu Shuizhao had a primary-school education, but they were unusual among Yue opera actresses. *Xuesheng jinian kan* 1946; and *Fanghua jukan* 1947.

20. This account of the professional and personal lives of Yue opera actresses in Shanghai is based largely on a variety of sources, including *Xuesheng jinian kan* 1946 and *Fanghua jukan* 1947, as well as interviews in 1995 and 1996 with many retired actresses, including Zhang Rongbiao, Zhang Yanqiu, Xiao-Bai Yumei, Yuan Xuefen, Fu Quanxiang, and Xu Yulan.

21. Interviews with Xiao-Bai Yumei, 1995, 1996, and with Wei Shaochang, 1996.

22. Lu Xun 1935.

23. Interviews with the witness Yuan Xuefen and Fu Quanxiang. Partly for his involvement with Ma's death, Lu was executed for being "counter revolutionary" by the PRC government in 1951. *Shanghai Yueju zhi* 1997, 362.

24. Zhang and Gao 1984.

25. Yuan 1994, 63.

26. Yuan 2002, 6.

27. Ibid., 7; and Yuan 1983, 59–61.

28. *Danghu chuan* [1920s?].

29. See *He Wenxiu* and *A Pair of Phoenix Jade Clasp* (Yu lianhuan), in *Suqu*. In *The Butterfly Lovers*, I found, for example, several obscene jokes in a piece sung by the first generation of women actors of Shengxian opera in the early 1930s. *Shengxianxi jijing* 1996.

30. *Sanxiao yinyuan* 1930s, 18.

31. Another example is in *Xiang Hudie* mid-1940s, 28–36.

32. Both Shengxian and Yuyao were part of Shaoxing Prefecture.

33. *Shaoxingxi bao*, March 13, 1941.

34. Two aspects contributed to the historical transition of Yue opera from all-male to all-female. First, the institution of the all-girls opera schools blossomed in Shengxian and adjacent counties in the early 1930s, as discussed in chapter 1. And the second was the artistic aspect of this transition, discussed here.

35. Xiao Wo, "Shaoxing diduban de jiantao" (A critique of Shaoxing *didu* opera). In *Shaoxing shangbao liangzhounian jinian tekan*, October 1935.

36. As discussed in "Introduction: Opera, Gender, and the City," in this volume, Hollywood's love melodramas were popular in Shanghai in the 1920s and 1930s, before the rise of women's Yue opera. Most Yue opera actresses active in the 1930s and 1940s, including Yuan Xuefen, Fu Quanxiang, and Xiao Dangui, were known to be admirers and eager students of Hollywood movies, and many Yue opera audience members were also moviegoers. Moreover, Hollywood style had a significant impact on Chinese film and theatrical arts. Paul Pickowicz has pointed out the relationship between Hollywood films and Chinese left-wing films; see Pickowicz 1993.

37. Xiao Wo, "Shaoxing diduban de jiantao" (A critique of Shaoxing *didu* opera). In *Shaoxing shangbao liangzhounian jinian tekan*, October 1935.

38. Zhang Linghui 1977.

39. *Shaoxingxi bao*, March 14, 1941.

40. Interviews with Xiao-Bai Yumei, Fu Quanxiang, and Xu Yulan, 1995, 1996.

41. Fan Li and Wen Zhong are both pseudonyms, pronounced the same as the names of the two ministers of the ancient Yue state [present-day Zhejiang] who helped the king of Yue rebound from a total defeat at the hands of the king of Wu and regain glory and power. The adoption of these names by the two modern Zhejiang natives was clearly a gesture of resistance against Japan and showed their intention to help establish their native opera in Shanghai. Fan Li's first script is indeed the patriotic *Hua Mulan*, which is discussed later in this chapter.

42. Yuan Xuefen 1983, 60.

43. Ibid.

44. Interview with Yuan Xuefen, 1995. Also see Yuan Xuefen 1983, 60–61. Zhang and Gao 1984.

45. *Shanghai chunqiu* 1948. Also see *Zhongguo xiqu quyi cidian* 1981, 64–65.

46. Interview with Han Yi, 2002.

47. Yuan Xuefen 1983, 60–61.

48. Fan Ruijuan 1994, 357.

49. For an extensive description of the spoken-drama movement and resistance to the Japanese invasion, see Hung 1994.

50. For a description of the spoken-drama movement in "island" Shanghai during the Japanese occupation, see Ke 1994, vol. 2.

51. Han Yi's story is based on interviews conducted in Shanghai in summer 2002.

52. *Xuesheng jinian kan* 1946, 20.

53. Ibid.; interviews with Cheng Rong, 1995; also see Cheng Rong's essay in Gao and Lu 1994, 385–92.

54. Note that the Soviet Union and Japan were not at war until August 1945, when the Red Army entered Japanese-occupied Manchuria after the United States dropped an atomic bomb on Hiroshima. Soviet Union Radio did not cease operating in Shanghai till sometime during the postwar period.

55. *Xuesheng jinian kan* 1946; interview with Chen Shulian, 1995.

56. Gao and Lu 1994, 176–205.

57. Fan Ruijuan 1994, 361.

58. Zhang Guifeng 1982. In Chinese operas, the clown is an important supporting role that can be used to portray many different characters and make them somewhat comic.

59. *Xuesheng jinian kan* 1946; Fan Ruijuan 1994; and other articles in Gao and Lu 1994.

60. Zheng Chuanjian, a veteran Kun opera performer who became the choreographer for a number of Yue opera companies in the 1940s, taught Yue opera actresses Kun opera dance and helped design many famous Yue opera dance pieces.

61. See *Shanghai Yueju zhi* 1997, 76–80; also see *Fanghua jukan* 1947.

62. The emphasis on Mulan being a filial daughter and a loyal general at the same time probably began as early as the Tang dynasty, as seen in Wei Yuanfu's poem about Mulan, quoted in Liu Wanzhang 1940.

63. *The China Press*, September 11, 1938. Reproduced in a photograph in Wei Shaochang 1995.

64. The top CCP leader, Zhou Enlai, attended Yuan's performance, while influential intellectuals such as Tian Han and Hong Shen attended Xu Yulan's performance. See *Shanghai Yueju zhi* 1995, vol. 2: 17.

65. *Xuesheng jinian kan* 1946, 48, 171–72.

66. *Shanghai Yueju zhi* 1997, 163–64.

67. Bai Yushuang was famous for her bold erotic performances, and her performances in Shanghai in the mid-1930s, including the original *Widow Ma's Inn*, caused a sensation and established her superstar status in *ping* opera. The Yue opera *Widow Ma's Inn* was adapted from *ping* opera.

68. *Yueju huabao*, January 12, 1941.

69. Interview with Wu Ping, 1996.

70. Di Renjie (630–700) was a high official in the Tang dynasty who served during the reigns of Emperor Gao Zong and Empress Wu Zetian. *Cihai* 1989, 923.

71. *Widow Ma's Inn* is much more than an erotic play. In fact, the seduction scene is the only erotic scene in the entire play. The play and Xiao's performance are discussed in chapter 6.

72. *Record of Retributions* is sometimes also titled *Mrs. Diao* (Diao Liu shi). *Shengxianxi jijing* 1996, 154–56.

73. Although the Nationalist Shanghai municipal government did take action against more modern entertainment places such as dance halls toward the end of its rule, it did not have the will or the resources to check on the numerous local operas that were put on every day in large and small theaters across Shanghai.

74. Wendy Larson makes a similar argument that the traditional framework of gender relations continued to dominate the discourse of women's liberation in the early Republican period. See Larson 1998.

75. Xu Jin 1947.

76. *Xinmin wanbao*, August 22, 1947.

77. *Fanghua jukan* 1947.

78. Yue Jia 1992.

79. In its details, this act seems not very different from the 1930s audio recording. While the singing by two male actors in the recording sounds a bit faster and coarse, the lyrics, dramatic turns, and scenes are rather similar. Another recording made in the late 1930s by two actresses shows a similar situation. *Shengxianxi jijing* 1996, 58–59, 99–100.

80. *Xuesheng jinian kan* 1946, 53, 172–73.

81. Ibid., 173.

82. Ibid., 53, 172–73.

83. Fan Ruijuan 1989.

84. Ibid.

85. *Shanghai Yueju zhi* 1995, vol. 1: 59, 62.

86. *Shanghai Yueju zhi* 1997.

3. *Patrons and Patronage*

1. My take on the Shanghai middle class is in agreement with that of such scholars as Wen-hsin Yeh and Hanchao Lu. Yeh discussed the "petty urbanites" as the middle and lower-middle class in Republican Shanghai, while Lu regarded as middle class all the residents of *shikumen*, the three-story townhouses built on narrow lanes that led off the main roads. Indeed, the majority of Yue opera audience members were "petty urbanites" living mostly in such houses regardless of their occupation and gender. See Wen-hsin Yeh 1992; and Hanchao Lu 1999.

2. *Zhongguo xiqu quyi cidian* 1981, 65.

3. Interviews with Han Yi, 2002.

4. Quoted in Luo Suwen 1993.

5. Chen Fengyuan 1939, 39.

6. *Shanghai chunqiu* 1948, vol. 2: 58.

7. See *Shanghai Yueju zhi* 1995, vol. 4: 6–19.

8. Ibid.

9. Interviews with Zhang Rongbiao and Zhang Yanqiu, November 1995.

10. Interviews with Xiao-Bai Yumei, 1995–96.

11. *Shaoxingxi bao*, March 14, 1941.

12. Interviews with Cheng Rong, 2002.

13. Interviews with Han Yi, 2002.

14. The stratification of audiences for various local operas was embedded in native-place sociology, which is discussed in the next section.

15. Interview with Dai Xinghuang, 2001.

16. Chen Zhengxiang 1970.

17. For extensive studies on native bonds and organizations in large cities, see Goodman 1995; and Rowe 1989.

18. For a discussion of native-place politics and discrimination against Subei natives in Shanghai, see Honig 1993, 1986.

19. Zhu, Hu, and Xu 1939, 166.

20. See Honig 1986.

21. See Honig 1986, 1993.

22. Zhu, Hu, and Xu 1939.

23. Shanghai Tebieshi Gongyongju 1943, 14.

24. For detailed discussions of Ningbo-Shaoxing immigrants and their economic power in Shanghai, see Susan Mann Jones 1974; Mann 1984; Goodman 1995; and Cole 1986.

25. See *Sekko zaibatsu*, October 15, 1929; and Yamagami 1937. Also see Goodman 1995; and Susan Mann Jones 1974.

26. "Shanhai ni okeru sensōgyo no jōkyō" 1941.

27. See *Cibai* 1989; and *Shengxian zhi* 1989, 584.

28. See Tang 1989, 800; and Shen, Jiang, Zheng 1996, vol. 2: 130.

29. *Shanghai Yueju zhi* 1995, vol. 2: 104–5. *Shaoxingxi bao*, February 2, 1941.

30. Quoted in Wei 1989, 5.

31. Chen Xi 1941.

32. Republican Shanghai's factory workers represented a new industrial class that enjoyed relatively stable wages and generally earned more than junior white-collar workers and clerks as well as lower-class laborers and domestic servants. Many of them, as Haochao Lu argued, earned wages that easily placed them in the ranks of the lower to middle class. See Hanchao Lu 1999.

33. Zhu, Hu, and Xu 1939. According to Zhang Qi, a respected authority on the communist labor movement, the Chinese Communist Party sponsored the book project. Party and labor movement leaders in Shanghai, including Liu Changsheng, Liu Ningyi, Ma Chungu, and Zhang Qi, organized the investigations and the writing of the book; the communist historian Gu Zhun conducted the final editing. Zhu Bangxing, Hu Lin'ge, and Xu Sheng were fictitious names, and the Yuandong Publishing House in Hong Kong was simply a fabrication. The book was actually printed in Shanghai. Chapters were written by communist labor movement cadres who penetrated various industries as ordinary workers and gained firsthand knowledge of the conditions. The project's purpose was to provide the CCP with data on which it would develop its labor movement guidelines. See Zhang Qi 1984.

34. Ibid., 31, 125, 179.

35. For a detailed study of female cotton-mill workers in Shanghai, see Honig 1986.

36. In comparison, in 1939, the retail price for rice was ¥0.12 per *jin* (1 *jin* = 0.5 kilogram or 1.1023 pound); ¥0.92 for each cake of soap; ¥0.426 for each *jin* of cooking oil; and ¥0.131 for each *chi* (1 *chi* = 1.0936 feet) of cloth. *Shanghai jiefang qianhou wujia ziliao huibian* 1958, 89. These statistics and those that follow cannot be taken as absolutely accurate, given the severe inflation of the late 1930s and possible errors in the sources, which are almost impossible to verify. The numbers, however, do provide a general sense of the economics of viewing opera.

37. Zhu, Hu, and Xu 1939, 95–96.

38. Ibid., 7.

39. Ibid., 180.

40. Ibid., 125.

41. Ibid., 123, 130–33, 186–87.

42. *Yue ou* 1939, vol. 4 (December). Also, according to Xiao-Bai Yumei, who performed at the New World during the late 1930s, Yue opera was one of the most popular local operas performed there. Within the small theater where Yue opera was staged, several rows of benches were placed in front of the stage with a rope closing off the area. Spectators paid an entrance fee of twenty-five cents at the door. Those who paid another forty cents to the Yue opera company were seated on the benches and served tea and a hot-pressed towel, while those who chose to stand and view the performance from behind the closed area did not have to pay the extra fee. Yue opera usually had afternoon shows

and evening shows. During the interim, the stage was taken over by comic shows in local Shanghai dialect. Interviews with Xiao-Bai Yumei, 1995–96.

43. Chen Fengyuan 1939, 39.

44. Zhu, Hu, and Xu 1939, 95–96.

45. Interviews with Wei Shaochang, 1996.

46. Wei Shaochang edited *Shaoxing Opera Daily*, *The Song of Yue* (Yue ou), and *Yue Opera Pictorial* (Yueju huabao) in the late 1930s and early 1940s.

47. Interview with Wu Ping, 1996.

48. Interviews with Cheng Rong, 1995.

49. For a discussion on Ningbo women's domesticity, see Mann 1994.

50. Interview with Zhang Xingzhou, 1996.

51. Zhu, Hu, and Xu 1939, 699–719.

52. The highest and lowest figures in the statistics have been discounted. Shanghai Tebieshi Gongyongju 1941, 29–30.

53. Zhu, Hu, and Xu 1939, 700.

54. Interview with Wu Ping, 1996. Wen-hsin Yeh also describes the everyday lives of white-collar employees and their sense of modernity in her essay on Shanghai's China Bank. See Wen-hsin Yeh 1995.

55. Round-table discussion by women writers in *Zazhi*, vol. 13, no. 3 (April 1944): 55. Here and there in her writings, Su Qing also mentioned her mother, relatives, and herself attending Yue opera.

56. Interviews with Teng Jiazhen and Song Zhiyou, 1996.

57. Interview with Chen Shulian, 1995.

58. *Yueju bao*, December 5, 1948.

59. Ibid., July 24, 1949.

60. See Zhang Ailing's work of the 1940s. Zhang Zijing, Zhang Ailing's younger brother, also described his father's and stepmother's decadent lifestyle in his memoir. See Zhang Zijing 1996.

61. For an extensive description of courtesans' involvement with actors in early twentieth-century Shanghai, see Hershatter 1997.

62. Other actresses I interviewed did not dispute Xiao-Bai's account of her father's morality.

63. Interviews with Xiao-Bai Yumei, 1995–96.

64. Hershatter describes liaisons between courtesans and actors as a widespread practice in the early twentieth century. Yet, courtesans often married their rich customers, with many carrying their old habit of flirting with actors into their married lives, as in the case of Lin Daiyu, the famous courtesan who adopted the name of the heroine of *Dream of the Red Chamber*. Hershatter 1997, 116–17, 149–50.

65. Interviews with Xiao-Bai Yumei, 1995–96.

66. Actresses certainly did engage in sexual relations, with theater bosses or audience members, and some got married. The operagoing public and potential patrons usually

lost interest in married actresses, as if they were then no longer available. For reasons discussed in this chapter and in greater detail in chapter 2, married actresses inevitably lost their popularity. Many popular actresses thus chose to remain single until their early thirties, very late given the marriage conventions of the time.

67. Wei Shaochang, whose parents were patrons of Yao Shuijuan, attributed Yao's rise in part to this circumstance: "The fact that there were only actresses backstage facilitated the development of adoptive mother and sworn sister relationships between actresses and rich patrons." Wei 1982, 95.

68. Adoptive family relations—such as adoptive mother, father, brother, and sister—were commonly known in traditional Chinese society. In northern China, an adoptive mother was dubbed *gan ma* and an adoptive father was called *gan die*; in the Yangzi River delta, the terms were *guofang xiang* for an adoptive mother and *guofang ye* for an adoptive father. This practice was especially popular among gangsters and underworld organizations in modern periods. The women's Yue opera practice may be seen as an indication of the circle's involvement with gangsters, an inevitable and frequent phenomenon for lowbrow entertainment genres of the time. But just as adoptive relationships were not unknown among the general population, adoptive relationships in women's Yue opera did not necessarily have gangster connections.

69. Interviews with actresses and fans of Yue opera, 1995–96.

70. Usually, one performance for one charity project, although on rare occasions, the actress would perform twice.

71. Interviews with Xiao-Bai Yumei, 1995–96. *Mma* means "mother" in Shanghai dialect.

72. *Shaoxingxi bao*, February 3, 1941.

73. *Yue ou* 1939, vol. 1 (July).

74. Xiao Dangui was the only other actress who nominally had her own theater in the mid-1940s, although it was controlled by Zhang Chunfan.

75. *Yao Shuijuan zhuanji* 1939.

76. Interview with Wei Shaochang, 1996.

77. *Banyue xiju*, vol. 3, issue 2 (December 5, 1940). Cited in Wei 1989, 4.

78. Wei 1989, 4.

79. Interview with Gao Jin, 1996. Interview with Dai Xinghuang, 2001. Dai was at that time the head of the company for which Gao Jin was the top actress.

80. *Yueju bao*, August 4, 1946.

81. Interviews with Xiao-Bai Yumei, 1995–96.

82. Zhao Xiaosi 1994, 155, 161–64, 198–99.

83. *Xuesheng jinian kan* 1946, 153–54.

84. Interviews with Cheng Rong, 2002.

85. Ibid.

86. Interview with Zhou Baokui, 1996. While leading actresses were equipped with gorgeous paraphernalia and costumes and performed earnestly, the rest of the team was not as well equipped and often less enthusiastic in their performance. This began to change

only after 1949, when the state took control of performing arts and demanded that every actor take his or her role seriously in order to raise production values overall.

87. The same can also be said of other popular-entertainment forms, including Suzhou story-singing, Shanghai opera, Beijing opera, and, later, comic shows in Shanghai dialect. For a discussion of Suzhou story-singing on the radio, see Bensen 1995.

88. Ibid. For a history of radio in Shanghai, see *Shanghai yanjiu ziliao xuji* 1937, 563–67.

89. For a discussion of life in Republican Shanghai, see Hanchao Lu 1995.

90. The *huqin* is a two-string instrument played with a bow. Interview with Wu Ping, 1996.

91. *Shanghai Yueju zhi* 1995, vol. 5: 44.

92. *Yueju zhuankan* 1940.

93. Suzhou story-singing, Shanghai opera, Beijing opera, and comic shows also contracted with radio stations for live broadcast programs. Hours and deals varied with individual cases.

94. Shi 1939.

95. Qiu Wenguang 1985.

96. *Shanghai Yueju zhi* 1995, vol. 5: 104.

97. These recordings are hard to find today but, fortunately, are available in the Audio and Video Division of the Shanghai Municipal Library. The recordings did what radio could not do—provided faithful historical records of the development of Yue opera during that period. *Shengxianxi jijing* 1996.

98. The Shanghai Yiming Publishing House (Shanghai Yimin Shuju) printed and distributed many Yue opera lyric handbooks in the 1930s and 1940s from several locations in residential lanes. *Fragrant Butterflies* (Xiang hudie), for example, was distributed from K22 Chengxing Lane, Paike Road, while *Marriage as a Result of Three Smiles* was printed on East Xihua Road across Zhaofeng Road in Hongkou. See *Xiang hudie* mid-1940s; and *Sanxiao yinyuan* 1930s.

99. Interviews with Cheng Rong, 1995.

100. Unfortunately, her son set all of her collections, several suitcases of playbills and lyric books, on fire during the Cultural Revolution, in response to the campaign of cleaning the "four old traditions"—old thinking, old habits, old customs, and old traditions. Interview with Wu Ping, 1996.

101. *Shanghai yanjiu ziliao xuji* 1937, 533.

102. Wang Changnian 1947, 203–7; *Shanghai zhi* 1946, 131–37.

103. *Shanghai geming wenhua dashi ji* 1991, 249–50; and Zhang and Gao 1984, 173.

104. Xiao Yueying 1983, 258.

105. *Shanghai Yueju zhi* 1995, vol. 4: 100.

106. Today's digital technology seems to be coming to Yue opera's aid. CDs, video compact discs (VCDs), and DVDs help maintain a sizable basic audience at a time when live performances have been cut to the minimum.

4. *Staging in the Public Arena*

1. *Shijie chenbao*, May 7, 1946; and *Xinmin bao*, May 7, 1946. Quoted in *Xuesheng jinian kan* 1946, 186.

2. *Xinmin bao*, May 7, 1946. Quoted in *Xuesheng jinian kan* 1946, 186.

3. *Shanghai geming wenhua dashi ji* 1991, 167, 169.

4. Ibid., 187.

5. Ibid., 218, 281.

6. Ibid., 169.

7. Ibid., 10, 169, 187–88.

8. The owner of *Wenhui Daily* invited Chu Yukun, a CCP member, to be editor in chief, and the paper resumed publication on August 18, 1945. The Shanghai *Dagong Daily*'s editor in chief was Xu Zhucheng, a CCP member and former editor in chief of *Wenhui Daily*. *Dagong Daily* resumed operations on November 11, 1945. See *Shanghai geming wenhua dashi ji* 1991, 166.

9. Zhang and Gao 1984, 110.

10. Yue opera researcher Gao Yilong provided me with an introduction to Ding, whom I interviewed in February 1996. For Ding's book, see Ding Ying 1946.

11. Ding Jingtang 1995.

12. In fact, there was very little organized resistance in occupied Shanghai, except for some Nationalist intelligence forces carrying out special tasks, such as assassinating important collaborators.

13. The journal was published by the son and daughter-in-law of Liu Chenggan, a famous book collector from Wuxing, Jiangsu. See Ding Jingtang 1982.

14. Ibid.

15. Ibid.

16. Ding Jingtang 1995.

17. Ibid.

18. Zhang and Gao 1984.

19. *Shishi xinbao*, April 28, 1946.

20. *Shishi xinbao*, May 10, 1946. Quoted in *Xuesheng jinian kan* 1946, 186.

21. *Shishi xinbao*, May 17, 1946.

22. *Wenhui bao*, May 9, 1946.

23. *Shijie chenbao*, May 8, 1946. The 1946 production of the Yue opera *Sister Xianglin* adds the thread of a love story between Sister Xianglin and the son of the Lu family, Ah Niu. The two are childhood sweethearts, but class difference and the arranged marriage system make it impossible for them to be married. As discussed in chapter 2, it was a common practice of the New Yue Opera reforms to add a love story to patriotic or socially meaningful plays so as to cater to the tastes of the Yue opera audience. Yuan Xuefen and Nan Wei consulted with Xu Guangping, and a supportive Xu gave her consent to this addition. Left-wing intellectuals such as Tian Han also expressed understanding of the necessity of this addition. All agreed, however, that the addition was trivial at best and

distorted the spirit of Lu Xun's original story at worst. In subsequent revisions and restagings of the play during the PRC period, the love story was taken out completely. See *Xianglin sao* 1949; *Xuesheng jinian kan* 1946, 137; and *Xianglin sao* 1978.

24. *Xinwen bao*, October 28, 1946.

25. Tian Han, "Juyi dazhonghua zhi lu," *Zhou bao* 1946, vol. 38 (May 25).

26. *Shanghai geming wenhua dashi ji* 1991, 206–7. Also quoted in *Shanghai Yueju zhi* 1997, 313; and Zhang and Gao 1984, 135.

27. *Shanghai geming wenhua dashi ji* 1991, 180–81. Also quoted in *Shanghai Yueju zhi* 1997, 313; and Zhang and Gao 1984, 135.

28. Interview with Xu Yulan, 1995. Also see Zhang and Gao 1984.

29. Interview with Fu Quanxiang, 1995.

30. *Shanghai Yueju zhi* 1995, vol. 2: 41–42; Yin 1982, 16; and Zhang and Gao 1984, 126–27.

31. Interviews with Fu Quanxiang, Xiao-Bai Yumei, and Xu Yulan, 1995–96. A contemporaneous joke in Shanghai teased Shengxian natives for having two distinctive local products: Shengxian opera and Shengxian hooligans. The Shengxian hooligans, according to the actress Zhou Baokui, were really just country folks with loud voices, a coarse manner, and an eagerness to resort to physical fights. Interview with Zhou Baokui, 1996. For a brief discussion of Shengxian hooligans in Shanghai and their relationship with Shengxian opera, see Cole 1986.

32. *Dagong bao*, August 29, 1946.

33. *Shijie chenbao*, September 11, 1946; *Xinmin wanbao*, September 18, 1946.

34. *Shen bao*, September 11, 1946.

35. *Shijie chenbao*, September 11, 1946.

36. Zhang and Gao 1984, 129–30.

37. Ibid., 128.

38. *Zhongyang ribao: Shanghai ban*, September 15, 1946.

39. See advertisement in *Xinwen bao*, October 10, 1946.

40. See Zhang and Gao 1984, 131.

41. Interviews with Cheng Rong, 2002.

42. On January 5, 1947, Yuan Xuefen published "Words Before My Retirement" in *The New Citizen Evening News*. Quoted in Zhang and Gao 1984, 137–38.

43. Yuan Xuefen complained that she was the only one who conscientiously pursued Yue opera reform and that other actresses simply followed suit without understanding the true meaning of reform. Interview with Yuan Xuefen, 1995.

44. Ibid.

45. *Xinwen bao*, January 6, 1947.

46. Quoted in Zhang and Gao 1984, 145–46.

47. The theater employees revolted against the management, but their request for a raise was firmly rejected. It is, however, not clear how the labor dispute within the theater affected the Yue opera fund-raising performances. *Luobinhan*, August 13 and 16, 1947.

48. In one account, Wang Xiaolai, head of the Shengxian native-place organization

in Shanghai, said to Fu Quanxiang and Zhu Shuizhao, the two "diplomats" for the ten sisters: "You young girls are really bold. You plan for such a grand performance but haven't even sent a thank-you gift to our little brothers. All right, I will help you out myself. Give me a hundred million yuan and I will quiet them down." Fu and Zhu agreed to pay half the amount and wrote a check to Wang. When they asked for a receipt, Wang withdrew his demand. The story, although unverified, is consistent with known practices of the time. Quoted in Zhang and Gao 1984.

49. *Luobinhan*, August 28, 1947.

50. See Zhang and Gao 1984, 158–59.

51. *Luobinhan*, August 5, 1947.

52. Ibid., August 16, 1947.

53. Ibid., August 28, 1947.

54. *Xinmin wanbao*, August 28, 1947.

55. Ibid., August 22, 1947.

56. *Xinwen bao*, August 28, 1947.

57. Xiang Zhen 1992; and Zhou Baokui 1990.

58. This account is based on miscellaneous sources, including Zhang Chunfan's statement to the police, witness accounts, my interviews with witnesses, and the written recollections of witnesses.

59. Interviews with various Yue opera personalities, including Han Yi, 2002; Yuan Xuefen, 1995; Fu Quanxiang, 1995; Xu Yulan, 1995; and Zhou Baokui, 1996.

60. *Dagong bao*, October 15, 1947.

61. Ibid., October 17, 1947.

62. Ibid.

63. *Shen bao*, October 18, 1947.

64. Ibid.

65. Ibid.

66. *Dagong bao*, October 20, 1947.

67. Ibid., October 27, 1947.

68. Ibid., October 31, 1947.

69. *Shen bao*, November 12, 1947.

70. *Xinwen bao*, December 28, 1947.

71. Zhang Chunfan, as the main suspect in Xiao's case, was deprived of any right to Xiao's legacy. *Xinwen bao*, December 15, 1947. A few years later, in 1951, Zhang was arrested and executed by the newly established Shanghai People's Government. Xiao Dangui's suicide was cited as one of his main crimes.

72. Interview with Fu Quanxiang, 1995.

73. Interviews with Yuan Xuefen and Xu Yulan, 1995.

74. Descriptions of Xiao as an unhappy woman are given in various sources, including a story in the tabloid *Robin Hood* (*Luobinhan*, August 25, 1947); Xu Yulan's biography (Zhao Xiaosi 1994); Yuan Xuefen's biography (Zhang and Gao 1984); and my interviews with Fu Quanxiang, Xu Yulan, and Yuan Xuefen, 1995.

75. *Dagong bao*, October 27, 1947.

76. See *Shen bao*, November, 12, 1947.

77. Lu Xun 1935.

78. Ibid.

5. *The Opera as History*

1. Interview with Yuan Xuefen, 2003. Also see Yuan Xuefen 2002, 121.

2. *Shanghai Yueju zhi* 1997, 379–80.

3. The suggestion that Xie Jin is a master of melodrama follows Pickowicz, who contested claims made by PRC film historians that Xie and other left-wing filmmakers practiced social realism. See Pickowicz 1993.

4. "*Wutai jiemei*" 1982, 305–6.

5. Xie Jin, "Director's elaboration," in "*Wutai jiemei*" 1982, 274–76.

6. "*Wutai jiemei*" 1982, 153.

7. In the original script, Chunhua contemplates the question of what kind of play she should perform for the rest of her life, and the final version changes the uncertainty into a clear-cut answer. See ibid., 148.

8. Xie Jin, "Director's elaboration," in "*Wutai jiemei*" 1982, 274.

9. Interview with Fu Quanxiang, 1995.

10. See *Yueju shijie* 1941, January–June.

11. *Yueju bao*, September 22, 1946.

12. *Shanghai Yueju zhi* 1997, 332.

13. Ibid., 23.

14. *Shanghai Shi Shehui Ju dang'an* 1946–49.

15. Interview with Qiu Yawei and Qiu Wenguang, 1996.

16. *Shanghai Yueju zhi* 1997, 313.

17. Interview with Li Taicheng, 1996.

18. *Shanghai Yueju zhi* 1997, 4.

19. Interviews with Han Yi, 2002.

20. *Shanghai Yueju zhi* 1997, 4.

21. The Shanghai Yue Opera House and the Shanghai Beijing Opera House were first established in 1950 as the East China Yue Opera Experimental Company and the East China Beijing Opera Experimental Company; they took on their current names in 1955, when the East China administrative district was abolished. The Shanghai Yue Opera House was at first designated the only state theater in Shanghai directly under the Cultural Affairs Bureau of the central government but was later given back to Shanghai for logistic reasons. See *Shanghai Shi Wenhua Ju dang'an* 1949–66, B9–2–28. The Shanghai Shanghai Opera Company and the Shanghai Huai Opera Company were established in February and May 1953, respectively. See *Shanghai Huju zhi* 1999, 25; and *Shanghai Huaiju zhi* 1998, 22.

22. According to statistics in *Shanghai Shi Wenhua Ju dang'an* 1949–66.

23. Ibid.

24. Ibid.

25. Interview with Li Taicheng, 1996.

26. *Zhongguo xiqu quyi cidian* 1981, 559.

27. *Shanghai Yueju zhi* 1997, 120–21.

28. Ibid.

29. Interviews with Han Yi, 2002.

30. *Shengxianxi jijing* 1996, 287–90; and interviews with Han Yi, 2002.

31. Fanghua Company also produced *Tale of the Western Chamber* in 1952, starring the famous male impersonator Yin Guifang. Not much is known about the play, except that it was a popular success. See *Shanghai Yueju zhi* 1997, 120–21.

32. Yuan Xuefen 2002, 141–45. Also see *Shanghai Yueju zhi* 1997, 27.

33. Interviews with Cheng Rong, 2002.

34. Interview with Wu Xiaolou, 1996.

35. Interview with Zhou Baokui, 1996.

36. "Detailed outline," in "*Wutai jiemei*" 1982.

37. "Epilogue," in "*Wutai jiemei*" 1982.

38. "*Wutai jiemei*" 1982, 241–42.

39. Performers as famous as Mei Lanfang and Zhou Xinfang, while no longer subject to the whim of every patron, still felt obliged to perform at Du Yuesheng's ostentatious sixtieth birthday party in 1947. Most Yue opera stars also performed at the party, but Yuan Xuefen stuck to her principles and did not go.

40. *Lianhe wanbao*, June 8, 1946. Quoted in Zhang and Gao 1984, 124.

41. See Zhang and Gao 1984, 123–24.

42. As she claimed some thirty-two years later. Yuan Xuefen 1978.

43. *Shanghai geming wenhua dashi ji* 1991, 209.

44. *Shanghai Shi Wenhua Ju dang'an* 1949–66.

45. Interview with Li Taicheng, 1996.

46. *Shanghai Shi Wenhua Ju dang'an* 1949–66.

47. "Epilogue," in "*Wutai jiemei*" 1982.

48. Jin Chunming 2001, 118.

49. Ibid., 117–19, 130–32.

50. See *Shanghai Yueju zhi* 1997, 39–42.

51. Yuan Xuefen 1978.

52. Zhang and Gao 1984, 123.

53. Interview with Lu Shijun, 1996; and conversations with Yue opera actresses and Yue opera scholar Gao Yilong, 1995–96.

54. Interviews with Han Yi, 2002.

55. Jin Chunming 2001, 215.

56. Ibid., 244–45.

57. Ibid., 293–96.

58. *Deng Xiaoping wenxuan*, vol. 3: 372. Quoted in Jin Chunming 2001, 294–95.

59. Interview with Li Taicheng, 1996.

60. Interview with Lu Shijun, 2001.

61. Interview with Lu Shijun, 1995.

62. See Gao and Lu 1994.

63. Based on my notes on Wu Boying's speech at "The Symposium on the Current Situation and Future Development of Yue Opera," November 14, 1995, Shanghai.

64. *Shanghai Yueju zhi* 1997, 105–53.

65. The following discussion of the play is based on the version performed in Beijing in 1999, which was made into a video compact disc (VCD) in 1999. I attended a performance of the same version in Shanghai in May 2002.

66. Yin does not specify the reason for this police detainment. They might have been charged with performing "obscene plays," one of the most common lodged against women's opera performances in the countryside at the time. Yin 1982, 12.

67. *Fanghua jukan* 1947, 70–71.

68. Interviews with Han Yi, 2002.

69. Yin's and Zhu's breakup in 1948–49 was well known in Yue opera circles. Yin herself did not mention this incident in her published recollections.

70. Interview with Su Jinzou, 2002.

71. Interviews with Xue Yunhuang, 2002–3.

72. Interview with Su Jinzou, 2002.

73. Interview with Shan Yangping, 2002. Also see the Shanghai Yue Opera House's Web site, http://www.yueju.net.

74. Interviews with Xue Yunhuang, 2002–3.

75. *Wutai jiemei* 1999.

76. Interview with Qian Huili, 2002.

77. Interviews with Shan Yangping, 2002–3.

78. Promising actresses Hu Minhua and Fang Xuewen, for example, were in the New York area, while Wang Zhiping returned from Japan and Xiao Ya from the United States to resume their acting careers at the turn of the twenty-first century. Fang Xuewen later also returned and rejoined the Fanghua Company in Fuzhou, Fujian.

79. The three-part television drama, *Mist and Storm on the Qinhuai River* (Qinhuai yanyun), tells about the romantic encounter between the noted scholar Qian Qianyi and the famous courtesan Liu Rushi at the end of the Ming dynasty. Interviews with Shan Yangping, 2003. *Shanghai Yueju zhi* 1997, 65, 278.

80. Interview with Su Jinzou, 2002.

6. *A Feminine Aesthetics*

1. Wen Yi, "Shanghai 'Lin Meimei' chang 'zui' Rongcheng ren" (Shanghai "Cousin Lin" charms Chengdu audiences), *Xinmin wanbao* [Shanghai], April 21, 2004.

2. Luo Suwen also pointed out the differences in taste between Shanghai and Beijing audiences that affected the development of Shanghai-style Beijing opera. See Luo Suwen 1993.

3. This observation is based on random conversations with educated Chinese men over many years.

4. Interview with Wu Ping, 1996.

5. Interview with Cheng Liping, Li Jiang, and Zheng Yinyin, July 2002.

6. *Fanghua jukan* 1947.

7. Huang Sha 1983, 363.

8. For details on how the *chai* scale system was created, see Yuan Xuefen 2002, 15–21; and Zhou Baocai 1983, 322–26.

9. Lian Bo 1983, 347.

10. Zhang Lihui 1983.

11. The following discussion is based on interviews as well as information from contemporaneous sources, such as *Xuesheng jinian kan* 1946.

12. The dominant color in major operas such as Beijing opera was black, and cotton was the most common material for costumes. This situation began to change only with the newfound prominence of female roles in the early twentieth century, and Shanghai provided material support for this change. Mei Lanfang, for example, had many costumes made in Shanghai. See Mei Lanfang 1954.

13. Interviews with Han Yi, 2002.

14. Interview with Wu Ping, January 1996.

15. Interview with Cheng Rong, May 2002.

16. Interview with Wu Ping, January 1996.

17. Ibid.

18. *Zhongguo xiqu quyi cidian* 1981, 3.

19. Interviews with Cheng Rong, 1995.

20. Gong Hede 1994, 544.

21. Li Huikang 1995, 31.

22. See Qiu Yawei 1992, 274–75. Lyrics in *Shengxianxi jijing* 1996, 274–75.

23. *Yueju bao*, December 12, 1948.

24. Ibid.

25. Jiang Zhikang 1995, 85.

26. Ibid., 84.

27. Interview with Xu Yulan, December 1995.

28. Xu Yulan 1985, 140.

29. Ibid., 141.

30. Ibid., 152.

31. Cao Xueqin, *Honglou meng*, chapter 26.

32. Fang and Li 1983, 262–64.

33. *Shanghai Yueju zhi* 1997, 320–24.

34. Interviews with Cheng Liping, Li Jiang, and Zheng Yinyin, July 2002.

35. Zhang Dai 1597–1679, *juan* 5.

36. Larson 1998, 198, 188–97.

37. Ibid., 206.

38. Ibid., 198–206, 205.

39. Discussion with Yin Yicui, 2001.

40. *Ma Guafu kaidian* 1944. Also see *Shengxianxi jijing* 1996, 151–52.

41. *Shanghai Yueju zhi* 1997, 109.

42. The Yue opera fan Wu Ping, who saw the play in the mid-1940s, remembered that the play ends with the widow committing suicide when she realizes that the minister is actually Di Renjie. Interview with Wu Ping, 1996.

43. Wolf 1975.

44. Mann 1987.

45. *Xuesheng jinian kan* 1946, 154.

46. *Yueju shijie* 1941, January–June.

47. Chen Letian was a *qigong* master who claimed a great number of followers in the 1980s.

48. Interview with Fu Quanxiang, 1995.

49. *Shanghai Yueju zhi* 1997.

50. With the success of women's Yue opera in Shanghai, the daughters of Shanghai residents also began to join the opera as actresses in the 1940s.

51. Qi Yaxian 1992, 3–4.

52. Ibid., 4.

53. Ibid., 13.

54. Yang Hansheng 1945. Professor Suetsugu Reiko in Tokyo found this source and kindly provided a copy of the article for me.

55. Ibid.

56. Wang Xiaochuan 1958.

57. Yi Bing 1959.

58. Ibid.

59. *Xuesheng jinian kan* 1946, 50.

60. *Shengxianxi jijing* 1996, 178–79; *Shanghai Yueju zhi* 1997, 356.

61. *Xuesheng jinian kan* 1946, 50. *Shengxianxi jijing* 1996, 178–79, 217–18, 305.

62. Li Jinfeng 1995, 313–14.

63. Yin Guifang 1951; Fu Jun 1995.

64. According to the Redologist Xu Gongshi's calculations. Quoted in Xiang Jing'an, "*Honglou meng* zhong jiujing xie le duoshao renwu" (How many characters are there in *Dream of the Red Chamber?*), *Guangjiao jing* (Wide angle), March 2004, Hong Kong.

65. Xu Jin wrote: "The novel does not contain 'Baoyu Mourns for Daiyu,' but many previous theatrical renditions do. It seems to me that opera especially needs it to meet the audience's psychological needs. For even though Daiyu has died, the audience still wants to see an emotional exchange between the two protagonists. I think that this act not only reinforces the audience's sympathy for the two lovers but also helps the image

of Baoyu—by showing his determination to break with feudal forces, the play joins Baoyu's spirit with that of Daiyu." Xu Jin 1962, 135.

66. *Shanghai Yueju zhi* 1997.

67. Interview with Cheng Liping, 2002.

7. *Conclusion*

1. Shanghai's settlers included people from foreign countries. Although this group was demographically insignificant, its social and cultural influence should not be overlooked.

2. Chinese women who were educated in the elite rhetoric of women's liberation and gender equality tended to have these kinds of views.

3. See Jin Jiang 2001; and Zheng Wang 2001.

4. Yang Hua, "Qingbo de Yueju" (Frivolous Yue opera). Available at http://www.xys.org (posted May 2002). There are many obvious factual errors in this short Internet piece, indicating that the author is not an opera specialist.

5. Catherine Yeh's study on Shanghai courtesans at the turn of the twentieth century provides another illustration of how public women and their performance of love dramas (both in real life and in role-play games) helped redefine a modern culture of love while assigning more favorable roles to their profession and to themselves within this culture. See Catherine Yeh 2006.

6. Butler 1993, 10.

7. Levenson wrote: "Intonation matters, in English as well as in Chinese. We may describe an item in the historical record as historically (really) significant, or as (merely) historically significant. The distinction is between an empirical judgment of fruitfulness in time and a normative judgment of aridity in the here and now" (Levenson 1958, 85).

8. See Nishimura 2004.

9. See Bian 2005; and Yixin Chen 2004.

10. For detailed discussions of the Three Transformations policy of the 1950s, see Jiang Jin 2005.

11. See the Shan Yangping Forum, http://sh.netsh.com/bbs/3610/.

12. See http://www.qianhuili.net/.

Chinese Character Glossary

Ai Xia	艾霞
aimeiju	愛美劇
An E	安娥
Anhui	安徽
Bai Yang	白楊
Bai Yushuang	白玉霜
Baimao nü	白毛女
Baishe zhuan	白蛇傳
Baishui tan	白水灘
bangzi	梆子
Banyue xiju	半月戲劇
Bao Tianxiao	包天笑
Baoyu yu Daiyu	寶玉與黛玉
Baqian li lu yun he yue	八千里路雲和月
beidan	悲旦
Beiguo Jiangnan	北國江南
bentan	本灘
biaozi	婊子
Biyu zan	碧玉簪
bu haokan	不好看
Bu Wancang	卜萬蒼
buwan xiaosheng	補丸小生
Cai Chusheng	蔡楚生
Cai Lanying	蔡蘭英
Cai Yuying	蔡萸英
caicha	採茶
Can Xue	殘雪
Cao Cao yu Yang Xiu	曹操與楊修
Cao Xueqin	曹雪芹
Cao Zhi yu Zeng Luo	曹植與曾洛
Caochuan jiejian	草船借箭
chai diao	尺調
chang daxi	唱大戲
chang shu wan liang	唱書完糧
chang tanghui	唱堂會
Chang Xiangyu	常香玉
chang xinwen	唱新聞
Chang'e	嫦娥
changgong	唱功
changji	娼妓
Changle	長樂
Changsheng dian	長生殿
changshu	唱書
Changzhou	常州
chayuan	茶園
Chen Dieyi	陳蝶衣
Chen Shulian	陳疏蓮
Chen Wanyuan	陳萬元
Chen Yi	陳毅
Chen Yusun	陳虞孫
Cheng Changgeng	程長庚
Cheng Rong	成容
Cheng Yanqiu	程硯秋

Chenxiang shan	沉香扇	*Dongzhou lieguo zhi*	東周列國志
chi	尺	ducao	毒草
Chongqing	重慶	"Du *Xixiang*"	讀西廂
Chongren	崇仁	Du Yuesheng	杜月笙
chou	丑	er nü si qing	兒女私情
chuanqi	傳奇	exing Haipai	惡性海派
Chuju	楚劇	Fan Li (Dimin)	樊籬(迪民)
Churen	處仁	Fan Ruijuan	範瑞娟
Cui Yingying	崔鶯鶯	*Fang mianhua*	紡棉花
da baobuping	打報不平	Fang Qing	方卿
Da piguan	大劈棺	Fang Yafen	方亞芬
Da Shijie	大世界	Fei Mu	費穆
Dagong bao	大公報	Feng Jiajin	封加進
dagu	大鼓	*Fengyu tan*	風雨談
Dai Qing	戴晴	Fu Quanxiang	傅全香
"Daiyu fengao"	黛玉焚稿	funü wenti	婦女問題
"Daiyu jinfu"	黛玉進府	*Funü yu wenxue*	婦女與文學
"Daiyu zanghua"	黛玉葬花	Fuzhou	福州
Dalai Juchang	大來劇場	gan die	乾爹
Danghu chuan	蕩湖船	gan ma	乾媽
Dangren hun	黨人魂	ganqing	感情
Daoguang	道光	Gao Jianling	高劍琳
dashu	大書	Gao Jin	高瑾
daxi	大戲	Gao Yilong	高義龍
Dazhong Jushe	大中劇社	Gao Yuesheng	高月昇
Deng Xiaoping	鄧小平	*Ge Nenniang*	葛嫩娘
Deng Yingchao	鄧穎超	gezaixi	歌仔戲
Di Renjie	狄仁傑	Gong Hede	龔和德
Diantong huabao	電通畫報	Gu Wenyou	顧文友
diaojiaoxi	吊腳戲	*Guaming de fuqi*	掛名的夫妻
diduban	的篤班	Guan Sushuang	關肅霜
diduxi	的篤戲	Guangdong	廣東
difang xi	地方戲	*Guangxu Di yu Zhenfei*	光緒帝與珍妃
Ding Cong	丁聰	gudao	孤島
Ding Jingtang	丁景唐	"Guifei zuijiu"	貴妃醉酒
Ding Ling	丁玲	"Guihua ting"	桂花亭
Ding Shi'e	丁是娥	Guiji	會稽
Ding Ying	丁英	Guilin	桂林
Dingjun shan	定軍山	Guo Moruo	郭沫若
Dong Qian	董倩	guofang niang	過房娘
Dong Tianmin	董天民	guofang ye	過房爺
Dongyang	東陽		

guojia juyuan	國家劇院
guoju	國劇
Guomindang	國民黨
Guopo shanhe zai	國破山河在
Guotai Daxiyuan	國泰大戲院
guoying jutuan	國營劇團
Haipai	海派
Haipai Jingju	海派京劇
Hairui baguan	海瑞罷官
Han Yi (Hong Jun)	韓義（洪鈞）
Hang-Jia-Hu	杭嘉湖
Hangju	杭劇
Hangzhou	杭州
hao kan	好看
hao ting	好聽
Haohao xiansheng	好好先生
He Lunzhang	何倫章
He Wenxiu	何文秀
Hebei	河北
hen mei	很美
Hong Shen	洪深
Honglou meng	紅樓夢
Hongse niangzi jun	紅色娘子軍
Hu Feng	胡風
Hu Shi	胡適
Hu Zhifei	胡知非
Hua Mulan	花木蘭
huaben	話本
huadan	花旦
huadeng	花燈
huagu	花鼓
Huaiju	淮劇
Huali yuan	華麗緣
hualian	花臉
Huang Jinrong	黃金榮
Huang Sha	黃沙
Huang Zuolin	黃佐臨
Huangjin Daxiyuan	黃金大戲院
Huangmeixi	黃梅戲
Huangpu (Jiang)	黃浦（江）
huangse xiaobao	黃色小報
Huangze	黃澤
Huanjin ji	浣錦記
Hudie meng	蝴蝶夢
"Hui shiba"	回十八
Huju	滬劇
Hunan	湖南
hunhun e'e	渾渾噩噩
Huo Dingjin	霍定金
huobao ju	活報劇
huqin	胡琴
Huxi	滬西
Jia Baoyu	賈寶玉
Jia Guilian	賈桂蓮
jian mian li	見面禮
Jiang Bo	江波
Jiang Laowu xunqing ji	蔣老五殉情記
Jiang Qing	江青
Jiang Zeming	江澤民
Jiangbei	江北
Jiangbeixi	江北戲
Jiangnan	江南
Jiangsu	江蘇
Jianguo ribao	建國日報
Jiangxi	江西
jiaohua	教化
jiating ju	家庭劇
Jiaxing	嘉興
Jiehun shinian	結婚十年
jiemei qing	姐妹情
jiguan bao	機關報
Jiming zao kantian	雞鳴早看天
jin	斤
Jin Qibing	金其炳
Jin Yuqing	金育青
Jin Zhitang	金芝堂
jinbu liliang	進步力量
jing	淨
Jingchao pai	京朝派
Jingju	京劇
Jingpai	京派
Jingu qiguan	今古奇觀
Jinhua	金華

Jinlong bian	金龍鞭
Jinpingmei	金瓶梅
"Jin-Yu liangyuan"	金玉良緣
Jiuxing Daxiyuan	九星大戲院
jixing	畸形
Juan She	娟社
juwu bu	劇務部
Juzhou	居州
kan re'nao	看熱鬧
Kangxi	康熙
kangzhan wenhua	抗戰文化
keai de shagua	可愛的傻瓜
koutou	叩頭
Kuaihuo lin	快活林
kuku diao	哭哭調
"Kuling chuzou"	哭靈出走
Kunming	昆明
Kunqu	昆曲
kuxi	苦戲
Lan gu'niang	懶姑娘
Langdangzi	浪蕩子
laodan	老旦
laosheng	老生
Laozha Xiyuan	老閘戲院
Lei sa xiangsi di	淚灑相思地
Leng Shan (Jin Zhaoyuan)	(冷山) 金兆元
li	理
Li Chunlai	李春來
Li Gongpu	李公樸
Li Hongzhang	李鴻章
Li Jiang	李江
Li Jianwu	李健吾
Li Taicheng	李太成
Li Tingfu	李廷甫
Li Xiuying	李秀英
Li Yuru	李玉茹
Lian Bo	連波
Lian sheng	聯聲
Liang Shanbo yu Zhu Yingtai	梁山伯與祝英臺
Liang Zhu aishi	梁祝哀史
liangzi	糧子
Lianhe ribao	聯合日報
Lianhe wanbao	聯合晚報
lianhua luozi	蓮花落子
Lianhua nü	蓮花女
Liao Lin	廖臨
Libai liu	禮拜六
Lin Daiyu	林黛玉
Lin Gu	林谷
Lin Zexu	林則徐
Lin'an	臨安
Lingyu xiangxiao ji	玲玉香消記
Liu Changsheng	劉長勝
Liu Chen	劉諶
Liu Housheng	劉厚生
Liu Jinding	劉金定
Liu Shaoqi	劉少奇
Liu Xiangnü baojuan	劉香女寶卷
Liu Xiao	劉曉
Liuyin ji	柳蔭記
Longyou	龍遊
"Loutai hui"	樓臺會
Lu Ang	盧昂
Lu Dan'an	陸澹盦
Lu Gendi	陸根棣
Lu Shijun	盧時俊
Lu Xun	魯迅
Lu Yin	盧隱
Lü Zhong	呂仲
luantan	亂彈
Lüju	呂劇
Lun yanyuan ziwo xiuyang	論演員自我休養
Luohan qian	羅漢錢
Luoyang	洛陽
lutou xi	路頭戲
Ma Chaoshui	馬潮水
Ma Guafu kaidian	馬寡婦開店
Ma Lianliang	馬連良
Ma shi wentong	馬氏文通
Ma Wencai	馬文才
Ma Zhanghua	馬樟花

Mai caotun 賣草囤
Mai po ji 賣婆記
Mai qingtan 賣青炭
mao'erxi 髦兒戲
Matang Cun 馬塘村
mei 美
Mei Baojiu 梅葆玖
Mei Duo 梅朵
Mei Lanfang 梅蘭芳
Meilong zhen 梅龍鎮
Meng Lijun 孟麗君
Meng Xiaodong 孟小冬
minban gongzhu jutuan 民辦公助劇團
Mingxing Daxiyuan 明星大戲院
Modeng jia'nü 摩登袈女
Mu Shiying 穆時英
mubiao 幕表
Mulan 木蘭
nan ban 男班
nan nü heyan 男女合演
Nan Wei 南薇
nan xiaosheng 男小生
Nanjing 南京
nankan 難看
Nanshi 南市
nanxi 南戲
Ningbo 寧波
nü ban 女班
Nü Wa 女媧
nü xi 女戲
nü xiaosheng 女小生
nü xizi 女戲子
nü yue 女樂
Nülan Wuhao 女藍五號
nüzi Shaoxing wenxi 女子紹興文戲
nüzi Yueju 女子越劇
Ouyang Yuqian 歐陽予倩
Paitou 牌頭
Pan Yueqiao 潘月樵
Panfu suofu 盤夫索夫
pihuang 皮黃
Ping-Hu tongche 平滬通車
pingju 評劇
pingtan 評彈
Pipa ji 琵琶記
Pu Tong 溥侗
Pudong 浦東
Qi Fanniu 戚飯牛
Qi Rushan 齊如山
Qi Yaxian 戚雅仙
Qian Huili 錢惠麗
Qianjin funü 前進婦女
Qianlong 乾隆
Qiliang Liao gong yue 悽涼遼宮月
Qimei tu 七美圖
qing 情
qingbai 清白
qinglou 青樓
qingqing baibai zuoren, renren zhenzhen yanxi 清清白白做人，認認真真演戲
qingyi 青衣
Qiongren hen 窮人恨
qipao 旗袍
qishi miezu 欺世滅祖
Qiu Guangxian 裘廣賢
Qiuyue guying 秋月孤影
renqing 人情
Renren zhoubao 人人週報
renyan kewei 人言可畏
rou 柔
rou mei 柔美
rouzi 肉子
Ruan Lingyu 阮玲玉
san gai 三改
san hua 三花
Sandu 三都
Sange modeng nüxing 三個摩登女性
Sanguo yanyi 三國演義
Sanjie 三界
Sankan yumei 三看御妹

Sanmen	三門
Sanxiao yinyuan	三笑姻緣
Sanyue chunchao	三月春潮
Sha Wenhan	沙文漢
Shaanxi	陝西
Shan Yangping	單仰萍
shandian xiaosheng	閃電小生
Shandong	山東
Shang Fangchen	商芳臣
Shang Shuihua	商水花
Shang Xiaoyun	尚小雲
Shanghai chanye yu Shanghai zhigong	上海產業與上海職工
Shanghai shenghuo	上海生活
Shanghai Yueju zhi	上海越劇志
"Shangshi"	傷逝
Shangyu	上虞
Shanhe lian	山河戀
Shanhu yin	珊瑚引
Shao Xunmei	邵循美
Shaoxing	紹興
Shaoxing daban	紹興大班
Shaoxing wanbao	紹興晚報
Shaoxing wenxi	紹興文戲
Shaoxing xikao quance	紹興戲考全冊
Shaoxingxi bao	紹興戲報
Shen bao	申報
Shen Congwen	沈從文
Shen Fu	沈浮
Shen nü	神女
Shen Xiling	沈西苓
Shengxian	嵊縣
Shengxian guanhua	嵊縣官話
Shengxian zizhi zhangcheng	嵊縣自治章程
Shengxianxi	嵊縣戲
Shengzhou	嵊州
Shenqu	申曲
shenying shizhe	神瑛侍者
Shi Dakai	石達開
Shi Dongshan	史東山
Shi guguai	十古怪
Shi Jihua	史濟華
"Shi wo cuo"	是我錯
Shi xiqi	十稀奇
Shi Yinhua	施銀花
Shi Zhecun	施蟄存
Shiba mo	十八摸
"Shibali xiangsong"	十八里相送
Shidai ribao	時代日報
Shijia Ao	施家嶴
shikumen	石庫門
Shiliupu	十六鋪
shimin wenhua	市民文化
Shishi xinbao	時事新報
Shuang jin hua	雙金花
Shuang zhu feng	雙珠鳳
Shuihu zhuan	水滸傳
Shuo Yue quanzhuan	說岳全傳
shuoxi shifu	說戲師傅
Sichuan	四川
sida mingdan	四大名旦
sida qishu	四大奇書
sigong diao	四工調
Sijichun Ban	四季春班
Siming Shan	四明山
Sizhou cheng	泗洲城
sizhu	絲竹
Song Meiling	宋美齡
Song Qingling	宋慶齡
Song Zhiyou	宋之由
su	俗
Su Qing	蘇青
Su Jinzou	蘇進鄒
Su San	蘇三
Subei	蘇北
Sulian Diantai	蘇聯電臺
Sun Kexian	孫克咸
Sun Yu	孫瑜
Suzhou	蘇州
Tan Xinpei	譚鑫培
tanci	彈詞
Tang Degui	唐德貴
Tang Diyin	湯蒂茵

Tang Jishan	唐季珊
tanhuang	灘簧
Tao Xingzhi	陶行知
taofan shu	討飯書
taofan xi	討飯戲
Taohua shan	桃花扇
taose xinwen	桃色新聞
Teng Jiazhen	滕家振
Tian Han	田漢
Tian Xiu	田秀
Tianchan Wutai	天蟾舞臺
Tiandi	天地
Tianjin	天津
Tianxiang Daxiyuan	天香大戲院
Tixiao yinyuan	啼笑因緣
Tixiao yinyuan tanci	啼笑因緣彈詞
Tong Lijuan	童禮娟
Tong Zhiling	童芷苓
Tongshang Lüguan	通商旅館
tongtian	通天
tongxing lian	同性戀
Tu Xinghua	屠杏花
tuqi	土氣
Wang Anyi	王安憶
Wang Chanzhi	王璨芝
Wang Jingwei	汪精衛
Wang Jinshui	王金水
Wang Shifu	王實甫
Wang Wenjuan	王文娟
Wang Xiaolai	王曉籟
Wang Xifeng	王熙鳳
Wang Xinghua	王杏花
Wang Yulin	王玉林
Wang Yurong	王玉蓉
Wang Zhiping	王志萍
Wanjia denghuo	萬家燈火
Wanxiang	萬象
Wei Changsheng	魏長生
Wei Jinshan	魏晉山
Wei Meiduo	魏梅朵
Wei Shaochang	魏紹昌
Wen Bizheng	文必正
Wen Tianxiang	文天祥
Wen Yiduo	聞一多
Wen Zhong (Guan Jian)	聞仲（關鍵）
Wencui	文粹
Wenhui bao	文匯報
wenmingxi	文明戲
wenxi	文戲
Wenyi fuxing	文藝復興
Wenzhou	溫州
wenzi xiaobao	蚊子小報
wode shenti shi qingbai de	我的身體是清白的
Wu Chen	吳琛
Wu Han	吳晗
Wu Kaixian	吳開先
Wu Kang	吳康
Wu Ping	吳萍
Wu Xiaolou	吳小樓
Wu Yonggang	吳永剛
wugong	武功
Wuhan	武漢
Wuju	婺劇
wupeng chuan	烏蓬船
wusheng	武生
Wutai jiemei	舞臺姐妹
xi zhong xi	戲中戲
xia hai	下海
Xia Yan	夏衍
Xia Yuerun	夏月潤
Xia Yueshan	夏月珊
xiandai xing	現代性
xiandai	現代
Xiang Jintang	相金堂
Xianglin sao	祥林嫂
xiansheng	先生
xiao	簫
xiao baihua	小百花
Xiao Dangui	筱丹桂
Xiao fangniu	小放牛
xiao shimin	小市民

Xiao Wo	笑我
Xiao Yueying	筱月英
Xiao-Bai Yumei	小白玉梅
xiaogeban	小歌班
xiaojie zuojia	小姐作家
Xiaoshan	蕭山
xiaoshu	小書
xiaoxi	小戲
xiban	戲班
Xie An	謝安
Xie Daoyun	謝道韞
Xie Jin	謝晉
Xie Tieli	謝鐵驪
xieyi	寫意
xin guoying jutuan	新國營劇團
Xin nüxing	新女性
Xin Shijie	新世界
xin xenxue	新文學
Xin Wutai	新舞臺
Xin Yanqiu	新艷秋
Xin Yueju	新越劇
Xinchang	新昌
Xindeng	新登
xing	性
xing pengzi	興蓬子
Xing Yuehong	邢月紅
Xinhua ribao	新華日報
xinju	新劇
Xinmin wanbao	新民晚報
Xinwen bao	新聞報
xinwenyi gongzuozhe	新文藝工作者
xinwenyi qingnian	新文藝青年
Xishi gui Yue	西施歸越
xiushen qijia zhiguo pingtianxia	修身，齊家，治國，平天下
Xixiang ji	西廂記
Xiyou ji	西遊記
xiyuan	戲院
xizi	戲子
Xu Datong	徐大通
Xu Fangfeng	徐芳鳳
Xu Guangping	許廣平
Xu Jin	徐進
xu shi	敘事
Xu Yulan	徐玉蘭
Xue Baochai	薛寶釵
Xue Xie	學協
Xue Yanqin	雪艷琴
Xue Yunhuang	薛允璜
Xuesheng jinian kan	雪聲記念刊
Xuesheng shenghuo	學生生活
Xun Huisheng	荀慧生
ya	雅
Yan Duhe	嚴獨鶴
Yan Huizhu	言慧珠
Yan Lanzhen	嚴蘭貞
Yan'an	延安
yang gang	陽剛
Yang Guifei	楊貴妃
Yang Hansheng	陽翰笙
Yang Shaochun	楊少春
Yang Xiaolou	楊小樓
Yang Yuelou	楊月樓
yangge	秧歌
Yangjia jiang	楊家將
Yangshupu	楊樹浦
Yangxifu hui niangjia	養媳婦回娘家
Yangzhou	揚州
yanqing	言情
Yao Min'ai	姚民哀
Yao Shuijuan	姚水娟
Ye Qinfang	葉琴芳
Yi Bing	伊兵
Yijiang chunshui xiang dong liu	一江春水向東流
Yilü ma	一縷麻
yin	陰
Yin Guifang	尹桂芳
yin rou	陰柔
Yin Yicui	殷一璀
ying	硬
Ying Yunwei	應雲衛

"Yingtai kuling" 英臺哭靈
yinshu 淫書
yinxi 淫戲
Yiyang 弋陽
Yongzheng 雍正
"You Shanglin Yuan" 遊上林宛
yu jiao yu le 寓教於樂
Yu lianhuan 玉連環
Yu Ling 于伶
Yu Longsun 俞龍孫
Yu Qiaqing 虞洽卿
Yu Shangyuan (Yui Shang-Yuen) 余上沅
Yu Shuiwen 俞水文
yuan fang 圓房
Yuan Meiyun 袁美雲
Yuan Xuefen 袁雪芬
Yue ou 越謳
Yueju 越劇
Yueju 粵劇
Yueju bao 越劇報
Yueju fazhan shu 越劇發展書
Yueju shijie 越劇世界
Yueju zhuankan 越劇專刊
Yuhang 餘杭
Yuju 豫劇
Yunnan 雲南
Yutang Chun 玉堂春
Yuyao 餘姚
Yuzan ji 玉簪記
zaju 雜劇
Zaochun eryue 早春二月
zaopo 糟粕
Zazhi 雜誌
Zhabei 閘北
Zhan Chengdu 戰成都
Zhang Ailing 張愛玲
Zhang Chunfan 張春帆
Zhang Chunqiao 張春橋
Zhang Damin 張達民
Zhang Dai 張岱
Zhang Daofan 張道藩
Zhang Du 張讀
Zhang Gong 張拱
Zhang Hailing 章海靈
Zhang Henshui 張恨水
Zhang Jinfeng 張金鳳
Zhang Junqiu 張君秋
Zhang Junxiang 張駿祥
Zhang Lihui 章力揮
Zhang Linghui 張玲蕙
Zhang Rongbiao 張榮標
Zhang Ruihong 章瑞虹
Zhang Xiangqing 張相卿
Zhang Xingzhou 張行周
Zhang Yanqiu 張豔秋
Zhang Yongmei 張永梅
Zhang Yunbiao 張雲標
Zhang Zaiyang 張載陽
Zhang Zhiyi 張執一
Zhang Zifan 張子範
zhanghui ti 章回體
Zhao Jingshen 趙景深
Zhao Naixue 趙耐雪
Zhao Ruihua 趙瑞花
Zhao Zhigang 趙志剛
Zhedong Daxiyuan 浙東大戲院
Zhejiang 浙江
Zheng Chuanjian 鄭傳鑒
Zheng Guofeng 鄭國鳳
Zhenguan shengshi 貞觀盛世
Zhenzhu ta 珍珠塔
Zhong Min 鍾泯
Zhongguo Daxiyuan 中國大戲院
Zhonghun qu 忠魂曲
Zhongsheng dashi 終生大事
Zhongyang ribao 中央日報
Zhou bao 週報
Zhou Baocai 周寶財
Zhou Baokui 周寶奎
Zhou Enlai 周恩來
Zhou Shoujuan 周瘦鵑
Zhou Wang yu Daji 紂王與妲己
Zhou Xinfang 周信芳

Zhou Xuan	周璇	Zhuge Liang	諸葛亮
Zhu Chunhua	竺春花	Zhuji	諸暨
Zhu Shuizhao	竺水招	Zhujia Zhuang	祝家莊
Zhu Xiangyun	朱翔雲	Zhuo Wenjun	卓文君
zhu xuanlü	主旋律	*Zhuofang Cao*	捉放曹
Zhu Yunlai	朱雲萊	*Ziluolan*	紫蘿蘭
zhuangyuan	狀元	*Ziyou ren*	自由人
"Zhufu"	祝福	zuogong	做功

References

Arkush, R. David. 1989. "Love and Marriage in North Chinese Peasant Operas." In Perry Link, Richard Madsen, and Paul G. Pickowicz, eds., *Unofficial China: Popular Culture and Thought in the People's Republic*. Boulder, CO: Westview Press.

Bai Mao. 1940. "Gei gudao yingye de congshizhe" (To the film industry workers in "island" Shanghai). *Xiju yu wenxue* (Drama and literature), vol. 1, no. 4 (June).

Bender, Mark. 1999. "Shifting and Performance in Suzhou Chantefable." In Vibeke Bordahl, ed., *The Eternal Storyteller: Oral Literature in Modern China*. Richmond, England: Curzon Press.

Bensen, Carlton. 1995. "The Manipulation of *Tanci* in Radio Shanghai during the 1930s." *Republican China*, vol. 20, no. 2 (April).

Bian, Morris L. 2005. *The Making of the State Enterprise System in Modern China: The Dynamics of Institutional Change*. Cambridge, MA: Harvard University Press.

Butler, Judith. 1993. *Bodies That Matter: On the Discursive Limits of "Sex."* New York: Routledge.

Cao Xueqin. Qing dynasty. *Honglou meng* (Dream of the red chamber).

Chen Fengyuan (Chin Hōgen). 1939. *Shin Shina sobyō* (A literary sketch of the new China). Taipei: Taiwan *Xinmin bao* she.

Chen, Jack. 1949. *The Chinese Theatre*. London: Dennis Dobson.

Chen Qingsheng. 1995. *Kang Ri zhanzheng shiqi de Shanghai wenxue* (Wartime literature in Shanghai). Shanghai: Shanghai renmin chubanshe.

Chen Xi. 1941. "Wo yu Yueju de yijian" (My opinion of Yue opera). *Shen bao*, May 3.

Chen, Yixin. 2004. "Understanding Twentieth Century China—An Interview with William Kirby." *The Chinese Historical Review*, vol. 11, no. 1 (Spring).

Chen Zhengxiang (Chen Cheng-Siang). 1970. *Shanghai* (Shanghai). Research Report, no. 38, Geographical Research Centre, Graduate School, The Chinese University of Hong Kong.

Cheng, Weikun. 1996. "The Challenge of the Actresses: Female Performers and Cultural Alternatives in Early Twentieth Century Beijing and Tianjin." *Modern China*, vol. 22, no. 2 (April).

Cheng Yanqiu zhuanji (A special issue dedicated to Cheng Yanqiu). 1938. Edited by Wu Jiangfeng. Shanghai: Huangjin Daxiyuan.

Cihai. 1989. Reprinted in reduced format. Shanghai: Shanghai cishu chubanshe, 1997.

Cole, James. 1986. *Shaoxing: Competition and Cooperation in Nineteenth-Century China*. Tucson: University of Arizona Press.

Dagong bao (Dagong daily). 1940s. Shanghai.

Danghu chuan (The river boat). [1920s?] Ningbo-storytelling script. Shanghai: Renhexiang shuzhuang.

Ding Jingtang. 1982. "Xianglin sao—Lu Xun zuopin zhong zhi nüxing yanjiu zhi yi: Fuji" (Sister Xianglin—A study of female characters in Lu Xun's work: An appendix). In *Xuexi Lu Xun zuopin de zaji* (Notes on my studies of Lu Xun's work), enlarged edition. Shanghai: Wenyi chubanshe, 1983.

———. 1995. "Wu Kang, ni zoude taizao!" (Wu Kang, you died too early!) In *Huainian Wu Kang tongzhi* (Memories of comrade Wu Kang). Edited and published by the editorial committee, Shanghai.

Ding Yi. 1992a. "Xiaogeban de diyici yanchu" (The initial staging of little opera). In *Yueju suyuan* (Tracing the origins of Yue opera), edited by Shengxian Zhengxie Wenshi Ziliao Weiyuanhui, 26–32. Hangzhou: Zhejiang wenyi chuban she.

———. 1992b. "Yueju *Liang Zhu* de youlai he fazhan" (The origin and development of the Yue opera *Liang Shanbo and Zhu Yingtai*). In *Yueju suyuan* (Tracing the origins of Yue opera), edited by Shengxian Zhengxie Wenshi Ziliao Weiyuanhui, 234–40. Hangzhou: Zhejiang wenyi chuban she.

Ding Ying (pen name of Ding Jingtang). 1945. "Xianglin sao—Lu Xun zuopin zhong zhi nüxing yanjiu zhi yi" (Sister Xianglin—A study of the female characters in Lu Xun's work). Originally published in *Qianjin funü* (The progressive women), vol. 2 (November).

———. February 1946. *Funü yu wenxue* (Women and literature). Shanghai: Hujiang chubanshe.

Esherick, Joseph. 1987. *The Origins of the Boxer Uprising*. Berkeley: University of California Press.

Fan Ruijuan. 1989. "Wo yan Liang Shanbo" (How I performed the character Liang Shanbo). In Wu Zhaofen, ed., *Fan Ruijuan biaoyan yishu* (Fan Ruijuan's performing art). Shanghai: Shanghai wenyi chubanshe.

———. 1994. "Yueju gaige de yiwei gongchen—Yi Nan Wei xiansheng" (A contributor to Yue opera reform—Recollections about Mr. Nan Wei). In Gao Yilong and Lu Shijun, *Chongxin zouxiang huihuang: Yueju gaige wushi zhounian lunwen ji* (Resume the past glory: A collection of essays dedicated to the fifth anniversary of Yue opera reform). Beijing: Zhongguo xiju chubanshe.

Fang Hairu and Li Yaokun. 1983. "Dui fazhan nan nü heyan Yueju de jidian kanfa" (A few points on developing gender-straight Yue opera). In *Yishu yanjiu ziliao* (Sources for research in art), vol. 6. Hangzhou: Zhejiang yishu yanjiu suo.

Fanghua jukan: Yin Guifang zhuanji (Fanghua company home magazine: A special issue dedicated to Yin Guifang). June 1947. Shanghai: Fanghua jutuan chubanshe.

Frith, Simon. 1988. "Art Ideology and Pop Practice." In Cary Nelson and Lawrence Grossberg, eds., *Marxism and the Interpretation of Culture*, 22–23. London: Macmillan.

Fu Jun. 1995. "Ji Yin Guifang siyan *Honglou Meng*" (Yin Guifang in her four times of acting in *Dream of the red chamber*). In Li Huikang, ed., *Yidai fengliu Yin Guifang* (The great actress Yin Guifang). Shanghai: Shanghai wenyi chubanshe.

Fu, Poshek. 1993. *Passivity, Resistance, and Collaboration: Intellectual Choices in Occupied Shanghai, 1937–1945*. Stanford, CA: Stanford University Press.

———. 2003. *Between Shanghai and Hong Kong: The Politics of Chinese Cinemas*. Stanford, CA: Stanford University Press.

Fu Quanxiang. 1989. *Kanke qianmian shi meijing* (Beautiful future comes after many hardships and frustrations). Shanghai: Baijia chubanshe.

Fuller, Peter. 1980. *Beyond the Crisis in Art*. London: Writers and Readers.

Furth, Charlotte. 1999. *A Flourishing Yin: Gender in China's Medical History, 960–1665*. Berkeley: University of California Press.

Gaimushō kōbun (Official documents of the Japanese Ministry of Foreign Affairs). 1930s and 1940s. Nippon Gaisei Kyōkai. Tokyo.

Gao Yilong. 1991. *Yueju shihua* (The story of Yue opera). Shanghai: Shanghai wenyi chubanshe.

Gao Yilong and Lu Shijun, eds. 1994. *Chongxin zouxiang huihuang: Yueju gaige wushi zhounian lunwen ji* (Resume the past glory: A collection of essays dedicated to the fifth anniversary of Yue opera reform). Beijing: Zhongguo xiju chubanshe.

Goldstein, Joshua. 1999a. "Theatrical Imagi-nations: Peking Opera and China's Cultural Crisis, 1890–1937." Ph.D. diss., University of California, San Diego.

———. 1999b. "Mei Lanfang and the Nationalization of Peking Opera, 1912–1930." *positions: east asia cultures critique*, vol. 7, no. 2 (Fall).

Gong Hede. 1994. "Xuanzexing de chongxin jian'gou—Tan Yueju de xingcheng jiqi yiyi" (Selective reconstruction—On the significance of the formation of Yue opera). In Gao Yilong and Lu Shijun, eds., *Chongxin zouxiang huihuang: Yueju gaige wushi zhounian lunwen ji* (Resume the past glory: A collection of essays dedicated to the fifth anniversary of Yue opera reform). Beijing: Zhongguo xiju chubanshe.

Goodman, Bryna. 1995. *Native Place, City, and Nation: Regional Networks and Identity in Shanghai, 1853–1937*. Berkeley: University of California Press.

Hall, Stuart. 1980. "Cultural Studies at the Centre: Some Problematics and Problems." In Stuart Hall, D. Hobson, A. Lowe, and P. Willis, eds., *Culture, Media, Language*, 15–47. London: Hutchinson.

Hamada Maya. 1993. "Josei sakka ni yoru rinkanki Shanhai no nichijō to mujun" (Women writers in occupied Shanghai). *Yasō* (The weeds), no. 52 (August). Tokyo.

Hayford, Charles Wishart. 1990. *To the People: James Yen and Village China*. New York: Columbia University Press.

He Keren. 1935. *Ruan Lingyu aishi* (A tragic biography of Ruan Lingyu). Shanghai: Xiangzhi Shuju. Edited and reprinted in He Keren et al., *Ruan Lingyu zhisi* (The death of Ruan Lingyu). Changsha: Yuelu shushe, 1986.

He Keren et al. 1986. *Ruan Lingyu zhisi* (The death of Ruan Lingyu). Changsha: Yuelu shushe.

Henriot, Christian. 2001. *Prostitution and Sexuality in Shanghai: A Social History, 1849–1949*. Cambridge: Cambridge University Press.

Hershatter, Gail. 1997. *Dangerous Pleasures: Prostitution and Modernity in Twentieth-Century Shanghai*. Berkeley and Los Angeles: University of California Press.

Honig, Emily. 1986. *Sisters and Strangers: Women in Shanghai's Cotton Mills*. Stanford, CA: Stanford University Press.

———. 1993. *Creating Chinese Ethnicity*. New Haven, CT: Yale University Press.

Hu Sha. 1982. *Pingju jianshi* (A brief history of *ping* opera). Beijing: Zhongguo xiju chubanshe.

Huang, Nicole. 2005. *Women, War, Domesticity: Shanghai Literature and Popular Culture of the 1940s*. Leiden and Boston: Brill Academic Publisher.

Huang Sha. 1983. "Yueju fengge de jicheng yu fazhan" (Carry on and develop Yue opera aesthetics). In *Yishu yanjiu ziliao* (Sources for research in art), vol. 6. Hangzhou: Zhejiang yishu yanjiu suo.

Hung, Chang-tai. 1994. *War and Popular Culture: Resistance in Modern China, 1937–1945*. Berkeley: University of California Press.

Jiang Jin. 2005. "Duanlie yu yanxu: 1950 niandai Shanghai de wenhua gaizao" (Rupture and continuity: Cultural transformation in Shanghai in the 1950s). *Shehui kexue* (Journal of social sciences), vol. 298 (June): 95–103.

Jiang, Jin. 2001. "'Times Have Changed; Men and Women Are the Same.'" In Zhong Xueping, Wang Zheng, and Bai Di, eds., *Some of Us: Chinese Women Growing up in the Mao Era*, 100–119. New Brunswick, NJ: Rutgers University Press.

Jiang Zhikang. 1995. "Guanzhong yanli de Yin Guifang" (Yin Guifang in the eyes of the audience). In Li Huikang, ed., *Yidai fengliu Yin Guifang* (The great actress Yin Guifang). Shanghai: Shanghai wenyi chubanshe.

Jin Chunming. 2001. *Zhonghua Renming Gongheguo jian shi* (A brief history of the People's Republic of China). Beijing: Zhonggong dangshi chubanshe.

Jin Xiangyin. 1992. "Nüzi Yueju diyi ban—Shi Jia Ao nüban" (The first women's Yue opera troupe—Girls' school from Shi Village). In *Yueju suyuan* (Tracing the origins of Yue opera), edited by Shengxian Zhengxie Wenshi Ziliao Weiyuanhui, 50–67. Hangzhou: Zhejiang wenyi chuban she.

Jones, Andrew F. 2001. *Yellow Music: Media Culture and Colonial Modernity in the Chinese Jazz Age*. Durham, NC: Duke University Press.

Jones, Susan Mann. 1974. "The Ningbo *Pang* and Its Financial Power at Shanghai." In Mark Elvin and William Skinner, eds., *The Chinese City between Two Worlds*. Stanford, CA: Stanford University Press.

Karl, Rebecca. 2002. *Staging the World: Chinese Nationalism at the Turn of the Twentieth Century*. Durham, NC: Duke University Press.

Ke Ling. 1994. *Ke Ling sanwen jingbian* (The best selection of essays by Ke Ling). 2 volumes. Hangzhou: Zhejiang wenyi chubanshe.

Ko, Dorothy. 1994. *Teachers of the Inner Chambers, Women and Culture in Seventeenth-Century China*. Stanford, CA: Stanford University Press.

Lanyun ji (The music of the orchid: A special issue dedicated to Xu Yulan). 1948. Edited by Shou Yaozong, Xu Zhiyuan, Zhang Zibai, and Zhang Shouju. Shanghai: Lukaiji shubaoshe.

Larson, Wendy. 1998. *Women and Writing in Modern China*. Stanford, CA: Stanford University Press.

Lee, Leo Ou-Fan. 1999. *Shanghai Modern: The Flowering of a New Urban Culture in China, 1930–1945*. Cambridge, MA: Harvard University Press.

Levenson, Joseph. 1958. *Confucian China and Its Modern Fate*. Vol. 3, *The Problem of Historical Significance*. Berkeley: University of California Press.

Li, Hsiao-T'i. 1996. "Opera, Society and Politics: Chinese Intellectuals and Popular Culture, 1901–1937." Ph.D. diss., Harvard University.

Li Huikang, ed. 1995. *Yidai fengliu Yin Guifang* (The great actress Yin Guifang). Shanghai: Shanghai wenyi chubanshe.

Li Jinfeng. 1995. "He Yin tuanzhang xiangchu de rizi" (The days I spent with Yin Guifang, the head of the company). In Li Huikang, ed., *Yidai fengliu Yin Guifang* (The great actress Yin Guifang). Shanghai: Shanghai wenyi chubanshe.

Lian Bo. 1983. "Cong yinyue changqiang shitan juzhong fengge" (Discussing Yue opera aesthetics in terms of music and singing). In *Yishu yanjiu ziliao* (Sources for research in art), vol. 6. Hangzhou: Zhejiang yishu yanjiu suo.

Liang Shanbo: Shi'er ge yue huaming (The story of Liang Shanbo and Zhu Yingtai in twelve-month flowers). [1930s?] Shuzhou, Jiangsu: Hengzhi shushe.

Liang Shanbo baojuan (The Buddhist treasury story about Liang Shanbo). Spring 1924. Suzhou story-singing script. Shanghai: Shanghai wenyi shuju.

Liang Shanbo yu Zhu Yingtai (Liang Shanbo and Zhu Yingtai). [1920s?] Shanghai storytelling script. 3 volumes. Shanghai: Shanghai renhexiang shuju.

Liang Shanbo yu Zhu Yingtai (Liang Shanbo and Zhu Yingtai). 1955. Yue opera script. Adapted by Xu Jin, Song Zhiyou, Chen Yu, Cheng Rong, and Hong Ying. Shanghai: Shanghai wenyi chubanshe.

Liang Shanbo yu Zhu Yingtai (Liang Shanbo and Zhu Yingtai). 1979. Yue opera script. Narrated by Yuan Xuefen and Fan Ruijuan. Adapted by Xu Jin et al. Shanghai: Shanghai wenyi chubanshe.

Liang Shanbo yu Zhu Yingtai fufu gongshu huanhun tuanyuan ji (A story about the reincarnations of the couple Liang Shanbo and Zhu Yingtai). [1920s?] 2 volumes. Shanghai: Shanghai chunyin shuzhuang.

Liang Shanbo Zhu Yingtai quanzhuan: Aiqing xiaoshuo (Love story: The complete story of Liang Shanbo and Zhu Yingtai). 1935. By Ma Weishi. Shanghai: Shanghai xiaoshuoshe.

Link, Perry. 1981. *Mandarin Ducks and Butterflies, Popular Fiction in Early Twentieth Century Chinese Cities*. Berkeley: University of California Press.

Liu Qikui. 1987. "Wang wei hanjian wenhua gaishu" (An outline of the Wang Jingwei puppet government's collaboration culture). In *Wang Jingwei hanjian zhengquan de xingwang* (The rise and fall of the Wang Jingwei puppet government), edited by the Modern History Division of the Department of History, Fudan University. Shanghai: Fudan University Press.

Liu Wanzhang. 1940. *Mulan'ge zhu* (Annotated Mulan lyric prose). Changsha, Hunan: Commercial Press.

Liujin suiyue: Huaijiu lao yuefenpai guanggao huazhan (An exhibition of nostalgic posters). 1996. National Museum of History, Taipei.

Liuyin ji (Liang Shanbo yu Zhu Yingtai). [1930s?] Sichuan opera script. In *Suqu* (Collection of opera scripts). Preserved in Fu Ssu-nien Library, Institute of History and Philology, Academia Sinica, Taipei.

Lu Gong, comp. 1955. *Liang Zhu gushi shuochang ji* (A collection of various versions of the story of Liang Shanbo and Zhu Yingtai in storytelling traditions). Shanghai: Shanghai chuban gongsi.

Lu, Hanchao. 1995. "Away From Nanking Road: Small Stores and Neighborhood Life in Modern Shanghai." *The Journal of Asian Studies*, vol. 54, no. 1 (February).

———. 1999. *Beyond the Neon Lights: Everyday Shanghai in the Early Twentieth Century*. Berkeley: University of California Press.

Lu Xun. 1922. "She xi" (Community opera shows). In *Na han* (The war cry). Shanghai: Shanghai renmin chubanshe, 1973.

———. 1924. *Zhu fu* (The New Year's sacrifice). Hong Kong: Chao Yang Publishing, 1973.

———. 1935. "Lun 'Renyan kewei'" (On "Gossip is frightening"). In He Keren et al., *Ruan Lingyu zhisi* (The death of Ruan Lingyu). Changsha: Yuelu shushe, 1986.

Luo Di. 1991. *Xiqu yu Zhejiang* (Opera and Zhejiang). Hangzhou: Zhejiang renmin chubanshe.

Luo Suwen. 1993. "Lun jindai xiqu yu dushi jumin" (Modern theater and city dwellers). In *Shanghai yanjiu luncong* (Research on Shanghai series), vol. 9. Shanghai: Shanghai Academy of Social Sciences Press.

———. 2005. "Gender on Stage: Actresses in an Actor's World (1895–1930)." In Bryna Goodman and Wendy Larson, eds., *Gender in Motion*, 75–96. New York: Rowman & Littlefield Publishers.

Luobinhan (Robin Hood). 1940s. Shanghai.

Lyell, William A., trans. 1997. *Shanghai Express.* Translated from Zhang Henshui, *Ping-Hu tongche*. Honolulu: University of Hawaii Press.

Ma Chaoshui. 1960. *Yueju fazhan shu* (On the early development of Yue opera). Manuscript in the Shengxian Yue Opera Museum.

Ma Guafu kaidian (Widow Ma's inn). 1944. Yue opera script. *Diduban Yueju dawang: Shaoxing wenxi jiaoben huibian* (King of *didu* Yue opera: Collection of plays in Shaoxing civil opera). Shanghai: Yimin shuju.

Ma Longwen and Mao Dazhi. 1982. *Hebei bangzi jianshi* (A short history of Hebei clapper opera). Beijing: Zhongguo xiju chubanshe.

Ma Shaobo, adapt. 1949. *Mulan congjun* (Mulan entering the army). Shanghai: Xinhua shudian.

Mackerras, Colin. 1972. *The Rise of the Peking Opera, 1770–1870—Social Aspects of the Theatre in Manchu China.* Oxford: Clarendon Press.

MacPherson, Kerrie. 1998. *Asian Department Stores*. Richmond, Surrey, England: Curzon Press.

Mann, Susan. 1984. "Urbanization and Historical Change in China." *Modern China*, vol. 10, no. 1.

———. 1987. "Widows in the Kinship, Class, and Community Sturctures of Qing Dynasty China." *Journal of Asian Studies*, vol. 46, no. 1 (February): 37–56.

———. 1994. "The Cult of Domesticity in Republican Shanghai's Middle Class." In *Research on Women in Modern Chinese History*, vol. 3, edited and published by the Institute of Modern History, Academia Sinica, Taipei.

———. 1997. *Precious Records: Women in China's Long Eighteenth Century*. Stanford, CA: Stanford University Press.

Mei Lanfang. 1954. *Wutai shenghuo sishi nian* (Forty years of my career on the stage). Recorded and edited by Xu Jichuan. Shanghai: Pingmin Publishing House.

Mulan congjun: Jiuguo Pingju (Mulan entering the army: A patriotic Beijing opera). 1938. Nanchang, Jiangxi: Qianfeng she.

Murphey, Rhoads. 1953. *Shanghai, Key to Modern China.* Cambridge, MA: Harvard University Press.

Nishimura Shigeo. 2004. *Nijū seiki chūgoku no seiji kūkan: "Chūka minzokuteki kokumin kokka" no gyōshukuryoku* (Political space in twentieth-century China: The binding power of "a citizen state of the Chinese nation"). Tokyo: Aoki shoten. *Nü sheng* (Women's voice magazine). Monthly, 1942–46. Shanghai.

Ōki Yasushi. 1989. *Minzoku shūkyō to geinō: Geinōshi kara mita Chūgoku to nōson no kōryū* (Popular religion and entertainment: A preliminary inquiry on the urban-rural interchanges in China viewed through entertainment history). *Tōyō bunka*, no. 69 (October). Tokyo: Tōyō Bunka Kenkyūjo.

Overmyer, Daniel L. 1985. "Values in Chinese Sectarian Literature: Ming and Ch'ing *Pao-chüan*." In David Johnson, Andrew Nathan, and Evelyn Rawski, eds., *Popular Culture in Late Imperial China.* Berkeley: University of California Press.

Perry, Elizabeth J. 1993. *Shanghai on Strike: The Politics of Chinese Labor*. Stanford, CA: Stanford University Press.

Pickowicz, Paul G. 1993. "The 'May Fourth' Tradition of Chinese Cinema." In Ellen Widmer and David Der-wei Wang, eds., *From May Fourth to June Fourth: Fiction and Film in Twentieth-Century China*. Cambridge, MA: Harvard University Press.

Qi Rushan. 1964. *Qi Rushan quanji* (The complete works of Qi Rushan). 8 volumes. Taipei: Chongguang chubanshe.

Qi Yaxian. 1992. *Qi Yaxian biaoyan yishu* (Qi Yaxian's performing art). Edited by Fu Jun. Shanghai: Shanghai wenyi chubanshe.

Qian Nanyang, comp. 1956. *Liang Zhu xiju jicun* (A collection of rare opera scripts of Liang Shanbo and Zhu Yingtai). Shanghai: Shanghai gudian wenxue chubanshe.

Qian Yonglin. 1992. "Xiaogeban sanjin Shanghai" (Three attempts to enter Shanghai by Shengxian little opera). In *Yueju suyuan* (Tracing the origins of Yue opera), edited by Shengxian Zhengxie Wenshi Ziliao Weiyuanhui, 42–49. Hangzhou: Zhejiang wenyi chuban she.

Qiu Wenguang. 1977. "Yueju suoyi" (Miscellaneous recollections of Yue opera). *Zhejiang yuekan* (Zhejiang monthly), vol. 98 (June). Taipei: Taiwan Zhejiang Native-Place Organization. Also in Qiu Yawei, ed. 1986. *Yihuai Shengxian* (Memories of Shengxian). Taipei: Taipei Shengxian Native-Place Organization.

———. 1985. "Zuile xiashi ling xiangying" (Listening to native tones is my favorite hobby). *Zhejiang yuekan* (Zhejiang monthly), vol. 192 (April). Taipei: Taiwan Zhejiang Native-Place Organization. Also in Qiu Yawei, ed. 1986. *Yihuai Shengxian* (Memories of Shengxian). Taipei: Taipei Shengxian Native-Place Organization.

Qiu Yawei, ed. 1986. *Yihuai Shengxian* (Memories of Shengxian). Taipei: Taipei Shengxian Native-Place Organization.

Ren Wensi. 1992. "'Luodi changshu' fayuandi Matang Cun kaocha" (Field investigation at Horse Pond Village, where Shengxian story-singing originated). In *Yueju suyuan* (Tracing the origins of Yue opera), edited by Shengxian Zhengxie Wenshi Ziliao Weiyuanhui, 1–17. Hangzhou: Zhejiang wenyi chuban she.

Rowe, William. 1989. *Hankow: Conflict and Community in a Chinese City, 1796–1895*. Stanford, CA: Stanford University Press.

Rui Heshi and Fan Boqun. 1984. *Yuanyang hudie pai wenxue ziliao* (Material of the butterfly school literature). Fuzhou: Fujian renmin chubanshe.

Sanxiao yinyuan (Marriage resulted from three smiles). 1930s. Women's Shengxian opera script. Shanghai: Yimin shuju.

Sekko zaibatsu (The Zhejiang financial magnates). October 15, 1929. In *Shanhai Mantetsu chōsa shiryō* (Investigation materials of the Shanghai office of the Southern Manchuria Railway Company), vol. 6. Shanghai.

Shanghai chunqiu (Spring and autumn in Shanghai). 1948. Reprinted in *Shili Yangchang hua Shanghai* (Speaking about colonial Shanghai). Hong Kong: Modern Publishing House, 1970.

Shanghai geming wenhua dashi ji, 1937–1949 (A chronicle of the development of revolutionary culture in Shanghai, 1937–1949). 1991. Zhonggong Shanghai Shiwei Dangshi Ziliao Zhengji Weiyuanhui, Zhonggong Shanghai Shiwei Dangshi Yanjiushi, and Zhonggong Shanghai Shiwei Xunchuanbu Dangshi Ziliao Zhengji Weiyuanhui (Committee for Collecting Historical Materials on Party History, Shanghai Committee of the Chinese Communist Party, et al.). Shanghai: Shanghai fanyi chuban gongsi.

Shanghai gonggong zujie shigao (History of the international settlement in Shanghai). 1980. Shanghai: Shanghai renmin chubanshe, 1984.

Shanghai Huaiju zhi (Shanghai Huai opera gazetteer). 1998. Edited and published by the Historical and Gazetteer Editorial Board, Shanghai Cultural Affairs Bureau, and the *Shanghai Huaiju zhi* editorial board.

Shanghai Huju zhi (Shanghai Shanghai opera gazetteer). 1999. Edited by Wang Pei, Chen Jianyun, and Lan Liu. Shanghai: Shanghai wenhua chubanshe.

Shanghai jiefang qianhou wujia ziliao huibian (1921 nian–1957 nian) (Commodity prices in Shanghai before and after the liberation [1921–1957]). 1958. Edited by the Shanghai Institute for Economic Research, Chinese Academy of Sciences and Institute for Economic Research, and the Shanghai Academy of Social Sciences. Shanghai: Shanghai renmin chubanshe.

Shanghai Jingju zhi (Shanghai Beijing opera gazetteer). 1999. Edited by Xu Xingjie and Cai Shicheng. Shanghai: Shanghai wenhua chubanshe.

Shanghai shenghuo (Shanghai life). Yan Duhe, honorary editor. Published monthly starting in 1936. Shanghai.

Shanghai Shi Shehui Ju dang'an (Archival documents of the Social Bureau of the Shanghai Municipal Government). 1946–49. Shanghai Municipal Archives.

Shanghai Shi Wenhua Ju dang'an (Archival documents of the Shanghai Cultural Affairs Bureau). 1949–66. Shanghai Municipal Archives.

Shanghai Tebieshi Gongyongju (Bureau of Public Services, Shanghai Special Municipality). 1941. *Zhonghua Minguo sanshi nian shangbannian yewu baogao* (Business report for the first half of 1941). Shanghai.

———. January 1943. *Zhonghua Minguo sanshiyi nian yewu baogao* (Business report for 1942). Shanghai.

Shanghai yanjiu ziliao (Sources for research on Shanghai). 1935. Compiled by Shanghaitong She. Shanghai: Shanghaitong She.

Shanghai yanjiu ziliao xuji (The second volume of sources for research on Shanghai). 1937. Compiled by Shanghaitong She. Shanghai: Shanghaitong She.

Shanghai Yueju gaige wushinian tekan, 1942–1992 (Special issue to commemorate the fiftieth anniversary of Yue opera reform, 1942–1992). 1992. Edited by Lu Shijun.

Shanghai Yueju zhi (Shanghai Yue opera gazetteer). 1995. Unpublished draft. Compiled by The Editorial Committee. 4 volumes. Shanghai.

Shanghai Yueju zhi (Shanghai Yue opera gazetteer). 1997. Edited by Lu Shijun and Gao Yilong. Beijing: Zhongguo xiju chubanshe.

Shanghai zhi (Shanghai gazetteer). 1946. In the library of the Institute of Modern History, Academia Sinica, Taipei.

Shanhai Mantetsu kikan (The Shanghai Southern Manchuria Railway quarterly). 1937–45. Compiled by Minami Manshū Tetsudō Kabushiki Gaisha Shanhai Jimusho (Shanghai office of the Southern Manchuria Railway Company). Shanghai.

"Shanhai ni okeru sensōgyō no jōkyō" (An investigation of Shanghai's native banks). 1941. *Shanhai* (Shanghai), vol. 1013 (December). Shanghai.

"Shaoxing shangbao" liangzhounian jinian tekan (A special issue for the second anniversary of *Shaoxing commercial daily*). October 1935. Shaoxing: Shaoxing shangbao she.

"Shaoxing shangbao" niankan (The annual magazine of *Shaoxing commercial daily*), vol. 2. 1935. Shaoxing: Shaoxing shangbao she.

Shaoxing wanbao (Shaoxing evening news). 1935. Shaoxing, Zhejiang.

Shaoxing wenxi nüzi changzuo diduban (Women's *didu* opera, Shaoxing civil opera). Mid-1940s. 31 volumes. Shanghai: Yimin shuju.

Shaoxing zhi sichou (The silk industry of Shaoxing). January 1937. Published by Jianshe Weiyuanhui Jingji Diaochazu Tongjike (Statistics Division, Economic Investigation Department, Committee on Construction).

Shaoxingxi bao (Shaoxing opera daily). January–March 1941. Shanghai.

Shaoxingxi kao (Shaoxing opera scripts). 1939. Shanghai: Shanghai Yuesheng chubanshe, 1942.

She Huimin. 1992. "Yueju *Biyu zan* de jici gaibian" (Revisions of the Yue opera play *Emerald hairpin*). In *Yueju suyuan* (Tracing the origins of Yue opera), edited by Shengxian Zhengxie Wenshi Ziliao Weiyuanhui. Hangzhou: Zhejiang wenyi chuban she.

She Ren. 1943. "Shanghai wenhuajie zong jiantao" (A general examination of Shanghai's culture). *Shanhai* (Shanghai) (February).

Shen bao (Shanghai newspaper). Published 1872–1949. Shanghai.

Shen Yixing, Jiang Peinan, and Zheng Qingsheng, eds. 1996. *Shanghai gongren yundong shi* (History of the labor movement in Shanghai), vol. 2. Shenyang: Liaoning renmin chubanshe.

Shengxian Yueju Shaoxingxi kao (Shengxian Shaoxing Yue opera scripts). 1930s. Shanghai: Yimin shuju.

Shengxian zhi (A Shengxian gazetteer). 1989. Hangzhou: Zhejiang renmin chubanshe.

Shengxianxi jijing (Collection of lyrics from Shengxian operas). 1996. Edited by Qiu Yawei, Zhang Jishun, and Qiu Wenguang. With 17 audiocassettes. In *Shengxun*, series no. 2. Taipei: *Shengxun* zazhi she.

Shengxun (Shengxian affairs). 1987–99. Edited by Qiu Yawei. Taipei: Taipei shi Shengxian Tongxianghui (Shengxian Native-Place Association in Taipei).

Shi Jiaoru, ed. 1939. *Shaoxing xikao quance* (A complete collection of Shaoxing opera lyrics). Shanghai: Yuesheng chuban she.

Shijie chenbao (World morning news). 1940s. Shanghai.

Shishi xinbao (The new current affairs). 1940s. Shanghai.

Shuoxi lunyi: Shanghai Yueju Yuan jianyuan sanshi zhounian wutai yishu wenxuan (Discussing the arts of the theater: Selected essays on the art of the stage on the thirtieth anniversary of the founding of the Shanghai Yue Opera House). 1985. Compiled by Shanghai Yueju Yuan. Shanghai.

Stock, Jonathan P. J. 1997. "Huju and Musical Change: The Rise of a Local Operatic Form in East China, to 1920." *ACMR Reports: Journal of the Association for Chinese Music Research* [Pittsburgh], vol. 10, no. 1 (Spring).

Su Qing. 1944a. *Huanjin ji* (A collection of essays from Huanjin). Shanghai: Tiandi chubanshe. Reprint, Hong Kong: Lili chubanshe, 1946.

———. 1944b. *Jiehun shinian* (Ten years of my married life). Shanghai: Tiandi chubanshe. Reprint, Shanghai: The Su Qing Publisher, 1945.

———. 1947. *Xu "Jiehun shinian"* (Sequel to *Ten years of my married life*). Hong Kong: Lili chubanshe.

———. 1995. *Su Qing sanwen jingbian* (A selection of Su Qing's best essays). Compiled by Yi Qing, Yi Xin, and Xiao Lan. Hangzhou: Zhejiang wenyi chubanshe.

Sun Chongtao and Xu Hongtu. 1995. *Xiqu youling shi* (History of opera performers). Beijing: Beijing wenhua yishu chubanshe.

Suqu (Collections of popular opera scripts). Preserved in the Fu Ssu-nien Library, at the Institute of History & Philology, Academia Sinica, Taipei.

Tanaka Issei. 1985. "The Social and Historical Context of Ming-Ch'ing Local Drama." In David Johnson, Andrew J. Nathan, and Evelyn Rawski, eds., *Popular Culture in Late Imperial China*. Berkeley: University of California Press.

Tang Zhenchang, ed. *Shanghai shi* (History of Shanghai). 1989. Shanghai: Shanghai renmin chubanshe.

Tao Juyin. 1979. *Gudao jianwen—Kangzhan shiqi de Shanghai* (The things I witnessed in "island" Shanghai). Shanghai: Shanghai renmin chubanshe.

Tao Lanying. 1943. "Xianhua xiaojie zuojia" (Chat about the young lady writers). *Chunqiu* (Spring and autumn), vol. 8 (May 15).

Tiandi (Heaven and Earth). 1942–45. Edited by Feng Heyi (Su Qing). Shanghai: Tiandi chubanshe.

Wakeman, Frederic, Jr. 1995. *Policing Shanghai, 1927–1937*. Berkeley: University of California Press.

Wang Changnian. 1947. *Da Shanghai zhinan, 1947* (Tourist guide for the great Shanghai, 1947). Shanghai: Dongnan wenhua fuwushe.

Wang Dewei. 1988. *Zhong sheng xuan hua: San ling yu ba ling nian dai di Zhongguo xiao shuo* (Clamoring: Chinese fiction in the 1930s and 1980s). Taipei: Yuan liu chu ban gong si.

Wang Lin, ed. 1991. *Pingxi zai Tianjin fazhan jianshi* (A brief history of the development of *ping* opera in Tianjin). Tianjin: Tianjin renmin chubanshe.

Wang, Qingping. 1998. *The Commercial Production of the Early Qing Scholar-Beauty Romances*. Ph.D. diss., Stanford University.

Wang Xiaochuan, ed. 1958. *Yuan Ming Qing sandai jinhui xiaoshuo xiqu shiliao* (Historical records of banning and destroying works of fiction and opera scripts in the Yuan, Ming, and Qing dynasties). Beijing: Zuojia chubanshe.

Wang, Zheng. 1999. *Women in the Chinese Enlightenment: Oral and Textual Histories*. Berkeley: University of California Press.

———. 2001. "Call Me 'Qingnian' But Not 'Funü': A Maoist Youth in Retrospect." In Zhong Xueping, Wang Zheng, and Bai Di, eds., *Some of Us: Chinese Women Growing Up in the Mao Era*, 27–52. New Brunswick, NJ: Rutgers University Press.

Ward, Barbara E. 1985. "Regional Operas and Their Audiences: Evidence from Hong Kong." In David Johnson, Andrew Nathan, and Evelyn Rawski, eds., *Popular Culture in Late Imperial China*. Berkeley: University of California Press.

Wei Shaochang. 1962. *Yuanyang hudie pai yanjiu ziliao* (Materials for research in the butterfly school), vol. 1. Shanghai: Shanghai wenyi chubanshe.

———. 1982. "Yueju manhua" (Informal talks about Yue opera). *Xiwen*, vol. 3 (June). Hangzhou.

———. 1984. *Yuanyang hudie pai yanjiu ziliao* (Materials for research on the butterfly school), vol. 2. Shanghai: Shanghai wenyi chubanshe.

———. 1989. "Yueju zai Shanghai de xingqi he yanbian" (The rise and development of Yue opera in Shanghai). In *Xiqu jingying* (The best of Chinese operas), vol. 2. Shanghai: Shanghai renmin chubanshe.

———. 1990. *Wo kan yuanyan hudie pai* (My view of the "mandarin ducks and butterflies" school). Hong Kong: Zhonghua shuju.

———. 1995. *Lishi de jianzheng—Yao Shuijuan dancheng bashi zhounian jinian* (Witness to history—A memorial collection of photos for the eightieth anniversary of Yao Shuijuan's birthday). Shanghai.

Wenhui bao (Wenhui daily). 1940s. Shanghai.

Wolf, Margery. 1975. "Women and Suicide in China." In Margery Wolf and Roxane Witke, eds., *Women in Chinese Society*. Stanford, CA: Stanford University Press.

Wu Fuhui. 1995. *Dushi xuanwo zhongde Haipai xiaoshuo* (Shanghai-style fiction in the urban eddies). Changsha: Hunan jiaoyu chubanshe.

Wutai jiemei (Stage sisters). 1999. A Yue opera playbill by Shanghai Yue Opera House.

"Wutai jiemei": Cong tigang dao yingpian (*Stage sisters*: From outline to film). 1982. Shanghai: Shanghai wenyi chubanshe.

Xiang hudie (Fragrant butterflies). Mid-1940s. In *Shaoxing wenxi nüzi changzuo diduban* (Women's *didu* opera, Shaoxing civil opera). 31 volumes. Shanghai: Yimin shuju.

Xiang Zhen. 1992. "Du pai banzhang Qiu Guangxian" (The serious troupe owner Qiu Guangxian). In *Yueju suyuan* (Tracing the origins of Yue opera), edited by Shengxian Zhengxie Wenshi Ziliao Weiyuanhui. Hangzhou: Zhejiang wenyi chuban she.

Xianglin sao (Sister Xianglin). 1949. Comic book. Shanghai: Jiaoyu chubanshe.

Xianglin sao (Sister Xianglin). 1978. Yue opera script. Original story by Lu Xun. Adapted by Wu Sheng, Zhuang Zhi, Yuan Xuefen, and Zhang Guifeng. Shanghai: Shanghai wenyi chubanshe.

Xiao Yueying. 1983. "Yueju gaige gei wo de yishu yingxiang" (The influence of the Yue opera reform on my performing art). In *Yishu yanjiu ziliao* (Sources for research in art), vol. 6. Hangzhou: Zhejiang yishu yanjiu suo.

Xin Yu si (New Threads). http://www.xys.org. Chinese-language Web site for the U.S.-based monthly online journal. Started Feburary 1994.

Xinmin bao (The new citizen daily). 1940s. Shanghai.

Xinmin wanbao (The new citizen evening news) [sometimes *Xinmin bao wankan*]. 1940s. Shanghai.

Xinwen bao (Daily news). Published 1893–1949. Shanghai.

Xiqu jingying (The best of Chinese operas). 1989. 2 volumes. Published as special issues of *Shanghai wenshi ziliao xuanji* (Selections from materials in the culture and history of Shanghai), nos. 61 and 62. Shanghai: Shanghai renmin chubanshe.

Xu Chengbei. 1990. *Mei Lanfang yu ershi shiji* (Mei Lanfang and the twentieth century). Beijing: Sanlian shudian, 1994.

Xu Dafeng. 1939. "Shanghai de xin yinxiang" (New impressions of Shanghai). *Shanghai shenghuo*, year 3, no. 10 (October 17).

Xu Gongsu and Qiu Jinzhang. 1933. *Shanghai gonggong zujie zhidu* (The structure of the international settlement of Shanghai). In *Shanghai gonggong zujie shigao* (History of the international settlement in Shanghai). 1980. Shanghai: Shanghai renmin chubanshe, 1984.

Xu Hansheng, ed. 1935. *Shang Xiaoyun zhuanji* (A special issue dedicated to Shang Xiaoyun). Beiping: Jingjin yinshuju.

Xu Jin. 1947. "Xue bu" (Learning to walk). *Yueju shijie* (The Yue opera world), no. 1 (September 1). Shanghai: Yinhua chubanshe.

———. 1962. "Cong xiaoshuo dao xi—Tan Yueju *Honglou meng* de gaibian" (From novel to opera play—About the adaptation of *Dream of the red chamber*). In *Shuoxi lunyi: Shanghai Yueju Yuan jianyuan sanshi zhounian wutai yishu wenxuan* (Discussing the arts of the theater: Selected essays on the art of the stage on the thirtieth anniversary of the founding of the Shanghai Yue Opera House), compiled by Shanghai Yueju Yuan. Shanghai, 1985.

———. 1994. "Qiantan Yueju yishu de gexing tese" (The characteristics of the art of Yue opera). In Gao Yilong and Lu Shijun, eds., *Chongxin zouxiang huihuang: Yueju gaige wushi zhounian lunwen ji* (Resume the past glory: A collection of essays dedicated to the fifth anniversary of Yue opera reform). Beijing: Zhongguo xiju chubanshe.

Xu Yulan. 1985. "Wo yan Jia Baoyu" (I perform Jia Baoyu). In *Shuoxi lunyi: Shanghai Yueju Yuan jianyuan sanshi zhounian wutai yishu wenxuan* (Discussing the arts of the theater: Selected essays on the art of the stage on the thirtieth anniversary of the founding of the Shanghai Yue Opera House), compiled by Shanghai Yueju Yuan. Shanghai.

Xuesheng jinian kan (Commemorative publication of Xuesheng Company). May 1946. Shanghai: Xuesheng juwu bu.

Yamagami Kanao. 1937. *Sekko zaibatsu no kisoteki kōsatsu* (A study of the foundation of Zhejiang financial magnates). *Shanhai Mantetsu kikan* (The Shanghai Southern Manchuria Railway quarterly), vols. 1 and 2. Minami Manshū Tetsudō Kabushiki Gaisha Shanhai Jimusho (Shanghai office of the Southern Manchuria Railway Company). Shanghai.

Yang Dongping. 1994. *Chengshi jifeng: Beijing he Shanghai de wenhua jingshen* (Wind of the seasons: The cultural spirits of Beijing and Shanghai). Beijing: Dongfang chubanshe.

Yang Hansheng. 1945. "Zhongguo xiju zhong de xin jiu nüxing" (Old and new women's images in Chinese theater). *Xiandai funü* (Modern women), vol. 6, no. 3 (Shanghai edition, no. 1, October): 15–18.

Yang Yi. 1993. *Ershi shiji Zhongguo xiaoshuo yu wenhua* (Chinese fiction and culture in the twentieth century). Taipei: Yeqiang chubanshe.

Yao Shuijuan zhuanji (A special issue dedicated to Yao Shuijuan). 1939. Compiled by Juanshe (The Juan Association). Shanghai: Yao Shuijuan zhuanji chubanshe.

Yeh, Catherine. 2006. *Shanghai Love: Courtesans, Intellectuals, and Entertainment Culture, 1850–1910*. Seattle: University of Washington Press.

Yeh, Wen-hsin. 1992. "Progressive Journalism and Shanghai's Petty Urbanites: Zou Taofen and the Shenghuo Weekly, 1926–1945." In Frederic Wakeman, Jr., and Wen-hsin Yeh, eds., *Shanghai Sojourners*. Berkeley: Institute of East Asian Studies, University of California: Center for Chinese Studies.

———. 1995. "Corporate Space, Communal Time: Shanghai's China Bank." *American Historical Review*, vol. 100, no. 1 (February).

Yi Bing. 1959. "Ping Yueju *Honglou meng*" (On the Yue opera *Dream of the red chamber*). In *Shuoxi lunyi: Shanghai Yueju Yuan jianyuan sanshi zhounian wutai yishu wenxuan* (Discussing the arts of the theater: Selected essays on the art of the stage on the thirtieth anniversary of the founding of the Shanghai Yue Opera House), compiled by Shanghai Yueju Yuan. Shanghai, 1985.

Yin Guifang. 1951. "Cong Jia Baoyu zhege renwu jiangqi" (Speaking about the character Jia Baoyu). Edited by Li Huikang. In Li Huikang, ed., *Yidai fengliu Yin Guifang* (The great actress Yin Guifang), 394–95. Shanghai: Shanghai wenyi chubanshe, 1995.

———. 1982. "Wo zouguo de yishu daolu" (My career as an artist). In *Yueju yishujia huiyi lu* (Memoirs by Yue opera artists), 8–18, edited by the editorial division, *Wenhua yule* (Culture and entertainment). Hangzhou: Zhejiang renmin chubanshe.

Ying Zhiliang. 2003. *Zhongguo Yueju fazhan shi* (History of Yue opera in China). Beijing: Zhongguo xiju chubanshe.

Yishu yanjiu ziliao (Sources for research in art), vol. 6. 1983. Hangzhou: Zhejiang yishu yanjiu suo.

Yu Shangyuan (Yui Shang-Yuen), ed. 1927. *Guoju yundong* (National theater movement). Zhongguo Xijushe congshu. Shanghai: Xinyue shudian.

Yuan Xuefen. 1978. "Chong yan *Xianglin sao*" (Restaging *Sister Xianglin*). In *Xianglin sao* (Sister Xianglin). Yue opera script. Original story by Lu Xun. Adapted by Wu Sheng, Zhuang Zhi, Yuan Xuefen, and Zhang Guifeng. Shanghai: Shanghai wenyi chubanshe.

———. 1983. "Ganku deshi cunxin zhi—Yueju gaige sishi nian de huigu he renshi" (Recollections and understanding of Yue opera reform in the past forty years). In *Yishu yanjiu ziliao* (Sources for research in art), vol. 6. Hangzhou: Zhejiang yishu yanjiu suo.

———. 1994. "Qianghua jingpin yishi, tuijin Yueju gaige" (Think more on producing masterpieces, push forward Yue opera reform). In Gao Yilong and Lu Shijun, eds., *Chongxin zouxiang huihuang: Yueju gaige wushi zhounian lunwen ji* (Resume the past glory: A collection of essays dedicated to the fifth anniversary of Yue opera reform). Beijing: Zhongguo xiju chubanshe.

———. 2002. *Yuan Xuefen zishu: Qiusuo rensheng yishu de zhendi* (Yuan Xuefen's own story: The search for the true meaning of art and life). Shanghai: Cishu chubanshe.

Yue Jia. 1992. "Yueju *Meng Lijun* bianyan shimo" (How the Yue opera *Meng Lijun* was produced). In *Yueju suyuan* (Tracing the origins of Yue opera), edited by Shengxian Zhengxie Wenshi Ziliao Weiyuanhui. Hangzhou: Zhejiang wenyi chuban she.

Yue ou (The song of Yue). 1939. Shanghai.

Yue yuan shen yun (Beautiful displays of Yue opera). 2001. Edited by Chen Shenglai, Hu Jinjun, and Liu Wenguo. Shanghai: Shanghai shuhua chuban she.

Yueju baimei tu (Photographs of the one hundred Yue opera actresses). December 1947. Shanghai: Yuelian chubanshe.

Yueju bao (Yue opera news). 1946–49. Shanghai.

Yueju huabao (Yue opera pictorial). 1940–41. Shanghai.

Yueju lingxiou xikao (Lyrics by the leading Yue opera actresses). 1940s. Shanghai: Yuelian chubanshe.

Yueju ribao (Yue opera daily). 1940s. Shanghai.

Yueju shijie (The Yue opera world). 1941. Shanghai.

Yueju shijie (The Yue opera world). Started September 1947. Shanghai: Yinhua chubanshe.

Yueju suyuan (Tracing the origins of Yue opera). 1992. Edited by Shengxian Zhengxie Wenshi Ziliao Weiyuanhui. Hangzhou: Zhejiang wenyi chuban she.

Yueju xikao daquan (The complete Yue opera scripts). 1940s. Shanghai: Daming shuju.

Yueju yishu jia huiyi lu (Memoirs by Yue opera artists). 1982. Edited by the editorial division, *Wenhua yule* (Culture and entertainment). Hangzhou: Zhejiang renmin chubanshe, 1984.

Yueju zhuankan (A special publication for Yue opera). April 1940. Shanghai: Sanyou Shiye She.

Zaoqi Yueju fazhan shi (A history of the early development of Yue opera). 1983. Compiled by Shengxian Wenhuaju Yueju fazhan shi bianxie zu. Hangzhou: Zhejiang renmin chubanshe.

Zazhi (The miscellany). 1938–45. Shanghai.

Zeng Yongyi. 1976. "Nanban nüzhuang yu nüban nanzhuang (Men playing women and vice versa). In *Shuo xiqu* (Talk about opera). Taipei: Lianjing shudian, 1983.

———. 1988. *Taiwan gezaixi de fazhan yu bianqian* (The development of boy-singers' opera in Taiwan). Taipei: Lianjing shudian.

Zhang Ailing (Eileen Chang). 1943. "Daodi shi Shanghai ren" (Alas, Shanghainese). *Zazhi* (The miscellany), vol. 11, no. 4 (August). Shanghai. The essay was later published in Zhang Ailing, *Liuyan* (Gossip), 1945.

———. 1945. *Liuyan* (Gossip). Reprint, Taipei: Huangguan chubanshe, 1968, 1995.

———. 1992. *Zhang Ailing sanwen quanbian* (The complete collection of Zhang Ailing's essays). Compiled by Lai Fengyi. Hangzhou: Zhejiang wenyi chubanshe.

———. 2006. *Zhang Ailing ji: Yujinxiang* (A collection of Zhang Ailing's novellas: Tulip). Beijing: Beijing chubanshe chuban jituan and Beijing shiyue wenyi chubanshe.

Zhang Dai. 1597–1679. *Taoan mengyi* (Dream recollections from the Clay Studio). Reprinted in *Taoan mengyi, Xihu mengxun* (Dream recollections from the Clay Studio, Back on West Lake in dreams). Beijing: Zuojia chubanshe, 1995.

Zhang Faying. 2002. *Zhongguo jiayue xiban* (Private opera troupes in China). Beijing: Xueyuan chubanshe.

Zhang Gansheng. 1991. *Minguo tongsu xiaoshuo lungao* (On popular fictions in the Republican period). Chongqing: Chongqing chubanshe.

Zhang Guifeng. "Yi qingnian shiqi de yanxi shenghuo" (Recollections of the career life in my youth). 1982. In *Yueju yishu jia huiyi lu* (Memoirs by Yue opera artists), edited by the editorial division, *Wenhua yule* (Culture and entertainment). Hangzhou: Zhejiang renmin chubanshe, 1982, 1984.

Zhang Henshui. 1935. *Ping-Hu tongche* (Shanghai express). Shanghai: Baixin shudian.

Zhang Jishun, comp. 1992a. *Yueju chuantong shuochang: Luodi changshu* (Traditional storytelling and singing in the early period of Yue opera). Hangzhou: Zhejiang wenyi chubanshe.

———. 1992b. "Yueju de bangui xisu" (The rituals and customs of Yue opera troupes). In *Yueju suyuan* (Tracing the origins of Yue opera), 97–104, edited by Shengxian Zhengxie Wenshi Ziliao Weiyuanhui. Hangzhou: Zhejiang wenyi chuban she.

Zhang Lihui. 1983. "Shanghai yishu yanjiusuo suozhang Zhang Lihui tongzhi de kaimuci" (Opening speech by Zhang Lihui, head of the Shanghai Institute for Research in Arts). In *Yishu yanjiu ziliao* (Sources for research in art), vol. 6. Hangzhou: Zhejiang yishu yanjiu suo.

Zhang Lihui and Gao Yilong. 1984. *Yuan Xuefen de yishu daolu* (The artistic path of Yuan Xuefen). Shanghai: Shanghai wenyi chubanshe.

Zhang Linghui. 1977. "Mantan Yueju" (Chat about Yue opera). *Zhejiang yuekan* (Zhejiang monthly), vol. 89 (June). Taipei: Taiwan Zhejiang Native-Place Organization.

Zhang Qi. 1984. "Qian yan" (Preface). In Zhu Bangxing, Hu Lin'ge, and Xu Sheng, *Shanghai chanye yu Shanghai zhigong* (Shanghai's industries and workers). 1939. Edited by Shanghai gongren Yundong Shiliao Weiyuanhui (Committee on Historical Materials of the Shanghai Labor Movement). Shanghai: Shanghai renmin chubanshe.

Zhang, Yingjin. 1996. *The City in Modern Chinese Literature and Film: Configurations of Space, Time, and Gender.* Stanford, CA: Stanford University Press.

Zhang Zijing. 1996. *Wode jiejie Zhang Ailing* (My older sister, Zhang Ailing). Taipei: Shih bao wenhua chuban gongsi.

Zhao Xiaosi. 1994. *Xu Yulan zhuan* (Biography of Xu Yulan). Shanghai: Shanghai wenyi chubanshe, 1995.

Zhejiang sheng nongcun diaocha (Survey of the rural area of Zhejiang). 1934. Shanghai: Commercial Press.

Zhejiang yuekan (Zhejiang monthly). 1970s–1990s. Taipei: Taiwan Zhejiang Native-Place Organization.

Zheng Yimei. 1987. "Guanyu *Libai liu* zhoukan—Dai xu" (About the *Saturday* weekly—Preface for the reprint of the magazine). In the reprint of *Libai liu* (Saturday), originally published in Shanghai, 1914–23. Nanjing: Jiangsu Guangling guji keyinshe.

Zhongguo xiqu juzhong da cidian (Dictionary of Chinese opera genres). 1995. Shanghai: Shanghai cishu chubanshe.

Zhongguo xiqu quyi cidian (Dictionary of Chinese opera and storytelling). 1981. Shanghai: Shanghai cishu chubanshe.

Zhongguo Yueju (Yue opera in China). 1989. Edited by Qian Facheng. Hangzhou: Zhejiang renmin chubanshe.

Zhongyang ribao: Shanghai ban (Central daily: Shanghai edition).

Zhou bao (Weekly). 1946. Edited by Tang Tao and Ke Ling. Shanghai.

Zhou Baocai. 1983. "Huigu wo jingli de Yueju yinyue gaige" (My experience with Yue opera music reform). In *Yishu yanjiu ziliao* (Sources for research in art), vol. 6. Hangzhou: Zhejiang yishu yanjiu suo.

Zhou Baokui. 1990. "Wode Yueju laodan shengya" (My career as an actress specializing in old female roles). *Wenhua yule* (Culture and entertainment magazine), no. 6 (June).

Zhou Huiling. 1996. "Nü yanyuan, xieshi zhuyi, 'xin nüxing' lunshu—Wan Qing dao wusi shiqi Zhongguo xiandai juchang zhong de xingbie biaoyan" (Actresses, realism, and the discourse of 'new women'—Gender performance in modern Chinese theaters from the late Qing to the May Fourth period). *Research on Women in Modern Chinese History*, vol. 4 (June). Edited and published by the Institute of Modern History, Academia Sinica, Taipei.

Zhu Bangxing, Hu Lin'ge, and Xu Sheng. 1939. *Shanghai chanye yu Shanghai zhigong* (Shanghai's industries and workers). Hong Kong: Yuandong chubanshe. New edition, edited by Shanghai Gongren Yundong Shiliao Weiyuanhui (Committee on Historical Materials of the Shanghai Labor Movement). Shanghai: Shanghai renmin chubanshe, 1984.

Zong Fei. 1940. "Luanlun xing yu ouran xing" (Incest and contingency). *Xiju yu wenxue* (Drama and literature), vol. 1, no. 4 (June).

Index

Illustrations are indicated in italic type.